Gustav Shpet's Contribution
to Philosophy and Cultural Theory

Comparative Cultural Studies,
Steven Tötösy de Zepetnek, Series Editor

The Purdue University Press monograph series of Books in Comparative Cultural Studies publishes single-authored and thematic collected volumes of new scholarship. Manuscripts are invited for publication in the series in fields of the study of culture, literature, the arts, media studies, communication studies, the history of ideas, etc., and related disciplines of the humanities and social sciences to the series editor via email at <clcweb@purdue.edu>. Comparative cultural studies is a contextual approach in the study of culture in a global and intercultural context and work with a plurality of methods and approaches; the theoretical and methodological framework of comparative cultural studies is built on tenets borrowed from the disciplines of cultural studies and comparative literature and from a range of thought including literary and culture theory, (radical) constructivism, communication theories, and systems theories; in comparative cultural studies focus is on theory and method as well as application. For a detailed description of the aims and scope of the series including the style guide of the series link to <http://docs.lib.purdue.edu/clcweblibrary/seriespurdueccs>. Manuscripts submitted to the series are peer reviewed followed by the usual standards of editing, copy editing, marketing, and distribution. The series is affiliated with *CLCWeb: Comparative Literature and Culture* (ISSN 1481-4374), the peer-reviewed, full-text, and open-access quarterly published by Purdue University Press at <http://docs.lib.purdue.edu/clcweb>.

Volumes in the Purdue series of Books in Comparative Cultural Studies
<http://www.thepress.purdue.edu/comparativeculturalstudies.html>

Gustav Shpet's Contribution to Philosophy and Cultural Theory, Ed. Galin Tihanov
Comparative Central European Holocaust Studies, Ed. Louise O. Vasvári and
  Steven Tötösy de Zepetnek
Marko Juvan, *History and Poetics of Intertextuality*
Thomas O. Beebee, *Nation and Region in Modern American and European Fiction*
Paolo Bartoloni, *On the Cultures of Exile, Translation, and Writing*
Justyna Sempruch, *Fantasies of Gender and the Witch in Feminist Theory and Literature*
Kimberly Chabot Davis, *Postmodern Texts and Emotional Audiences*
Philippe Codde, *The Jewish American Novel*
Deborah Streifford Reisinger, *Crime and Media in Contemporary France*
Imre Kertész and Holocaust Literature, Ed. Louise O. Vasvári and Steven Tötösy
  de Zepetnek
Camilla Fojas, *Cosmopolitanism in the Americas*
Comparative Cultural Studies and Michael Ondaatje's Writing, Ed. Steven Tötösy
  de Zepetnek
Jin Feng, *The New Woman in Early Twentieth-century Chinese Fiction*
Comparative Cultural Studies and Latin America, Ed. Sophia A. McClennen and
  Earl E. Fitz
Sophia A. McClennen, *The Dialectics of Exile*
Comparative Literature and Comparative Cultural Studies, Ed. Steven Tötösy de
  Zepetnek
Comparative Central European Culture, Ed. Steven Tötösy de Zepetnek

Gustav Shpet's Contribution to Philosophy and Cultural Theory

Edited by Galin Tihanov

Purdue University Press
West Lafayette, Indiana

Library of Congress Cataloging-in-Publication Data

Gustav Shpet's contribution to philosophy and cultural theory / edited by Galin Tihanov.
    p. cm. -- (Comparative cultural studies)
 Includes bibliographical references and index.
 ISBN 978-1-55753-525-2
1. Shpet, Gustav, 1879-1937. I. Tikhanov, Galin.
B4259.S5664G89 2009
197--dc22
                        2009007471

Contents

Acknowledgements

This book is the result of a collective effort; I wish to extend heartfelt thanks to all contributors for their unfailing support, good will, and responsiveness to my comments and suggestions. The authors of this volume have brought to it valuable knowledge and genuine passion for the work of Gustav Shpet, thus making the whole enterprise both feasible and enjoyable. It is also a great pleasure to thank a number of colleagues who have been working over the years on Gustav Shpet, or in related fields, and have assisted my editorial tasks through abundant gestures of kindness: John Bowlt, Jenny Brine, Katya Chown, Igor Chubarov, Aleksandr Dmitriev, Evgeny Dobrenko, Wolfgang Eismann, Maria Candida Ghidini, Anna Han, Catriona Kelly, Modest Kolerov, Georgii Levinton, John Malmstad, Tatiana Martsinkovskaia, Olga Mazaeva, Anita Michalak, Zoran Milutinović, Nikolai Nikolaev, Vladimir Novikov, Giulietta Ottaviano, Irina Paperno, Elena Pasternak, Nikolaj Plotnikov, Boris Poizner, Irina Prokhorova, Catia Renna, Andrei Rogatchevski, Tatiana Shchedrina, Marina Shtorkh, Gerry Smith, Grigorii Tulchinskii, Michela Venditti, Boris Wolfson, Sergei Zenkin, and Viktor Zhivov. I should also like to thank the anonymous reviewers of the manuscript for their comments and suggestions.

Adelina Angusheva, spouse and fellow scholar, has been of enormous help all along in more ways than I would be able to acknowledge here. I am grateful for her inspiration and trust.

Thanks are due to Springer Verlag, AAASS, and Cornell University Press for their permission to republish in this volume, in updated versions, the texts of Steven Cassedy, Peter Steiner, and Thomas Seifrid. Stephen Hutchings and Jonathan Starbrook at The University of Manchester kindly facilitated a grant towards the copyright fees. My own research, including the two bibliographies in the volume, was funded by the Alexander von Humboldt Foundation. Finally, I would like to thank Steven Tötösy de Zepetnek, editor of the Purdue University Press monograph series of Books in Comparative Cultural Studies, for welcoming this volume in the series. His advice and constructive patience are greatly appreciated, as is the kind editorial assistance of Rebecca Corbin and Dianna Gilroy.

G.T.
7 October 2009

Gustav Shpet's Life and Works: Introduction to the Volume

Galin Tihanov

Why Shpet?

Gustav Gustavovich Shpet (1879-1937) has emerged as one of the most prominent Russian philosophers of the twentieth century. The principle promoter of Husserlian phenomenology, at the same time creatively modifying Husserl and at times departing from him, Shpet was also an early advocate of hermeneutics. He left behind seminal work spanning philosophy, aesthetics, psychology, literary and theater theory, and the history of Russian thought. Significantly, many of his concerns anticipate preoccupations that have dominated the discourses of cultural theory and the philosophy of language over the last few decades.

Shpet's publications on phenomenology and hermeneutics are indispensable for gaining a proper understanding of the variety of trends and perspectives in these fields of European philosophy in the years immediately before and after World War One. With his translation of Hegel's *Phänomenologie des Geistes*, Shpet is also a central figure in the revival of academic research on, and the broader philosophical appropriation of, Hegel in the Soviet Union in the 1930s. Shpet was the author of significant studies in aesthetics and the philosophy of language, where he was endeavoring to revive Humboldt's legacy, in particular the idea of "inner form." His membership of the Moscow Linguistic Circle and contacts with Roman Jakobson put him at the forefront of the polemics surrounding the Formal Method. Studying Shpet's work, above all his *Esteticheskie fragmenty* (*Aesthetic Fragments*), affords a unique insight into the scene of Russian and European aesthetics, cultural, and literary theory at the time, and a better understanding of the transition (or return, depending on one's concept of history) from Formalism to philosophical aesthetics that a group of younger scholars, inspired by Shpet, sought to accomplish in the mid-1920s. Moreover, throughout the 1920s, Shpet was an important figure occupying positions of leadership at the Institute of Scientific Philosophy and at GAKhN (Gosudarstvennaia akademiia khudozhestvennykh nauk [The State Academy of Artistic Sciences]). Knowledge of Shpet's career and his institutional affiliations during

1

this period facilitates a better grasp of the complex environment in which the Soviet humanities and social sciences functioned in the earlier years of Stalinism.

It thus becomes clear that Gustav Shpet was a major philosopher in his own right, an important interpreter of Husserl, Humboldt, and Hegel, an active participant in the polemics about the emerging trends in Russian literary and cultural theory in the 1910s and 1920s, and a figure of significant institutional impact in the shaping of the Russian and Soviet humanities and social sciences. Examining closely Shpet's work and life would enable scholars in a wide range of disciplines—philosophers, intellectual historians, theorists of culture and literature, linguists, psychologists—to gain a deeper insight into the multitude of directions and factors determining the state of philosophical and cultural debates in both Russia and the West in the early twentieth century.

Shpet's Life and Intellectual Career

Shpet's intellectual career can be subdivided into four periods. One could take as a starting point for the first of these periods the year 1903 when Shpet published his first scholarly reviews. This period ends with Shpet's turn to phenomenology in 1912-13. The second period, Shpet's most creative and fruitful, begins in 1912-13 and finishes in 1923. The third period, marked by Shpet's close involvement in the work of GAKhN, begins in 1923-24 (Shpet was elected Vice President of GAKhN in 1924) and ends in 1930 with his forced retirement from the Academy. The final stage of his life comprises the time between 1930 and 1937.

Shpet was born on 7 April 1879 in Kiev. His mother, who had to raise him all by herself (the father had disappeared before his son's birth), was Polish and never learned to write in Russian (Polivanov 10). Shpet finished high school in Kiev and then enrolled at the University of Kiev, initially in the Faculty of Physics and Mathematics. After two years of study, in 1900, he was expelled for participating in activities organized by the Social Democrats (Poleva 7), and, according to his daughter, Marina Shtorkh, exiled to the Province of Herson for six months (Shtorkh, "V Rossii"). To this time dates his knowledge of Marxism, for which he had sympathy in his youth but rejected soon afterwards, although he did continue reading Marx into the latter half of the 1910s, along with texts by anarchists and reformist socialists (Shpet, "Sotsializm"). On being re-admitted to the University, Shpet enrolled in the Faculty of History and Philology and began to attend the famous psychology seminars of Georgii Ivanovich Chelpanov (later a patron and promoter of Shpet's career). In 1904 Shpet married Mar'ia Krestovskaia; in 1907 he moved to Moscow, following Chelpanov. Shpet became *Privat-Dozent* and undertook teaching at the University of Moscow and the Higher Women's Courses. In 1910-11 he travelled to Germany, Scotland, and France to expand his knowledge of philosophy and psychology.

This first period of Shpet's life and work, until 1912, is marked by the formative influence of European Enlightenment philosophy. Of particular importance for Shpet's early years were Hume and Kant, in whose orbit his thought moved for about ten years after 1903. The first mature works Shpet wrote were on the problem of causality in Hume and Kant, and on Hume's scepticism and Kant's response to it. In this early period Shpet reviewed, translated, and edited works on philosophy and psychology, notably by Heinrich Rickert and William James.

Shpet's second, and most creative, period (1912-23) can be said to have commenced with his trip to Göttingen in 1912-13. Here, most likely in the Fall of 1912, he made Husserl's acquaintance, an event of enormous significance for Shpet's evolution as a thinker. Shpet's embrace of phenomenology, but also his departure from Husserl in certain aspects, are documented in his first major work, *Iavlenie i smysl* (*Appearance and Sense*; 1914). Despite Lev Shestov's advice that Shpet initiate a German translation of the book, the idea did not materialize. At the same time, Shpet's personal life changed dramatically. He divorced his first wife and married Natalia Konstantinovna Guchkova, who would remain his partner for the rest of his life.

On returning from Germany, Shpet worked on his dissertation, *History as a Problem of Logic,* and on a book on hermeneutics (first published in 1989-92). He attempted a synthesis of phenomenology and hermeneutics, moving gradually closer to the latter of these two currents. The philosophy of history and of the historical sciences now became one of Shpet's major preoccupations: here he drew on Dilthey and especially on Wilhelm von Humboldt. At the same time Shpet remained interested in psychology and metaphysics; his important essay, "Consciousness and Its Owner" ("Soznanie i ego sobstvennik"), appeared in 1916.

On 1 October 1918, the Bolshevik regime abolished all academic degrees and titles and replaced them by the single title of Professor. Following this decree, 175 *privat-dotsenty* at Moscow University, including Shpet, received the title of Professor (Pavlov 102). It is precisely in the years immediately preceding and following the October Revolution of 1917 that Shpet's creativity seems to have peaked. This is the time when the ideas informing his later work were generated. During this relatively brief spell Shpet wrote an important article on ethnic psychology, "The Subject and the Tasks of Ethnic Psychology" (1917-18), which became the nucleus of his future *Introduction to Ethnic Psychology.* He also finished, in July 1918, his book "Germenevtika i ee problemy" ("Hermeneutics and Its Problems"), the study which had propelled his turn to Humboldt and thus bore on his later work *Vnutrenniaia Forma Slova. Etiudy i variatsii na temy Gumbol'ta (The Inner Form of the Word: Études and Variations on Humboldt's Themes*; 1927). That is also the time when Shpet wrote his most significant work on aesthetics and literary theory, the *Aesthetic Fragments (Esteticheskie fragmenty)*, the three parts of which took less than a month to complete (26 January to 19 February 1922). Finally, during this period he published important articles on theater, the philosophy of art, and the methodology of art history, and offered his own interpretation of the early stages of the evolution of Russian philosophy, as well as detailed studies of two important Russian thinkers, Herzen and Lavrov. His *Outline of the Development of Russian Philosphy (Ocherk razvitiia russkoi filosofii,* part I; 1922) triggered, as I show elsewhere (Tihanov, "Gustav Shpet v zerkale") both enthusiasm (Koyré) and skepticism (Florovskii).

The years 1922-23 saw the end of this inordinately fruitful stage of Shpet's career and signalled a gradual change in his fortunes. Shpet became increasingly disillusioned with the regime, soon after he had requested—and, most likely with Anatolii Lunacharskii's support, achieved—that his name be removed from the list of intellectuals who were to be exiled from the country in 1922. (The Berlin-based émigré newspaper *Rul'* reported in early September 1922 that Shpet had been arrested on the night of 16 August, together with the "entire Berdiaev Circle." No other source has so far verified this information, nor was Shpet known as an exponent of Berdiaev's philosophy; see the report in Artizov 589-90.) The closure of the Department of Philosophy at the University a year earlier had left Shpet deprived of institutional base, suffering the anomy of an academic without students and colleagues. With seemingly endless opportunities in sight—but without the prospect of a single worthwhile solution—Shpet would scatter his energy in various directions, living a life of enforced multifariousness. In this third period of Shpet's life, his attention was claimed frequently by more projects than anyone could have reasonably hoped to bring to fruition. He never completed the promised sequel to the first volume of his *Outline of the Development of Russian Philosophy*, nor did he publish the continuation of what was the first part (*vypusk*) of his *Introduction to Ethnic Psychology* (*Vvedenie v etnicheskuiu psikhologiiu*). Shpet was engaged in theater discussions, in literary disputes, in the work of various professional societies and artistic associations, and in prize juries (we see him, for example, on a GAKhN Committee set up in 1926 to judge the entries to a competition for the best translation of Boileau's *Art poétique*; see Iarkho 676-77). At various points during the 1920s Shpet was closely involved with the Institute of Scientific Philosophy, where he served as founding Director (1921-23), with the Higher Literary Courses (*Vysshie gosudarstvennye literaturnye kursy Mosprofobra*) in 1925-27 (see Baranskaia 335-41), and—over a considerably longer period of time—with GAKhN. But even GAKhN, increasingly isolated and under growing ideological pressure by 1927, was doomed to fall under party control in 1929. In October 1929, Shpet was discharged from his duties as Vice President of GAKhN. In January 1930 his membership was terminated and he was forced to retire; even this did not spare him the humiliation of a Party-led purge, to which he was subjected along with twenty-four other members of GAKhN in the summer of 1930 (for detailed chronology of the purges at GAKhN, see Iakimenko; for the public press campaign against Shpet, see Tihanov, "Multifariousness"). He was banned from scholarly work and was only allowed to undertake translations, if "proper ideological supervision" was secured. All this explains why between 1924 and 1929 Shpet was unable to produce as much work of substance as in the decade between 1912-13 and 1923. His two important books of the third period, *Introduction to Ethnic Psychology* (published in 1926; see Petritskii 25) and *The Inner Form of the Word* (1927) were revisiting ideas which were formulated, as we have seen, in the late 1910s. In fact, after 1927 Shpet appears to have produced no more than an updated version of his short article "Literatura" (published in 1982) and an unfinished text (published in 2002) on

Chernyshevskii, work on which was abandoned in 1929, the year of Shpet's deposition as Vice President of GAKhN.

The final period of Shpet's life and intellectual career, from his forced retirement from GAKhN in January 1930 until his execution in 1937, is marked by constant insecurity. Although Shpet was involved actively in work for the theater and in translation, notably in the preparation of the prestigious eight-volume Academia edition of Shakespeare's works, his belief in the meaningfulness of philosophy and scholarship was irretrievably destroyed. He undertook translations, adaptations, editorial work, internal reviewing, and other duties that could provide a source of income for his large family (five children from his two marriages). Shpet's entrance into these new spheres of activity was facilitated by his already extensive network of contacts in the world of literature, publishing, and the theater. After 1930 he was able to translate an imposing body of literature, mainly from the English Romantic and realist canon, as well as philosophical works by Berkeley and Hegel, most importantly the latter's *Phänomenologie des Geistes*. Much of this work was done in Eniseisk and Tomsk, where Shpet was exiled following his first arrest and trial in 1935. In October 1937 he was re-arrested in Tomsk and shot there on 16 November. The precise date of his death remained unknown until June 1989 when a little note by N.V. Serebrennikov was published in the Paris newspaper, *Russkaia Mysl* (Serebrennikov, "Novye").

The Present Volume

While Shpet's interdisciplinary work has been enjoying growing attention since the 1980s, predominantly in Russia, the research produced over this period, particularly that in English and the other Western European languages, has not yet succeeded in coalescing to a representative and reliable body of scholarship that introduces a wider audience to the most seminal aspects of Shpet's contribution to psychology, cultural and literary theory, and the humanities at large. It is hoped that the present volume will begin to change this situation. It offers original research by leading scholars based in the US, the UK, Russia, Germany, Switzerland, and France, covering all central areas of Shpet's multidisciplinary work. Equal attention is paid to Shpet's significance, past and present, in the broader context of Western philosophy, and to his roots in the history of Russian thought

The volume is organized into five parts. The authors of the articles in part one map out Shpet's contribution to several key areas: the philosophy of history and historiography (Peter Steiner), hermeneutics (Robert Bird), psychology (Vladimir Zinchenko and James Wertsch), and literary and theater theory (Galin Tihanov). In his article, Peter Steiner focuses on one conspicuous lacuna in our knowledge of Shpet: the methodology of historiography that he advanced in the 1910s. His argument is that in many respects it anticipated the "linguistic turn" that took place in Western historiography during the last quarter of the twentieth century and that is most often identified with Hayden White's work. But while White analyzes the historian's discourse in terms of *tropology* and *narratology*, for Shpet, *predication* is the key logical mechanism that informs the production of texts about the past. The divergence of these two approaches, Steiner concludes, can be explained through the hidden Kantian underpinnings of White's thought that contrasts sharply with the explicit Hegelianism of Shpet's theorizing.

Robert Bird discusses Shpet's hermeneutics in the light of his concept of detachment, subsequently adopted by Aleksei Losev, most notably in his 1930 *Dialectics of Myth*. The comparison of Shpet and Losev highlights their common debt to the earlier aesthetics of Viacheslav Ivanov. Together these three thinkers form a Russian tradition of hermeneutic thought. Their common cause is illustrated by their contacts in the walls of the State Academy of Artistic Sciences in the 1920s.

Next, Vladimir Zinchenko and James Wertsch reveal Shpet's important, though little appreciated, influence on Russian and Soviet psychology. For a variety of reasons, psychologists in the USSR went to great lengths to hide the impact Shpet had on their work. The authors take up one case in particular, that of Lev Semenovich Vygotskii, whose writings have had a major impact in Russia and more recently in the West. Vygotskii was well known for his ideas about inner speech, but Shpet's rich account of the inner form of the word never really surfaced in Vygotskii's writings, despite the fact that he attended some of Shpet's lectures and seminars. The authors outline these and other historical dimensions of the impact that Shpet did—and did not—have on Soviet psychology and identify a few fields where such an impact could have been very beneficial.

In the last article of the section, Galin Tihanov examines and evaluates Shpet's literary and theater theory and his contribution to the work of the Moscow Linguistic Circle and to the study of verbal art at GAKhN. Tihanov also reconstructs Shpet's contacts with the Russian Symbolists and the Imagists, as well as Shpet's activities as translator and his theater affiliations. The article is based on extensive research of published and unpublished sources, including Shpet's estate at the Russian State Library in Moscow, and contains a wealth of new information which could also be of interest to Shpet's future biographers.

The second group of essays turns specifically to Shpet's presence on, and importance for, the Russian philosophical scene of his time. In his contribution, James Scanlan argues that, although not known primarily as a historian of philosophy, during one decade of his life (roughly 1914-23) Gustav Shpet produced a body of brilliant and original studies of the evolution of philosophical thinking in his homeland, focusing on what he considered the unenlightened and pragmatic orientation of Russian culture that militated against the development of "true" or "genuine" theoretical philosophy in the spirit of Plato, Hegel, and modern-day phenomenology. The other two papers in this section submit, contrary to received opinion, that Gustav Shpet was prepared to treat Russian religious philosophy seriously (although he never embraced it and persistently questioned its intellectual foundations). Steven Cassedy examines Shpet's modifications of Husserl's phenomenology and portrays a thinker grounded as much in Western thought as in Russian religious thought of the late nineteenth and early twentieth centuries. On Cassedy's imaginative reading, Shpet's philosophy combines Husserl's analysis of the structure of consciousness with the fundamental Platonism of Orthodoxy, the doctrine of incarnation and the related notion that matter is to be venerated. Maryse Dennes attempts to demonstrate that Vladimir Solov'ev's legacy, as well as that of Russian religious thought more generally, has a special role in Gustav Shpet's work. She focuses on Shpet's pre-1917 writings, *Appearance and Sense* (1914) and "Consciousness and Its Owner" (1916), in which Shpet quotes from Pavel Florenskii, Vladimir Solov'ev, and Sergei Trubetskoi. By examining Shpet's reactions to them, Dennes also poses the question of the relationship between the principle of *sobornost'* and that of hermeneutic inquiry in Shpet's philosophy.

The articles in part three focus on Shpet's work in the context of the Western European mainstream, examining his philosophy in the framework of three different versions of phenomenology (Hegel, Husserl, Sartre). Thomas Nemeth argues that despite his obvious enthusiasm for phenomenology, Shpet expressed reservations towards a number of Husserl's procedures and teachings. His acceptance of Husserl's transcendental turn was cautious and restrained, his following of Husserl's project of "philosophy as a rigorous science"—hesitant and qualified. Shpet found Husserl's dichotomy between experiencing intuition and essential intuition wanting. Despite phenomenology's laudable goal of calling attention to consciousness as a specific form of being, it overlooked, among other things, an entire class of conscious acts, namely, hermeneutic acts. Nemeth focuses not only on the nature of Shpet's disagreements with Husserl's position as it stood in 1914, but also on how in time these differences led Shpet to make a "social turn" via linguistics and aesthetics.

George L. Kline traces Shpet's appropriation of Hegel by examining in detail his translation of Hegel's *Phänomenologie des Geistes,* which Shpet completed while in exile, shortly before being re-arrested and shot. He furnishes convincing proof of the remarkable quality of Shpet's translation by analyzing examples in Shpet's text that render key points of Hegelian doctrine as well as Hegel's wit and irony. Shpet's frequent verbatim and near verbatim repetitions of the 1913 Russian translation were presumably the result of his sense that, time being desperately short, he needed to focus on the technical distinctions of Hegel's terminology, such as that between *Vermittlung* (mediation) and *Vermitteln* (act of mediating). He conveyed such distinctions brilliantly, although without full consistency. Shpet's translation, Kline concludes, is a towering achievement, one that ranks with the best in the major European languages. Next, Ulrich Schmid demonstrates how Shpet essayed to fuse different positions into a coherent logical method for the interpretation of history. At its basis lies the Hegelian assumption that history has no necessary evolution but is governed by rationality. Shpet, admittedly, modifies Hegel's optimism by pointing to the fact that history is far from reaching an end as Hegel had suggested for his own age. However, for a while Shpet himself saw the Russian Revolution as an important step towards the rationalization of Russian reality; he came to sympathize with the voluntaristic views of thinkers such as August von Cieszkowski or Alexander Herzen. Finally, Shpet tried to create a strictly logical hermeneutics of history on the grounds of Husserl's phenomenology: in Shpet's view, historical reality is given exclusively in the word which embodies one single, objective sense. This rigid conceptualization, Schmid suggests, led Shpet to a tragic misinterpretation of early Soviet history: he searched for a rational sense where there was only politics of power.

Alexander Haardt opens his article with the assertion that by 1927, in *The Inner Form of the Word*, Shpet's phenomenological descriptions of eidetic structures had taken on a dialectical dimension derived from Hegel's *Phänomenologie des Geistes*. Haardt applies this method of a "dialectical interpretation" to Shpet's own poetics, as laid out in his *Aesthetic Fragments*. The characterization offered there of the essential features of poetry or poetic discourse—a characterization largely informed by Shpet's Platonist interpretation of Husserl's phenomenology—is analyzed in its one-sidedness and is juxtaposed with an alternative descriptive model of poetry or literature, that of Jean-Paul Sartre's *What is Literature?* Sartre is ultimately bound to a Cartesian interpretation of Husserl, and thus sets priorities quite different from those of the author of the *Aesthetic Fragments*.

The essays in part four examine Shpet's philosophy of language and semiotics. Thomas Seifrid considers the implicit meditations on selfhood within Shpet's philosophy of language. Shpet's reiteration of Husserl's ideas, Seifrid submits, betrays an ontological anxiety over where to house the self, given the insubstantiality of the individual ego. In recompense, Shpet turns to the idea of language, and the greater emphasis he places on this topic is another way in which he departs from Husserl. In works like "Germenevtika i ee problemy" ("Hermeneutics and Its Problems") and *Vvedenie v etnicheskuiu psikhologiiu* (*Introduction to Ethnic Psychology*) he outlines his vision of language and language-like entities as models for the existence of order and meaning in the world. It is these structures that serve as ultimate repositories of selfhood. This concept of selfhood in Shpet, Seifrid argues, is more closely tied with native Russian, rather than the more visible Western (especially German), philosophical influences on Shpet's work.

Craig Brandist's paper deals with the reception of German and Austrian philosophical thought in the work of Shpet and the Bakhtin Circle, particularly as it relates to the philosophy of language. Shpet was particularly influenced by the works of Husserl that followed his idealist turn, while the Bakhtin Circle was more interested in the work of members of the phenomenological movement who refused to follow Husserl in this direction, most notably Max Scheler. Shpet was also more indebted to the work of Anton Marty than was the Bakhtin Circle (especially Voloshinov, who drew more heavily on the work of Karl Bühler). Shpet started with phenomenology but gradually moved away from it, whereas Bakhtin began from a neo-Kantian position, which he attempted to supplement with phenomenological "concreteness." While this conditioned a certain convergence of their positions, especially when they considered the same philosophical issues, they ultimately followed different intellectual trajectories.

Dušan Radunović seeks to explore thematic and conceptual correspondences between Shpet's concept of language and Voloshinov's theory of verbal interaction.

Radunović argues that, although the two thinkers belong to different philosophical traditions, there are significant affinities between their philosophical concerns. With the question of meaning at the center of his discussion, Radunović addresses Shpet's and Voloshinov's notion of the subject and the role of sociality in the development of their conceptions of meaning. Radunović maintains that the two thinkers shared dissatisfaction with traditional semantics and its inability to account for the complexity of meaning. Despite this shared dissatisfaction, he concludes, Shpet and Voloshinov offered in the end radically different interpretation of the significance of semantics.

The volume also contains, for the first time in English translation, three essential sections of Shpet's book-length study of hermeneutics, as well as a synopsis of his paper on the limits of "scientific literary scholarship." Finally, in order to encourage and assist further research on Shpet, the volume features a bibliography of Shpet's published works, including translations into English and other languages, and an extensive bibliography of literature on him.

Works Cited

Artizov, Andrei. et al., eds. *"Ochistim Rossiu nadolgo . . ." Repressii protiv inako-mysliashchikh, konets 1921—nachalo 1923 g.: dokumenty*. Moscow: MFD and Materik, 2008.

Baranskaia, N.V. *Stranstvie bezdomnykh. Zhizneopisanie*. Moscow: n.p., 1999.

Iakimenko, Iu.N. "Iz istorii 'chistok apparata': Akademiia khudozhestvennykh nauk v 1929-1932." *Novyi istoricheskii vestnik* 1 (2005): 150-61.

Iarkho, Boris. *Metodologiia tochnogo literaturovedeniia. Izbrannye trudy po teorii literatury*. Ed. M.I. Shapir. Moscow: Iazyki slavianskikh kul'tur, 2006.

Pavlov, A.T. "Filosofiia v Moskovskom universitete v poslerevoliutsionnye gody. 1917-1941." *Filosofskie nauki* 9 (2003): 100-17.

Petritskii, V.A. "K tvorcheskoi biografii G.G. Shpeta (po materialam ekzempliara "Vvedeniia v etnicheskuiu psikhologiiu" s inskriptom filosofa)." *Shpetovskie chteniia v Tomske 1991*. Ed. O.G. Mazaeva. Tomsk: Izdatel'stvo Tomskogo universiteta, 1991. 21-26.

Poleva, Nataliia. "Osnovnye daty biografii G.G. Shpeta." *Gustav Gustavovich Shpet. Arkhivnye materialy. Vospominaniia. Stat'i*. Ed. T.D. Martsinkovskaia. Moscow: Smysl, 2000. 7-14.

Polivanov, Mikhail. "Ocherk biografii G.G. Shpeta." *Litsa. Biograficheskii al'manakh* 1 (1992): 7-43.

Serebrennikov, N.V. "Novye dannye o gibeli G.G. Shpeta." *Russkaia mysl'* [Paris] 3778. 2 June 1989: 13.

Shpet, Gustav. "Sotsializm ili gumanizm." Ed. T.G. Shchedrina. *Kosmopolis* 1 (2006): 77-90.

Shtorkh, Marina. "V Rossii dobrogo cheloveka staviat vyshe obrazovannogo" [An Interview with Natal'ia Ivanova-Gladil'shchikova]. *Izvestiia. Prilozhenie "Nauka."* 22 February 2002.

Tihanov, Galin. "Gustav Shpet v zerkale Georgiia Florovskogo (1922-1959)." *Issledovaniia po istorii russkoi mysli: ezhegodnik* 8 (2009): 140-49.

Tihanov, Galin. "Multifariousness under Duress: Gustav Shpet's Scattered Lives." *Russian Literature* 63.2/3/4 (2008): 259-92.

Part One

Mapping Out the Field

Tropos Logikos: Gustav Shpet's Philosophy of History

Peter Steiner

Recollecting the heady atmosphere at the Moscow University before WWI when belonging to a particular camp of contemporary German philosophy was *de rigueur*, Boris Pasternak wrote: "The devotees of the Göttingen Husserlites found support in Shpet" (35). This cryptic remark (Shpet's name is not mentioned again in *Safe Conduct*) caught my attention for several reasons. The first is quite trivial: when writing his autobiographical novel, Pasternak could not have known that his then-seven-year-old son Evgenii—whimsically compared in the book to the philosopher Hermann Cohen—would once upon a time marry Shpet's granddaughter Elena. Two other reasons deserve a more detailed explication.

As his life and violent death illustrate, Gustav Gustavovich Shpet (1879-1937) was the son of a turbulent era (see Polivanov; Martsinkovskaia). He became enmeshed in politics rather early, after his freshman year at Kiev University, when he joined the Marxist Social Democratic Party. Arrested and exiled from the city for his radical activities, he nevertheless managed to return and graduated in 1905. After moving to Moscow two years later, his star rose fast on the Russian intellectual horizon: research trips abroad, articles and books on philosophy, historiography, psychology and, in 1918, a coveted professorship at Moscow University. Surviving the revolution and the civil war, Shpet apparently declined the opportunity to emigrate in 1922 and found a *modus vivendi* with the Soviet government. Until 1929 he served as Vice President of the State Academy for the Study of the Arts (GAKhN: Gosudarstvennaia akademiia khudozhestvennykh nauk), which became a well-known Moscow intellectual and cultural center during the post-Civil War era. There he continued his multifaceted research, focusing eventually on the study of language. The year 1929 marked the second intrusion of politics into Shpet's scholarly career. The hurricane of Stalinism blew away his protective academic shell: GAKhN was closed and he found himself relegated to the gray zone of a public quasi-existence: a six year long limbo preceding Siberian exile and eventual execution. During this time he earned his bread mainly as a translator but was prohibited from publishing his own writings.

13

In 1929-30 he was subjected to a vicious press campaign that painted him as an undesirable remnant of reactionary ideology who insidiously misused his administrative position at GAKhN to publish (at the proletariat's expense) books clearly hostile to its cause. *Safe Conduct*—and this is my second reason for mentioning Pasternak's text—coming out as a book in 1931 might well have been the last publication in which Shpet could have still read his name unsullied by negative epithets.

Finally, Pasternak's laconic remark cast Shpet in a very specific intellectual mold, as prime promoter of Husserlian phenomenology in Russia. This view, I would like to stress, was prevalent among Shpet's contemporaries. Thus, a fellow student from Kiev University, Vasilii Zen'kovskii (unlike Shpet, luckily emigrating from Russia in the 1920s) stated in his *Istoriia russkoi filosofii* (*History of Russian Philosophy*) that Shpet was "a most orthodox follower of Husserl" who "treated all those thinking differently with contempt and irritation" (369-72). Zen'kovskii's grudge, one might surmise, has something to do with an inhospitable review of his book on causality in psychology Shpet published some thirty-five years earlier (see Shpet, "Kriticheskie zametki"). In a more sympathetic manner, Roman Jakobson mentioned Shpet several times while reflecting about the roots of inter-War structuralist linguistics and poetics. He remembered him as the conduit through which that newly rising interdisciplinary paradigm became impregnated with fundamental phenomenological postulates: "In the Moscow Linguistic Circle of the early twenties, continuous and ardent debates led by Gustav Shpet—in Husserl's opinion, one of his most remarkable students—were concerned with the linguistic use of the *Logische Untersuchungen* and especially with Edmund Husserl's and Anton Marty's avowed and suggestive return to 'the thought of a universal grammar'" (Jakobson, "Retrospect" 713; "Toward the History" 281).

There are good reasons why Shpet's coevals viewed him in this particular way. His stays at the University of Göttingen, where he encountered Edmund Husserl and became acquainted with his *Ideas*, is one of the most famous *topoi* of the Russian philosopher's biography. Furthermore, the correspondence between the two thinkers from 1913 to 1918 attests to their convivial relationship, just as Shpet's dedication of his first book, *Appearance and Sense*, to Husserl evinces a deep-seated respect. Yet scrutiny of Shpet's writings reveals a much less passive attitude toward Husserl's ideas than his contemporaries seemed to perceive. Shpet was thrilled by the intellectual rigor of this philosophical school and borrowed some of its concepts and methods, but in a highly selective manner. Kline's remark that "it would be more accurate to call [Shpet] a neo-Husserlian . . . since on central philosophical issues he was closer to both Plato and Hegel than to (early) Husserl," characterizes well, I believe, the overall orientation of his thought ("Meditations" 144). For even his abovementioned trip to Göttingen was carried out for a research purpose alien to the usual phenomenological agenda of the pre-WWI period. He went abroad to gather materials for his dissertation, published in 1916 under the title *Istoriia kak problema logiki. Kriticheskie i metodologicheskie issledovaniia* (*History as a Problem of Logic*). It was most likely Shpet's concern with the theory of history which revealed to him the limits of Husserl's transcendental phenomenology, as he pointed out in *Appearance and Sense*: its inability to deal with the social dimension of our consciousness. A historical fact (like all other cultural products) is a reality fundamentally unlike simple physical things and to experience it adequately requires a particular mental act unacknowledged in the Husserlian scheme of human perception. The unique source of historical knowledge, Shpet asserted, is a special "intelligible intuition" through which we construe what no longer is ("Filosofiia i istoriia" 437).

Shpet's philosophy of history, advanced in the above-mentioned dissertation and subsequently further refined in the lengthy essay "History as a Subject-matter of Logic" (written in 1917 but published only five years later) did not elicit, it seems, much of a public response among his contemporaries. Whether this lack of reaction is attributable to the inclement sociopolitical context of war and revolution or to the unabashedly iconoclastic tenor of his ideas remains to be decided. The fact is that in the early 1920's Shpet himself turned away from the field of history, focusing his attention on aesthetics, linguistics, and social psychology instead. In my opinion, however, Shpet's philosophy of history belongs among the most original intellectual contributions across all the disciplines in which he engaged. To some degree it anticipated the "linguistic turn" that took place in Western historiography during the last quarter of the twentieth century for which Hayden White's well-known book *Metahistory* (1973) stands as a convenient shorthand. What makes Shpet's thought akin to his are the following principles about history that he advanced in his writings on this subject: 1) sources of historical knowledge are words rather than facts; 2) a historian neither describes nor explains, but interprets; 3) history is above all a historiography, a representation of the past from a new perspective; and 4) its methods are not narrowly mono-disciplinary but are applicable to other types of writing as well.

Turning now to Shpet's writings themselves, let me start with the titles of the two publications mentioned above that bring together in a somewhat enigmatic manner the words *history* and *logic*. This combination, it must be stressed, does not imply the stance dubbed "historicism" by Karl Popper: the assumption that history follows a preordained logic of its own and, therefore, the study of the past enables us to make valid predictions about the course of future events (see Popper; Kline, "Shpet as Interpreter"). Shpet was well aware of how homonymic the word *history* is, "signifying simultaneously an actual process as well as the discipline [*nauka*] about it" (*Istoriia* 49). These two are heterogeneous and logic pertains solely to discourse about data, not to the unfolding of data per se. In Shpet's parlance, logic, as I illustrate later, refers to historiography, that is, the production of texts about the past.

Compared to *history*, Shpet's use of the term *logic* is far more resistant to incisive yet economic exposition. It is a cardinal term of his theorizing, popping up with a fearful frequency in all his writings. The multiplicity of subjects treated under this heading and Shpet's own intellectual development vastly enlarged its extension. This, however, is less a symptom of intellectual failure than a sign of his time. For the philosophers concerned with the theory of logic at the turn of the last century, a commentator informs us, this discipline "was still in the melting pot: not only its proper scope, subject matter, concept and methods, but also its standing with respect to mathematics, psychology, and . . . the theory of meaning were all problems yet to be solved" (Bell 87). Thus, instead of mapping the vicissitudes of this term in Shpet's discourse, let me broadly highlight some salient features of his understanding of logic by juxtaposing it to the manner in which Edmund Husserl treated this pregnant concept in his trailblazing *Logische Untersuchungen.*

Setting as his objective to provide the self-evident foundation of all science, Husserl's approach was deliberately reductionist. He strove, first of all, to establish a *calculus ratiocinator*, pure logic prior to any actual languages and universal for all of them. To meet this formal constraint Husserlian logic dealt solely with ideal, categorial, and nontemporal linguistic forms capable of retaining their eidetic self-sameness in every actual repetition. Secondly, such a logic not only purged language of all empirical components but also concerned itself exclusively with semantics and syntax (universal grammar providing combinatory rules for pure meanings), leaving communication outside its purview. For Husserl, words were incapable of transmitting the logical meaning from one subject to another. No sooner than leaving the safe limits of one's consciousness—as a medium of intercourse—did they degenerate into mere indices of either speaker's mental state or of some segment of reality.

Shpet could not have been satisfied with Husserl's notion of pure logic on a number of counts. Practically speaking, the empirical sciences (among which he included history) ultimately operate with natural languages. And these are never pure embodiment of reason but much fuzzier entities—the archetypes of human culture in general. Says Shpet, "by the structure of word, I mean . . . an organically deep [system]: from the sensorily perceptible to the formally-ideal (eidetic) object, with all levels of relations between these two terms" (*Esteticheskie* 11). None of these linguistic features can be eliminated from the structural whole (as Husserl would have it) without destroying it. Put differently, when language is used even for the most formal purposes, its material substance remains present if only *in potentia*, as an unrealized, schematic possibility.

At the theoretical level too, Shpet's basic view of language was diametrically opposed to Husserl's. By conceiving of language primarily as a calculus, the German philosopher regarded it in and of itself as unimportant (see Kusch 55-76). Necessity forces us to use a particular language but it is not a prison house we cannot escape, for truth is just as accessible in all other languages due to the universal grammar they all share. On this issue Shpet was close to the Humboldtian position that emphasizes the constitutive nature of language in our interaction with the world at large. There is a sharp difference between experience and knowledge that is linguistic. The empirical becomes cognitive, Shpet maintained, only if informed with language. And, stressing his thought, he proclaimed that "the word is the principium cognoscendi of our knowledge." From this vantage point, then, rather than a method of searching for truth, logic is a discipline that "studies the word as an expression of knowledge" ("Mudrost' ili razum?" 294). This stance, as I will illustrate, has important implications for how Shpet conceived of historians' business. But to consider language merely in its world-disclosure capacity—as a universal medium through which we interpret the world around us—limits, according to Shpet, its potential in one important respect. It casts linguistic praxis solely in terms of a subject-object interaction: a single mind conferring meaning on the phenomena it attends. From very early on Shpet refused to see human consciousness from such a solipsistic perspective. He emphasized his abhorrence of "absolute social solitude" in *Appearance and Sense*: "'solitary confinement' is the destiny not of the individual, as such, but only of the insane" (160). And as he reiterated throughout his writings, especially in his 1916 essay, "Consciousness and Its Owner," human consciousness is never the private property of a single owner, but always a collective creativity ("Soznanie"; see also *Istoriia* 4). What we are and how we perceive reality is a function of the language that we share with other members of the same community. This "sharing" however, should not be understood as the passive acquisition of a ready-made cognitive lens. Language was for Shpet not a static *ergon* but a dynamic *energeia*. And nowhere does its processive nature demonstrate itself better than in communication, the give-and-take mechanism of questions and answers through which we traffic information about the world and piece together its picture.

Here we are getting to the heart of the matter. Given the all-pervasive manner in which language obtrudes itself on our interaction with the world and others, it seemed rather doubtful to Shpet that there is a human experience that might be truly primordial, originary, unmediated by it. Any introspective analysis of how we know what we know, he proposed, reveals the deep-seated linguistic underpinnings of our knowledge (whether direct or indirect) making in fact the perceptual a function of the verbal. This premise, however, has fundamental consequences for how we conceptualize our interaction with the world. Words are not physical objects observed from outside but signs, vehicles of a social meaning accessible only through the above mentioned "intelligible intuition": "understanding" or "comprehension" (*urazumenie*) to use Shpet's own terms (*Appearance* 160). To navigate this intricate semiotic web, however, requires a logic different from that employed by mathematically based natural sciences that deal solely with material realities. Such a logic ought to be, first of all, dialectical, according to Socrates' "definition of *dialogos* in its original and full sense," that is, "joint [*sovmestnyi*] thinking" (Shpet, "Filosofiia i istoriia" 428). And second, it should be hermeneutical, analyzing signs within the circular structure: "experience-expression-understanding" (Shpet, "Hermeneutics" 241).

The concept of "experience" that I just mentioned provides me with a convenient gateway into his argument. It proves rather vexing for the traditional historian who is guided by Leopold von Ranke's maxim to present the past *wie es eigentlich gewesen war*. Obviously, the past cannot be relived *stricto sensu*. Thus, those wishing to construct faithfully events that have transpired must have recourse to various ingenious schemes enabling them to step, so to speak, twice into the same river. Stakes in this exercise are high, though; failing to provide a causal explanation of past actions undermines the claim that history is a scientific enterprise on a par with physics or chemistry. But in the second half of the nineteenth century this one-fits-all epistemological approach came under concentrated attack. Wilhelm Dilthey and the Baden School (to mention just a few of those influencing Shpet) divided the systematic pursuit of knowledge into two distinctive spheres, each governed by its own methods: roughly speaking, the "nomothetic" natural sciences that strive to subsume all particulars under general covering laws and the "ideographic" *Geisteswissenschaften* (like history), which ascribe to every particular a unique value within its appurtenant cultural context. Shpet's own solution to this problem is unexpected in its boldness. He returned to the single-model approach, but in a surprising move he reversed its mimetic order. While in its canonic version history was relegated as a poor relative of the *strenge Wissenschaften* whose methods it was to emulate at any cost, Shpet proclaimed history the model for all systematic knowledge. In his own words: "To the nineteenth century conviction, still dominant today, that the logic of the natural sciences [*estestvoznanie*] is the logic of [all] empirical sciences [*empiricheskie nauki*] we . . . oppose the categorical assertion that it is the logic of history which of them all is the logic of the empirical sciences" (Shpet, "Istoriia, kak predmet" 12).

If one suspects that this stance has something to do with Shpet's belief in the world-disclosing capacity of language, one is probably right. Faithful to the tenets of phenomenology, Shpet rejected outright the postulate that the ultimate source of systematic knowledge (*nauka*) is a direct sense experience per se. These, he explained, are incompatible categories. "Knowledge, and particularly its system, is not an experience but a reflection about it, it is not an experience but the critique of an experience" (Shpet, "Istoriia, kak predmet" 6). One example of such a critique (discussed by Shpet) is Husserl's "noematic/noetic" model proposed in the *Ideas*. It bracketed off from human perception all that was subjective and transient, thus grounding knowledge in the essential structure of experience. Shpet, however, did not follow suit. The degree of formal reductions undertaken by the German thinker in the pursuit of a *reine Wesensschau* made his method, Shpet insisted, altogether too abstract for the empirical sciences.

More relevant for Shpet's own argument seems to be Husserl's discussion of the act of reflection through which we become consciously aware of our experience. Such meta-experience should simultaneously exhibit two features: it should be concurrent with experience, unlike memory, while, at the same time separable from it, available to subsequent mental processing. But Husserl was careful to distinguish reflection from judgment, a secondary interpretation of the experience liable to egregious distortions (see Kohák 105-20). As far as I can tell, the father of phenomenology did not outline any mechanism enabling reflection to remain undistorted in one's mind after the experience that triggered it has faded away. Shpet, however, proposed a solution to this problem. To fix the moments of sameness within the ongoing flux of living experience, a special medium is needed. This, he was happy to announce, is language: "To be able to stop the experience in front of you for a moment and render it the object of 'observation' you must be able to say: 'here it is, here is something,' 'this is what I want to be aware of,' etc. These originary, undefined, pure percepto-sentences [*pert-septivnye predlozheniia*] immediately elicit entire systems of new sentences . . . of a similar percepto-demonstrative form: 'this is something,' 'this is a symptom of that,' 'this is an effect of that,' etc., and, then, the entire manifold system of abstract, concrete, simple [and] complex sentences, etc., etc." (Shpet, "Istoriia, kak predmet" 17).

In transforming sensations into an idea—an object of knowledge—we articulate what we observe into distinct segments, attributing certain qualities to them in this process. And this mental act, Shpet's quote suggests, is identical with the logical act of predication (traditionally represented by the equation S = P): the most basic mechanism of a sentence-generating. According to this view, no systemic inquiry in any field can be language free. This is especially pertinent to the natural sciences that, as it has been believed since the advent of positivism, are the product of pure observation undiluted by any exogenous factors. But if, as Shpet wrote, "the mind's first *logical* act is the investiture [*oblechenie*] of experience with verbal form" (Shpet, "Istoriia, kak predmet" 18), even this type of knowledge is, from its very inception, language bound. And to push his parallel with history yet further, Shpet termed any interpretation of experience a "reading":

> The observer in fact deals with nothing but his own system of sentences about the object under study. This, in other words, means that in his cognition the observer deals with his own assertions about the object and he cognizes by reading the sentences he himself composes. The natural scientist, it appears, reads his own yet unrecorded composition while the historian reads a recorded one transmitted by others. One need only recall the extent of others' opinions, presuppositions and bookish theories that the observer carries into his actual observations to realize that this difference is altogether relative and, in any case, not a matter of principal. (Shpet, "Istoriia, kak predmet" 17)

The conclusion that Shpet drew from comparing these two kinds of interpretations is elegant in its simplicity. Because he is dealing with a far more intricate semiotic system as a reader, the historian is superior to the natural scientist. If, while reflecting upon his observations, the latter employs language still in a nascent state with many of its forms inchoate, imperfect, the historian deals with words in their full complexity. It is therefore only logical that it is precisely his hermeneutic methods that provide the best model for the art of interpretation in general.

At this moment I should not fail to observe that in discussing the concept of *perception* I have willy-nilly moved a step forward (or backward) in Shpet's hermeneutic circle. A self-conscious experience is merely a linguistic transubstantiation of sensations, that is, their understanding. But we should also recall that there is still a third term of which this circle is comprised: *expression*. In order not to break the circuit, private comprehension must be made intelligible to others, translated from inner speech into public discourse, which in scholarship usually implies a written text. This process is patent in the physical sciences where the qualitative jump from observable facts to theories about them is hard to miss. In history, on the other hand, where words just reflect other words, the distinction between the two seems rather putative and tends to be largely ignored—to the detriment of history, said Shpet. This discipline, like any other, straddles two distinct activities, Shpet contended: research proper and its exposition (*izlozhenie*). Among the historians of his time, however, the former was generally considered far more important than the latter, as if presentation of data were a mere appendage to archival work, a total rendition of its results in a fully transparent form. This generally accepted view, however, directly contradicts what was, in Shpet's mind, truly important in scholarship. "Strictly speaking, what characterizes systematic knowledge [*nauka*] is its second aspect alone [i.e., the communication of results]—however we arrive at knowledge, it is essential that we convey it in such a way that we do not inspire doubt, but we prove our point" (Shpet, *Istoriia* 32). To understand retrieved signs, the historian must be a reader; but to impart his understanding to others he must be a writer as well. True, a certain correlation (*respektivnost'*) exists between the two occupations, Shpet was willing to concede, but they are asymmetrical. "It is clear, that just as what is understood does not cover the entire content of the source, neither does what is transmitted, 'expose' its verbatim content" (Shpet, "Istoriia, kak predmet" 32-33). Each approach is selective in its own way and, therefore, requires its own methodology. Heuristics (which Shpet, following Gerardus Joannus Vossius's lead, occasionally also calls "historics") was in his view a necessary but ancillary subdiscipline that instructs a historian how to approach his material and how to analyze it (Shpet, *Istoriia* 34). It is fully subordinated to logic: "the discipline [*nauka*] of the form of expression of systematic historical knowledge [*nauka*]" (Shpet, *Istoriia* 62). At this point it might be useful to return to the claim with which this paper began, namely, that Shpet's philosophy of history anticipated to some degree the linguistic turn that emerged in Western historiography some sixty years after the publication of his studies on the subject. Yet does not his exclusive reliance on logic as the master matrix for the study of history writing contradict its explicit renunciation by the linguistically minded theoreticians who discovered their analytical tools in certain branches of literary theory: tropology and narratology?

Insofar as narration is concerned, this category played only a limited role in Shpet's theorizing. His typology of history writing, derived from Ernst Bernheim's *Lehrbuch der historischen Methode*, differentiates among three methods of rendering the past: 1) narrative, 2) didactic, and 3) genetic: narrative history is a story about events triggered by purely aesthetic needs and is, in this respect, related to other genres of verbal, "literary" creativity. While the value of such texts, Shpet argued, is primarily artistic, works of didactic history pursue pragmatic goals. They provide readers with "norms or maxims of behavior in the form of a 'historical moral.'" And finally, genetic history does not exhort but instead strives to explain how transpired events came about and developed (Shpet, *Istoriia* 25-26). This division is not merely classificatory but also genealogical. Narrative history is, in Shpet's opinion, a more primitive stage of historiography than the pragmatic, and the latter, in turn, has been superseded in the course of time by the genetic mode. Shpet himself complicated this scheme a bit by inserting into it one additional interphase: "philosophical history."

The transition from moralism to science that took place during the Enlightenment was stimulated by philosophical reflections about the subject and methodology of history that eventually molded it into the discipline we know today. Narrative, this developmental scheme suggests, was for Shpet a discursive strategy characteristic of one type of historical discourse but not of historiography in its entirety.

But there might be yet other reasons why Shpet did not pay much attention to the narrative aspect of history: his own historiographic practice. We should not forget that he was not only a philosopher of history but also an author of three books on the history of philosophy. Besides his 1916 *Istoriia kak problema logiki. Kriticheskie i metodologicheskie issledovaniia* (*History as the Problem of Logic*), which in some 400 pages outlines the formation of European historical thought in the eighteenth and early nineteenth centuries, he wrote in 1918 "Germenevtika i ee problemy" ("Hermeneutics and Its Problems")—a survey of and commentary on the state of this discipline from antiquity to his own time—and in 1922 published the first part of an ambitious *Ocherk razvitiia russkoi filosofii* (*Essay on the Development of Russian Philosophy*). As intellectual histories these texts are not stories (emplotments of past events according to genre-bound formulas) but chronologically organized discussions of ideas lifted from the past because of their supposed bearing on present thought.

Shpet's attitude toward tropology was more complex, however. It is clear that his dialogic and hermeneutic logic was a far cry from the discipline rejected by White because it supposedly treats the language of history as "a set of empty forms waiting to be filled with a factual and conceptual content or attached to preexistent referents in the world" (White, *Figural* 5). From very early on the Russian philosopher insisted that logic (in the sense of the purely formal discipline invoked by White) is incapable of treating historical concepts adequately because these embody what he provisionally termed "semiotic knowledge" that "requires an epistemology of its own" (Shpet, "Pervyi opyt" 381). In historical discourse, to paraphrase his thought, words are always already meta-signs: knots in a truly endless mesh of semiotic permutations, substitutions, refractions. But he described these semantic shifts in terms of the various dichotomies permeating language use—potential versus actual, meaning versus reference, context versus recontextualization—rather than as poetic tropes. This does not mean that Shpet altogether ignored the issue of figurative language. He discussed it in his book *Vnutrenniaia forma slova. Etiudy i variatsii na temy Gumbol'ta* (*The Inner Form of the Word*, subtitled significantly, *Etudes and Variations on Humboldt's Themes*) from a perspective which, in fact, is not so different from White's. There is no formal difference between poetic images and scientific concepts, he asserted in 1927. "An 'aerial ocean' is in its form as much a concept as 'atmosphere,' and 'atmosphere' (*atmos* + *sphaira*) is as much a trope as 'aerial ocean'" (Shpet, *Vnutrenniaia* 183). What does set the two apart are their respective modes of signification. Whereas a trope refers only indirectly, through the mediation of other words, a concept (where the initial figurative link between sound and meaning has been largely effaced) does so directly. Yet, if Shpet believed that historical concepts (unlike their scientific counterparts but very much like poetic figures) are signs of signs, signifying only in a roundabout manner, why did he never find it necessary to make a formal tropology part of his historiography?

To answer this question, let me create a provisional and rather inaccurate parallel between Shpet's and White's views of the historiographer. To both he seems, in a manner of speaking, a Jehovah-like figure hovering upon an amorphous mass of data about a past. And he says the word and the light is divided from darkness. But there is a difference in how he says what he says. To wit, one speaks in sentences, the other in images. The gap between these discursive modalities, arguably, is not unbridgeable. A trope can be easily viewed as an abbreviated predication: calling Achilles a lion is like saying that he is a lion in some respect or capacity. Let me also note in passing that for Shpet, predication was not logic's ultimate building block consisting of three irreducible terms: "S is P." The members of this triad, in his view, already carry certain attributes prior to entering any actual sentence (Shpet, "Istoriia, kak predmet" 20). Leaving such technicalities aside, the difference between logic and tropology seems to rest in the degree of discursive freedom they allow the speaker to exercise. In predication the synthetic power of consciousness is unfettered: S can be associated with P for whatever motives. White's tropology, on the other hand, consisting of metaphor, metonymy, synecdoche, and irony allows for just four types of associations, no more and no less. Why four, or precisely these four, one may well ask.

The actual make up of the tropology appointed by White to articulate historical discourse might be arbitrary, but is the function of the specific philosophical assumptions underlying his thought. According to F.R. Ankersmit's observation, there is a close affinity between the Whitean system of tropes and the Kantian transcendental categories of understanding. The intellectual thrust of tropology, he asserted, is "to develop a quasi-Kantian critique of historical knowledge and to closely associate his own theory of history with that impressive culmination point of Western scientific thought . . . *Metahistory* is no less an endeavor to provide with us with quasi-Kantian investigation of the cognitive foundations that support historical representation and meaning". But such transcendentalism is not just an idle intellectual game; it also serves a practical goal: "appropriating," "familiarizing" the uncanny past. This function, inherent in all Whitean tropes, is most palpable, Ankersmit continued, in metaphor: "Speaking generally, metaphor has been remarkably effective in organizing knowledge in ways that may serve our social and political purposes" (Ankersmit 10-13). From this perspective, then, the limiting nature of tropology is not a secondary byproduct of its existence, but the final cause of its being, its telos. The formal grid of possibilities it provides harnesses historical discourse to the utilitarian agenda of today, thus making imagination a technique for the purposive manipulation of the past, an instrument for steering its narrative in a desired direction.

Returning now to Shpet, in contrast to White's hidden Kantianism his attitude toward this transcendental philosophical tradition was critical, to say the least. There are no other figures in the history of ideas whom he upbraided so sharply as Immanuel Kant and his followers. Their apriorism, he charged, the imposition of a priori transcendental structures on human experience is but a version of epistemological determinism that rules out genuine philosophical inquiry. In the world so conceived, "reason does not embrace the heterogeneity of objects and does not discover in them the inexhaustible reservoir of its critical powers but, because of its inability to think in any other way, subjects existence to monotonous regulation and routine" (Shpet, *Istoriia* 4). Given this philosophical bent, it is no wonder that Shpet's logic of history did not propose a ready-made taxonomy of expressive forms available to each and every historiographer prior to their endeavor. But is, therefore, predication a more felicitous technique to be used in their interpretations? I return to this question soon.

Shpet elaborated on the concept of predication in the same 1927 book in which he dealt with the topic of figurative language. In keeping with the Humboldtian tenor of this work, the author prefaced his discussion of the "inner syntactic forms" with a warning that no static formula can ever capture the incessant semantic changeability of a living dialogue unfolding in a specific situation. "The sentence, as it lives in its linguistic element," he summed up his position, "is genuine synthetic evolution in the strictest sense of the word evolution—*evolutio libri*" (Shpet, *Vnutrenniaia* 110). Leaving aside the essential duality of all syntactic forms (always existing, if only potentially, within two contexts) predication is for Shpet, broadly speaking, an equation of incongruents. Every verbal assertion of the S is P type (unless a purely formal tautology) implies that S to some degree is and is not P. Yet, neither is it S's direct opposite: non-P. From this highly restricted perspective, then, a discourse evolves as a series of interconnected utterances, each qualifying the contradictions generated in previous statements and, in this process, simultaneously creating new contradictions. But is a self-contradicting predication a more felicitous starting point for writing about history than a well-defined set of tropes? The answer to this question depends entirely on the motive for one's engagement in this activity. White's tropology, Ankersmit suggests, has its distinct utility: it provides the historian with a precise tool for familiarizing the past, making it appropriate to the social or political concerns of the day. But what can be done with a never-ending permutation of sameness as being-other and otherness as being-same whose outcome is utterly unpredictable? Very little—if the past is conceived as an object of knowledge to be appropriated from without. But everything—if the two are merged in the act of self-reflection, thereby making history a precondition of knowledge and knowledge itself historical. This was Shpet's position.

Philosophy in the most general meaning of this word is, according to Shpet, knowledge's search for the very principles of knowledge, its own beginnings. But this process itself is also impregnated with history as thinkers of each successive era reflect upon the philosophical quests of their predecessors. The longer this line of inquiry gets, the greater the weight of the past. Shpet's comparison of classical antiquity with his own time illustrates this point: "With eyes wide open the philosophy of ancient Greece contemplated [*sozertsat'*] the very self in its own 'presence,' it began with contemplation. . . . We start with memory, with 'a legend' [*predanie*], we see the world through 'the dust of ages' . . . We and the ancient world look at the same things but for us panta rei has a new content and a new meaning: for us it is . . . above all the stream of history." The lesson to be learned from this development is clearly positive: the past is not inert ballast but a stimulating force. "In this sense our philosophy is turning above all into a historical philosophy. And the more it bestirs itself with the idea of the concrete as historical, the more it will become a historical philosophy" (Shpet, "Filosofiia i istoriia" 433-34). The influence of Hegel's thought on Shpet is undeniable. But there are also some contrasts between the two that are relevant to my topic. Though usually approving of Hegel, in his 1927 book Shpet pointed out a curious lacuna in the German philosopher's overarching system. Among all the realms in which spirit manifests itself (mapped so painstakingly by Hegel) one is surprisingly absent: language. It was Wilhelm Humboldt's linguistics which, according to Shpet, closed this intellectual gap. But this, in his eyes, did not make Humboldt a mere Hegelian acolyte stuck with the inglorious job of mopping up the spots untouched by the master's hand. Humboldt did not simply supplement what was missing in an otherwise perfect system but, significantly, succeeded in putting it on a new track. Wrote Shpet, "Just as Hegel would not have denied that language is an objectification of the spirit, Humboldt would have acknowledged that art, law, the state are objectifications of the spirit too. But Humboldt went further than Hegel and shifted the focus of the Hegelian project in such a way that the possibility of its continuation in Hegel's sense became realistic: this very art, law, [and] the state are the language of the spirit and the idea" (Shpet, *Vnutrenniaia* 34). Whence Shpet's own identification of the logic of history with historiography: the objectification of immaterial thought in tangible signs generated by properties specific to this medium.

My second comment about the difference between Hegel's and Shpet's views of history concerns their respective economies. Simplifying matters a good deal, it might be argued that the Hegelian developmental scheme is a closed system from which nothing ever gets lost. The spirit's path toward self-realization consists of a series of *Aufhebungen* (sublations): what is negated does not disappear in a void but through this very act becomes preserved, incorporated into its opposite and raised to a higher dialectical level. For Shpet, on the other hand, any cumulative view of the growth of knowledge (however dialectical) reeks of a technological attitude. In self-reflexive knowledge, of which philosophy is a paradigmatic case, re-cognition is never absolute. The Platonic metaphor of memory with which Shpet chose to characterize its beginnings hints not only at remembrance, information's retrieval, but also at its dissipation: forgetfulness, oblivion. Neither a cumulative growth of knowledge, nor a total amnesia, historical philosophy is a creative interplay of both: "In philosophy," Shpet wrote, "growth is always an ever new becoming [*porozhdenie*]—philosophy does not gather but productively wastes [*tratit*]" (Shpet, "Filosofiia i istoriia" 438). It is tempting to apply this conception of history to its author, to the fate of Shpet's own thought. At the beginning of this paper I interrupted the biography of our star-crossed hero in the early 1930s when, after being purged from his academic job, he was biding stormy weather as a translator. But then, in 1935, he was arrested together with several other scholars from the now defunct GAKhN (Boris Iarkho, Mikhail Petrovskii, etc.) and charged with belonging to a German-fascist counterrevolutionary organization. Luckily for him, initially he was "only" dispatched to Siberia for five years for his crimes (three members of the "group" were executed—among them a son of Shpet's mentor, the psychologist Georgii I. Chelpanov). Exile, however, proved just a short respite from his ordeal. Two years later, in the Siberian city of Tomsk, he was re-arrested and, following a secret court sentence as usual during Stalin's purges, shot in November 1937. And then, for some fifty years, he remained a specter, a virtual nonperson for any but a few. True, his official status changed in 1956 when Shpet, like many other victims of Stalin's regime, was posthumously rehabilitated. Nevertheless, the silence surrounding him was not broken in his homeland for another twenty years. If an individual entry (even a short one) in the *Great Soviet Encyclopedia* can be read as the sign of true acceptance by the Kremlin's ideological watchdogs, Shpet made it back fully only in 1978, albeit as a "philosopher-idealist" who, nota bene, died in 1940 (Mitiushin 469). And yet, during the following decade, as if from deep-rooted fear, his name was mentioned far more often abroad than in Russia, particularly among Western scholars interested either in the history of poetics or in the German phenomenological tradition. Only after 1989, when ideological taboos were abolished in the former Soviet Union, did Shpet emerge as one of the symbols of Russia's repressed intellectual past. Finally, after having been denied to his countrymen for so long, his works have begun to be reprinted and widely discussed. But even today, despite international effort, we still lack a synthesis of all of Shpet's theoretical endeavors. To wit, the hitherto most detailed study of his ideas, Alexander Haardt's *Husserl in Rußland* (1993), focuses primarily on Shpet's linguistics and aesthetics to the detriment of other dimensions of his truly multifaceted research agenda.

All this said, it is clear that on the balance sheet of intellectual history Shpet's historiographic ideas belong among the debits. They vanished: unknown, forgotten, prohibited. This waste, Bataille be my witness, cannot be called productive in any sense of the word! But can the wheel of fortune be turned, can we somehow profit today from his prescient thoughts about the philosophy of history? Is it not too late to bring Shpet back, to make him a voice in the ongoing dialogue of whether to construct, reconstruct or deconstruct the past? The melancholic part of my self-reflexive ego, like Aleksandr Blok's infant Jesus above "tsarskie vrata" (a royal door) of the iconostasis, cries in despair that all is lost, "chto nikto ne pridet nazad." But there is also the other part of myself, a hidden daemon with a weak but persistent voice that kept whispering in my soul as I was composing this tale: Besser spät als nie!

Note

The permission of American Association for the Advancement of Slavic Studies (AAASS) to reprint here an updated version of Peter Steiner's article is gratefully acknowledged.

Works Cited

Ankersmit, F.R. *History and Tropology: The Rise and Fall of Metaphor*. Berkeley: U of California P, 1994.

Bell, David Andrew. *Husserl*. London: Routledge, 1990.

Haardt, Alexander. *Husserl in Russland. Phänomenologie der Sprache und Kunst bei Gustav Špet und Aleksej Losev*. München: Fink, 1993.

Jakobson, Roman. "Retrospect." *Selected Writings*. Vol. 2. The Hague: Mouton, 1971. 711-24.

Jakobson, Roman. "Toward the History of the Moscow Linguistic Circle." *Selected Writings*. Vol. 7. Berlin: Mouton, 1985. 279-82.

Kline, George L. "Meditations of a Russian Neo-Husserlian: Gustav Shpet's 'The Skeptic and His Soul.'" *Phenomenology and Skepticism: Essays in Honor of James M. Edie*. Ed. Brice R. Wachterhauser. Evanston: Northwestern UP, 1996. 144-63.

Kline, George L. "Gustav G. Shpet as Interpreter of Hegel."*Archiwum historii filozofii i myśli społecznej* 44 (1999): 181-90.

Kohák, Erazim V. *Idea & Experience: Edmund Husserl's Project of Phenomenology in Ideas I*. Chicago: U of Chicago P, 1978.

Kusch, Martin. *Language as Calculus vs. Language as Universal Medium: A Study in Husserl, Heidegger and Gadamer*. Dordrecht: Kluwer, 1989.

Martsinkovskaia, T.D., ed. *Gustav Gustavovich Shpet. Arkhivnye materialy. Vospominaniia. Stat'i*. Moscow: Smysl, 2000.

Mitiushin, A.A. "Shpet, Gustav Gustavovich." *Bol'shaia sovetskaia entsiklopediia*. Vol. 29. Moscow: Sovetskaia entsiklopediia, 1978. 469.

Pasternak, Boris. *Safe Conduct: An Autobiography and Other Writings*. Trans. Babette Deutsch. New York: New Directions Publishing, 1958.

Polivanov, M.K. "O sud'be G.G. Shpeta." *Voprosy filosofii* 6 (1990): 160-64.

Popper, Karl Raimund. *Poverty of Historicism*. London: Routledge, 1957.

Shpet, Gustav. *Appearance and Sense: Phenomenology as the Fundamental Science and Its Problems*. Trans. Thomas Nemeth. Dordrecht: Kluwer, 1991.

Shpet, Gustav. *Esteticheskie fragmenty*. 2 vols. Peterburg: Kolos, 1923.

Shpet, Gustav. "Filosofiia i istoriia: Rech'." *Voprosy filosofii i psikhologii* 134 (1916): 427-39.

Shpet, Gustav. "Hermeneutics and Its Problems." Trans. Erika Freiberger-Sheihkoleslami. Ed. George L. Kline. Unpublished typescript. "Germenevtika i ee problemy," 1918.

Shpet, Gustav. "Istoriia, kak predmet logiki." *Nauchnye izvestiia Narkomprosa* 2 (1922): 1-35.

Shpet, Gustav. *Istoriia kak problema logiki: Kriticheskie i metodologicheskie issledovaniia*. Moscow: Tovarischchestvo tipografii A.I. Mamontova, 1916.

Shpet, Gustav. "Kriticheskie zametki k probleme psikhicheskoi prichinnosti: Po povodu knigi V. V. Zen'kovskogo *Problema psikhicheskoi prichinnosti*." *Voprosy filosofii i psikhologii* 127 (1915): 283-313.

Shpet, Gustav. "Mudrost' ili razum?" *Filosofskie etiudy*. Moscow: Progress, 1994. 222-336.

Shpet, Gustav. "Pervyi opyt logiki istoricheskikh nauk: K istorii ratsionalisma XVIII veka." *Voprosy filosofii i psikhologii* 128 (1915): 378-438.

Shpet, Gustav. "Soznanie i ego sobstvennik (Zametki)." *Filosofskie etiudy*. Moscow: Progress, 1994. 20-116.

Shpet, Gustav. *Vnutrenniaia forma slova. Etiudy i variatsii na temy Gumbol'dta*. Moscow: Gos. akademiia khudozhestvennykh nauk, 1927.

White Hayden. *Metahistory: The Historical Imagination in Nineteenth-Century Europe*. Baltimore: The Johns Hopkins UP, 1973.

White, Hayden. *Figural Realism: Studies in the Mimesis Effect*. Baltimore: The Johns Hopkins UP, 1999.

Zen'kovskii, Vasilii V. *Istoriia russkoi filosofii*. 2 vols. Paris: YMCA, 1950.

The Hermeneutic Triangle: Gustav Shpet's Aesthetics in Context

Robert Bird

From 1921 to 1930, numerous Russian thinkers found refuge in a Moscow institution called the State Academy of the Artistic Sciences (*GAKhN: Gosudarstvennaia akademiia khudozhestvennykh nauk*). GAKhN was an island of relatively independent scholarship and open intellectual debate, and it served as a locus of cultural continuity in the tumultuous period between the Civil War and the first Five Year Plan (see Misler). A large share of the credit for GAKhN is owed to Gustav Shpet, a member from its inception in 1921 (when it was still known as the Russian [*Rossiiskaia*] Academy of Artistic Sciences), head of the philosophical section from 1922, and Vice President of the institution from 1924. In these years Shpet maintained a prolific rate of scholarship in the most varied fields; in addition to numerous essays and papers, he published *Esteticheskie fragmenty* (*Aesthetic Fragments*; 1922-23), *Vnutrenniaia forma slova. Etiudy i variatsii na temy Gumbol'ta* (*The Inner Form of the Word: Etudes and Variations on Themes from Humboldt*; 1927), and *Vvedenie v etnicheskuiu psikhologiiu* (*An Introduction to Ethnic Psychology*; 1927). Like many of his colleagues, he paid a high price for his intellectual independence. When GAKhN was purged in 1930, he was hounded from his post and forbidden to teach or publish on philosophy. Five years after GAKhN was closed, Shpet was arrested and charged with leading a counter-revolutionary group centered at the Academy, and on 16 November 1937 he was executed for his crimes of thought.

The image of GAKhN as a kind of Noah's Ark for the remnants of Russia's intelligentsia fits the fragile, dialogical nature of Shpet's philosophy (see Shchedrina 217-20). All of his ideas were developed in intense dialogue with others, and his works typically took the form of commentaries on the works of previous, sometimes relatively obscure thinkers. Fittingly, he was the first Russian thinker to appropriate the term *hermeneutics* for the type of philosophy which views knowledge primarily as understanding, and which theorizes culture as an interpretive continuum. Although the historical deluge delayed its publication by seventy years, his 1918 book

"Germenevtika i ee problemy" ("Hermeneutics and Its Problems") still managed to be the first of its kind in Russia.

It is ironic that one of the major philosophical documents to have suffered the fate of near oblivion is a vast and impassioned defense of culture as a continuous community of interpretation. GAKhN, whose members included many of Shpet's close intellectual interlocutors, was the institutional image of this community which informed the immediate sources and contexts of Shpet's philosophical hermeneutics. In this essay I investigate Shpet's hermeneutics with special reference to two of his colleagues at GAKhN, the symbolist poet and theorist Viacheslav Ivanov (1866-1949) and the philosopher Aleksei Losev (1893-1988). I argue that Shpet's links to these two thinkers call particular attention to his key concept of detachment, which in turn helps illuminate an original tradition of hermeneutics and narrative theory.

Shpet's Phenomenological Hermeneutics

Shpet's "Germenevtika i ee problemy" consists largely of a critical overview of approaches to historical understanding by numerous (mainly German) historians and philosophers. In its major lineaments and characters Shpet's history of hermeneutics matches closely the standard story told in Western scholarship (see, e.g., Palmer; Grondin). However, Shpet was writing decades before his closest competitors; his account of the history of hermeneutic thought is independent and distinctive. Alexander Haardt's authoritative statement will guide my own investigation of the matter: "The most significant innovation in Shpet's history of hermeneutics was that he placed the task of a philosophical grounding for the hermeneutic canon squarely within a fundamental analysis of understanding," and that he pursued this by a "combination of semiotics and hermeneutics within the horizon of a 'phenomenology of understanding reason'" (127, 136). In short, Shpet was the first thinker for whom the field of hermeneutics united phenomenology, history, and art within a single, manifold problematic.

In the Europe of 1918 the hermeneutic problem was ripe. The atomism of modern society, exemplified by the mechanical slaughter of World War I, demanded new explanations of how inner experience becomes perceptible and communicable to others. Idealistic tendencies in philosophy were under a particular obligation to confront historical failures of communication and present alternatives. In German philosophy, various schools of thought (Neo-Kantianism, Philosophy of Life, phenomenology) were converging on the problem of how lived experience relates to sense perception. Russia was bound to be receptive to the aspirations of nascent hermeneutic philosophy, insofar as an established tradition of idealist metaphysics had been constantly challenged by a stubbornly disobedient historical process. As early as 1886, Vasilii Rozanov completed a major philosophical study (his debut work) entitled *O ponimanii* (*On Understanding*), which investigated how human interpretive activity shapes raw reality. In a very different way, Shpet also claimed "understanding" as "the central problem of [his] philosophy" ("Shpet" 51). Shpet's

formulation of the hermeneutic problem grew out of his earlier work on phenomenology, in which he had sought to marry the phenomenological reduction to a metaphysical horizon of vision. Moreover, in my view, some thinkers such as Viacheslav
Ivanov and Pavel Florenskii had been approaching a hermeneutic standpoint as they
sought to incorporate history into their symbolist metaphysics. Young thinkers such
as Aleksei Losev, Pavel Medvedev, and Mikhail Bakhtin were avidly watching all
of these developments and would soon develop them in their own accounts of language, art, and history. So, although the Russian revolution effectively canceled out
the immediate prospects for speculative philosophy, Shpet's hermeneutics must be
viewed as part of a rich philosophical ferment both at home and abroad.

    Like Heidegger, Shpet was a student of Husserl who sought to strengthen the
ontological ground of phenomenology, thereby opening it up to metaphysics. Both
Shpet and Heidegger posited ontology as the central problem for a philosophy that
sought to understand life and lived experience; however, they both sought a new
kind of metaphysics that would "achieve its tasks in this, the immanent world"
(Shpet, "Problemy" 388). In particular, the two philosophers shared the belief that
Dilthey's hermeneutics presented "the point from which we must now proceed"
(Shpet, "Germenevtika" 396; Shpet, "On Wilhelm Dilthey's Concept" 61). Thus,
central to Shpet's "Germenevtika" is his discussion of Dilthey, whom he generally praised for formulating understanding as a universal problem of knowledge.
Shpet accepted Dilthey's explanation of why understanding should be placed at
the center of philosophical attention. The key problem was "scientific knowledge
of the personality" (Shpet, "Germenevtika" 382), which Dilthey calls understanding. Empirical data are signs which can be used to trace social processes in which
people act as individuals and objects function as "instrumental being" (Shpet,
"Problemy" 410). However, this instrumental reading of external signs does not
exhaust human knowledge. Understanding is knowledge which "from sensual data
in human history turns to what is inaccessible to the senses, but what is nonetheless embodied and expressed in outer being" ("Germenevtika" 391). Shpet quotes
Dilthey as saying: "we call understanding a process in which we receive from sensual data psychical experience, of which sensual data are the manifestation" (*Istoriia* 880). This is why understanding is the basis of human community (as more
than the mere sum of its individuals): "mutual understanding ensures community
(*Gemeinsamkeit*) existing amongst individuals, and on the other hand community
represents the precondition for understanding" ("Germenevtika" 393). Reality that
has been understood can also be viewed as "concrete reality," which is properly
understood as the life not of individuals in society, but of personalities in the realm
of the human spirit. With this link to spirit, understanding becomes the center of
an entire metaphysics.

    The central category of understanding in Shpet's philosophy places particular
stress on his account of the mechanism of interpretation. Shpet took from Dilthey a
description of interpretation as a triad of terms: "experience, expression, understand-

ing" ("Germenevtika" 390). A psychical experience finds outer expression in signs, which are then understood by being read back to their origin in inner experience. Concrete reality, which has been expressed in this manner and which is therefore available for understanding, is separate from purely instrumental reality; Shpet calls it "detached reality" or simply "culture." Understanding is knowledge that detaches or suspends (in the sense of *Aufhebung*) the phenomenon in the realm of pure meaning; such detached representation renders phenomena available for critical analysis and ethical judgement. While Shpet extrapolated much of the preceding from Dilthey, he was concerned by Dilthey's inattention to the precise mechanism by which understanding is achieved in creative acts of interpretation. In Shpet's view, while Dilthey viewed the task of hermeneutics as "contrasting universally obligatory and objective interpretation to romantic arbitrariness and skeptical subjectivity" ("Germenevtika" 253), he often succumbed to reductive psychologism: "Dilthey did not formulate the . . . question . . . as to the logical expression of interpretation and understanding. This would have raised a general question about [the nature of] signs, by means of which we express not only our selves, not only something personal, but also something that can be communicated objectively" ("On Wilhelm Dilthey's Concept" 55).

Shpet's criticism of Dilthey issues directly from his phenomenological standpoint, according to which things present themselves in order to be understood; therefore understanding is a potential within empirical reality (*Iavlenie* 207). As Shpet wrote in his first book, *Iavlenie i smysl* (*Appearance and Sense*), "The being of reason consists in hermeneutic functions establishing the rational motivation which issues from entelechy, which is the 'bearer' of objective being, understood as the 'spirit of the object'" (209). In other words, signs can be trusted as manifestations of spirit, and thus phenomenological semasiology—the scientific study of signs—can stiffen the backbone of Dilthey's rather amorphous hermeneutic theory. Shpet accepted Dilthey's historicism and Husserl's ahistorical phenomenology as two complementary parts of a larger whole. Deriding Husserl's semasiology as "static" and "arid," and thus lacking "a comprehensive philosophical understanding in its living efficacy, in its dynamicity, in its all-penetrating rational spirituality" ("Germenevtika" 412-13), Shpet argued that it must be historicized in order for it to find its rightful place as a method of knowledge about human actors. What is more, Shpet incorporated dialectic logic in his semasiology ("Rabota" 35-38). In a response to Aleksei Losev's 1925 essay on the concept of "idea," Shpet objected to being lumped together with Husserl by claiming that "Husserl lacks the dialectic which G.G. [Shpet] introduces" (RGALI 941.14.11, 35). Understanding is the "knowledge of realized ideas" ("Germenevtika" 414); therefore one must ensure the existence both of "the ideal," and of its "realization" in history: "We proceed from sensual reality as from a riddle to its ideal basis, in order to solve the riddle by means of making sense of reality, by means of reason's discretion, within the reality of what has been realized and made incarnate" ("Germenevtika" 414). These passages demonstrate how erroneous it is to see Shpet in a one-sided fashion as a "precursor" of Soviet semiotics, as Viacheslav

Vsevolodovich Ivanov has done (Ivanov, *Ocherki*; *Izbrannye trudy*). Shpet's position vis-à-vis semiotics is closer to that of Aleksei Losev, who in the 1960s became
a notable critic of Iurii Lotman's school because of its refusal to read the potential
"sense" disclosed in arbitrary "signs" (see Losev, *Znak* 3-4).

It is, then, as an antidote to the amorphousness of historicism and the aridity of
semasiology that Shpet places the act of understanding (*ponimanie*) squarely at the
center of philosophical investigation: "One must begin with a fundamental analysis
of understanding, and only then may one hope to base on it a strict and consummate
methodology, most of all for the historical sciences, and then for all semasiological
logic, as it will appear after the verification of its premises in the light of historical
methodology" ("Germenevtika" 413). Shpet thought of philosophy as an intricate
balancing act between life and reason. The synthesis that Shpet sought is suggested
by his frequent substitution of the synonym "urazumenie" for "ponimanie" (see *Iavlenie* 207-08, "Rabota" 34-35). The goal is still the fathoming of living, feeling
experience in its amplitude, but this is to be achieved without sacrificing rationality
(*razum*), which is guaranteed by expressing sense in the logical medium of words.

As George L. Kline has noted, Shpet effectively supplemented Husserl with "a
characteristically Hegelian stress on history, tradition, community, culture, and the
network of interrelated social institutions and practices that constitute what Hegel
called objektiver Geist" ("Shpet as Interpreter" 182). However, Shpet contrasted
Hegel's "dialectic of the objectivized concept" to his own "real dialectic, a dialectic
of realized cultural sense," in which concept and materiality always go in tandem
(*Vnutrenniaia* 116). Shpet termed his philosophy "a dialectic which exposits and interprets, or else, embracing both formal and material tasks in their inherent concrete
unity, a hermeneutic dialectic" (*Vnutrenniaia* 116). In his "Germenevtika," he wrote
that "Dilthey and others, who appreciate the inspirational role of understanding in
history and the human sciences, came up with the formula 'experience—expression—understanding,' but circling within this formula did not provide a key to the
vortex of philosophical thought as a whole; on the other hand, the authors of semasiological studies have failed to see that such studies must be conducted through the
life of the spirit itself in order for them to receive philosophically vital and concrete
incarnation" (412). Put simply, understanding is the appropriate mode of knowledge for spirit; it follows that spirit is the appropriate content of understanding. An
act of understanding both endows reality with reason and reveals the innate reason
of things: "Spirit as the object of understanding is rational spirit" ("Germenevtika"
413). Understanding gets at "the truth" of "the absolute reality of the historical" or of
"spiritual historical reality." Understanding is the only sure foothold in the "constant
motion" of reality ("Germenevtika" 415). It resolves the problem of eternal regression by providing a basic beginning point for reliable knowledge that relies on no
auxiliary means and requires no further derivation ("Problemy" 406; *Istoriia* 860-
62). Our need and ability to understand is the basic fact of our existence.

Shpet's historicizing phenomenology has several notable counterparts in later
hermeneutic thinkers, most notably Paul Ricoeur. Like Ricoeur, Shpet emphasized

the need to include within the hermeneutic process its result—exposition and action—which raises the raw experience to the level of fully rational expression in a "verbal-logical form" and completes the "realization of reality" as "culture" (Shpet, *Vnutrenniaia* 113, 116). Since the knowledge one gains from understanding is completed only when it is applied in acts of exposition and application, Shpet discounts the possibility of learning dogmatic truths from past history: "The only lesson we can extract from this is that one must move and complete what has not yet been completed" ("Germenevtika" 280). Earlier Shpet had described the process of knowledge as a "'dialogue' with truth": "Since in the final analysis only one alternative can be accompanied by the ultimate 'yes,' the realized process of dialectic in its hermeneutic unfolding can yield only a single truth, but as long as the process remains unfinished, the prediction of possibilities remains absolutely free" ("Rabota" 37-38). For Shpet it is even an ethical requirement that understanding result in action; in addition to being, it has bearing also on the sphere of "duty" (*dolzhenstvovanie*; Shpet, *Istoriia* 857): "A proposition that we use as a norm . . . becomes such only in the process of application" ("Problemy" 381). Shpet's hermeneutics combines Hegelian historicism with a Kantian imperative for ethical action.

The parallel to Ricoeur is instructive in two other respects. First, just as Ricoeur's hermeneutic phenomenology has led him to a focused consideration of the concept of distance, so also was Shpet drawn to detachment. Ricoeur has defined narrative as "the distanciation of fable or *muthos*," which renders the world intelligible in terms of the person and places the person into an already meaningful world (Ricoeur 86). As for Shpet, human understanding changes the status of reality itself by creating a separate realm of meaning. Theorizing this distantiated realm of meaning leads both Ricoeur and Shpet to questions of aesthetic expression, which promise a more precise definition for the way perception suspends reality as (mythic, detached) meaning. As I shall argue, the link between understanding and detachment allows us to place Shpet in a specific tradition of Russian aesthetics which coalesced within the walls of GAKhN.

Hermeneutics and Aesthetics

In his work in hermeneutic philosophy, Shpet paid particular attention to the realm of aesthetics, where he always sought to reconcile the schematism of form with a freedom of interpretation. If, for Shpet, "all reality without remainder is a word addressed to us and already audible to us" ("Esteticheskie" 369), this is a word that is meaningful only in its human address: "An isolated word, strictly speaking, is bereft of meaning, it is not λόγος" ("Esteticheskie" 389-90). Similarly, art is defined not only by beauty, but also by its interpretability, without which it is only "ornament" ("Esteticheskie" 351). Thus the form of an aesthetic expression must be read as significant with respect to its sense. Alongside the broader detached sphere that Shpet calls concrete reality, art is distinguished by the precise manner in which its expressions are fully "externalized" and therefore rendered transparent for interpretation:

"Externality [*vneshnost'*] demands not conceptual modeling [*kontsipirovanie*], but understanding and interpretation" ("Esteticheskie" 364). Doubly detached from reality—first as rational content and then as fictional form—aesthetic objects are presented exclusively for the understanding of the reality to which they refer.

On 16 March 1922 Shpet presented to the philosophical section of GAKhN an essay entitled "Problemy sovremennoi estetiki" ("Problems of Contemporary Aesthetics"). Here Shpet confirmed his definition of aesthetic objects as marked by a double "detachment." If all detached reality is distinguished by its proximity to meaning, then art is further distinguished by a re-distanciation into palpable form, which makes its meaning fully immanent to sensual experience: "Detaching [*otreshaia*] being from its reality, the imagination doesn't crimple it and doesn't dump it into a mass of supporting material (μη ov), but incarnates it into communicable and meaningfully expressed forms" ("Problemy" 404). As "detached cultural being," aesthetic objects are inherently expressive: "Detached being avoids becoming insignificant because it has expression, and it *is* only what is expressed" ("Problemy" 405).

The most pressing problem for Shpet was to define the specificity of aesthetic being within the broader realm of concrete or understood reality (what he calls culture). He does this by asserting the aesthetic object's fictionality and lack of social usefulness. First, he clarifies the dual nature of the cultural object—as use-object and as sign:

> A social object as an object of social usage, of life and of consumption, is always a kind of "instrument" or "means." Such an object is essentially deprived of "self-sufficient" being. Any object of "culture" as a social object, taken not in its meaning but in its being, is also a "means" and is therefore not self-sufficient. However instruments of culture, as instruments of spiritual being by principle; or, to say the same thing, [as instruments] of the being of spiritual creativity, cannot have any being other than spiritual being. As instruments and means they are only "signs," which do not possess self-sufficient being but indicate it and thereby attain their proper meaning. The self-sufficient sphere of "meaning" which they indicate is the sphere of detached cultural being, including art. ("Problemy" 408)

Art is distinct among cultural objects because it has no immediate social use. However, as a sign, the aesthetic object remains instrumental in its being, insofar as it refers to something other than itself: "Being which surrounds us really is either self-sufficient being or the being of an instrument and 'sign.' Detached being . . . reflects the same distinction within itself. Art in its being is a 'sign,' 'imitation,' 'communication,' and 'expression.' The aesthetic object, as an object of detached being, is first of all a cultural object, a 'sign,' and an 'expression.' This is detached being, but not self-sufficient being; rather its being is *significative*" ("Problemy" 409).

Thus having identified this purely "spiritual" realm of detached meaning, Shpet proceeds to divide it into instrumental and significative subspheres. If the former merely makes things into disembodied signs, the latter contains things that have been both understood and presented for understanding, that is, in which the significative and expressive aspect is radically foregrounded and externalized. In his *Aesthetic Fragments* Shpet clarifies the status of this "significative being" with the concept of the "image" (*obraz*), which hovers between "thing" and "idea": "The image is not a 'thing,' because it does not pretend to real being in the real world, and the image is not an 'idea' because it does not pretend to eidetic being in the ideal world . . . It is a materialized idea and an idealized thing, *ens fictum*. Its relationship to being is not positive or negative, but neutral" ("Esteticheskie" 445). This neutrality or fictionality explains how the aesthetic object can be both immediate in its impact and transcendent in its meaning. It is not a characteristic of the object itself, but of its function within a life situation. Human cognition can fictionalize anything by "neutralizing" or suspending its relationship to being: "just like anything else in the world, 'nature' attains any meaning, including aesthetic meaning, only in context—in the context of culture. Nature for aesthetics is a fiction, because culture for aesthetics is also not reality. Aesthetics does not perceive, rather it contemplates and imagines. Fine culture is fictional; fictive culture is aesthetic" ("Esteticheskie" 348). In fact, the inner form of an aesthetic object is neither its material formation nor its intellectual content, but "the relation between the outer significative form and the object form of its thingly content" (*Vnutrenniaia* 117; see also "Esteticheskie" 400). In its dual being the art work dramatizes attitudes and relations—degrees of detachment—between signs and pure meanings, between instrumental being and self-sufficient being. In a certain sense, fiction thematizes detachment as a distinct potential within instrumental being. In this manner Shpet's investigation of art allows him to isolate the concept of detachment and to define it more precisely as a condition of understanding.

Just as aesthetics is germane to broader philosophical problems, so also art illumines life, indeed it may just be a precondition for ethical action. In his paper "Poznanie i iskusstvo" ("Cognition and Art"), presented and discussed at GAKhN in 1926, Shpet set out to define the cognitive value of art. He begins by distinguishing "art as knowledge" from "the knowledge of art itself (the science of art)" and "knowledge through art" ("Poznanie" 53). He asserts that while art and cognition share "the investigation of their object and creative forming of their material," they differ both in the type of reality they investigate and in their cognitive attitude: "cognition, as a function of the mind, directs itself towards real being and reveals its necessary bases as expressed by laws of reality, while art, as a product of the activity of the imagination, directs itself towards detached being, the artistic expression of which is mainly intended to create an emotional impression" ("Poznanie" 53). Here again, art appears as doubly detached from reality; it is a material externalization of cultural objects, which have already been suspended conceptually in the realm of understanding. Likewise, Shpet insists on the interdependency of cognition and art in forming the person as a cultural being: "artistic fantasy, ordering and organizing any 'dreaming,' is an aspect of the general development of the imagination which does not exclude the development of scientific imagination, and *vice versa*; both aspects are fused together and directed towards the transformation and correction of reality which exists and is perceived as disordered, just as [they are directed] towards the human person's mastery of his own emotional and willing life, towards its disciplining" ("Poznanie" 54). Art therefore plays a key role in communicating "living knowledge," which directs and even obligates "living work on real reality" ("Poznanie" 54).

The role of artistic detachment is crucial to Shpet's analyses of specific aesthetic concepts. For instance, in the 1922 essay "Theater as Art" ("Teatr kak iskusstvo"), Shpet describes "artistic realism" as an "artificial convention" that is merely a "homonym" of "the realism of being": "The main principle that is common to all arts ascertains that the 'reality' which is created by art is not the reality of vital and practical experience which surrounds us, it is not so-called empirical reality which is studied by the natural and historical sciences, but it is reality of particular features and a particular perception—detached reality" (120). Inquiring of the material and the means by which theater "detaches us from everyday reality around us," Shpet focuses on the mask by means of which the actor achieves the "sensual incarnation of some images which the actor creates himself" (122). Moreover, theatrical detachment creates a kind of perception and understanding which is distinct from the other arts, such as poetry, and the actor "must detach himself from his poetic perception of the 'role' and proceed to a new, individual perception, understanding and interpretation" (123). Extrapolating from Shpet's frequently voiced opposition to any concept of the synthesis of the arts ("Esteticheskie" 348-51; "Teatr" 112-15), one might conclude that, in his eyes, the types of detachment that distinguish the different artistic media require equally distinct perceptive postures on the part of the beholder. Instead of distinguishing between dramatic genres ("drama, tragedy, comedy") Shpet proposes the term "emplois," which he identifies as the "inner form" of the performance's expressivity. Like Bertolt Brecht's concept of "Gestus," Shpet's concept of the "inner form" shifts the center of a performance from the narrative content to the manner of its representation by actors on stage. In Brecht's "epic theater," which was implacably opposed to the synthetic spectacle of the *Gesamtkunstwerk*, "The audience identifies itself with the actor as being an observer, and accordingly develops his attitude of observing or looking on" (93). Shpet specifies that the "outer scenic form" is defined by the actor's "gesture, miming, intonation" ("Teatr" 130). For the viewer, this "outer sensuous form is turned into a symbol of the inner and 'real'" ("Teatr" 130). The viewer, as it were, reads the gestures on the mask to reveal the underlying attitude towards the "detached aesthetic object," which is "a symbol . . . not of a real person, but of a possible one" ("Teatr" 130-31). Without referring the spectator to a specific, abstract meaning, fictional art thematizes the very modes of detachment that render reality meaningful.

In this manner art communicates others' acts of interpretation in a fashion that renders them generative of new experience. It brings ideology into material life and allows life to be interpreted as ideology. From this perspective, Shpet's aesthetics is merely the clearest example of his overall hermeneutic philosophy. However it also reminds us that Shpet's project was less the speculative discovery of static truths than the investigation of diverse and changing human attitudes towards the search itself.

Shpet in the Russian Context

Shpet claims that, "As far as I know, this is the first time the problem has been posed in this way" ("Germenevtika," 414). He was certainly correct. There were, however, interesting precedents for Shpet's hermeneutics in Russian thought, among which Alexander Haardt has singled out Vladimir Solov'ev and Sergei Trubetskoi (117-18), with whom Shpet shared the view that the individual can only be understood within a distinct horizon of being (120-21). This view emerges with particular force in the 1916 essay, "Consciousness and Its Owner" ("Soznanie i ego sobstvennik"), where Shpet, citing Trubetskoi, writes that "the 'I' itself is the 'bearer' not only of its own 'personal' consciousness, but also of shared [obshchnyi] consciousness" ("Soznanie" 115). Shpet carried this idea of communal consciousness over into his aesthetics, writing in 1922 that, "The play and life of consciousness is the exchange of words, dialogue" ("Esteticheskie" 347). With this interpersonal vitality in mind, Aleksandr Mikhailov has placed Shpet's philosophy of understanding squarely in the tradition of Russian thought, which rests on an intuition of "stable, undifferentiated being" (Mikhailov 527). Shpet, who "so profoundly assimilated the views and language of German philosophy," still "very quickly gives new accents to the phenomenological philosophy, most importantly, that this is an understanding of reality as historical reality" (528). Mikhailov concludes that "Shpet was not only a phenomenological philosopher, not only a representative of Husserlianism in Russian philosophy; he was a representative of the Russian cultural tradition in the phenomenological movement" (530-31). Of course, it would be an oversimplification to identify historicism exclusively with Russian thought, especially when there is such abundant evidence of Shpet's profound indebtedness to Dilthey.

Shpet's direct influence upon later Russian thinkers is difficult to gauge, since the manuscript of his "Hermeneutics" remained unpublished until the 1990s and citation of Shpet in Soviet times was infrequent. There has been speculation about whether the poet and thinker Viacheslav Ivanov knew Shpet's text in manuscript (Szilard 175), but there is no direct proof of this. Bakhtin worked largely outside of the hermeneutic tradition, but his newly published text with the Dilthey-esque title, "Towards the Philosophical Grounds of the Human Sciences" reveals formulations strikingly similar to those of Shpet:

> You can't change the factual, thingly aspect of the past, but the meaning, expressive and speaking aspect can be changed, since it is unfinalizable and does not coincide with itself (it is free). The role of memory in this eternal transfiguration of the past. Knowledge is understanding of the past in its unfinalizability (in its non-coincidence with itself). . . . The problem of understanding. Understanding as a seeing of meaning, but not a phenomenal seeing, but a seeing of the living meaning of experience and expression, the vision of what is inwardly meaningful, so to speak, of a self-meaningful phenomenon. (9)

This admittedly cryptic passage seems indebted to Shpet's emphasis on the deep meaning of phenomena that lies beyond their surface signification as usable and exchangeable tokens. At the same time, Bakhtin's application of "unfinalizability" to the past results in phrases reminiscent of Hans-Georg Gadamer's "effective history," according to which the past is seen as fluid insofar as it is constantly reshaped in the present. Bakhtin relates these insights to the "human sciences," which, by constantly reinterpreting past expressions of human experience, achieve access to the deep meaning of phenomena and form the present. Despite Shpet's and Bakhtin's mutual interest in "grounding the human sciences," this rather academic-sounding problem has failed to gain traction in the largely para-academic world of Russian philosophy.

Shpet had a much more consequential influence on the philosophy of his colleague in GAKhN, Aleksei Losev. After joining GAKhN in 1923, Losev became one of its most active members and was in constant contact with Shpet in the 1920s. As A.A. Takho-Godi has shown, the campaign against Losev in 1930, culminating in his arrest and imprisonment, began during the purge of GAKhN, when Losev was accused of being "an idealist of Shpetian ferment" (Takho-Godi 12). In addition to his main post in Shpet's Philosophical Section, Losev collaborated with Shpet on the Commission for the History of Aesthetic Doctrines and was a member of the Commission for Compiling a Dictionary of Artistic Terminology, which Shpet chaired. On this latter commission, Losev quickly proved to be one of the most eager and competent contributors. At one point, two articles were assigned jointly to Shpet and Losev: on Eros and on the metaphysics of art (RGALI 941.14.11, 18). Neither of these was written, and it is difficult to imagine such distinct temperaments producing any single text. When Losev's first article on the concept "Idea" elicited much criticism for its esoteric argument and difficult style, Shpet, the chairman of the commission, concurred: "The reader will not be able to orientate himself according to this rationalistic classification (I call it rationalistic because the typology is abstract and does not coincide with the historical development of the concept). An entire series of authors is excluded from your scheme. One should issue from a historical understanding of 'idea' and present these interpretations—idea as form, as given, as constructive and regulative definition, as concept [*kontsept*], as sense [*smysl*], etc." (RGALI 941.14.11, 35). This disagreement was of little direct consequence: Losev's article was accepted after light revision, but the dictionary remained unpublished.

Both Shpet's influence and Losev's distinctiveness—recognizable in part in his attention to myth as a philosophical problem and in his greater willingness to subject his philosophy to more explicitly religious truths—can be discerned in Losev's adoption of the term "detachment" in his philosophical masterpiece *The Dialectics of Myth* (*Dialektika mifa*, 1930). Instead of equating "concrete reality" and "culture," Losev drew a sharp distinction between myth and art, which for him represent two different types of detachment from everyday reality. Losev basically equated aesthetic detachment with Kant's concept of aesthetic disinterestedness; the meaning of reality is telescoped by being detached from factual being and set off as fiction. By contrast, "Mythical detachment is detachment from the meaning and idea of everyday facts, but not from their facticity" (Losev, *Dialectics* 62). The borderline between artistic and mythical detachment is sometimes indistinct, but the latter is marked by Losev's insistence on the materiality of myth: "Myth is poetic detachment given as a thing" (*Dialectics* 177). Like Shpet, Losev links the detachment of art and myth to the concept of expression. Detached reality is not internal or external reality, rather, it is reality that manifests an interchange between the two: "Expression is always dynamic and mobile . . . Expression is the arena where two energies meet, from within and from without, and their mutual communication in some whole and indivisible image that is at once the one and the other" (Losev, *Dialectics* 55). As in Shpet's discussion of the art of acting, Losev attributes aesthetic power not to the aesthetic object itself "but the mode of its depiction, and, ultimately, the mode of understanding it" (*Dialectics* 56). Art and myth thus denote two possible attitudes that may exist between a subject and his world.

The major contrast to Shpet's treatment comes in the strict hierarchy which Losev establishes among types of detachment. For Losev, myth is an unquestionably truer detachment of reality than art or normal experience. "Myth," Losev asserted, "is the fullest perception [of reality]" (RGALI 941.12.49 20 obv.). Moreover, mythical detachment is distinguished precisely by its illumination of hierarchies within reality. When faced with the need to define myth positively, Losev avers that it is marked by "some detachment and some hierarchic character" (*Dialectics* 33). While he does not specify the origin of this hierarchy, it appears to be the contribution of the human subject in his interaction with reality. After all, myth exists only because there are people to perceive reality mythically, and the hierarchic quality of myth must refer primarily to the gradation of its human subjects, who must be elevated either in the cognitive or in the ontological sense. In the context of Orthodox spirituality, Losev would seem to be implicating the kind of spiritual detachment one finds in ascetic authors such as St. John of the Ladder (John Climacus), in whose *Ladder of Divine Ascent* detachment appears as *memento mori*, exile, poverty, pure prayer (i. e., free of images), and the vision of things spiritual. As in Shpet, the concept of detachment in Losev serves to refocus attention on the interaction of human subjects with their world, for which both philosophers use the term understanding. Despite his metaphysical tonalities, the overwhelming tendency in Losev is to present all his major categories as functions of the human subject. Defining myth as miracle, Losev avers: "It is a modification of the meaning of the facts and events rather than the facts and events themselves. It is a specific method of interpreting historical events rather than a search for some new events as such" (*Dialectics* 158).

It is instructive to note the contrast which Losev drew between his philosophy of myth and Ernst Cassirer's "philosophy of symbolic forms." After presenting Cassirer's work to the Philosophical Section of GAKhN in 1926, Losev called attention precisely to the concept of understanding: "Cassirer has not introduced a new concept of 'understanding' and his method is not [that of] understanding, otherwise he would be a religious thinker. He has introduced only a description of understanding. His application of the logic [of myth] and the construction of the logic of myth must be admitted to be correct. But in reality he does not reveal the essence of myth" (RGALI 941.14.25, 5; see also Dunaev 216-18). For Losev, then, myth is not only a descriptive or logical category; as mythical detachment it presupposes a particular medium of understanding, which is to say: a mode of living in truth.

The Base of the Triangle

In 1926 the ranks of GAKhN swelled to receive another new member, the poet and thinker Viacheslav Ivanov. Strangely enough, Ivanov was not even in Russia at the time; in fact he would never again set foot in his homeland. His only appearance within the walls of the Academy was on 16 July 1924, when he read some old poetry and a new satirical drama. When he left for Italy a month later, he was given the task of creating a Russian Institute for Archeology, History, and Art History in Rome under the aegis of GAKhN. Nothing came of this task (Bird 317-21), but it is symbolic of his role in the philosophical debate I have been tracing. Drawing inspiration from the timeless sources of ancient culture, and remaining largely aloof to the polemics of the 1920s, Ivanov was able both to anticipate the hermeneutic movement and to survive it, as a kind of living witness to its originary impulse and to its historical fragility.

Best known as an indefatigable advocate of Dionysian frenzy in art, Ivanov may not seem an obvious source for the measured historicism of hermeneutics and for an aesthetics of detachment. Indeed, Ivanov was usually suspicious of any notion of distanciation, which he associated with Apollo and the epic, the antipodes of Dionysus and tragedy. For instance, in his 1912 essay, "The Essence of Theater" ("Sushchestvo teatra"), Ivanov attributed to the "Apollonic moment" of tragedy the ability to lend the performance "formal rigor and plastic visuality . . . as a kind of fine protection" from "the direct blow of Dionysian lightning." However this "magic veil" also "de-magnetizes tragedy," distancing the action from the spectator "with purely-epic detachment" (201). Nonetheless, Ivanov's anxiety over engagement had the effect of focusing attention on art as the negotiation of ontological distance.

The key concept in Ivanov's negotiation of this distance was the symbol, which both Shpet and Losev adopted to denote detached reality. In his *Aesthetic Fragments* Shpet struck a distinctively Ivanovian note: "The symbol is creatively-prophetic and inexhaustibly-infinite. The allegory is theosophical, while the symbol is mystical" ("Esteticheskie" 358). Shpet typically spoke of the symbol in terms similar to those he applied to the "image" in the passage quoted above, as a "concrete relation" of such intensity that it is "the supreme level of aesthetic poetic ascent" (411). More specifically, Shpet averred that the symbol "is the relation between the logical sense and the syntagmata," that is to say, the poetic symbol is born of the stress that arises between meaning and grammar, between atemporal revelation and the narrative that bears it. Losev's use of the term "symbol" is clearly mediated by Shpet's. In *The Dialectics of Myth*, Losev writes of the symbol as "a complete equilibrium between the 'internal' and 'external,' the 'idea' and the 'outer shape,' the 'ideal' and the real'" (*Dialectics* 38). In a sense, Losev's concept of the symbol might seem to be completely detemporalized and incompatible with narrative. However, its timeless equilibrium—like that of myth itself—subsumes an entire history of imbalances and revolutions. The story in its unfolding (*mythos*) retains an identity with its unchanging kernel.

Ivanov's stress on the simultaneity of the symbol challenged subsequent thinkers such as Shpet and Losev to account for its embeddedness in history. In fact, Ivanov himself suggested a concept of myth as a narrative capable of gesturing beyond time itself. However, in later essays and, increasingly, in his own poetic works, Ivanov recognized the need for the intensive power of tragedy to be emplotted in time as an extensive narrative. Exemplary here are Ivanov's writings on Dostoevskii's "novel-tragedies." Ivanov characterized Dostoevskii's novelistic oeuvre as "a composite creation, which, without being especially fit for a Dionysiac state of mind, was at least Protean," a "tragedy in epic dress" (*Freedom* 6). Ivanov wrote that Dostoevskii maintained the storyteller's "art of holding the reader in suspense [*Spannung*] as he awaits the unravelment of an apparently hopeless tangle," but that Dostoevskii subordinated it to the task of constructing a "unified tragedy" (*Freedom* 10).

Following Ivanov, Shpet and Losev both elaborated concepts of the temporal unfolding of artistic images, that is, of narrative, in which the inner tension or suspense was seen as a central factor in overcoming the limits of linguistic reference. For Losev, it is impossible to identify an historical reality beyond the stories we tell of it, and therefore any criterion of "truth" must be intrinsic to narrative, more a matter of narrative structure than of extrinsic reference. Shpet's theory of narrative, by contrast, remained within the bounds of aesthetics. He viewed plots as typical unities, expressible by a single proper name, such as "Oedipus," which exemplifies its aesthetic attraction. However, this intensive aesthetic unity becomes meaningful for the perceiver when it is unfolded extensively in its "ideal necessary sequence" (Shpet, "Esteticheskie" 457). The distinct arts are differentiated by narrative structures as well as by the perceptive postures which they presuppose. For instance, Shpet contrasts the gradual development of a protagonist in a literary narrative to the "synthetic" presentation of his character in drama ("Teatr" 124-25). In a drama, the character's actions are "consequences" of his character, which is set from his first appearance on stage and which is wholly present in all of his discrete manifestations ("Teatr" 125). In each case, "'play' of forms" adds its own distinct kind of aesthetic enjoyment linked to particular "emotional feelings, moods, agitation, etc." which in turn "magnify the affective power of the form itself" (Shpet, "Esteticheskie" 457).

Shpet's insights into narrative were picked up by Lev Vygotskii (1896-1934), the pioneering psychologist and theorist of narrative. In a remarkable essay on Ivan Bunin's story "Light Breathing" ("Legkoe dykhanie") Vygotskii undertook to show how Bunin creates "that particular tension, that clogging of our interest, which . . . theorists of literature call *Spannung*" (190). The double motion of suspense and suspension link events together only to transform them into something completely different: "they are emancipated from the usual linkages . . . they are detached from

reality" (Vygotskii 190). This special atmosphere, the "light breathing" of Bunin's
story, is what transforms the raw data of reality into meaning. Vygotskii's theory of
narrative comprehension as a particular "detachment" of and from reality provides
a valuable extension of Shpet's more rarified aesthetic conceptions. It suggests how
narrative suspense engages the beholder in the form only to suspend this interest in
an act of self-reflection, which thematizes detachment as a mode of understanding
the world. In this manner, against the background of Ivanov's intuitive aesthetics of
symbolism, Shpet and Losev both developed variants of an influential hermeneutic
aesthetics that sought to mediate symbol and history. What for Ivanov was largely
an incursion of transcendence in the world becomes for these two phenomenologists
a key to describing the interaction between human consciousness and the world beyond. In particular, Shpet's and Losev's concepts of detachment prove to be central
components in their theories of narrative and myth.

Conclusion

At the close of his address at GAKhN on "The Problems of Contemporary Aesthetics," Gustav Shpet described the philosophy of culture as the "extreme" or "liminal"
(*predel'nyi*) branch of philosophy because "culture is itself reality at the limit—at
the limit of realization and of exteriorization" and because "cultural consciousness
is consciousness at the limit" (Shpet, "Problemy" 412). He might also have added
that a cultural space like GAKhN is a liminal space, a locus of intellectual endeavor
that could—and did—all too easily become a site of disappearance and extinction.
Viacheslav Ivanov's emigration saved him from the repressions that struck Losev
and Shpet in the 1930s. Shpet's fate was undoubtedly the gravest, but as the author
of the first Russian text on hermeneutics Shpet found himself at the apex of a remarkable philosophical triangle that is wedged at a turning point in Russian history,
signaling what was lost in the rupture, but securing the continuity of the tradition.

Works Cited

Bakhtin, M.M. "K filosofskim osnovam gumanitarnykh nauk." *Sobranie sochinenii.*
    Vol. 5. Moscow: Russkie slovari, 1996. 7-10.
Bird, Robert. "Viacheslav Ivanov i sovetskaia vlast'." *Novoe literaturnoe obozrenie*
    40 (1999): 305-31.
Brecht, Bertolt. *On Theater*. Trans. John Willett. New York: Hill and Wang, 1964.
Dunaev, A.G. "Losev i GAKhN (issledovanie arkhivnykh materialov i publikatsiia
    dokladov 20-kh godov)." *A.F. Losev i kul'tura XX veka: Losevskie chteniia*. Ed.
    Iu.F. Panasenko. Moscow: Nauka, 1991. 197-220.
Grondin, Jean. *Introduction to Philosophical Hermeneutics*. Trans. Joel Weinsheimer.
    New Haven: Yale UP, 1994.
Haardt, Alexander. *Husserl in Rußland. Phänomenologie der Sprache und Kunst bei
    Gustav Špet und Aleksej Losev*. München: Fink, 1993.

Ivanov, Vyacheslav. *Freedom and the Tragic Life*. Trans. Norman Cameron. London: Harvill, 1952.

Ivanov, V.I. "Sushchestvo tragedii." *Sobranie sochinenii*. Vol. 2. Brussels: Foyer Oriental Chrétien, 1971-87. 190-204.

Ivanov, V.V. *Ocherki po istorii semiotiki v SSSR*. Moscow: Nauka, 1976.

Ivanov, V.V. *Izbrannye trudy po semiotike i istorii kul'tury*. Vol. 1. Moscow: Iazyki russkoi kul'tury, 1998.

Kline, George L. "Gustav G. Shpet as Interpreter of Hegel." *Archiwum historii filozofii i myśli społecznej* 44 (1999): 181-90.

Losev, A.F. *The Dialectics of Myth*. Trans. Vladimir Marchenkov. New York: Routledge, 2003.

Losev, A.F. *Znak, simvol, mif*. Moscow: Izdatel'stvo Moskovskogo universiteta, 1982.

Mikhailov, A.V. "Sovremennaia istoricheskaia poetika i nauchno-filosofskoe nasledie Gustava Gustavovicha Shpeta." *Obratnyi perevod*. Moscow: Iazyki russkoi kul'tury, 2000. 526-34.

Misler, Nicoletta, ed. *RAKhN: The Russian Academy of Artistic Sciences.* Special issue, *Experiment / Eksperiment* 3 (1997).

Palmer, Richard E. *Hermeneutics: Interpretation Theory in Schleiermacher, Dilthey, Heidegger and Gadamer*. Evanston: Northwestern UP, 1969.

RGALI: Rossiiskii gosudarstvennyi arkhiv literatury i iskusstva, Moscow.

Ricoeur, Paul. "The Hermeneutical Function of Distanciation." *From Text to Action. Essays on Hermeneutics, II*. Trans. Kathleen Blamey and John B. Thompson. Evanston: Northwestern UP, 1991. 75-88.

Shchedrina, T. G. "*Ia pishu kak ekho drugogo . . .*" *Ocherki intellektual'noi biografii Gustava Shpeta*. Moscow: Progress-Traditsiia, 2004.

Shpet, Gustav. "Esteticheskie fragmenty." *Sochineniia*. Moscow: Pravda, 1989. 345-472.

Shpet, Gustav. "Germenevtika i ee problemy." *Mysl' i slovo: Izbrannye trudy*. Ed. T.G. Shchedrina. Moscow: ROSSPEN, 2005. 248-418.

Shpet, Gustav. *Iavlenie i smysl. Fenomenologiia kak osnovnaia nauka i ee problemy*. Moscow: Germes, 1914.

Shpet, Gustav. *Istoriia kak problema logiki: kriticheskie i metodologicheskie issledovaniia*. Ed. V.S. Miasnikov. Moscow: Pamiatniki istoricheskoi mysli, 2002.

Shpet, Gustav. "On Wilhelm Dilthey's Concept of the Human Sciences: Excerpts from 'Hermeneutics and Its Problems.'" Trans. Erika Freiberger and George L. Kline. *Russian Studies in Philosophy* 37.4 (1999): 53-61.

Shpet, Gustav. "Poznanie i iskusstvo (konspekt doklada)." *Gustav Gustavovich Shpet. Arkhivnye materialy. Vospominaniia. Stat'i.* Ed. T.D. Martsinkovskaia. Moscow: Smysl, 2000. 52-54.

Shpet, Gustav. "Problemy sovremennoi estetiki." *Psikhologiia sotsial'nogo bytiia. Izbrannye sotsiologicheskie trudy*. Ed. T.D. Martsinkovskaia. Moscow: Insititut prakticheskoi psikhologii; Voronezh: MODEK, 1996. 373-412.

Shpet, Gustav. "Rabota po filosofii." *Nachala* 1 (1992): 31-49.

Shpet, Gustav. "'Shpet' (Stat'ia dlia entsiklopedicheskogo slovaria 'Granat')." *Nachala* 1 (1992): 50-52.

Shpet, Gustav. "Soznaie i ego sobstvennik." *Filosofskie etiudy*. Moscow: Progress, 1994. 20-116.

Shpet, Gustav. "Teatr kak iskusstvo." *Gustav Gustavovich Shpet. Arkhivnye materialy. Vospominaniia. Stat'i*. Ed. T.D. Martsinkovskaia. Moscow: Smysl, 2000. 111-34.

Shpet, Gustav. *Vnutrenniaia forma slova. Etiudy i variatsii na temy Gumbol'ta*. Moscow: Gosudarstvennaia Akademiia Khudozhestvennykh Nauk, 1927.

Szilard, Lena. "Problemy germenevtiki v slavianskom literaturovedenii XX v. (fragment)." *Studia Slavica* 38.1-2 (1993): 173-83.

Takho-Godi, A.A. "'Filosof khochet vse ponimat': 'Dialektika mifa' i 'Dopolnenie' k nei." *Dialektika mifa: Dopolnenie k "Dialektike mifa."* By A.F. Losev. Moscow: Mysl', 2001. 5-30.

Vygotskii, L.S. *Psikhologiia iskusstva*. Moscow: Labirint, 1997.

Gustav Shpet's Influence on Psychology

Vladimir Zinchenko and James V. Wertsch

Gustav Gustavovich Shpet is re-emerging as a major figure in twentieth-century in-tellectual history. As the person who introduced Russia to phenomenology, he has had a powerful impact on a wide range of intellectual debates in Russia and beyond. This impact, however, was ignored or consciously downplayed in the USSR. Start-ing in the 1930s, Shpet became largely invisible in official Soviet scholarly dis-course, a tendency that was only exacerbated during the decades after his execution in 1937. This tendency is one of the factors that contributed to Shpet's being so little known in the West today.

In this article, we trace some of the lines of influence that Shpet had on psy-chology, a discipline that has usually not been closely associated with his name. It turns out that his impact on this discipline in the USSR was considerable. We pay particular attention in this regard to Shpet's impact on Lev Semenovich Vygotskii, a Russian psychologist whose ideas have come to widespread use throughout the world today. As will become apparent, however, the story of Shpet's influence on Russian psychology extends well beyond Vygotskii. When considering the fate of psychology in Russia, as well as on the worldwide scene today, one cannot help but recall Dostoevsky's comment after his staged execution (the pardon arriving at the last moment). At that moment in his life he wrote his brother Mikhail that "The dialectic has ended and life has begun." After October 1917, there is a sense in which life in academic disciplines like psychology in Russia ended and a dialectic began that has dragged on to our time. One of the most striking and impressive facts about the aftermath of the October Revolution, however, is that many Russian scholars managed to carry out their work despite tyranny and ideological censorship. In order to understand how this took place, it is essential to understand more about those lines of influence that tied figures like Shpet to other scholars.

The fate of Shpet, like that of so many other Soviet scholars, was horrendous. On several occasions he was dismissed from research and teaching positions. In 1935 he was arrested and sent to Eniseisk. In 1937 he was arrested again and an NKVD *troika* sentenced him to ten years in prison without the right to correspond with any-one. Later that same year he was re-arrested, tried again, and shot. In the criminal code of the 1930s, execution by shooting was called the "highest measure of social defense." According to this logic the executioner apparently was what one might call a "social worker." In 1956 the rehabilitation of Shpet began, but in certain—intellectual—respects it continues to this day. Shpet's scholarly life was varied, intense, and extremely productive. He published a great deal. However, there is almost a total absence of recognition or response on the part of his contemporaries working on topics such as art, aesthetics, psychology, consciousness, meaning, language, and thinking. In actuality, Shpet's circles of contact and influence were extensive. He was friends with Tairov and Alisa Koonen; Anna Akhmatova met Shpet and Boris Pil'niak in the company of the Lithuanian poet Yurgis Baltrushaitis and the composer Sergei Prokofiev. Shpet himself wrote about his acquaintance with the poets Andrei Belyi, Mikhail Kuzmin, Boris Pasternak, and Pavel Antokol'skii. In recalling his contact with Shpet, Andrei Belyi wrote:

> It was never possible to decide whether [Shpet] was joking or serious. In an academic setting, Academician Shpet was usually the same, but when dining he was a completely different person. Sometimes we thought that the second was a clever reconnaissance party for the first, and sometimes we thought the opposite. For Shpet, launching a formal attack on you constituted a friendly attempt to lead you from a formal meeting to an intimate discussion. None of the philosophers befriended us as he did, and no one held himself off from us so warily when making academic presentations. (274)

Shpet's tact and delicacy, which he displayed in connection with people of the arts, were apparently not very characteristic of his performance when interacting with colleagues, where he was at times merciless in his criticism.

In one way or another the problem of not knowing about Shpet, or knowing too little about his work, is only now beginning to be alleviated in psychology and more generally in the human sciences. In the 1920s and 1930s, however, this was not an issue. Shpet was much better known than Bakhtin, Vygotskii, or Rubinshtein. This is to say nothing of the younger A.N. Leont'ev and A.R. Luriia. His status as a major thinker in psychology began to be publicly recognized at the end of the Soviet period. For example, in 1988, in an article on "Shpet and his Place in the History of Psychology in our Country," A.A. Mitiushin wrote that Shpet "was a leading figure in the history of Russian science and philosophy. In the first three decades of our century he was one of the most noteworthy figures in the cultural life of Russia" (23). All this raises questions about Shpet's influence on psychology in Russia and how this influence seems to have disappeared so thoroughly. As preliminary hypotheses for his apparent disappearance from the scene, we ask: Might it be due to the fact that he was too well known during his own lifetime? Or is it the case that "the perpetual absence in our efforts of generally organized scientific work is a sign of our great cultural backwardness [*nekul'turnosti*]!" (Shpet, "Ocherk" 11).

Perhaps it is time to follow Shpet's advice to attend to our past in a serious and culturally sophisticated way. We of course realize that the problem of knowing who cites whom and for what reason is a complex one, and not only in repressed and censored scholarship. In this connection, it is worth noting the almost total absence of mutual citations among figures such as Bakhtin, Vygotskii, and the physiologist of motor control N.A. Bernshtein. They all seemed to be surprisingly unfamiliar with one another, despite the fact that they actually were well acquainted. It is also strange that there are no traces of the participation of Bakhtin, Bernshtein, and Vygotskii in the work of GAKhN, despite the fact that they were all deeply concerned with issues of art. In Vygotskii's case there is only a single purely formal citation in *Psikhologiia iskusstva* (*The Psychology of Art*) to an article of Shpet's on aesthetics. *Psikhologiia iskusstva* is an early work by Vygotskii, most of which, apparently, was written before the publication of Shpet's *Aesthetic Fragments*, which first appeared in 1922-23. Unlike it, Vygotskii's *Thought and Language* was first published in 1934, a little over a decade after Shpet's *Aesthetic Fragments* appeared and several years after the appearance of his *Vnutrenniaia Forma Slova. Etiudy i variatsii na temy Gumbol'ta* (*The Inner Form of the Word: Études and Variations on Humboldt's Themes*), which appeared in 1927. The problems explored in all three of these remarkable books are similar. Their overlapping concerns are reflected in the fact that they share key terms such as *culture, history, consciousness, thinking, thought, word, action, image, sign, meaning, sense, inner speech, element, unit of analysis,* and *experience.* An exception to this pattern arises in connection with the concept of the inner form of the word. From the perspective of timing and influence, it is noteworthy that already in his 1917 article, "Mudrost' ili razum?" ("Wisdom or Reason?"), Shpet had outlined a diverse set of forms belonging to the word. These included grammatical, stylistic, aesthetic and logical forms: "What is important to us is that these are not accidental and empirical forms, but essential and necessary, so they are stable and self-identical, just as an object is identical with itself in its formation. In an analogy with Humboldt's 'inner form of language,' these are logical, and I term them ideal inner forms of language" ("Mudrost'" 294-95).

It is striking that Vygotskii generally did not use the concept of the inner form of the word, even in places where it would seem appropriate or necessary, for example, when reviewing the ideas of Humboldt and Potebnia. In outlining their views in "The History of the Development of Higher Mental Functions," Vygotskii, as it were, renamed the inner form of the word as "meaning" and "inner image" and spoke of "inner comparison, inner picture or pictogram, conditional sounds connected with the inner image." (Vygotskii, "Istoriia razvitiia" 171). In *Thought and Language,* Vygotskii wrote of the "inner side of the word," that is, meaning, arguing that "there has been very little research on this aspect of the word" (Vygotsky, *Collected* 47). But in fact the inner form of the word had already been specially outlined in detail by Shpet in 1922. It is possible to read into Vygotskii's treatment of the inner side of the word ideas that Shpet had outlined regarding what he termed "the inner form." Indeed, Zinchenko did exactly this in publications connected with the centenary of

Vygotskii's birth (see Zinchenko, "Ot klassicheskoi"). Another major figure in Soviet psychology and philosophy, S.L. Rubinshtein, also did not go deeply into the inner side of the word. He spoke of the word as a unit of meaning and as a sign. True, he noted that "the external form of the word goes beyond the boundaries of the sign because the word has inner meaning. The meaning of a word is its semantic content which involves a generalized reflection of the object" (Rubinshtein 444-45).

It appears that Vygotskii did not so much supplement Shpet's ideas about the inner form of the word as he replaced them with the notion of the "inner plane of speech." In this connection, he argued that speaking requires the transformation from an inner plane to an external one, and understanding presupposes the reverse movement—from the external plane of speech to an internal plane. In our view, if Vygotskii had employed the full range and depth of Shpet's ideas about the inner form of the word in his account of inner speech and comprehension, he could have formulated things in a richer way. Perhaps it is even less surprising that Vygotskii's student, A.N. Leont'ev, a figure who went on to be a major shaping force in Soviet psychology, ignored Shept's profound meditations on meaning and sense. The psychological theory of consciousness outlined by Leont'ev, in which these concepts play a central role, is quite hermeneutic in general intent, but it is short on specifics. For example, Leont'ev's writings are significantly less concrete in this area than were Vygotskii's. Leont'ev also managed not to notice Bakhtin and his ideas on dialogism and the polyphony of consciousness.

It is impossible to imagine how the ideas in Shpet's book, *Appearance and Sense,* could have not been known to Bakhtin, Vygotskii, and Leont'ev (the latter two, after all, had attended lectures and seminars by Shpet at Moscow University). This is especially so since these three authors repeatedly cited Husserl. What this suggests, then, is that consciously or unconsciously, Vygotskii began a tradition in psychology of ignoring Shpet, a tradition that was preserved by P.P. Blonskii, L.M. Vekker, P.Ia. Gal'perin, V.V. Davydov, A.N. Leont'ev, A.A. Leont'ev, B.F. Lomov, A.R. Luriia, Ia.A. Ponomarev, S.L. Rubinshtein, A.A. Smirnov, A.N. Sokolov, and G.P. Shchedrovitskii. This also applies to many others who studied language, thinking, understanding, sense, and meaning. One almost never encounters references to Shpet, even in the writings of his own student, N.I. Zhinkin, who dedicated his life to studying the mechanisms of speech. This is true despite the fact that in lectures and discussion Zhinkin did speak a great deal about Shpet.

Before going into more detail on whether and how Shpet's ideas influenced others in Russia, it is worthwhile considering some frequently encountered explanations for why this influence appears not to exist. One line of reasoning behind the tradition of ignoring Shpet is that although he was a superior analyst and a still better critic, he actually produced very little by way of original work. This totally unfounded legend, the origins of which can be traced to Valentin Asmus and Vasilii Zen'kovskii, was supported indirectly by justified references to the difficulty in understanding Shpet's texts: "Shpet's exposition is characterized by the extremely abstract manner in which he set out his position in *Esteticheskie Fragmenty* (in a style that somewhat shocked the reader): exampla sunt idiosa" (Ivanov 682). Although he made brilliant use of the Russian language, it is true that Shpet wrote in a way that is difficult to understand. He consciously avoided examples, considering it more important for the reader to apply something than to develop abstract notions on the basis of illustrations. Perhaps he overestimated his readership, believing them to be capable themselves of finding examples that could illustrate one or another difficult point in his thought. In short, the subject of Shpet's thinking is not simple. In this connection it is worth remembering that he worked with Husserl for some time. After such collaboration, it is not possible to expect simplicity.

The dearth of Shpet's apparent influence in Soviet psychology is particularly striking, given the extent to which he participated in the discipline's theoretical debates and organizational efforts. As early as 1912 he weighed in with his vision of the shape the discipline might take in the future. On the eve of the opening of the Psychological Institute in that year, he wrote an article titled "One Path of Psychology and Where It Leads." In this article he clearly identified himself as a psychologist. Furthermore, Shpet was deeply involved in the formation of organizations devoted to psychology. For example: "In December of 1920 an Office for Ethnic and Social Psychology was created at Moscow State University on the initiative of G.G. Shpet. N.I. Zhinkin was selected as its secretary. The organization of this office was preceded by Shpet's historical and critical research in the area of 'folk psychology' and his sharp critical analysis of Wundt's conceptual system. The theoretical principles and foundations formulated by Shpet preserve their unquestioned significance even today" (Mitiushin 37). This is not to say that Shpet always identified himself with the discipline of psychology; in keeping with his reputation for being a forceful, indeed scorching critic, he sometimes approached it from a perspective that was not appreciated. In fact, in some publications Shpet wrote as an "anti-psychologist," sharply critical of "psychological naturalism" (Shpet, "Teatr" 420-21).

One key to understanding the dual position Shpet articulated in these debates on the significance of psychology is to keep in mind that throughout the entire history of twentieth-century psychology it was fashionable to reflect on the discipline by identifying some crisis that it was supposedly undergoing at the moment. This crisis was felt by many, but different parties saw it in their own way. For example, in his renowned work "Istoricheskii smysl psikhologiskogo krizisa" ("The Historical Significance of the Crisis in Psychology"), Vygotskii characterized the psychology he knew in a wholly uncomplimentary light. Looking back, one is staggered by the obvious incongruity between this formulation and the facts at the time. In 1927, in addition to Vygotskii and his emerging school of followers (e.g., Luriia, Leont'ev), scholars in pedagogy and psychotechnics were in full stride; members of the Bakhtin Circle were making contributions; and A.A. Ukhtomskii and N.A. Bernshtein who created the foundations of the physiology of activation (psychological physiology) were hard at work. We also have to mention A.A. Smirnov, B.M. Teplov, N.D. Levitov, P.A. Shevarev, and others who had comprised the Chelpanov Circle. And in the West, Gestalt psychology and other schools of thought were working at full strength with new names appearing all the time, names such as Kurt Lewin, Jean Piaget, Edward Tolman, and Frederic Bartlett. In reality all this hardly suggested a crisis. Instead it was a flowering of psychology that any period could envy. In the end, however, what came to transpire in science, including psychology, in the Soviet Union probably should be referred to by some term stronger than "crisis." Instead of crises of the sort one would normally expect in scientific evolution, Soviet science experienced a series of catastrophes. Vygotskii seems to have sensed the impending fate of his own work, and as a result he did not feel it necessary to publish his essay on the crisis in psychology during his lifetime (indeed, it was almost half a century after his death in 1934 that this paper appeared in the Russian edition of Vygotskii's writings).

When trying to understand the impact of various thinkers on Soviet psychology, we would argue that the self-definition of the individuals involved does not always provide the most useful insight. This applies to figures such as Bakhtin, Bernshtein, and Ukhtomskii, and also to Shpet. These names are not always mentioned in accounts of Soviet psychology, but without them, it is difficult to imagine the discipline taking the shape it did. Indeed, the first three never even called themselves psychologists. They never expressed a desire to be so labelled. As for Shpet, while it is obvious that he belonged and contributed to many disciplines, he did have a clear affiliation with psychology, at least during the early stages of his professional life. After starting off in this discipline, he went beyond its boundaries to consider issues of culture, philosophy, linguistics, aesthetics, and theater. But despite all his various inclinations, we would argue that he could not stop being a psychologist. He was already shaped by this discipline, and perhaps even against his will did a great deal for it.

Vygotskii's fate took him down a somewhat different path. It was only late in his career that he identified himself as member of the discipline of psychology, coming to it from his study of culture. He did indeed bring a wealth of knowledge about culture to his studies in this discipline, thereby giving rise to the "Cultural-Historical School of Psychology," a term that, incidentally, emerged only after his death. Fundamental to Vygotskii's formulation of human consciousness is the claim that language and other cultural tools play a fundamental role in shaping it. This theme of "mediation" (Wertsch, *Vygotsky*; *Voices*) runs throughout his writings, and was so central that near the end of his life he stated that "the central fact about our psychology is the fact of mediation" (Vygotskii, "Zapis'" 166). In developing his ideas about semiotic mediation, Vygotskii identified two main "semiotic potentials" (Wertsch, *Vygotsky*; *Voices*) in language that can be exploited in the formation of human mental functioning. He was concerned in part with the potential that language has for serving as a tool for abstract reflection, a concern that led him to study forms of conceptual reasoning that he viewed as developing, both in sociocultural history and in ontogenesis.

In much of his writing, Vygotskii celebrated this form of reasoning as the key to "higher" (i.e., uniquely human) mental functioning. But Vygotskii revealed some ambivalence about the power and prospects of Enlightenment rationality, at least as a sole formulation of human consciousness (Wertsch, "Vygotsky's Two Minds"), and in this connection he recognized another form of mental life. The key to his line of reasoning on this issue is the second semiotic potential he saw in language, namely the potential for linguistic signs to derive significance from context, including linguistic context, as opposed to abstract, decontextualized reflection. The form of mental functioning associated with this potential is something like a language-mediated stream of consciousness. It is in connection with this second semiotic potential that Vygotskii's debt to Shpet is particularly apparent. One concrete connection between Shpet and Vygotskii in this context can be seen in their discussions of meaning (*znachenie*) and sense (*smysl*). Instead of harnessing Shpet's ideas when dealing with these notions, Vygotskii cited the French psychologist Frederick Paulham (1856-1931), whose ideas are significantly less well developed than those outlined by Shpet in "Germenevtika i ee problemy" ("Hermeneutics and Its Problems"), which he completed in 1918. Nonetheless, the parallels between Shpet and Vygotskii are striking.

In Shpet's account meaning is a polysemous collection of significance that is fixed in dictionaries. In contrast, sense is a form of signification that emerges only in a concrete speaking context:

> The word seems polysemous only as long as it is not used in meaningful communication or when we encounter it and do not yet know what meaning it has in communication. One might think, however, that sometimes the use of one and the same word for accomplishing two or more goals of signification may be a part of intention. It is obvious, however, that uncovering these goals involves the analysis not of meaning but of an author's intention, an author who might have his own rhetorical form (allegory, personification, parables and so forth). In order to understand the use of words' meanings as tasks of interpretation, therefore, one must have in mind not only meaning as such. One must also attend to the multiple forms of using a word and the psychology of using it. (Shpet, "Germenevtika" 226)

Vygotskii arrived at a formulation of the distinction between meaning and sense that has many striking parallels with Shpet's account, despite the fact that Vygotskii made no mention of Shpet or his ideas. Specifically, in chapter 7 of *Thought and Language,* Vygotskii wrote: "A word's sense is the aggregate of all the psychological facts that arise in our consciousness as a result of the word. Sense is a dynamic, fluid, and complex formation which has several zones that vary in their stability. . . . In different contexts, a word's sense changes. In contrast, meaning is a comparatively fixed and stable point, one that remains constant with all the changes of the word's sense that are associated with its use in various contexts. . . . The actual meaning of a word is inconstant. In one operation the word emerges with one meaning; in another, another is acquired" (Vygotsky, *Collected* 275-76).

The parallels between Vygotskii's and Shpet's discussions extend well beyond their formulations of particular terms or distinctions such as those between meaning and sense. Indeed, focusing too heavily on parallels in terminology can lead to overlooking a more general and more important way in which Shpet influenced Vygotskii. This has to do with the general formulations the two employed when dealing with language and thought.

Vygotskii wrote, or rather dictated, chapter 7 of *Thought and Language* as he was dying of tuberculosis. The chapter entitled "Thought and Word" is the text where Shpet's influence is probably more apparent than anywhere else in his writings. The two terms in the title of this chapter reflect a formulation that is reminiscent of Shpet's on several counts. Specifically, *thought* and *word* reflect an opposition that Vygotskii saw as operating between the two potentials around which his writings on semiotically mediated mental functioning are organized. *Word* is a cover term for the potential that language has for the kind of explicit, expanded, systemically organized meaning and form outlined in his account of conceptual development. *Thought*, by contrast, is a cover term Vygotskii used in this chapter for the potential language has for "abbreviation" and for contextualized signification.

Throughout chapter 7 Vygotskii examined these two general semiotic potentials in terms of several other more specific oppositions. For example, he outlined a distinction between the *internal* and *external* form of the word, between social and inner speech (with *egocentric speech* serving as a link between the two), between written speech and inner speech and between sense and meaning. In all these cases Vygotskii stressed that the two members of the opposition were quite distinct with regard to form as well as function. In general, he took *language, social speech, written speech*, the *phonetic* or *auditory* aspect of speech, the *grammatical* categories of subject and predicate, and *meaning* to be associated with explicit, systemically organized, social, expanded form, whereas *thought, inner speech*, the *semantic* aspect of speech, the *psychological* categories of subject and predicate, and *sense* were viewed as being characterized by implicit, condensed and highly contextualized and abbreviated form and personal sense. In Vygotskii's view, the externality associated with the first set of terms is tied to the fact that they are concerned with the social, and hence public sphere, whereas the internality of the second set of terms is tied to the fact that they are concerned with a private, psychological world: "Inner speech is for oneself. External speech is speech for others" (Vygotsky, *Collected* 257).

Vygotskii framed the general line of reasoning he would employ in chapter 7 in terms of an opposition between "two planes of speech . . . the inner, meaningful, semantic aspect . . . [and] its external, auditory aspect" (Vygotsky, *Collected* 250). Of course, some distinction between material sign and meaning is a commonplace in linguistic and semiotic analysis, but Vygotskii's formulation in this chapter goes beyond this general observation and echoes a more concrete line of reasoning employed by Shpet. Specifically, Vygotskii laid out his argument in terms of an opposition between the unarticulated intentions and motives of a speaker, on the one hand, and the discrete articulation and organization imposed by language, on the other. The dialectic that emerges between these two poles of opposition is a defining property of human consciousness in his view and was what led Vygotskii to emphasize that this relationship, mediated by inner speech, is one of emergence rather than stasis.

Several elements of this line of reasoning appear to come straight out of Shpet's writings. Shpet warned that "We must look at language not as a dead product of a generative process [*ein Erzeugtes*], but instead as a generative process [*eine Erzeugung*]" (Shpet, "Vnutrenniaia" 55), and this is a central tenet of the argument he lays out in *Vnutrenniaia forma slova*. He repeated this assertion at several points in his review of Humboldt's position that language must be viewed as *energeia* and not as *ergon*: "For Humboldt it was a major revelation that language is energeia. For him everything comes down to this. All the other nuances in the description of this term must be understood in this sense: language is 'activity of the spirit' and 'the immanent work of the soul.' It is at the foundation of the very nature of being human . . . Language can be examined not only as substance, but as subject, not only as a thing, product or result of production, but as production process, as energeia" (Shpet, "Vnutrenniaia" 77-78). The extent to which this formulation of the problem is echoed in Vygotskii's writings is apparent in the way he mapped the task of chapter 7 of *Thought and Language*: "This central idea—a concept we will develop and clarify in the following discussion—can be expressed in the following general formula: The relationship of thought to word is not a thing but a process, a movement from thought to word and from word to thought. Psychological analysis indicates that this relationship is a developing process which changes as it passes through a series of stages . . . The movement of thinking from thought to word is a developmental process" (Vygotsky, *Collected* 250). This general formulation is something that Vygotskii outlined briefly in this chapter, but in our view he did not develop or utilize it to the level of sophistication that can be found in Shpet's writings. Rather, it seems that Vygotskii used it to establish the outlines for a set of arguments he wanted to make about a range of theoretical and empirical studies he had done.

As noted earlier, it is notoriously difficult to identify, let alone fully understand the intellectual influence of one thinker on another. In the case of Gustav Shpet, this is made all the more difficult because scholars from a range of disciplines in the Soviet Union seemed intent on forgetting him, at least in public discussion. However effective the tradition of ignoring Shpet may have been on the surface, it is becoming increasingly apparent that he had a deep influence on many areas of scholarship in Soviet Russia, and that influence continues today.

In seeking to outline Shpet's influence on psychology, a discipline that is often not closely associated with his name, we have been able to do little more than mention how this influence played out in general and give a bit more detail concerning one major figure, Lev Semenovich Vygotskii. In addition to being found in the latter's use of specific terms such as *meaning* and *sense*, Shpet's influence is to be seen in the general formulation of Vygotskii's line of reasoning about the relationship between language and thought.

What we have laid out is no more than a preliminary effort to identify and examine the ways in which Shpet influenced thinking in psychology as well as many other disciplines, both in the Soviet context and elsewhere. Because of Shpet's tragic, but all too common, fate in the Soviet Union, it is impossible to know how his impact on a range of disciplines in the human sciences might have evolved had he lived. With the new possibilities presented to us in the post-Soviet era to appreciate the power and significance of his ideas, however, it has already become apparent that we have much more work ahead of us to understand the powerful impact of this amazing intellect.

Note

The research and writing of this article was assisted by a grant from the Russian Foundation for Fundamental Studies (05-06 80509) to Vladimir Zinchenko and by a grant from the Spencer Foundation to James V. Wertsch.

Works Cited

Belyi, Andrei *Mezhdu dvukh revoliutsii*. Moscow: Khudozhestvennaia literatura, 1990.

Ivanov, V.V. *Izbrannye trudy po semiotike i istorii kul'tury*. Vol. 1. Moscow: Iazyki russkoi kul'tury, 1998.

Mitiushin, A.A. "G. Shpet i ego mesto v istorii otechestvennoi psikhologii." *Vestnik MGU. Seriia 14. Psikhologiia* 2 (1988): 33-42.

Rubinshtein, S.L. *Osnovy obshchei psikhologii*. Moscow: Pedagogika, 1989.

Shpet, Gustav. "Ocherk razvitiia russkoi filosofii." *Sochineniia*. Moscow: Pravda, 1989. 9-342.

Shpet, Gustav. "Germenevtika i ee problemy." *Kontekst 1989*. Moscow: Nauka, 1989. 231-67; *Kontekst 1990*. Moscow: Nauka, 1990. 219-59; *Kontekst 1991*. Moscow: Nauka, 1991. 215-55; Kontekst *1992*. Moscow: Nauka, 1993. 251-84.

Shpet, Gustav. "Mudrost' ili razum?" *Filosofskie etiudy*. Moscow: Progress, 1994. 222-336.

Shpet, Gustav. "Teatr kak iskusstvo." *Psikhologiia sotsial'nogo bytiia. Izbrannye sotsiologicheskie trudy*. Ed. T.D. Martsinkovskaia. Moscow: Insititut prakticheskoi psikhologii; Voronezh: MODEK, 1996. 413-37.

Shpet, Gustav. "Vnutrenniaia forma slova." *Psikhologiia sotsial'nogo bytiia. Izbrannye sotsiologicheskie trudy*. Ed. T.D. Martsinkovskaia. Moscow: Insititut prakticheskoi psikhologii; Voronezh: MODEK, 1996. 49-260.

Vygotskii, L.S. "Istoriia razvitiia vysshikh piskhicheskikh funktsii." *Sobranie sochinenii v shesti tomakh*. Vol. 3. *Razvitie psikhiki*. Ed. A.M. Matiushkin. Moscow: Pedagogika. 1983. 5-328

Vygotskii, L.S. "Zapis' osnovnykh polozhenii doklada L.S. Vygotskogo." By A.N. Leont'ev. *Sobranie sochinenii v shesti tomakh*. Vol. 1. *Voprosy teorii i istorii psikhologii*. Ed. A.R. Luriia and M.G. Iaroshevskii. Moscow: Pedagogika, 1982. 156-67.

Vygotsky, L.S. *Collected Works*. Vol. 1. *Problems of General Psychology*. Trans. Norris Minick. New York: Plenum, 1987.

Wertsch, J.V. *Vygotsky and the Social Formation of Mind*. Cambridge: Harvard UP, 1985.

Wertsch, J.V. *Voices of the Mind: A Sociocultural Approach to Mediated Action*. Cambridge: Harvard UP, 1991.

Wertsch, J.V. "Vygotsky's Two Minds on the Nature of Meaning." *Vygotskian Perspectives on Literacy Research: Constructing Meaning through Collaborative Inquiry*. Ed. C.D. Lee and P. Smagorinsky. Cambridge: Cambridge UP, 2000. 19-30.

Zinchenko, V.P. "Ot klassicheskoi k organicheskoi psikhologii. K 100-letiiu L.S. Vygotskogo." *Voprosy psikhologii* 5 (1996): 7-20; 6 (1996): 6-25.

Zinchenko, V.P. *Obraz i deiatel'nost'*. Moscow: Insititut prakticheskoi psikhologii; Voronezh: MODEK, 1997.

Gustav Shpet's Literary and Theater Affiliations

Galin Tihanov

Gustav Shpet's theoretical work on literature and theater has not been systematically studied, nor has sufficient attention been paid to his overall presence on the Russian cultural scene from the 1910s to the 1930s. As a result, our knowledge and appreciation of the scope of his writings and the variety of Russian literary and theater life in the first third of the twentieth century have remained less rich and well informed than they could otherwise have been. Shpet's participation in contemporary literature and theater assumed different forms: to start with, he wrote on both from a theoretical perspective grounded in his overall aesthetics; second, through personal friendships and affiliations, as well as through his membership, he played an important part in a number of informal circles or more formally structured groupings, such as the Moscow Linguistic Circle, which promoted literature, theater, and scholarship on them; and last but not least, Shpet was active as the Russian translator of, and commentator on, several works belonging to the canon of English literature. In what follows, I attempt a concise chronological examination of Shpet's contribution in these three intersecting areas. My prime concern will be to establish the factual basis of Shpet's involvement with literature and the theater and to assess briefly his contribution to literary and theater theory in the 1920s.

To a significant degree, this study is meant as a contribution to a proper scholarly biography of Shpet, which someone might undertake to write in the future (for a first very helpful attempt, see Shchedrina, *"Ia pishu . . ."*). To that end, I draw on previously unheeded published and unpublished sources, bringing together strains of research that have so far remained unconnected. The examination I undertake is ultimately intent on revealing Shpet's scattered talents and energy, and—in the years after 1927—his tragically multifarious life under the political duress of Stalinism. I begin by reviewing Shpet's immersion in Russian Symbolism and his contacts with the Imagists. Then I focus on his contribution to the work of the Moscow Linguistic Circle and the study of literature at GAKhN. In the final two sections I offer an analysis of Shpet's career as a translator and of his theater affiliations, both falling largely in the 1930s and shaped in no small measure by the ideological constraints of Stalinism.

Among the Symbolists

Shpet's literary and theater affiliations had commenced in earnest after his move to Moscow in 1907. In Kiev, where he studied at St. Vladimir University, he had given expression to his early literary ambitions by publishing brief newspaper notes under the pseudonym "Lord Genry" (M. Polivanov, "Ocherk" 15). There he also was Anna Akhmatova's teacher in psychology (later in life Shpet was one of Boris Pasternak's philosophy professors; on Shpet's contacts with Akhmatova, Pasternak, Mikhail Kuzmin, and Sofia Parnok; see Tihanov, "Multifariousness"). Yet it was Moscow, and Russian Symbolism, that became the ground of his first serious association with a major literary and artistic circle, "Obshchestvo svobodnoi estetiki" ("The Society of Free Aesthetics"), also known simply as "Estetika" ("Aesthetics"). "Estetika" was founded under the informal leadership of Valerii Briusov; other distinguished participants included Andrei Belyi, Mikhail Gershenzon, and the artist Valentin Serov, the literary scholars Sakulin and Dzhivelegov, and the philosophers Fedor Stepun and Boris Vysheslavtsev, to name but a few. Shpet befriended several fellow participants, notably Iurgis Baltrushaitis, who was to become a life-long friend, and the brothers Emilii and Nikolai Metner (Belyi, *Mezhdu* 242); most likely, his acquaintance with Pavel Sakulin also goes back to this time. A couple of years later Shpet joined the group around the Musaget publishing house, led by Emilii Metner, Belyi, and Lev Kobylinskii (Ellis), the latter also a friend of Shpet's (see Belyi, *Nachalo* 53). Although Belyi perceived Shpet as a late-comer, he had considerable respect for Shpet's taste and valued his background in philosophy (Belyi, *Nachalo* 75). Shpet asserted the "philosophical nature" (*filosofichnost'*) of Belyi's 1904 collection of poetry "Gold in Azure" ("Zoloto v lazuri"; Belyi, *Mezhdu* 306), but would warn him sarcastically on numerous occasions against playing with, or "parading," philosophy in his poems; in Belyi's words—reporting Shpet's—in order to be a truly philosophical poet, one does not need to wear "a shabby tail-coat borrowed from [Heinrich] Rickert's wardrobe" (Belyi, *Mezhdu* 307), nor, indeed, to mix the mystic aspects of a poem with the philosophical ones (Belyi, *Vospominaniia* 561; "Iz vospominanii" 338). Belyi confessed to being "in love" with Shpet's "subtle and sophisticated mind" (*Vospominaniia* 559-60). In September 1909, when it was still unclear whether Musaget would be launched as a journal or as a full-fledged publishing house (Belyi, *Mezhdu* 374), Belyi regarded Shpet as a potential contributor to the journal who could write on Fichte and on Polish philosophy and culture (Shpet, himself of Polish descent, would read Belyi the poetry of Słowacki and Mickiewicz in Polish; see Belyi, *Vospominaniia* 560). Emilii Metner, too, believed at the time that Shpet would make a good contributor to the philosophical section of the journal (Shchedrina, *"Ia pishu . . ."* 78). Yet a year later, in October 1910, Shpet's outspokenness led Belyi to write to Metner that Shpet was "brilliant, but apparently hostile to us" (qtd. in Shchedrina, *"Ia pishu . . ."* 56). Despite this early crisis, Shpet and Belyi worked together once again after the Revolution, in the Moscow branch of the Free Philosophical Association (*Vol'fila*), established in September 1921. Belyi became the chairman of the branch's council; Shpet was elected one of his deputies (Gut 94; Lavrov and Malmstad 269). A few years later, in 1927, Belyi wrote to Ivanov-Razumnik that his gradual estrangement from Shpet had to do with the latter's attraction to alcohol, which Belyi did not wish to share (Lavrov and Malmstad 463). Belyi briefly resumed the acquaintance in 1933, about a year before his death (see his two letters to Shpet of April and August 1933 in Shtorkh 64-65).

Shpet was not the only philosopher to participate in the activities around the Musaget publishing house; Vladimir Ern, Sergei Bulgakov, Sergei Gessen, Nikolai Berdiaev, and Mikhail Gershenzon were also frequently seen there. (After the October Revolution and before being sent into exile in 1922, Bulgakov and Berdiaev participated in the logico-philosophical student circle that Shpet and the mathematician Luzin directed at Moscow University; see Granin 30-31.) From 1910 to 1914, Musaget published the Russian version of *Logos*, the international journal of philosophy, edited by Fedor Stepun and Sergei Gessen. Within the membership of Musaget, there was a clear divide between those who were in favor of the line represented by *Logos* and those who opposed it as being too neo-Kantian and not heeding in sufficient measure other currents in contemporary philosophy. Shpet, Ern, and Bulgakov (the latter occasionally ridiculed by Shpet as using a "pomade prepared from religious superstition [*iz popovskogo dukha*] and memories of a peculiar Marxism"; Belyi, *Mezhdu* 306) were in the camp of the opponents; in Shpet's case this was no doubt motivated by a rejection of neo-Kantianism in favor of phenomenology.

Among the Symbolists, Shpet became more intimately acquainted not only with Belyi, Baltrushaitis, Ellis (and Nikolai Feofilaktov, the principal illustrator of *Vesy*), but also with Viacheslav Ivanov. Their contacts are yet to be studied in detail, but it would appear from the scattered evidence available that over time the relationship grew from Shpet's respect for and interest in Ivanov the poet and thinker into a friendship in which Ivanov recognized Shpet's seriousness as a philosopher and commentator on literature. Lev Shestov mentions an evening at his home on 8 December 1914, where he and his guests—Ivanov, Shpet, and Berdiaev—spent the time in captivating discussions (Baranova-Shestova 130); Shpet's letters to his second wife, Nataliia Guchkova, reveal (Shchedrina, *Gustav Shpet* 225, 248, 258) that in the summer of 1915 he and Lev Shestov would often visit Ivanov to hear him read from his poetry, sometimes in the company of Bal'mont, Baltrushaitis, and Remizov (Shpet later received a brief mention in Remizov's *Vzvikhrennaia Rus'*; Remizov 232), at others in Mikhail Gershenzon's. Shpet described Ivanov's poems read on one such occasion (7 June 1915) as "superb" (*prevoskhodny*). Ivanov was clearly an authority in Shpet's eyes not just as a poet, but also as a mentor inculcating in Shpet a relentless work discipline (Serebrennikov 228). Shpet presented Ivanov with three of his publications (Obatnin 323-24), all with personal inscriptions: *Iavlenie i smysl* (1914); *Filosofskoe nasledstvo P.D. Iurkevicha* (1915) and *Istoriia, kak problema logiki* (1916). In 1920, Boris Gornung participated in long discussions on the future of Russian culture, in which Ivanov would side with Lunacharskii, while Gornung was enjoying support from Shpet (B. Gornung, *Pokhod* 331). Later, during

Ivanov's first years in Italy, Shpet was apparently instrumental in GAKhN electing Ivanov as one of its "member-candidates" in December 1926 (Bird 320; Kondiurina 238). Shpet endeavored to assist Ivanov by offering to buy on behalf of GAKhN his Moscow library (Kondiurina 373), while Ivanov wanted to entrust Shpet with overseeing the final stage of publication, including the proofreading, of his translation of Aeschylus' *Oresteia* trilogy (Kondiurina 235, 239, 240) which was supposed to be published by GAKhN. The task was deemed by Ivanov to demand so much knowledge and organizational talent as to be impossible to assign to anyone but Shpet. The publication, however, did not materialize (Bird 331).

Behind these personal ties to some of the major poets of Russian Symbolism, we have to see (and here only briefly refer to) the larger picture: Symbolism left its crucial imprint on Shpet's subsequent aesthetic theory, contributing to the formation of his overall conservative platform (Nikolaev 265-67). Shpet's appreciation of "seriousness" and his fight against "emptiness, utilitarian attitudes [*utilitarnosti*], barbarism" found support in the philosophical ambition and gravitas of Symbolism, whose praise Shpet continued to sing into the 1920s in his *Aesthetic Fragments* (Shpet, "Esteticheskie" 357-59), while at the same time rejecting Naturalism and Futurism and criticizing Akhmatova's acmeist poetry (Shpet, "Esteticheskie" 371).

Shpet and the Imagists

If it is fair to suggest that Shpet's affiliations with Russian Symbolism had not been researched in sufficient detail, the same is true to an even larger extent of his contacts with the Russian Imagists. Shpet's sympathy for the Imagists, an avant-garde group active from 1919 to 1927 and including Vadim Shershenevich, Sergei Esenin, and Anatolii Mariengof, among others, would come as a surprise when one recalls his (already mentioned) unambiguous and sharp criticism of Futurism, the most significant manifestation of the Russian literary avant-garde, in the first installment of the *Aesthetic Fragments* (Shpet, "Esteticheskie" 361-63).

Shpet's contacts with the Imagists occurred at a time when, on the demise of Symbolism and the fading of Acmeism after the outbreak of the Revolution and the Civil War, it was imperative for the intelligentsia to reposition itself vis-à-vis the new political realities and the new aesthetic trends. Esenin was apparently the first of the future Imagists to make Shpet's acquaintance. Belyi saw behind this friendship a shared proclivity to alcohol-induced merriment (*Mezhdu* 310), but there was undoubtedly more to it than that. Shpet was among the members of the Moscow Union of Writers (other members included Mikhail Gershenzon, Mikhail Osorgin, and Georgii Chulkov) who in December 1918 considered a request from Esenin for a document certifying his possession of live stock, to enable the poet to protect himself against tax and requisition (Esenin 7 [2]: 202, 284). The contacts between the two probably intensified in 1919 when Esenin joined the short-lived literary association "Dvorets Iskusstv," of which Shpet, along with Sakulin, Vengerov, Tsvetaeva, and others, was also a member (Savchenko 204). More importantly, beyond the drinking companionship and the day-to-day business, Shpet was undoubtedly interested in Esenin's poetry. The peak of this interest and of their literary contacts seems to fall in the years 1920-1921, when Esenin presented Shpet with inscribed copies (Esenin 7 [3]: 60 and 7 [1]: 158) of his books *Confessions of a Hooligan* (*Ispoved' khuligana*) and *Pugachov* (the latter inscription, "Milomu Gustavu/Gustavovichu/S liubov'iu liutoi" is dated December 1921, while the publication date indicated in the book is 1922). A copy of the collective publication *Imazhinisty* was inscribed by Esenin, Mariengof, and Riurik Ivnev (Esenin 7 [1]: 117 and 447) to Shpet's daughter Lenora (1905-1976) in December 1920 (the publication date indicated in the book is 1921). As Mariengof reports in his memoir *A Novel without Lies* (*Roman bez vran'ia*), in the summer of 1921 he and Esenin organized a gathering at which they read from their new works (Esenin read from *Pugachov* on this occasion); Shpet, Meyerhold, the artist Georgii Iakulov, and the sculptor Sergei Konenkov were present (Mariengof 130; Iur'ev and Shumikhin 383).

Shpet must have lent a sympathetic year to Esenin's and Mariengof's works, for in the first half of September 1921 the Imagists, insulted by an article in which Lunacharskii referred to them as "charlatans who wish to fool [*morochit'*] the public" (Lunacharskii, "Svoboda" 6), published a challenging response in the journal *Pechat' i revoliutsiia*, calling Lunacharskii to a "public discussion on Imagism, where Prof. Shpet, Prof. Sakulin and other representatives of science and the arts will be invited in the capacity of competent judges" (Esenin, Mariengof, and Shershenevich 249). The letter, a different version of which was also sent to the journal *Kniga i revoliutsiia* (but did not appear there), was signed by Esenin, Mariengof, and Shershenevich. The original—now considered lost—was handwritten by Mariengof, yet the actual instigator of the letter, according to Matvei Roizman (1896-1973), himself a minor Imagist poet, was Shershenevich, as he was allegedly the only one personally familiar with both Sakulin and Shpet, occasionally calling at their homes (Roizman 145).

The accuracy of Roizman's memoirs ought to be questioned here on two counts. Shershenevich may well have played a part in suggesting Sakulin for the role of a "competent judge," but more likely than not his name was put forward as a result of a collective discussion rather than by Shershenevich alone. As for Shpet's name, it is more likely that Esenin and Mariengof were the actual force behind his "nomination" rather than Shershenevich.

Two arguments seem to be corroborating these conjectures. While Shershenevich was clearly grateful to Sakulin for giving his adolescent literary ambitions an early (and decisive) impetus, which Shershenevich duly recorded in his own memoirs (Iur'ev and Shumikhin 428, 460), Esenin, too, felt he was indebted to Sakulin, as the latter had been similarly supportive of his own beginnings as a poet (Kuniaevy 58; unfortunately, the Kuniaevys reproduce uncritically Roizman's statement that Shershenevich was the sole initiator of the letter to *Pechat' i revoliutsiia*). Thus it is extremely unlikely that Esenin—the fact of whose personal acquaintance with and debt to Sakulin Roizman completely neglects—will not have had a say in the conversations on Sakulin's role in the proposed public dispute with Lunacharskii. On the other hand, Shershenevich cannot be taken to have been unconditionally fascinated with Shpet. Back in December 1918, he had put Shpet's name on a list of twenty Russian literati whom Shershenevich, on behalf of the Professional Union of Poets (*Professional'nyi soiuz poetov*), wanted to see elected on the council (*sovet*) of the Literary Department of the Narkompros (Drozdkov 148-49). His motion, however, was rejected. Less than a year later, in 1919, Shershenevich opened his poem "A Lyrical Construction" ("Liricheskaia konstruktsiia") with the impenetrably (to most readers today) ironic line "All who in Chelpanov's cradle nursed their thought!" ("Vse, kto v liul'ke Chelpanova mysl' svoiu/vynianchil!"; Shershenevich 204). Georgii Chelpanov (1862-1936) was widely known as Shpet's mentor at Kiev University and his patron in Moscow (Belyi, *Mezhdu* 306); Shpet was considered Chelpanov's most gifted pupil who eventually overtook his teacher in terms of prestige and recognition (Belyi, *Mezhdu* 307). (Chelpanov is mentioned once again, again in a rather ambiguous context, in Shershenevich's 1920 manifesto "2x2=5" [Shershenevich 407].) Shershenevich's opening line from "A Lyrical Construction" was thus not just collectively addressed to Chelpanov's pupils, but may well have envisaged Shpet in particular. This makes it more likely for Esenin and Mariengof, rather than Shershenevich himself, to have put forward Shpet's name as a judge in the discussion with Lunacharskii, which in the end never took place (Lunacharskii declined the offer in a response published in the same issue of *Pechat' i revoliutsiia*). If Shershenevich was not overenthusiastic about Shpet, by the mid-1930s the latter's disappointment over Shershenevich's career as a poet was equally unconcealed; in a letter of 21 November 1936 to his son Sergei, Shpet remarked: "And Shershenevich, alas, has failed" ("A iz Shershenevicha, uvy, nichego ne vyshlo"; qtd. in Serebrennikov 177).

Shpet's contacts with the Imagists appear to have been relatively short-lived. He does not seem to have kept up his friendship with Esenin; later this gave Shpet's daughter Tatiana Maksimova-Shpet reason to speculate that "there was . . . no friendship [between them], but there was mutual acceptance [*vzaimnoe priniatie*]" ("Vospominaniia", 119). Nor did Shpet deepen his acquaintance with Mariengof (although as late as 1926 Shpet promised Boris Gornung to introduce him to Mariengof [B. Gornung, *Pokhod* 397]). Shpet's links with the Imagists did not have any noteworthy effect on his aesthetic views or on his immediate political fortunes. The mention of his name in the Imagists' letter apparently did not put off Lunacharskii, who knew Shpet from his time in Kiev, from helping the philosopher in 1922—so the story told repeatedly by Shpet's immediate family goes—to stay on in Russia after his name had been placed on the infamous list of intellectuals to be exiled from the country. It was only in 1929, after the process of Stalinization had advanced to the point where a reversal was no longer in sight, that Lunacharskii joined the chorus of ideology-driven criticism of Shpet's work, castigating his writings at a meeting at the Land and Factory (*Zemlia i fabrika*) publishing house in October 1929 as "most harmful" (*vredneishie sochineniia Shpeta* [Lunacharskii, "Nashi" 436]). Lunacharskii's speech appeared on 28 October 1929 in *Literaturnaia gazeta*; the next day, Shpet was released from his duties as Vice President of GAKhN—an unambiguous example of media deployment as an instrument of cadre politics under Stalin.

Shpet and the Study of Literature in the Moscow Linguistic Circle and GAKhN

The Moscow Linguistic Circle (MLC) existed formally from March 1915 to November 1924. On 14 March 1920, Shpet was elected a member of the Circle, following his presentation of a paper entitled "Aesthetic Features in the Structure of the Word" ("Esteticheskie momenty v strukture slova"), in the discussion of which Osip Brik took part (Krusanov 461). Although Shpet attended only one more meeting of the Circle (4 April 1920), through his younger disciples he influenced its work in no small measure. In an article on the history of the MLC written in November 1976 for *The Short Literary Encyclopaedia* (*Kratkaia literaturnaia entsiklopediia*), but only published twenty years later, Roman Jakobson noted that Shpet's phenomenology of language left "an evident mark on the evolution of the Circle in the concluding phase of its life" (Jakobson, "Moskovskii" 367); elsewhere, he praised Shpet's important role as an "outstanding philosopher of Husserl's school" (Jakobson, "An Example" 534), whom Husserl himself considered "one of his most remarkable students" (Jakobson, "Retrospect" 713). (Jakobson also recalled that Shpet had urged him to acquaint himself with the ideas of Anton Marty.) After Jakobson's departure for Estonia and then Prague in 1920, Shpet's (and later, through him, GAKhN's) influence gradually became so overpowering that it eventually led to the split of the Circle (Nikolaev 228). In the final stages of the Circle's existence, several younger members—Boris Gornung, Buslaev, Zhinkin—joined GAKhN, where Shpet was elected Vice President in 1924; the library of the Circle was also transferred to GAKhN (Toman 66).

Shpet's impact on the work of the MLC flowed above all from the publication of his *Aesthetic Fragments*. But his contributions to the work of the Circle were noted even before that. On 4 April 1920 Shpet participated in a most interesting discussion on plot (*siuzhet*), where he and Petr Bogatyrev sided with Vinokur's insistence on the essentially verbal (*slovesnaia*) nature of plot, against Osip Brik's suggestion that in painting and sculpture plots are possible that are of a nonverbal character (Shapir 299-300). This discussion bears an early testimony to Shpet's belief in a universal semiotic code that enables the processes of translation and expression between different sign systems (literature, painting, sculpture etc.; Shpet advances this idea most comprehensively in his article, "Literatura," which was written as an entry for GAKhN's *Dictionary of Artistic Terms* [*Slovar' khudozhestvennykh terminov*]; the article was first published in 1982). Finally, at a meeting of the Circle on 21 March 1922, it was proposed that Shpet be invited to become a member of the editorial board of the linguistic section of the Circle's publishing house (in his capacity as a philosopher)—an idea which, after long discussions, failed to gain approval among the membership (the planned publishing house did not materialize in the end; see Toddes and Chudakova 240-41).

With the appearance of the *Aesthetic Fragments* (written in January-February 1922, published in 1922-23) Shpet's influence on the Moscow Linguistic Circle became much more visible and substantive. Of particular significance was the second instalment of the *Aesthetic Fragments*, where Shpet offered the first ever definition of poetics as grammar: "Poetics in the broad sense *is the grammar of poetic language and poetic thought*" (Shpet, "Esteticheskie" 408; unless indicated otherwise, all translations are mine). This initially metaphorical use of *grammar* was later taken up by Roman Jakobson in the late 1950s and the early 1960s in his well-known program for the study of the "Poetry of Grammar and Grammar of Poetry," where *grammar* evolved from a metaphor to a term with distinct scope and content. In the same place Shpet also speaks for the first time of the "poetic" (rather than simply aesthetic) "function of the word," thus foreshadowing Jakobson's later authoritative emphasis on the poetic function of language.

The second vital contribution of Shpet in the *Aesthetic Fragments* is his definition of the structure of the word and its differentiation from the concept of system, the latter applied by Shpet mostly to entire discourses rather than to isolated words (although sometimes he blurs the boundary between these two levels by using indiscriminately the Russian *slovo* to stand for both *word* and *discourse*). Again in the second installment, Shpet writes:

> What is meant by "structure" of the word is not the morphological, syntactic, or stylistic construction—in short, not the arrangements of linguistic units "on the plane" [*ploskostnoe*], but on the contrary—the organic, depth-wise arrangement of the word, from the sensually conceivable [wording] to the formal-ideal (eidetic) object, at all levels of the relations located [*raspolagaiushchikhsia*] between these two terms. The structure is a concrete construction whose individual parts can vary in "size" [*"razmere"*] and even in quality, but not a single part of the whole *in potentia* can be removed without destroying that whole. ("Esteticheskie" 382)

The system, on the other hand, is a set of structures where each structure preserves its own particularity. The biological organism—Shpet's example—is precisely such "a system of structures," where each structure (bones, nerves, blood vessels, etc.) remains concrete and distinct. This differentiation between structure and system was welcomed by some linguists in the 1920s, notably Viktor Vinogradov (Vinogradov 265), who read into Shpet's argument a privileging of the notion of structure (depth) over that of system (horizontality), and thus—one can add—an implicit criticism of de Saussure's influential preference for synchronicity (Shpet was aware of Saussure's *Cours* since about the end of June 1922 when he received the unpublished translation of the first part prepared by Aleksandr Romm, another member of the Moscow Linguistic Circle; see Toddes and Chudakova 235 and Reznik; on Romm, see Depretto).

Finally, Shpet's *Aesthetic Fragments* should be credited with anticipating the trend of detecting in scientific discourse traces of figurativeness, a feature that brings the discourses of science and literature closer to each other than customarily thought. "Figurativeness [*obraznost'*] is not only a trait of 'poetry' . . . it is a general property of language, which belongs to scientific discourse as well" (Shpet, "Esteticheskie" 443). This statement questioned Husserl's certainty that the discourse of science can be strictly differentiated from everyday discourse; it offered an approach that—although not pursued further by Shpet himself—was revived by Derrida and Hayden White in the 1970s and 1980s (Steiner, "*Tropos Logikos*"). (Already in *The Inner Form of the Word* [1927], Shpet seemed to be backtracking from his assertion of the porous boundaries between various types of discourses; *Vnutrenniaia* 157.)

But we can also see from this statement why Shpet was perceived as an outright enemy by the Petersburg Formalists (especially Shklovskii and Eikhenbaum) and as insufficiently radical by Jakobson. Despite the pioneering distinction between the poetic and aesthetic function of language, Shpet remained interested mainly in the latter. He denied poetry—and literature in general—their special status as sole exponents of discursive metaphoricity bestowed upon them by the Formalists. And although he resolutely opposed the psychological interpretation of the image (as practised by Potebnia), both in the *Aesthetic Fragments* and in the *Introduction to Ethnic Psychology* (because of that opposition the latter work earned him Jakobson's conditional praise; see Jakobson's letter to Shpet in Shchedrina, *Gustav Shpet* 505-06), Shpet nonetheless sought to explain the image as hovering between the object and the idea; he endeavored to clarify the relation of the image to the inner form of the word, to its logical and ontological dimensions. Last but not least, he was also receptive to the subjective-biographical aspects of the literary work of art, singling out the importance of the authorial voice ("Esteticheskie" 464-71).

Ultimately—and here lies the crucial difference between Shpet and the Formalists—literature for him was not a self-sufficient system to be explained away with reference to the specifically poetic function of language; literature for Shpet—even when all his semiotic inclinations are taken into account—is just one of the spheres of creativity whose outcomes are appropriated by what he calls "aesthetic consciousness." As a phenomenologist, Shpet's prime concern was to understand under what conditions an utterance becomes the object of aesthetic experience. This question is inextricably linked to the question of sense, so consistently ignored by the Formalists: "how should one express a given sense [*smysl*], so that its perception is an aesthetic one?" ("Esteticheskie" 448). Equally, it presupposes attention to form in its necessary relation to content, as both the *Aesthetic Fragments* and Shpet's article "Literatura" demonstrate. Hence Shpet's interest in both "poetic language" *and* "poetic thought" (Shpet, "Esteticheskie" 408). Small wonder, then, that the Formalists were hostile to Shpet's *Aesthetic Fragments* and the output of his younger followers in the MLC and at GAKhN. Eikhenbaum wrote on 30 June 1924 to Grigorii Vinokur—who was very sympathetic to Shpet's ideas, reviewed favorably his *Aesthetic Fragments*, openly acknowledged Shpet's influence on his own work (Vinokur 106), and even tried (unsuccessfully) to urge Jakobson and Eikhenbaum to shed their reservations towards the philosopher—that in the end he "doesn't believe" in Shpet, "it's all empty rhetoric" ("eto pustoe krasnorechie"; qtd. in Chudakova and Toddes 17). Shklovskii, too, preserved a highly sceptical and sarcastic attitude, as is clear from his reaction to Shpet's work as a translator of verse as late as 1934. (Shpet was also the target of irony in the joyous hymn of the younger generation of Formalists, the so called "mladoformalisty"; Kumpan and Konnechnyi 282-83).

The value of the *Aesthetic Fragments* is thus twofold. First, despite the fact that on several counts Shpet in fact presaged important developments in (post)structuralism and semiotics, his book presented the philosophically most sophisticated (and earliest) substantive, if at times oblique, polemic with Formalism, preceding both Engel'gardt's and Medvedev's later critiques. Second, and even more importantly, it offered a positive program for the study of the verbal work of art from the positions of phenomenological aesthetics (Shpet's occasional departures from Husserl notwithstanding), cross-bred with hermeneutics. Here the concept of inner form is of particular significance. Formulated as early as 1917 in his essay "Mudrost' ili razum?" ("Wisdom or Reason?"), Shpet's crucial concept of inner form harked back to Wilhelm von Humboldt's philosophy of language and culture. It was sharpened in Shpet's work on the history and the current state of hermeneutics (in "Hermeneutics and Its Problems," completed in 1918) and then occupied center stage in both the *Aesthetic Fragments* and the *Introduction to Ethnic Psychology*, not to mention Shpet's 1927 monograph specifically dedicated to the study of the inner form of the word. Inner form was also an important theoretical instrument in the research of Shpet's younger colleagues at GAKhN. In 1923, Shpet gave at GAKhN a paper on "The Concept of Inner Form in Wilhelm Humboldt," followed in 1924 by papers from Buslaev ("The Concept of Inner Form in Steinthal and Potebnia") and Kenigsberg ("The Concept of Inner Form in Anton Marty"). This direction was followed up in the collective GAKhN volume *Artistic Form* (*Khudozhestvennaia forma*) of 1927, where Shpet's disciples offered an exploration of form from the perspectives of aesthetics and semantics. Equidistant from both Marxism and Formalism, this volume was ultimate proof of this younger generation of scholars having little time or regard for either, a position that no doubt put them, their teacher, and their institution, the State Academy for Artistic Sciences, in a very difficult position.

Finally, we also need to consider Shpet's extensive notes on the novel (1924), a document of his theoretical preoccupations that brings into sharp relief the differences between his and Mikhail Bakhtin's approaches. The notes, which remained unpublished until 2007, were perhaps part of Shpet's larger (also unpublished) work titled "Literaturovedenie," announced in 1925 as one of GAKhN's projects (see Shchedrina's comments in Shpet, *Iskusstvo* 507).

Shpet relies very much on authors, notably Hegel, Erwin Rohde, and György (Georg) Lukács, who later also feature prominently (explicitly or implicitly) in Bakhtin's discussion of the novel. Shpet borrows from Hegel and Lukács, as does Bakhtin, the conceptual framework that juxtaposes epic and novel (Shpet, *Iskusstvo* 57-58). But while Bakhtin overturns Lukács's scheme and emancipates the novel, transforming it from an underdog of literary history into a celebrated *écriture* that transcends the restrictions of a mere genre, Shpet abides by the old opposition and validates the role of the novel as a "negative" genre. For Shpet, the novel is marked by a string of fatal absences. It lacks "composition," "plan," and, most importantly, "inner form" (*Iskusstvo* 57). For Shpet "inner form" is, let us recall, a crucial evidence for the potential of art to produce serious, nonarbitrary versions of reality. The lack of "inner form" stands, more widely, for the lack of necessity and compelling direction in the work of art. The novel is thus no more than a "degradation" of the epic (63): the epic offers access to an *idea* (in Plato's sense), whereas the novel furnishes only *doxa* (66). The novel, with its arbitrary inventions, is the result of the disintegration of myth (84). The novel therefore has no "plot in the strict sense of the word," only a "theme" that deals not with the "construction of an idea" (what plot should really do), but simply with the "empiric commonality of the motif" (79, "empiricheskaia obshchnost' motiva," "ona ne obshcha, a obshchna"). Lagging behind not just the epic but also the Greek tragedy, the novel knows no catastrophe, only irresolvable conflict, antinomy (67). In concord with his condescending evaluation of Russian philosophy, Shpet interprets the whole of Russian literature as a "novel," for there was, allegedly, no sense of epic reality in it (79); even *War and Peace* is called not an epic but an ironic, and therefore, "romantic" novel, romantic being the damning label attached to any narrative permeated by arbitrariness. We thus begin to understand why in the *Aesthetic Fragments*, as well as in his notes on the novel, Shpet gestures towards the novel as a mere "rhetorical" form: the epic is about an "organic embodiment of the idea," the novel is all about "an analysis of opportunities" (81), about the multitude of equally valid free wills and the choices the individual faces after leaving the epic cosmos. The novel is not about *incarnatio*, it is only about *inventio* and *elocutio* (81), the skills involved in unfolding and charting the ephemeral and accidental private world of opportunities without conclusion, of journeys without destiny.

It is against this background that Bakhtin's utter dissatisfaction with Shpet's denigration of the novel becomes clear. Bakhtin too, one would recall, began from the premise of negativity: the novel does not have a canon of its own; it is possessed of no constant features which generate the stability and cohesion marking most other genres. He reinterprets this negativity, however, into a forte: the novel knows no ossification, its energy of self-fashioning and re-invention is unlimited, its versatility accommodates and processes vast masses of previously submerged and neglected discourses. In brief, the novel is anything but a merely "rhetorical form" in the pejorative sense Shpet gives this term in the *Aesthetic Fragments*, in his notes on the novel, and in *The Inner Form of the Word* (Bakhtin 268). For Shpet, the novel signals impasse; it holds no prospect: "When a genuine flourishing of art occurs, the novel has no future" (*Iskusstvo* 84). The novel, unlike poetry, is a genre for the masses, it corresponds to their "average moral aspirations" (88). Bakhtin, by contrast, extolled the democratic charge of the novel and dreamt, as we know, of a literature colonized by the novelistic.

Shpet's literary theory thus emerges as a complex amalgam of innovation and regression. He foreshadowed important tenets of semiotics and structuralism while remaining critical of the Formalists; at the same time, however, his aesthetics and philosophy of art and his distinct distrust of historical poetics barred him from keeping pace with significant contemporary developments in genre theory. His interpretation of the novel alludes to his deeper roots in an artistic and philosophical tradition alien to the new departures in literature, art, and theory heralded and stimulated by the efforts of the avant-garde. This regressive entrenchment is even more salient in Shpet's theater theory (which I discuss in the final section of this article).

Shpet's Literary Translations

Shpet's contribution to Russian culture should be measured not just by the scope and the quality of his original work. He was an indefatigable promoter of Western philosophy; his translations span an impressive range of authors from Berkeley to Hegel and Rickert (Shpet's translation of Berkeley's *Three Dialogues between Hylas and Philonous* was published in 1937 without a mention of Shpet's name; see Serebrennikov 144). His single most important translation of a philosophical text, that of Hegel's *Phenomenology of Spirit*, is a major accomplishment and the result of selfless work and perseverance during the last two years of his life (the translation did not appear until 1959). Here, however, I focus on Shpet's contributions as translator of verse and prose, an aspect of his career that has so far failed to attract serious scholarly attention. The added value of such research is twofold: 1) it helps to reveal Shpet's extensive network of contacts with a number of both significant and lesser known twentieth-century Russian poets active as translators, as well as the part he played in a string of journals and almanacs in the 1920s and 2) even more importantly, Shpet's work as translator after his expulsion from GAKhN assists us in grasping the practice of literary translation as an instrument of ideological power and a site of competing political tenets in the 1930s.

Shpet's first known translations of verse are a distich by Plato and a fragment from Alcaeus (Levinton and Ustinov, "Ukazatel'" 194; the two texts are reproduced in L. Gornung, "Moi" 178-79), published in the third issue (September 1923) of the obscure typewritten literary journal *Hermes* (*Germes*). (These translations are absent from the bibliography of Shpet's translations compiled by Mitiushin, "Bibliografiia" 91-2; Shpet's translation of Berkeley's *Three Dialogues* is also omitted there.) The journal was launched in the summer of 1922 by a group of aspiring poets and philologists. The person behind the first two issues was Boris Gornung (1899-1976), a member—as we have seen—of the Moscow Linguistic Circle in its later years. He formed an editorial board that included, among others, his brother Lev Gornung (1902-1993), the philologist Maksim Kenigsberg (1900-1924)—to whose memory Shpet's *Vnutrenniaia forma slova* is dedicated—and Kenigsberg's friend (later his wife) Nina Vol'kenau. The last two issues (out of four) saw a change in the editorial board, which was now chaired by Kenigsberg and was joined by Buslaev (chairman of the MLC at the time the first issue of *Hermes* was published) and Viktor Mozalevskii. Kenigsberg's untimely death in 1924 meant that only the first part of the fourth issue was prepared, already without Boris Gornung's participation as a member of the editorial board (B. Gornung, "O zhurnale" 188). More importantly, at the beginning of 1924 a "scholarly-artistic" (*nauchno-khudozhestvennyi*) advisory board was formed, chaired by Shpet and including some of his GAKhN colleagues, notably Aleksandr Gabrichesvkii, Mikhail Petrovskii, and the classicist Aleksandr Chelpanov (the eminent psychologist's son). Shpet and his colleagues had great plans for the second part of the fourth issue, which was supposed to carry a number of scholarly articles; instead, these were all published some three years later, long after the journal had ceased to exist: Shpet's article on Humboldt evolved into a book (*Vnutrenniaia forma slova*, 1927), whereas the articles to be written by Petrovskii, Zhinkin, Guber, and Volkov appeared in 1927 in GAKhN's aforementioned collective volume *Khudozhestvennaia forma* (B. Gornung, "O zhurnale" 188).

Shpet's close involvement with these young literati continued over the next few years, until around 1926-27 (B. Gornung, *Pokhod* 331). Joined by Nikolai Berner and Aleksandr Romm (on Berner, see Ustinov 5-64), Boris Gornung conceived the typewritten literary almanac *Mnemosyne* (*Mnemozina*); he confirmed in a letter to Mikhail Kuzmin of September 1924 that Shpet had been the driving force behind the formation of the new group that launched *Mnemosyne* (Levinton and Ustinov, "K istorii" 209). Another almanac, *Hyperborean* (*Giperborei*), which saw the light of day in Moscow toward the end of 1926 (Vorob'eva 177), was the result of collaboration, under Shpet's guidance, between the Gornung brothers and several GAKhN scholars, including Nikolai Volkov and Boris Griftsov. A second issue of *Hyperborean* was in preparation in 1927 but was banned by the GPU (Vorob'eva 178). Shpet's translation of Plato's distich was republished in *Mnemosyne*, while *Hyperborean* brought out his article "Literatura" (K. Polivanov, "Mashinopisnye" 46), the 1929 manuscript version of which was eventually published in Tartu in 1982. Since *Hermes* and *Hyperborean* were produced in just 12 copies each (B. Gornung, "O zhurnale" 186; Vorob'eva 179—unlike his brother, Lev Gornung asserts that *Hermes* was produced in three copies only; see L. Gornung, "Moi" 175), the likely impact of Shpet's contributions there was probably rather limited (although Boris Gornung did insist that these periodicals were read by hundreds of people in Moscow, Petersburg, Kiev, Kazan, and Nizhnii Novgorod; see *Pokhod* 349). Among the better-known poets, only Kuzmin and Sofiia Parnok published in *Mnemosyne*.

In the 1920s Shpet was still translating sporadically, and mostly for pleasure; not so in the 1930s when, after his removal from GAKhN, translation became his principal way of earning a living. The remaining years of Shpet's life (1930-37) were spent translating into Russian a vast amount of literature, mainly from the nineteenth-century English canon. No doubt Shpet was handsomely equipped for a career as professional translator. He stated in a declaration to the Prosecution, written in 1937, that he had, in addition to Russian, command of thirteen foreign languages: English, German, French, Italian, Spanish, Polish, Swedish, Norwegian, Danish, Ukrainian, Bulgarian, Latin, and Greek (Serebrennikov 190); the number of languages he could translate from was even larger, seventeen (Shpet, "Pis'mo" 587)—and was magnified to nineteen in petitions to Stalin written on different occasions by Shpet's wife and the actor Vasilii Kachalov (Serebrennikov 284, 287). Shpet himself indicated that he undertook editorial work on translations from the canon of the English, Polish, German, and the Scandinavian literatures (Shpet, "Pis'mo" 589). He also acted as evaluator of translations for various publishers, most frequently for Academia.

In Shpet's translation of prose after 1930, Dickens figured prominently. Both *Hard Times* and *Bleak House* (the latter abridged for children and adolescents) appeared in 1933 in Shpet's translation. His translation of Dickens's *Pickwick Papers* was, however, rejected (M. Polivanov, "Ocherk" 30) and Shpet had to resign himself to being allowed to compile a volume of commentaries published in 1934. Vladimir Milashevskii, the artist who illustrated the *Pickwick Papers*, noted in one version of his memoirs that both Shpet and Evgenii Lann (who translated the book together with A.V. Krivtsova) were hostile towards his illustrations, insisting instead that the edition carry the original illustrations by Robert Seymour, Robert Buss, and Hablot Browne. In the end, Kornei Chukovskii succeeded in breaking Shpet's vociferous opposition, and a compromise was reached: Dickens's text was illustrated by Milashevskii, while the original drawings were reproduced in Shpet's volume of commentaries (Iuniverg 51-53). Shpet was also considering a multivolume edition of Dickens and even a Dickens Encyclopaedia (see his respective book proposals, both written in 1933, at RGB, f. 718, k. 17, ed. khr. 4). While in exile, he tried unsuccessfully to get Academia to commission him the translation of *David Copperfield* and the editorship of what was meant to be the first complete Russian translation of Harriet Beecher Stowe's *Uncle Tom's Cabin*; he also translated Oliver Goldsmith's play *She Stoops to Conquer or the Mistakes of a Night* (the translation, apparently unpublished at the time, is preserved in RGB, f. 718, k. 11, ed. khr. 10 and 11). Earlier on he had served as the editor of the two-volume translation of Thackeray's writings, for which he wrote the notes to *Vanity Fair* (1933-34) and had prepared a partial translation of Sterne's *Tristram Shandy* (preserved in RGB, f. 718, k. 12, ed. khr. 5). He also edited Constance Garnett's English translation of *Anna Karenina* (1933).

Shpet's only known translation of German prose are Schiller's letters to Goethe, on which he worked in 1935-37 (the translation is preserved in RGB, f. 718, k. 13, ed. khr. 6); Goethe's letters to Schiller were entrusted to Mikhail Petrovskii (1887-1937), a literary scholar and Shpet's former colleague at GAKhN, later an exile in Tomsk where he worked as a scholar-bibliographer at the university library before being rearrested and shot (Serebrennikov 115, 263). Despite Shpet's reluctance to communicate with someone he believed had betrayed him during the inquest, meeting Petrovskii in Tomsk proved eventually impossible to avoid (Serebrennikov 215, 226, 235). A translation published in 1937 (with an introduction by Lukács) did not carry the name of either Shpet or Petrovskii.

It is, however, Shpet's work as translator of verse in the 1930s that gives us access to the intricate politics of translation under Stalinism. The 1930s saw the most sustained and energetic campaign to bring to the Soviet reader the works of the eighteenth- and nineteenth-century European canon. The idea was initially Gorkii's, but his pet project (for which the publishing house Vsemirnaia Literatura [1918-1924] had been founded) lost momentum after he left the country in the autumn of 1921. It is not by accident that the idea came back precisely in the 1930s. Establishing a new canon of widely read classic works was part of Stalin's cultural politics designed to produce a sentiment of unity and a picture of public consensus built around the supposedly shared aesthetic (read: ideological) values embodied in the Russian and Western literary tradition of the past two centuries. This new canon was more inclusive of works previously stigmatized as representative of the abstract bourgeois humanism that the party-minded art had been encouraged to fight and leave behind. In particular, from the mid-1930s onwards, bourgeois realism was in fashion once again, protected by attempts to reach consolidation around a shared antifascist ideological platform. The new line did soften for a moment the perception of rigidity that Stalin's cultural policies produced abroad. In 1935, Erenburg, Babel', and Pasternak were able to join the Paris Congress for the defense of culture on an equal footing with their Western colleagues. Pasternak's reluctance there to assign art clearly defined political tasks was indicative of this freshly licensed humanistic outlook.

At home, the subscription to the new canon was meant to conceal the deep rifts and the contest between the irreconcilable national perspectives and the often incommensurable cultural orientations of the different social strata within the multinational state. To attain this goal, translation had to be a closely monitored activity (control was made easier by setting up a translation sector within the Writers' Union; the sector met for its first conference in January 1935), and it also had to be proactive and "practice-orientated," that is, delivering not just samples of great literary style and craftsmanship but above all versions of the classics that would have a purchase on the everyday lives of their Soviet readers. Thus it comes as no surprise that the practice of literary translation in the 1930s was marked by a serious discord between the principles of faithfulness (to the original) and usefulness (to the target audience). The former principle was branded as "literalism" and had to give way to a culture of translation based on lower artistic expectations and higher political returns. The political war over the principles of translation was plain to see in the polemics surrounding two of the most ambitious projects of the 1930s: the multivolume editions of Goethe's and of Shakespeare's works. The first two volumes of the Goethe edition, in the organization of which Shpet's pupil and friend Aleksandr Gabrichevskii was closely involved, were met with protests at the allegedly low use-value of the translations, which, it was suggested, had failed to provide the Soviet readership with those much needed "current phrases" (*khodiachimi vyrazheniiami*) that could be of help to propagandists, philosophers and scholars (see, e.g., Shaginian, "Lirika"). Similarly, the Academia edition of Shakespeare's works was attacked (notably by Chukovskii and Mirskii) for the misleading "precision" of some of the translations, which allegedly made the access of the Soviet reader to Shakespeare more difficult by obscuring rather than revealing his genius (for more on the political stakes in the contemporary wars in translation theory, see Tihanov, "Multifariousness").

Shpet brought to his work as translator of verse his unconditional professionalism, sober-mindedness, and rigor that also marked his style of philosophizing. Small wonder, then, that he would often be reproached for siding with the "literalists." Sometimes this was justified by his occasionally excessive faithfulness to the original; at others, he was simply the victim of an overarching ideological imperative—the "democratisation" of the classics—that he felt unable to follow. Shpet's translations of verse in the 1930s included Byron's dramatic poems "Manfred," "Cain," and "Heaven and Earth," as well as "Age of Bronze," and Tennyson's "Enoch Arden," the latter translated in September-October 1935 and first published sixty years later (Serebrennikov 17-38, 321). Not surprisingly, given the polemics on the philosophy of translation, his translations of Byron's poems were met with some hostility. Anna Radlova, the wife of stage director Sergei Radlov and a poet in her own right, wrote to Lev Kamenev (in response to Shpet's critical remarks on her translations of *Othello* and *Macbeth*) that she was not prepared to accept Shpet's taste and translation techniques demonstrated in his own rendition of Byron (Kuzmin 228-29). Radlova meant by this Shpet's unbending insistence on precision that on occasion favored the literal over the creative. Shpet defended himself by responding to Kamenev that eminent poets such as Kuzmin and Pasternak had praised his translation (Kuzmin 229). Accusations of literalism were also levelled by Chukovskii and Shklovskii. In February 1934, the latter ridiculed in a letter to Tynianov Shpet's explanatory notes: "it seems that Shpet glossed the word 'crocodile' in Byron by adding a note giving the Latin for it" ("Shpet, kazhetsia, k Baironu na slovo krokodil dal primechanie, nazvavshi etogo krokodila po-latyni" [qtd. in Panchenko 204]). Clearly, Shklovskii had an axe to grind (because of Shpet's pronounced anti-Formalist orientation), but for once he was not exaggerating, nor was he making things up (see Shpet's gloss in Bairon 406).

When considering Shpet's career as translator of verse, one has to give prominence to his work on the prestigious eight-volume Shakespeare edition published by Academia in 1936-1949, under the general editorship of Sergei Dinamov (himself a victim of Stalin's purges, shot in April 1939) and Aleksandr Smirnov (a high-flying literary scholar, the author of *Tvorchestvo Shekspira* [1934] and in 1946 one of the three official evaluators of Mikhail Bakhtin's doctoral dissertation *Rabelais in the History of Realism*). In a letter to Stalin written in November 1935 in Eniseisk (probably never sent), Shpet took pride in his role as a member of the working group preparing the edition and pleaded that he be allowed to resume his editorial duties. Before his arrest he had read a number of draft translations by "experienced translators such as Mikhail Kuzmin and Osip Rumer" and had "subjected these to brutal correction" (*zhestokoi pravke*), although he knew that not everybody would agree with his demand for "super-philological exactitude" (*sverkhfilologicheskoi tochnost'iu*; see Shpet, "Pis'mo" 592). Shpet referred to Smirnov and the poets Kuzmin, Pasternak, and Antokol'skii as potential guarantors for the quality of his work ("Pis'mo" 592). Shpet's defensive mention of "super-philological exactitude" in this letter is an unmistakeable response to those of his critics who favored the utilitarian principles of translation over precision and philological soundness. The tension between these two attitudes came to be felt acutely as work on the Shakespeare edition progressed. Over time, Smirnov and Shpet had established a smooth and efficient cooperation, with Shpet editing meticulously the translations of several key plays, including *Macbeth* (in this case his contribution amounted in effect to co-translating the play) and *King Lear*. The balance was disturbed when Mirskii was appointed a consultant to the edition, thus strengthening the positions of the utilitarian wing around Chukovskii. In his letters to Shpet, Smirnov objected to this appointment and to Mirskii's written evaluation of the work that had been done so far. He even contemplated leaving his editorial duties but was dissuaded by Kamenev (the relevant letters by Smirnov, of 9 June and 1 November 1934, are in Shpet's estate in RGB, f. 718, k. 25, ed. khr. 25). The situation turned truly unpleasant when Smirnov revealed to Shpet that Chukovskii was plotting to oust the philosopher from the edition (Smirnov to Shpet, letter of 31 January 1935; RGB, f. 718, k. 25, ed. khr. 38, l. 9). Dethroned and fallen from grace after the purges at GAKhN, Shpet was no longer able to defend himself. An article responding to Mirskii's criticisms of S.M. Solov'ev and Shpet's translation of *Macbeth* seems to have remained unpublished; Shpet had to contend himself with a letter seeking Kamenev's support (the typescript of the article and the letter are both at RGB, f. 718, k. 20, ed. khr. 3). The depressing irony in this otherwise banal story of ideological and personal rivalry is that Mirskii himself was soon to become an outcast; he perished two years after Shpet, another victim of Stalinism.

Shpet's Theater Affiliations

Shpet must have been moving in theater circles as early as 1905, while still in Kiev, for Aleksandr Tairov, the founder of the famous Chamber Theater (*Kamernyi teatr*), acknowledged in his *Zapiski rezhissera* (1921) Shpet's beneficial influence on his formative time there (Tairov 68). Shpet, Tairov and his spouse, the actress Alisa Koonen, preserved their friendship in later years; in the journal of the Chamber Theater, *The Craft of Theater* (*Masterstvo teatra*), Shpet published his main article on theater, "Theater as Art" ("Teatr kak iskusstvo").

After the October Revolution, a Theater Department (*TEO*, "*Teatral'nyi otdel*") was established within the People's Commissariat of Enlightenment (*Narkompros*) to regulate the work of theaters throughout the country. At its foundation in 1918, TEO consisted of four sections administering, supervising, and studying 1) theater history; 2) the organization and management of the existing theaters and circuses; 3) the repertoire; and 4) theater pedagogy. A section dealing predominantly with questions of theory was later added but then dissolved before being re-established early in 1921, when the writer and critic Andrei Belyi, the philosopher Fedor Stepun, and Shpet himself were appointed as its only members (Iufit 72). In discharging his duty of promoting the study of theater theory and disseminating the results of such studies, Shpet published in 1921 a highly interesting and controversial short piece on the process of the differentiation of labor in the modern theater (see Shpet, "Differ-entsiatsiia"). Historically, Shpet argued, the playwright and the actor were identical; the first step in the process of differentiation was the separation of the actor from the author. The next step meant that the author also lost the actual function of staging the play: the stage director and the set designer were born. Finally, Shpet claims, the time has arrived for the role of interpreting the meaning of the play to be entrusted to an independent agent—neither the author, nor the stage director, nor the actor should be entitled to impose their interpretations which are anyway often, quite naturally, in conflict with one another. The hermeneutic function, Shpet insists, is a difficult one; it requires a degree of specialization, education, and skill that neither the actor nor the stage director necessarily possess. Without a professional interpreter, the "intel-lectual sense of the play" (*razumnyi smysl p'esy*) will be lost, and the actors will try to compensate for it by emphasizing instead the bodily techniques of the spectacle ("Differentsiatsiia" 204).

Shpet's attention to the process of differentiation within the stage performance has been compared in the past to Tynianov's pronouncement in his article "Illustra-tions": "We live in the age of differentiation of activities" (318; for an interpreta-tion aligning Shpet with Tynianov, see S.V. Stakhorskii's commentaries in Shpet, "Differentsiatsiia"). This is rather surprising, given the fact that, unlike Tynianov, Shpet posited the process of differentiation as an instrument of revealing, to recall his expression, the "intellectual sense of the play." In addition to the controversial ideological implications of this insistence on a single interpreter and, by extension, a single correct interpretation, there is here also a hint of skepticism towards avant-garde theater (cf. the protest against emphasizing the bodily techniques of the spec-tacle), not inconsistent with Shpet's only slightly later attack on Futurism and the avant-garde in his *Aesthetic Fragments*.

Shpet's reservations towards the theater of the avant-garde became much more prominent in his main contribution to theater theory, the article "Theater as Art" (completed in September 1922 and published in December of the same year). Pub-lished in an issue dedicated to the eighth anniversary of the Chamber Theater and preceded there by an article by Tairov, Shpet's piece was an uneasy attempt at a compromise between, but also a critique of, the two wings of avant-garde theater theory. He distanced himself from Tairov's radical insistence that theater be regarded as completely detached from the task of dialectically comprehending the world that exists outside art (Schmid 112); at the same time, Shpet also sought to resist the demand that theater and life be completely fused. The very title of Shpet's article, "Theater as Art," signalled his insistence on theater being and remaining art, *pace* all activist aspirations (regardless of their political provenance) that sought to blend life and art (Evreinov; Vsevolodskii-Gerngross). In the same article, Shpet criticizes Wagner's thesis of the synthetic nature of theater (Shpet, "Teatr" 112), which later theorists had taken up and solidified into one of the cornerstones of avant-garde performance practice. (Tairov, as is well known, wanted to rename his Chamber Theater "Sinteticheskii teatr," an idea flying in the face of Shpet's theoretical platform.) Liubov' Gurevich, one of Shpet's contemporaries, noted that in his theater theory Shpet, rather than following Wagner and the avant-garde, was still the captive of Diderot's "paradoxe sur le comédien" (Gurevich 14; more on this see in Tihanov, "Gustave Chpet").

Shpet's position against the synthesis of the different arts, which also rever-berates strongly in his *Aesthetic Fragments*, was waging wars on more than one front. It was attacking not only the avant-garde, but also, obliquely, the religious notion of theater as an extension and modification of the church ritual, an approach made available, before Shpet entered the scene of theater theory, by Pavel Floren-skii ("Khramovoe deistvo kak sintez iskusstv," 1918). In the end, when it comes to theater theory, Shpet's career was marked by a tormenting discrepancy: when he wrote on theater (the very early 1920s), he did not do any work for the theater; when, in the 1930s, he began working for the stage (both as translator and as adviser), he had stopped writing on theater. Thus the two streams—writing on theater and work-ing for the theater—were never brought together in his career. A salient paradox of Shpet's theater affiliations was also the fact that while he maintained close contacts with two of the greatest experimenters in the history of Russian theater, Tairov and Meyerhold, he never got involved in an avant-garde theater production. On the con-trary, when Meyerhold decided to stage Alexandre Dumas's *La Dame aux camé-lias* (premiered on 19 March 1934), Shpet not only took on the translation (Zinaida Raikh—Meyerhold's spouse—and Mikhail Tsarev were listed in the program notes as Shpet's cotranslators; see Sitkovetskaia 55), but he steered the rehearsals as well, achieving, according to one of the actors, a "miracle": Meyerhold, the inveterate theater experimenter, staged the play in a realistic spirit (Mitiushin, "Commentary" 89). Meyerhold did insert a few short texts that were not part of the original, and he also reshaped some others to give them a modern feel (Sitkovetskaia 55), but on the whole the play was done in a way that put historical verisimilitude first.

Shpet's preference for realism as an aesthetic foundation of the modern theater led him to a close association with Stanislavskii's Moscow Art Theater, at a time when its innovative force had admittedly been on the wane for a number of years. On 24 January 1928, the People's Commissariat of Enlightenment approved the artistic council (*Khudozhestvennyi sovet*) of Stanislavskii's theater; being at the time (still) the holder of a high office at GAKhN, Shpet became a member of the council from the quota of the "public organizations" (*ot obshchestvennykh organizatsii*). From the same quota the renowned expert on Marx and Marxism David Riazanov and the prominent literary critics Viacheslav Polonskii and Aleksandr Voronskii were elected (Trabskii 186). Preserved are Shpet's comments as part of the council's discussions in 1928 on Leonid Leonov's play *Untilovsk* and Valentin Kataev's *The Embezzlers* (*Rastratchiki*), a stage adaptation of his better known novel by the same title (see the minutes reproduced in Markov 562-63; 566-67). At Stanislavskii's invitation, in 1932-34 Shpet led the organization of a new Actors' Academy (*Akademiia vysshego akterskogo masterstva*), a project which did not materialize (cf. Aristov 108-15). At the same time he was also involved in the failed initiative of establishing an Academy of Operatic Art (*Akademiia opernogo iskusstva*) at the Bolshoi Theatre (Aristov 114). In 1933, Shpet was one of the initiators of a small working group, whose task was to read and comment on Stanislavskii's book manuscript which was to be completed in 1935 and published the following year in English translation in the US as *An Actor Prepares* (Stanislavskii, *Sobranie sochinenii v vos'mi tomakh* 8: 345, 366; the notes to Stanislavskii's letters in the eight-volume edition of his works wrongly assume that the manuscript was that of the first part of *Rabota aktera nad soboi* published in Russian in 1938, shortly after Stanislavskii's death. The Russian version had been revised by Stanislavskii and differed from the American one; Shpet played no part in these revisions, since they took place while he was already in exile.) Shpet was also one of the organizers of the nation-wide discussion of Stanislavskii's memoirs *Moia zhizn' v iskusstve* (cf. Maksimova 163; Shchedrina, *"Ia pishu . . ."* 258). In the same year, 1933, Shpet was asked to translate the libretto of *Rigoletto*, but then Stanislavskii's deputy artistic director, Bogdanovich, rejected the translation and recommissioned it, which resulted in Stanislavskii having to write an apologetic letter to an offended Shpet (cf. Stanislavskii, *Sobranie sochinenii v deviati tomakh* 9: 535; 768). Still, in a letter of October 1934 to his wife, the actress Maria Lilina, Stanislavskii hoped that Shpet might assume responsibility for the literary aspects of the work of the Moscow Art Theatre (but feared intrigues from Nemirovich-Danchenko; cf. Stanislavskii, *Sobranie sochinenii v deviati tomakh* 9: 611). As late as 1938, Shpet's spouse, not aware of his death, wrote to Stalin to ask for a favorable intervention, referring, among other plans, to her husband's project of a nine-volume history of the Moscow Art Theater (Serebrennikov 287-88).

Shpet's immediate knowledge of the Russian theater scene included (as suggested also in Stanislavskii's letter cited above) an acquaintance with Nemirovich-Danchenko, whose memoirs Shpet was to read while already in exile (Serebrennikov 202). These high-profile contacts at the Moscow Art Theater, but above all his friendship with Vasilii Kachalov and Ol'ga Knipper-Chekhova, two of its most famous actors, meant that Shpet was able to rely on the theater profession to raise a voluble concern when he was arrested in 1935. Kachalov and Knipper-Chekhova were among the signatories to petitions asking for Shpet's relocation from Eniseisk to Tomsk, a university town with a library and better conditions for scholarly and literary work, and for permissions enabling his family to continue to reside in Moscow after he had been exiled (Serebrennikov 256-57). Finally, Kachalov alone wrote a letter to Stalin asking for Shpet's full rehabilitation, not knowing that he had already been shot (Serebrennikov 283-84).

In 1936, already an exile in Tomsk, Shpet renewed his acquaintance, dating back to the GAKhN years, with the playwright Nikolai Erdman (1902-1970) who had been involved at the early stages of his career with the Imagists. Erdman, too, was exiled and lived at the time in Tomsk, working as the dramatist of the local theater from September 1935 to the end of October 1936 (Serebrennikov 242). Shpet afforded himself some familiarity in addressing Erdman as "Mandat" (Serebrennikov 237), the Russian title of Erdman's most successful comedy staged by Meyerhold in 1925. Erdman acquainted Shpet with a younger stage director who wanted to do *Othello* for the Tomsk theater and who sought Shpet's advice on the interpretation of the play. Having written copious commentaries on ten of Shakespeare's plays for the Academia edition ("Pis'mo" 589), Shpet was undoubtedly well prepared to help. The production, however, did not materialize, nor did the plan to secure for Shpet Erdman's post in the theater on the latter's departure (Serebrennikov 242).

Conclusion

Our knowledge of Shpet's significant contribution to literary and theater theory—where in the 1920s he was poised between innovation (anticipating some of the tenets of [post]structuralism) and regression (reverting, away from the radicalism of the Formalists, back to more traditional aesthetics and philosophy of art); of his extensive contacts with writers, playwrights and other literati; of his work for the theater and as translator, enables us to appreciate the multifarious texture of his intellectual life, particularly in the late 1920s and the 1930s, a stage in his career marked by diversity under duress. During that time Shpet was forced to apply his energy to a growing number of pursuits, none of which could give him the opportunity to advance his own agenda as a thinker and scholar. The propitious volatility of the first post-revolutionary decade, still tolerant and conducive to creativity, had gradually been supplanted by a climate of ideological control and suppression, the brutality of which left its stamp on Shpet's declining fortunes and his eventual catastrophe. The last—and at the same time most pronounced and most persistent—Westernizer in the history of twentieth-century Russian thought was relegated after 1927 to an increasingly marginal and unfulfilling existence. Rejecting the props of both Marxism and Russian religious philosophy, Shpet was left weathering the storms of history alone, facing his impending end with consummate dignity.

Works Cited

Aristov, Vladimir. "G.G. Shpet i proekt sozdaniia im Akademii Moskovskogo khu-dozhestvennogo teatra." *Voprosy psikhologii* 3 (2009): 108-15.

Bairon, Dzh. G. [George Gordon Byron]. *Misterii*. Trans. G.G. Shpet. Moscow: Academia, 1933.

Bakhtin, Mikhail. "Discourse in the Novel." *The Dialogic Imagination: Four Essays*. By Mikhail Bakhtin. Ed. Michael Holquist. Trans. Michael Holquist and Caryl Emerson. Austin: U of Texas P, 1981. 259-422.

Belyi, Andrei. *Nachalo veka*. Moscow: Gosudarstvennoe izdatel'stvo khudozhest-vennoi literatury, 1933.

Belyi, Andrei. *Mezhdu dvukh revoliutsii*. Leningrad: Izdatel'stvo pisatelei v Leningrade, 1934.

Belyi, Andrei. *Vospominaniia o A.A. Bloke*. Munich: Wilhelm Fink, 1969.

Belyi, Andrei. "Iz vospominanii o russkikh filosofakh." Ed. J. Malmstad. *Minuvshee: Istoricheskii al'manakh* 9 (1992): 326-51.

Bird, Robert. "Viacheslav Ivanov i sovetskaia vlast' (1919-1929)." *Novoe literaturnoe obozrenie* 40 (1999): 305-31.

Chudakova, M., and E. Toddes. "Nasledie i put' B. Eikhenbauma." *O literature. Raboty raznykh let*. By Boris Eikhenbaum. Ed. O.B. Eikhenbaum and E. Toddes. Moscow: Sovetskii pisatel', 1987. 3-32.

Depretto, Catherine. "Alexandre Romm (1898-1943), lecteur du *Marxisme et la philosophie du langage* (1929)." *Slavica Occitania* 25 (2007): 399-416.

Drozdkov, V.A. "Shershenevich i Esenin: biograficheskie i tvorcheskie paralleli v kontekste sporov o soderzhanii imazhinistskoi poezii." *Russkii imazhinizm. Istoriia. Teoriia. Praktika*. Ed. V.A. Drozdkov et al. Moscow: Linor, 2003. 139-68.

Esenin, Sergei, Mariengof, Anatolii, Shershenevich, Vadim. "Pis'mo v redaktsiiu zhurnala 'Pechat' i revoliutsiia.'" *Pechat' i revoliutsiia* 2 (1921): 248-49.

Esenin, Sergei. *Polnoe sobranie sochinenii*. Ed. Iu.L. Prokushev. 7 vols. Moscow: Nauka-Golos, 2000.

Gornung, B.V. "O zhurnale 'Germes.'" *Piatye Tynianovskie chteniia: Tezisy dokladov i materialy dlia obsuzhdeniia*. Riga: Zinatne, 1990. 186-89.

Gornung, B.V. *Pokhod vremeni. T. 2: Stat'i i esse*. Moscow: RGGU, 2001.

Gornung, L.V. "Moi vospominaniia o professore Gustave Gustavoviche Shpete (Kommentarii K.M. Polivanova)." *Shestye Tynianovskie chteniia. Tezisy dokladov i materialy dlia obsuzhdeniia*. Riga: n.p., 1992. 172-85.

Granin, D. *Zubr*. Moscow: Profizdat, 1989.

Gurevich, L. *Tvorchestvo aktera. O prirode khudozhestvennykh perezhivanii aktera na stsene*. [1926.] Moscow: GITIS, 2002.

Gut, Taja, ed. *Andrej Belyj. Symbolismus, Anthroposophie. Ein Weg*. Dornach: Rudolf Steiner, 1997.

Iufit, A.Z., ed. *Sovetskii teatr. Dokumenty i materialy, 1917-1967. Russkii sovetskii teatr, 1917-1921*. Leningrad: Iskusstvo, 1968.

Iuniverg, L., ed. "Iz literaturnogo naslediia V. Milashevskogo." *Russian Philology and History. In Honour of Professor Victor Levin*. Jerusalem: The Hebrew University of Jerusalem, 1992. 39-58.

Iur'ev, K.S., and S.V. Shumikhin. *Moi vek, moi druz'ia i podrugi. Vospominaniia Mariengofa, Shershenevicha, Gruzinova*. Moscow: Moskovskii rabochii, 1990.

Jakobson, Roman. "An Example of Migratory Terms and Institutional Models (On the Fiftieth Anniversary of the Moscow Linguistic Circle)." *Selected Writings*. By Roman Jakobson. Vol. 2. The Hague: Mouton, 1971. 527-38.

Jakobson, Roman. "Retrospect." *Selected Writings*. Vol. 2. The Hague: Mouton, 1971. 711-22.

Jakobson, Roman. "Moskovskii lingvisticheskii kruzhok." Ed. M.I. Shapir. *Philologica* 3.5-7 (1996): 361-80.

Kondiurina, A.A. et al., eds. "Perepiska V.I. Ivanova i O.A. Shor." *Archivio Italo-Russo* 3 (2001): 151-455.

Krusanov, A.V. *Russkii avangard, 1907-1932. Istoricheskii obzor.* Vol. 2.1: *Futuristicheskaia revoliutsiia, 1917-1921.* Moscow: Novoe literaturnoe obozrenie, 2003.

Kumpan, K., and A. Konechnyi, eds. "Gimn Formalistov. Publikatsiia, soprovoditel'nyi tekst i kommentarii." *Natales grate numeras? Sbornik statei k 60-letiiu Georgiia Akhillovicha Levintona.* Ed. A.K. Baiburin and A.L. Ospovat. St. Petersburg: Izdatel'stvo Evropeiskogo universiteta v Sankt-Peterburge, 2008. 266-94.

Kuniaevy, S. and S. Kuniaevy. *Zhizn' Esenina.* Moscow: Tsentrpoligraf, 2002.

Kuzmin, Mikhail. *Dnevnik 1934 goda.* Ed. G. Morev. St. Petersburg: Ivan Limbakh, 1998.

Lavrov, A.V., and John Malmstad, eds. *Andrei Belyi i Ivanov-Razumnik. Perepiska.* St. Petersburg: Atheneum and Feniks, 1998.

Levinton, G.A., and A.B. Ustinov. "Ukazatel' soderzhaniia zhurnala 'Germes.'" *Piatye Tynianovskie chteniia: Tezisy dokladov i materialy dlia obsuzhdeniia.* Riga: Zinatne, 1990. 189-97.

Levinton, G.A., and A.B. Ustinov. "K istorii mashinopisnykh izdanii 1920-kh godov." *Piatye Tynianovskie chteniia: Tezisy dokladov i materialy dlia obsuzhdeniia.* Riga: Zinatne, 1990. 197-210.

Lunacharskii, A.V. "Svoboda knigi i revoliutsiia." *Pechat' i revoliutsiia* 1 (1921): 3-9.

Lunacharskii, A.V. "Nashi zadachi v oblasti khudozhestvennoi literatury. Stenogramma doklada na izdatel'skom aktive ZIFa." *Sobranie sochinenii v vos'mi tomakh.* By A.V. Lunacharskii. Vol. 2. Moscow: Khudozhestvennaia literatura, 1964. 426-39.

Maksimova, T.G. "Iz vospominanii." *Gustav Gustavovich Shpet. Arkhivnye Materialy. Vospominaniia. Stat'i.* Ed. T.D. Martsinkovskaia. Moscow: Smysl, 2000. 157-69.

Mariengof, A. *A Novel without Lies.* Trans. J. Alaniz. Birmingham: Glas, 2000.

Markov, P.A. *V Khudozhestvennom Teatre. Kniga zavlita.* Moscow: Vserossiiskoe teatral'noe obshchestvo, 1976.

Mitiushin, A.A. "Commentary." *Soviet Studies in Philosophy* 28.3 (1989-90): 89-91.

Mitiushin, A.A. "Bibliografiia pechatnykh trudov G.G. Shpeta." *Nachala* 1 (1992): 89-92.

Nikolaev, N.I. "M.M. Bakhtin, Nevel'skaia shkola filosofii i kul'turnaia istoriia 1920-kh godov." *Bakhtinskii sbornik* 5 (2004): 210-80.

Obatnin, G.V. "Materialy k opisaniiu biblioteki Viacheslava Ivanova." *Europa Orientalis* 21.2 (2002): 261-343.

Panchenko, Ol'ga, ed. "Iz perepiski Iu. Tynianova i B. Eikhenbauma s V. Shklovskim." *Voprosy literatury* 12 (1984): 185-218.

Polivanov, K.M. "Mashinopisnye al'manakhi 'Giperborei' i 'Mnemozina.' Ukazatel' soderzhaniia." *De Visu* 6 (1993): 46-49.

Polivanov, M.K. "Ocherk biografii G.G. Shpeta." *Litsa. Biograficheskii al'manakh* 1 (1992): 7-43.

Remizov, A. *Vzvikhrennaia Rus'.* Paris: Tair, 1927.

Reznik, Vladislava. "A Long Rendezvous: Aleksandr Romm's Unpublished Works on Ferdinand de Saussure." *The Slavonic and East European Review* 86.1 (2008): 1-25.

Roizman, M.D. *Vse, chto pomniu o Esenine.* Moscow: Sovetskaia Rossiia, 1973.

Savchenko, T.K. "Sergei Esenin i Aleksandr Kusikov." *Russkii imazhinizm. Istoriia. Teoriia. Praktika.* Ed. V.A. Drozdkov et al. Moscow: Linor, 2003. 202-13.

Serebrennikov, N.V., ed. *Shpet v Sibiri: Ssylka i gibel'.* Tomsk: Vodolei, 1995.

Schmid, Herta. "Gustav Špets Theatertheorie im Kontext der historischen Avantgarde der Künste." *Balagan* 2.1 (1996): 88-116.

Shaginian, Marietta. "Lirika Gete v iubileinom izdanii." *Literaturnaia gazeta* 49 (23 October 1933): 1.

Shapir, M.I. "Kommentarii." *Filologicheskie issledovaniia: Lingvistika i poetika.* By G.O. Vinokur. Ed. T.G. Vinokur and M.I. Shapir. Moscow: Nauka, 1990. 256-365.

Shchedrina, T.G. *"Ia pishu kak ekho drugogo . . ." Ocherki intellektual'noi biografii Gustava Shpeta.* Moscow: Progress-Traditsiia, 2004.

Shchedrina, T.G., ed. *Gustav Shpet: zhizn' v pis'makh. Epistoliarnoe nasledie.* Moscow: ROSSPEN, 2005.

Shershenevich, V.G. *Listy imazhinista.* Iaroslavl': Verkhne-Volzhskoe knizhnoe izdatel'stvo, 1997.

Shpet, Gustav. "Differentsiatsiia postanovki teatral'nogo predstavleniia." *Sovremennaia dramaturgiia* 5 (1991): 202-04.

Shpet, Gustav. "Esteticheskie fragmenty." *Sochineniia.* By Gustav Shpet. Moscow: Pravda, 1989. 343-472.

Shpet, Gustav. *Iskusstvo kak vid znaniia. Izbrannye trudy po filosofii kul'tury.* Ed. T.G. Shchedrina. Moscow: ROSSPEN, 2007.

Shpet, Gustav "Pis'mo Stalinu." *Tvorcheskoe nasledie Gustava Gustavovicha Shpeta v kontekste filosofskikh problem formirovaniia istoriko-kul'turnogo soznaniia (mezhdistsiplinarnyi aspekt). G.G. Shpet/Comprehensio. Chetvertye Shpetovskie chteniia.* Ed. O. Mazaeva. Tomsk: Izdatel'stvo Tomskogo universiteta, 2003. 586-92.

Shpet, Gustav. "Teatr kak iskusstvo." *Gustav Gustavovich Shpet. Arkhivnye materialy. Vospominaniia. Stat'i.* Ed. T.D. Martsinkovskaia. Moscow: Smysl, 2000. 111-34.

Shpet, Gustav. *Vnutrenniaia forma slova (etiudy i variatsii na temy Gumbol'ta* [sic]*).* Moscow: Gosudarstvennaia akademiia khudozhestvennykh nauk, 1927.

Shtorkh, M.G., ed. "Pis'ma k G.G. Shpetu." *Nachala* 1 (1992): 63-69.

Sitkovetskaia, M.M., ed. *Meierkhol'd repetiruet. V dvukh tomakh. T. 2.* Moscow: Artist. Rezhisser. Teatr (ART), 1993.

Stakhorskii, S.V., ed. *Iz istorii sovetskoi nauki o teatre. 20-gody. Sbornik trudov.* Moscow: GITIS, 1988.

Stanislavskii, K.S. *Sobranie sochinenii v vos'mi tomakh. T. 8. Pis'ma 1918-1938.* Moscow: Iskusstvo, 1961.

Stanislavskii, K.S. *Sobranie sochinenii v deviati tomakh. T. 9. Pis'ma 1918-1938.* Moscow: Iskusstvo; Moskovskii khudozhestvennyi teatr, 1999.

Steiner, Peter "*Tropos Logikos*: Gustav Shpet's Philosophy of History." *Slavic Review* 62.2 (2003): 343–58.

Tairov, A. *Zapiski rezhissera. Stat'i, besedy, rechi, pis'ma*. Moscow: Vserosiiskoe teatral'noe obshchestvo, 1970.

Tihanov, Galin. "Gustav Shpet: Literature and Aesthetics from the Silver Age to the 1930s." *Primerjalna književnost* 29.2 (2006): 1-19.

Tihanov, Galin. "Multifariousness under Duress: Gustav Shpet's Scattered Lives." *Russian Literature* 63.2/3/4 (2008): 259-92.

Tihanov, Galin. "Gustave Chpet: Problèmes théoriques de literature et de theater dans les années 1920 (le CLM et le GAKhN)." *Slavica Occitania* 26 (2008): 33-48.

Toddes, E., and M. Chudakova. "Pervyi russkii perevod "Kursa obshchei lingvistiki F. de Sossiura [Saussure] i deiatel'nost' Moskovskogo lingvisticheskogo kruzhka (Materialy k izucheniiu bytovaniia nauchnoi knigi v 1920-e gody)." *Fedorovskie chteniia 1978*. Moscow: Nauka, 1981. 229-49.

Toman, J. *The Magic of a Common Language. Jakobson, Mathesius, Trubetzkoy, and the Prague Linguistic Circle*. Cambridge: MIT Press, 1995.

Trabskii, A.Ia., ed. *Sovetskii teatr. Dokumenty i materialy, 1917-1967. Russkii sovetskii teatr, 1926-1932. Chast' pervaia*. Leningrad: Iskusstvo, 1982.

Tynianov, Iurii. *Poetika. Istoriia literatury. Kino*. Moscow: Nauka, 1977.

Ustinov, A. "Dve zhizni Nikolaia Bernera." *Litsa. Biograficheskii al'manakh* 9 (2002): 5-64.

Vinogradov, V. "Iz istorii izucheniia poetiki (20-e gody)." *Izvestiia AN SSSR. Seriia literatury i iazyka* 34.3 (1975): 259-72.

Vinokur, G.O. "Slovarnaia avtobiograficheskaia zametka." *Vvedenie v izuchenie filologicheskikh nauk*. By G.O. Vinokur. Ed. S.I. Gindin. 1925-26. Moscow: Labirint, 2000. 105-07.

Vorob'eva, M. "Neizvestnyi 'Giperborei.'" *Bibliofil* 3 (2000): 177-83.

"Vospominaniia T.G. Maksimovoi-Shpet ob otse." *Voprosy psikhologii* 3 (2009): 116-21.

Part Two

The Russian Context

The Fate of Philosophy in Russia: Shpet's Studies in the History of Russian Thought

James P. Scanlan

Gustav Shpet's historical essays on philosophy in Russia occupy a special place in the study of that subject. Neither a Marxist nor a defender of the prominent religious tradition in Russian thought, Shpet saw little philosophical merit in the earlier figures most esteemed by those dominant groups. He approached his country's philosophy with a fresh and highly critical eye, and if his essays dismayed both the social radicals and the religious thinkers, it was because he managed to provide a valuable new picture of Russian thought from a perspective that sought to avoid their established orthodoxies.

Shpet was not, of course, primarily a specialist in the history of Russian thought. Yet during one decade of his life (roughly 1914-1923) he produced a body of brilliant and learned writings on the subject. The first was a long essay on the Russian idealist philosopher Pamfil Iurkevich, published in 1914. This was followed after the Russian revolution by the publication of three articles dealing with the Russian Populist theoretician Petr Lavrov (1920-1922), a monograph on Alexander Herzen entitled *Herzen's Philosophical World View* (1921) and his major work in the field—*An Essay on the Development of Russian Philosophy, Part One* (1922; reprinted in 1989 and 1991). Although he was able to publish nothing more on the subject during his lifetime, Shpet's archive as described by Russian scholars who have examined it (Emeli'anov and Livshits 40-42; Emel'ianov and Lobutin 24; Shchedrina 37-40) contains several additional items relating to the history of Russian philosophy. These include a 69-page manuscript portion of part 2 of the *Essay*, a working bibliography for the *Essay* running to over 400 titles, and lengthy texts of two articles—one on Nikolai Chernyshevskii (1929, published in 2002; see Shpet, "Istochniki disertatsii") and the other on Vissarion Belinskii (1923, published in 1991).

Shpet's views on the history of Russian philosophy are discussed here as they relate to three periods: from the beginnings to the mid-1840s, the later nineteenth century, and the twentieth century before his arrest and execution in 1937.

Shpet on Early Philosophical Thought in Russia

Shpet's reputation as a severe critic of Russian thought rests largely on part 1 of his widely-read *Essay*. It should be noted, however, that in the book itself Shpet asked readers not to judge his opinions solely on the basis of the appraisals in that volume: remarking that it was composed in haste during a time of turmoil in Russian life, he wrote that he wished its tone in many places were "less revealing of the shifts in my emotional states" ("Ocherk" 11). Because only that volume appeared, however, critics have been left with a treatment of early Russian philosophy that is called "contemptuous" by Nikolai Losskii (Lossky 324) and "harsh, often scornful, and always captious" by Vasilii Zen'kovskii (Zenkovsky 830). At the same time, even the work's detractors find value in its fastidious study of primary sources and its attention to Russian thinkers otherwise largely ignored.

Shpet's uncomplimentary treatment is nowhere more evident than in his denial of philosophical importance to figures often cited as Russian pioneers in the field. An example is his assessment of Grigorii Skovoroda, the eighteenth-century religious moralist who expressed the wish to be a Russian Socrates. Shpet belittles Skovoroda's accomplishments, writing caustically that "our Socrates found himself without a Plato, which of course greatly diminished his Socratic significance" ("Ocherk" 83). More than that, Shpet rejects any claim that Skovoroda was a noteworthy thinker, asserting that the actual philosophical content of his works was "minimal in the extreme" and denying that his exposure to philosophy extended much beyond Cicero and Plutarch. He finds little evidence that the would-be Socrates even knew Plato at first hand ("Ocherk" 84-86).

Mikhail Lomonosov and Aleksandr Radishchev—two other eighteenth-century thinkers often regarded as major early Russian philosophers—suffer similar diminution at Shpet's hands. Without denying that they were, respectively, a capable early scientist and a pioneering social radical, Shpet sees the two as having no substantial impact on Russian philosophy or culture in general. He writes, with wicked sarcasm: "One [Lomonosov] traveled to Europe, studied what needed to be studied, returned and began to teach what no one needed, and only toward his two-hundredth anniversary did his descendants guess who among us was 'our own Newton.' The other [Radishchev] likewise traveled to Europe, learned what they didn't teach and didn't learn what they taught, and after a hundred and fifty years a grateful posterity recognized him as 'the first Russian revolutionary'" ("Ocherk" 40). Radishchev is dismissed as little more than a compiler. His essay on immortality, regarded as a major theoretical treatise by Soviet Marxist scholars, is described by Shpet as "beneath criticism—a pupil's synopsis of four or five books he had read" ("Ocherk" 78).

Such criticisms are not isolated instances of iconoclasm. Rather, they represent Shpet's settled conviction that Russia had virtually no philosophical life before the nineteenth century. The earliest ages of Russian history, through the Kievan and Muscovite periods, he sees as lost in essentially unbroken intellectual darkness— "the darkness of Russian *neveglasie*," he calls it, using an Old Church Slavonic term for ignorance ("Ocherk" 33). Shpet concedes that with Peter the Great, "the stifling fog of universal ignorance" finally began to lift ("Ocherk" 24), but he sees progress in the development of philosophical culture as agonizingly slow even in the new atmosphere. The reason, he argues, was linguistic isolation from the classical sources of modern culture. Although Christianity came to Russia from the Byzantine world, the language devised by the missionaries Cyril and Methodius to disseminate it deprived the new Christians of access to the treasures of Greco-Roman culture. "They baptized us in Greek," Shpet writes, "but the language they gave us was Bulgarian. What could the language of a people devoid of cultural traditions, of literature, of history, bring with it?" ("Ocherk" 28).

At its highest pitch, Shpet's criticism grows into a sweeping condemnation of Russian culture reminiscent of Peter Chaadaev's earlier indictment. "Our social and state system has always been based on ignorance," he writes. "Our history is the organization of innate, elemental Russian ignorance" ("Ocherk" 261). In such an atmosphere, he argues, ideas are valued not for their own sake but for their usefulness; "ignorance," he adds, "is impressed by the practical successes of knowledge" ("Ocherk" 32). Thus even when ideas are borrowed from others, they are appropriated for their utility only. From the beginning Russian philosophy has been philosophy in the service of extra-philosophical purposes. In Shpet's view true philosophy, by contrast, must be free, unfettered—a science committed to no external ends.

As Shpet reconstructs its history, Russian philosophy began its life in the service of the Church. In the Kievan Academy of the seventeenth century, philosophy came to Russia as "the handmaiden of theology" ("Ocherk" 24): its work was to buttress Orthodoxy and encourage morals. Thus although the academy professors were in a sense a source of "enlightenment," their work did not promote genuine philosophy. The subservient position of philosophy gave it a distinctive atmosphere and character: its prevailing psychological trait was a feeling of being restrained, and it typically shunned clear outlines, distinct forms, and well-defined formulas ("Ocherk" 182). Its thought was "lazy," like a slave's, Shpet charges, and it produced almost no truly philosophical works ("Ocherk" 156).

With Peter the Great a second period in the life of Russian thought began, marked by a new form of subjection. The government succeeded the clergy as Russia's intelligentsia; philosophy, previously subordinated to the interests of religion, was now called to support the state. In this regard Russian intellectual history differed fatefully from that of Western Europe, Shpet argues. There, a creative aristocracy became the second intelligentsia, and it produced the Renaissance. But in Russia there was no aristocracy competent to return to the classical sources of culture. Intellectual leadership was provided instead by the government, and in Shpet's eyes government in all its forms is inherently uncreative, occupied of necessity with "the national instinct of self-preservation" ("Ocherk" 46). Lacking inner creativity, the government intelligentsia could progress only by borrowing, and what was borrowed was limited again by the standard of utility. When Moscow University was opened (with German professors) in 1755, Shpet writes, it served not science but the state ("Ocherk" 38).

The domination of the government intelligentsia, however—like that of the clerical intelligentsia before it—finally came to an end. What replaced it was the liberal, socialist—or, as Shpet calls it, "nihilistic"—intelligentsia, which represented the demands of free culture against government rule. But such was the continuing power of "ignorance" and of the utilitarian orientation in Russian intellectual life that this third intelligentsia, too, called philosophy to the service of an extra-philosophical ideal—no longer the state or the church but now the people. Its commitment to serving the people made the opposition as much the slave of utility as the government had been, though with an opposite goal; Shpet characterizes the struggle between them as "a squabble between an ignorant state, in the person of the government, and the free culture of ignorance, in the person of the opposition intelligentsia" ("Ocherk" 46). In a few disapproving sentences he portrays the atmosphere produced by the "nihilist" opposition: "It took its mission to be enlightenment, not creativity, and it adopted measures to protect itself against heterodoxy—that is, it desired, not to educate [*obrazovat'*], but to nurture [*vospitat'*] . . . The general formula of utility became the slogan of the day—utility in art, literature, science, philosophy—'insatiable utility'" ("Ocherk" 47).

The tragedy of philosophy in Russia, then, according to Shpet, is that it has been forced to lead not its own life but a life of service to three successive intelligentsias: "We have needed the spirit," he writes, "for the church, for the state, and for the people, but not for itself, not so that church, state, and people might live in it and by it" ("Ocherk" 318). The philosopher in Russia has been called upon to be successively a preacher, a ruler, and a champion of the people—none of them roles compatible with the idea of philosophy as "pure knowledge," the object of a disinterested love ("Ocherk" 50). Hence Shpet calls the history of philosophy in Russia a history of "prescientific philosophical thought"—thought that has known itself only as subordinate, not free ("Ocherk" 51).

Shpet does not contend, however, that the demands of free philosophy went entirely unheard throughout that history. None of the three intelligentsias, he comments, " prevailed even for a moment without opposition from the voice of the cultured conscience" ("Ocherk" 318). Indeed much of the *Essay* is devoted to seeking out the expressions of that voice. With the independence of philosophy as his controlling interest, Shpet does find a few landmarks in the history of Russian philosophy—landmarks different from those picked out by writers in the Marxist and Russian religious traditions.

Among those who "took our first steps in the direction of serious philosophy" ("Ocherk" 170), Shpet singles out Fedor Sidonskii (1805-1873), a professor at St. Petersburg Theological Academy, in whose 1833 book, *An Introduction to the Science of Philosophy*, Shpet sees a certain independence and originality. Those features do not protect Sidonskii, however, from the wittily acid criticism at which Shpet excels in the *Essay*: "Sidonskii," he writes, "is a skeptic who is afraid of not being a philosopher, and a philosopher who is afraid of not being an Orthodox Christian. He wanted to obtain pure philosophical water by combining Kant with

Jacobi, but the resulting explosion of detonating gas wrecks his whole philosophical laboratory" ("Ocherk" 167). Orest Novitskii (1806-1884) fares somewhat better: he is credited with delivering at St. Vladimir University in Kiev in 1837 a speech that Shpet calls "the *first* Russian philosophical work written with truly philosophical style, flair, and sympathetic understanding of the tasks of philosophy" ("Ocherk" 204). Shpet is also favorably inclined toward the work of Sylvester Gogotskii (1813-1889), another Kiev philosopher, in whom, he says, "our philosophy found the true path." Gogotskii's emphasis on the independence of philosophy represented, Shpet believes, the highest intellectual achievement possible in Russia at the time ("Ocherk" 266).

In the one published volume of the *Essay*, Shpet does not carry his account beyond these voices crying in the wilderness of the mid-1840s; he mentions the names of Vissarion Belinskii and others from time to time, but does not dwell on their views. For evidence of his interpretation of later nineteenth-century Russian philosophy, we must turn to his separate studies of a few individual thinkers of that period.

Shpet on Later Nineteenth-Century Russian Thinkers

In these studies, Shpet expands on his basic critique of Russian philosophy as "practical" rather than "genuine," but he also softens it in ways that allow for a somewhat more nuanced assessment of his chosen thinkers. Of course, not all of these subjects are spared outright rejection. In his lengthy work on Chernyshevskii, for example, he treats that influential thinker as a dilettante who concerned himself with philosophical issues only "in immediate application to the resolution of issues of the day" (Emel'ianov and Livshits 42); in another essay, he simply pronounces Chernyshevskii "philosophically incompetent" ("K voprosu" 117). But in the cases of four other figures—Belinskii, Herzen, Iurkevich, and Lavrov—we find at least grudging acknowledgement of their significance in the halting approach toward "genuine" philosophy in Russia.

Vissarion Belinskii

Shpet's long and dazzlingly erudite essay on Belinsky's brief Hegelian period of the late 1830s is the least complimentary of these individual studies, as is shown by the faint praise with which he justifies allotting Belinskii a place in the history of Russian philosophy: "Given the general poverty, it is necessary to include . . . even names that in a happier history would be destined for indisputable oblivion" ("K voprosu" 144). Still, he calls Belinskii an "instrument" of "the spirit of European philosophy in Russia" ("K voprosu" 144): Belinskii recognized the importance of Hegel—a true philosopher, for whom Shpet had unbounded admiration—and he took the Russian public a bit further toward a correct understanding of the Hegelian philosophy. Above all, he rightly noted the central place in that philosophy of the celebrated formula, "what is real is rational; what is rational is real" ("K voprosu"

120-21). Furthermore, according to Shpet, Belinskii opened a new stage in the development of Russian aesthetics with his insistence that "the subject of poetry is reality" ("K voprosu" 161).

Despite those commendations, the bulk of Shpet's article is devoted to a minutely detailed critique of Belinskii's understanding of Hegel. The crux of the matter, according to Shpet, is that Belinskii, although he accepted the equation of reality with rationality, had a woefully inadequate grasp of what Hegel meant by "reality." In the name of "reconciliation with reality," Belinskii was ready to accept as rational and thus to justify, in Shpet's words, "every little thing one might encounter . . . everything accidental, cruel, diseased, despotic" ("K voprosu" 164). Looking specifically at the political sphere, Shpet castigates Belinskii for praising Russian autocracy on the grounds that Hegel called monarchy the highest form of government, when in fact Hegel made that claim only for a limited, constitutional monarchy ("K voprosu" 147).

Shpet explains Belinskii's distortions of Hegelianism by the fact that he had no direct acquaintance with the German philosopher's writings ("K voprosu" 144). Unable to read them, he relied on others who knew German—Nikolai Nadezhdin, Nikolai Stankevich, Mikhail Katkov, and above all Mikhail Bakunin—for information about the Hegelian system, and all those figures, Shpet argues, viewed Hegel through the prism of Fichte—a philosopher whom Shpet himself disdained almost as much as he admired Hegel. Hence Belinskii inevitably adopted a Hegelianism tainted by "the hysterics of Fichte's ill-starred philosophizing" ("K voprosu" 126). According to Shpet, Fichte's action-oriented philosophy had a special appeal for the practical-minded Russians, who wanted philosophy to resolve questions of everyday life—something Shpet considered impossible. They sought to transform "pragmatic problems" into philosophical problems, and in so doing they left the sphere of philosophy altogether ("K voprosu" 147-48). Belinskii moved from philosophy "into the emptiness of a 'world view'" (Shpet, "K voprosu" 167)—a term (*mirovozzrenie*) that Shpet defines elsewhere as "a philosophical theory in the service of practice" (*Filosofskoe mirovozzrenie* 19), or what in the present day we might call an ideology.

Alexander Herzen

Shpet's monograph on the thought of Alexander Herzen, based on an address delivered in January 1920 at a meeting marking the fiftieth anniversary of Herzen's death, is both like and unlike Shpet's other major writings in the history of Russian philosophy. As in the other studies, he is concerned with the intellectual ancestry of his subject and examines it closely; in particular he stresses the beneficent influence of Hegel on Herzen's thought. But he devotes far more attention to the connection between philosophy and life than he does in any of the other works, and he discusses Herzen's views on ethical and social issues that nowhere concerned him in the other historical writings. Moreover, at many points in the monograph Shpet himself engages in something very much like the preaching he otherwise scorns as unphilosophical.

Some of this uncharacteristic behavior may be explained by the memorial context of Shpet's address, but it also reflects his understanding of the nature of Herzen's thought. Herzen's fundamental interests, Shpet argues, were always practical: he sought to create a new world by translating reason into action, and hence he was not concerned with theoretical problems as such. His attention to philosophy, then, was precisely the kind of impure, utilitarian attention that Shpet finds incompatible with "true" philosophy. It is no accident that Shpet titles his monograph not "The Philosophy of Herzen" but "The Philosophical World View of Herzen."

Because of Herzen's devotion to the implementation of thought in life, Shpet is tempted to deny him philosophical significance altogether. In more generous moments, however, he sees in the young Herzen the potential for dealing seriously with philosophical ideas; Herzen did, after all, arrive independently at a critique of law and of history comparable to that of the German "left Hegelians." This critique could have been significant for Russian philosophy, Shpet suggests, but unfortunately Herzen took up "nonphilosophical 'factual' practice" (*Filosofskoe mirovozzrenie* 10) instead, and as a result Russian philosophy did not "reach the point at which philosophy in itself . . . is a *deed*, and even more, is *life itself*, though of a special sort that does not initiate 'deeds' and 'acts' but only cautions, at least, against many of them" (*Filosofskoe mirovozzrenie* 18).

At the same time, Shpet is himself clearly sympathetic to much of Herzen's practical program; he not only goes on to expand at length on the "world view" behind the program but injects his own, sometimes impassioned support for the values and attitudes it represents. Why does Shpet, with his disdainful view of "impure" philosophy, devote so much attention to these extra-philosophical concerns, and why does he second Herzen's "practical" commitments so warmly? An answer to these questions must wait for the concluding section of this essay.

Pamfil Iurkevich

The long article on Iurkevich—the only one published before the Bolshevik revolution—foreshadows the general interpretation of Russian thought advanced by Shpet later in the *Essay* but is far more favorable to its subject than the essays on Belinskii and Herzen. Iurkevich is described as having worked in an age marked by a negative attitude toward philosophy (the age of the dominance of the radical intelligentsia) but as being nonetheless an ardent champion of philosophy and of the freedom of the philosophical spirit. Shpet does not rehearse the details of Iurkevich's principal encounter with the radical intelligentsia—his polemic with Chernyshevskii in the 1860s—but he leaves no doubt as to where his own sympathies lie. Philosophically, it was a very uneven contest, Shpet writes, inasmuch as Iurkevich had on his side "knowledge, subtle understanding, independent thought," and an interest in enduring truth ("Filosofskoe nasledstvo" 654; Shpet's grandson, M.K. Polivanov, suggests poignantly that the same could have been said of Shpet himself in the confrontation with Soviet authorities that led to his execution [15]).

In all of Shpet's writings no Russian philosopher is praised as warmly as Iurkevich is praised in this essay. Calling him "one of the most interesting of Russian thinkers," Shpet speaks of Iurkevich's "exceptionally brilliant interpretation" of Plato, of his "profoundly thought-out" comparison of Plato and Immanuel Kant, and in general of "the depth and power of [his] philosophical genius" ("Filosofskoe nasledstvo" 653, 681, 687). He heartily approves of Iurkevich's attack on the narrow "materialism" of the time—all the more since it was joined with a recognition of the shortcomings of contemporary idealism as well. In his critique of the Kantian philosophy, Iurkevich was in the forefront of philosophical progress in his day, according to Shpet. Iurkevich recognized that in criticizing Kant on the givenness of objects it was necessary to return to Plato, and in this regard Shpet finds Iurkevich's ideas "striking in their finished, considered, truly philosophical character" ("Filosofskoe nasledstvo" 686). "It was necessary," Shpet writes, "to go through Kant's school anew and completely, in order to reveal fully the inconsistency of his negative philosophy as a whole, to find in it everything that can reconcile it with the tradition of a truly positive philosophy, and finally, on the basis of this tradition and returning always to Plato, to find new outlets and paths" ("Filosofskoe nasledstvo" 687). Inasmuch as Shpet himself was attempting to do something very much like that (following Edmund Husserl and the other German philosophers he admired), he must have considered himself a continuer of Iurkevich's effort: "We must strive . . . to show," he wrote, "that in the history of our thought, his [Iurkevich's] ideas have not remained fruitless" ("Filosofskoe nasledstvo" 687).

For all his virtues, however, even Iurkevich did not fully satisfy Shpet's demanding model of true philosophy. For in the end Iurkevich had recourse to moral values and to faith in order to ground particular philosophical conclusions, and that was a cardinal sin Shpet could forgive in no thinker. "To bet on morals in theoretical philosophy," he wrote, "is to play *va banque*: . . . losing is guaranteed! Once theoretical philosophy must appeal to morality it would be better for it to cease existing, for if it cannot be beyond good and evil, then it cannot be at all" ("Filosofskoe nasledstvo" 696). And no less destructive of true philosophy is the reliance on faith as a source of knowledge that supposedly transcends reason. Faith and reason cannot be "joined" in a philosophical system, Shpet insists; they are "incompatible, like oil and water" ("Filosofskoe nasledstvo" 719). Philosophy is an enterprise of free reason, and reason cannot be free if there is another authority beyond it.

Peter Lavrov

Shpet's principal essay on Lavrov, dated August 1919 in the text though not published until 1922, tells a similar story of a philosophical enterprise with good beginnings. Although his praise in this case is not expressed so enthusiastically, Shpet finds a great deal to agree with in the philosophy of Lavrov—more, in fact, than in the philosophy of Iurkevich—despite lamenting that Lavrov, too, ultimately went astray. Shpet contends that Lavrov's "anthropological point of view," often dismissed as derivative or eclectic, must be regarded as an independent and original construction;

thinkers such as Kant, Ludwig Feuerbach, Auguste Comte, and John Stuart Mill, he argues, were not so much specific influences on Lavrov as shapers of the intellectual atmosphere in which he worked out his own philosophical ideas ("Antropologizm" 74-75). The philosophers who could be regarded as definite sources of inspiration for Lavrov Shpet identifies as Herzen, Pierre Proudhon, and above all Hegel, of whom Lavrov is said to have had a very complete knowledge ("Antropologizm" 101); but Shpet denies that Lavrov can be called either a disciple of any one of them or an eclectic follower of all three ("Antropologizm" 74).

Lavrov's general approach to philosophy, as Shpet presents it, is one he manifestly shares. First, Lavrov (along with Hegel) recognized that the task of philosophy is to "understand reality"—thus, by implication, that it is not to guide action, buttress morals, defend state power, or serve any other extraneous end ("Antropologizm" 111). Second, Lavrov realized that philosophy must be "a science, absolute knowledge, a scientific system," which in Shpet's language means that it must consist of interpersonal, objective knowledge rather than speculation, opinion, or faith ("Antropologizm" 102). In this regard Shpet applauds Lavrov's opposition to both materialism and spiritualism; Lavrov recognized, he states, that each of these positions is not science but metaphysics. At a time when most people believed that the future of philosophy hinged on which side was victorious in the struggle between materialism and spiritualism, Shpet argues, Lavrov was one of those more penetrating thinkers who "looked for and saw the philosophy of the future from another perspective" ("Antropologizm" 104). Third, Shpet concurs with Lavrov's principle of the primacy of consciousness—the principle that "man knows only his own consciousness," and consequently that the content of reality, which it is philosophy's mission to know, can be approached only through the systematic examination of what is given to human consciousness ("Antropologizm" 114-15).

Up to this point, Shpet not only agrees with Lavrov but sees him as having fixed on the central task of philosophy in the present day: "To establish the primitive givenness of consciousness in its full sense," Shpet writes, "is the work and the task of our time" ("Antropologizm" 123). Beyond that point, however, Shpet finds that Lavrov's approach suffers from a fundamental flaw, having to do with his understanding of "consciousness." Lavrov's "anthropological principle," Shpet avers, focuses on the empirical individual, and as such it tacitly identifies consciousness with the sensory or the perceptual (*chuvstvennost'*); for the empirical individual, consciousness is what is sensorily given. Lavrov thus remains in Shpet's eyes a phenomenalist who fails to recognize that consciousness, as Shpet expresses it, "is given to us not only sensorily . . . but in thinking, and, as an act, only in thinking" ("Antropologizm" 123). Moreover, because of his phenomenalist approach Lavrov is inclined to stress the personal character of what is given to consciousness. But that, of course, is of no interest to philosophy, which seeks impersonal, objective knowledge; it is meat only for the empirical sciences of psychology and anthropology.

Altogether, then, Lavrov failed to follow the path of true philosophical development, which Shpet identifies as the path leading to modern phenomenological analysis: "From phenomenalism through immanentism to the recognition of consciousness as an object not of the senses but of thought; as the ideal subject, not of anoetic recognition, but of the cognition of pure intellectual intuition. . . . This is the path taken by the history of philosophy," Shpet writes, "while Lavrov was occupied . . . with other questions" ("Antropologizm" 135). On balance, however, Shpet appears to view Lavrov's philosophy as not only the most advanced in nineteenth-century Russian thought but as important by world standards; "his anthropologism as an interpretation of the problem of reality is more important than his psychologistic mistake" ("Antropologizm" 136).

Shpet on Twentieth-Century Russian Philosophy and Its Prospects

Although Shpet's principal subject was Russian philosophy in the nineteenth century and earlier, he was writing in revolutionary Russia, for twentieth-century readers. Accordingly, much of what he has to say in these historical works, and especially in the Herzen monograph and the *Essay*, relates to the intellectual life of his own day and reflects his own intense interest in the more recent history of Russian thought, in the fate of philosophy in a Marxist state, and in the future of philosophical culture in Russia.

Shpet's view of the past accomplishments of Russian philosophy was far from favorable, as we have seen. Still, there had been some advances. Iurkevich, Lavrov, and a few others had understood the true task of philosophy. After the Iurkevich-Chernyshevskii debate there was, Shpet maintains, a productive retreat of philosophers from the public forum: "Our philosophy," he writes, "shut itself in. Our best philosophical names remained unknown to the 'broad intelligentsia public,' [but] in patient, slow construction they erected a foundation for a sturdy and lasting building" ("Ocherk" 48). On the strength of this progress—in which he himself, of course, was playing a part—Shpet was prepared in 1922 to say that Russian philosophy had at last begun to approach "the highest historical and dialectical stage" of the development of philosophy—that is, the stage of "philosophy as knowledge" ("Ocherk" 12). It is regrettable that these few sentences are the only descriptions we have from Shpet of the powerful development of Russian philosophy that took place in the late nineteenth and early twentieth century, for he wrote nothing on such productive philosophers of that period as Aleksei Kozlov, Aleksandr Vvedenskii, Lev Lopatin, or even the hugely influential Vladimir Solov'ev, who was hardly unknown to the broad intelligentsia public and whose teacher was the much-admired Pamfil Iurkevich.

Shpet was acutely aware in 1922, however, that nonphilosophical events could have a profound effect on the further progress of Russian philosophy, and in the *Essay* he alluded repeatedly to the contemporary situation in revolutionary Russia. Five years after the Bolshevik revolution, he was still uncertain as to its cultural significance. Like many in Russia who had accepted a social transformation they did not actively seek, Shpet faced the Marxist future with ambivalence: he had hopes, but strong fears as well.

In the *Essay* Shpet speaks of "a new dawn," and he expresses the conviction that in the wake of the revolution a new intelligentsia is being born that will create a new ideology ("Ocherk" 15). He admits, however, that this conviction exists largely as a faith, and his expressions of it are tentative and hypothetical: "If my faith in a Russian Renaissance, in a new, healthy national intelligentsia, in a new aristocracy, if you will—an aristocracy of talent—has a basis, and if this Renaissance brings with it also a new philosophy at the stage of development that I consider *higher*, then our revolution in the philosophical-cultural aspect of 'consciousness' must inspire optimistic moods. And such an optimism, in my eyes, is a healthy optimism" ("Ocherk" 16-17). He stresses that this ideology of the future must be a creative product; it must be genuinely new: "Otherwise," he adds ominously, "there would be nothing more unsuccessful than our revolution" (15).

Shpet's call for a new ideology of yet unknown content shows, of course, that although he accepted the revolution he by no means accepted its Marxist principles. He suggested early in the preface to the *Essay* that in a historical work such as his it would be useful to be a Marxist. Speaking of the demand for "explanations" of historical development, he writes: "In that connection one can scarcely find anything more convenient than Marxism. I should like to be a Marxist . . ." ("Ocherk" 13). The ellipses are Shpet's and they point to a longer story that the *Essay* was not prepared to tell. And not only in the *Essay* but in Shpet's other writings of the period there are many indications of his negative attitude toward Marxism and its philosophy; taken together, they reveal very clearly Shpet's conviction that Marxism could not be the source of philosophical creativity in Russia.

For one thing, Shpet denies that Marxism has any significant philosophical content beyond a materialist metaphysics. Writing of Lavrov's contention that it is inappropriate to apply the term "materialism" to the philosophies of Feuerbach, Marx, or Engels, Shpet acknowledges the justice of the remark in the case of Feuerbach but denies it in the cases of Marx and Engels, apparently ascribing a materialist ontology to both of them as well as to their Russian followers: "What remains that is 'philosophical' in Marxism," he asks rhetorically, "if its materialism is thrown out?" ("Antropologizm" 88n). Philosophically, Marxism is no more than a variety of materialism in Shpet's view, and as such it is subject to the severe criticisms of materialism presented throughout his historical writings—essentially, that it is only a faith masquerading as knowledge, and a self-contradictory faith at that.

Moreover, Shpet finds no creative development even of materialism among Russian thinkers. In an interesting footnote to his major article on Lavrov, Shpet observes that after the appearance of Chernyshevskii's *Anthropological Principle in Philosophy* materialism became, as Shpet puts it, "if not a public opinion, at least a journal opinion among us," but he goes on to deny any philosophical significance to this intellectual fashion: "It is curious," he writes, "that apparently we have not had a single philosophical representative of materialism. I, at least, know of not one original (not translated) philosophical book or article that defends materialism" ("Antropologizm" 94n). Addressed to an audience familiar not only with Lenin's

Materialism and Empirio-Criticism but with the materialist writings of Plekhanov and other Russian Marxists, the point of this remark must have been strikingly clear: the Marxist heritage in Russia is devoid of philosophical creativity. And that message was further reinforced in the *Essay* when Shpet suggested that the Marxist intelligentsia as such had ceased to exist after the revolution, since it had turned from thought to practice, becoming "agents" rather than thinkers ("Ocherk" 15). Hence the urgent need for "a new intelligentsia."

But Shpet's apprehensions ran far deeper than his conviction that Marxist philosophy as such carried no promise for Russia's future. He feared that a Marxist state was a positive threat to all philosophical culture. In the *Essay* and the article on Herzen's world view, this fear looms larger than any hopes for the constructive development of philosophy in Russia. Shpet saw no reason to think that, once "the opposition intelligentsia has become the government" ("Ocherk" 49), its "service" orientation would disappear; indeed, as transformed into a government interest, this utilitarian orientation could only be expected to increase, given the inherently conservative impulses of every state. That he believed the Marxist state in Russia was characterized by these impulses, Shpet left no doubt: "All governments in Russia have always looked and now look at education from a utilitarian point of view," he wrote ("Ocherk" 42); because culture is essentially free, it is at war with government "everywhere in history" (46); "the conditions in which philosophy [in Russia] continues and exists today are the same conditions in which it has existed up to this day. Ignorance is a kind of historical constant in the evolution of Russian creativity" (49). These and many similar statements by Shpet are deliberate expressions of his fears for the future of philosophy in Marxist Russia.

What hopes Shpet did harbor were maintained despite, and ultimately against, the political direction of the revolution. Still alive in Russia, he believed, was the creative spirit expressed by Pushkin when he wrote, in his 1828 poem "The Poet and the Crowd": "We were born for inspiration, for sweet sounds and prayers." "These words," Shpet adds, "will not now be torn from the history of Russian culture by any electrifiers or Salieris, and they will move Russian man until the Russian language itself is abolished" ("Ocherk" 319). Pushkin advanced the ideal of a creative spiritual aristocracy; but the burden of Russian thought since Pushkin's day, in Shpet's eyes, had been in the direction of a kind of leveling, populist nationalism—rather than the truly creative, autochthonous (*pochvennyi*) nationalism advocated by Pushkin, Dostoevskii, and others. In this regard there was little difference, Shpet thought, between Westernists, Slavophiles, and Bolsheviks—all of whom he calls "*narodnik*" and "oriental" in their thinking. "It is no accident," he writes (in a paragraph appearing in the 1922 book edition of the *Essay* but unaccountably missing from its 1989 and 1991 reproductions in article form), "that the romantic Kremlin of Slavophilism is the real Kremlin of Bolshevism" (*Ocherk razvitiia* 85). Certainly the Bolshevik state shows no signs of appreciating a creative intellectual aristocracy or a truly original nationalism; instead, he comments bitterly (referring to Communist orthographic decrees), the state proclaims it necessary "in the name of the idea of 'universal equality,' to write not 'Parthenon' . . . but 'Parfenon' . . . , and not 'God' but 'god'" ("Ocherk" 223). Whether there exists in the revolution an autochthonous intelligentsia capable of promoting Pushkin's ideal, Shpet writes (again in the missing paragraph mentioned above), one may only "guess" and "ardently desire" (*Ocherk razvitiia* 86).

Shpet's darkest fear, however—a fear amply justified by Russia's ensuing history—was that the revolution not only would fail to promote true culture but would destroy the individuality and freedom needed in order for philosophy to prosper. It is only in this light that we can explain Shpet's warm and sustained endorsement of Herzen's "world view" in his 1921 monograph. Herzen's thought became for Shpet the occasion for an impassioned defense of the humanistic values that make possible a creative aristocracy and the flowering of philosophy. If, in Shpet's interpretation, Herzen's concerns were fundamentally nonphilosophical, they were not irrelevant to philosophy: they were concerns for the preconditions of all philosophy, and it is these preconditions that Shpet identifies and defends in his article.

The individual person (*lichnost'*), Shpet writes, was the "fiery center" of Herzen's outlook, and individual dignity requires "absolute freedom" (*Filosofskoe mirovozzrenie* 24, 34). Shpet lauds Herzen for adhering steadfastly to these ideals of individual dignity and freedom against all temptations to endorse fatalism, reject individual responsibility, and yield to the importunate demands of "abstractions" such as justice, state, and society. The person, Shpet agrees, must not be subordinated to any other value—a conviction, as George L. Kline has shown, for which Herzen was deeply indebted to Hegel (186-89).

Two forms of subordination are singled out for special attack by Shpet, and in each case we can clearly see a warning addressed to his own Marxist day. The first form is subordination of the individual to society. Shpet points out that, although for Herzen the individual attains full reality in society and the path of individual self-development runs from "the narrowly personal to the all-embracing and universal," it is nonetheless essential to reject all formal constraints on the individual (*Filosofskoe mirovozzrenie* 37). We must realize, he argues, that there can be no set criterion for fixing the borderline between individual and social morality, and thus no grounds for limiting the individual by considerations of justice or equality (34). In this regard Shpet heartily seconds Herzen when the latter faults Proudhon for sacrificing the independence of the individual person to the demands of justice. Shpet finds Herzen more consistent than Proudhon: "To the extent that Proudhon was right in his condemnation of communism," he writes, "to that extent it is necessary to give oneself unreservedly to the cult of the individual person" (68). In a society ruled by a Communist Party in the name of "universal justice," such remarks must have struck Shpet's readers with particular force.

The second subordination, which Shpet attacks with equal vigor, is the subordination of the individual to the future. Herzen's values and ideals are firmly located in the present, Shpet observes, and it is in that circumstance, he asserts, that "the world view that radiates from the individual as its center approaches its noblest summit" (*Filosofskoe mirovozzrenie* 44). Herzen recognized correctly that fixation on a utopian ideal is incompatible with humanistic values: it is not only impersonal but barbarous, for it leads to willingness to sacrifice the present generation to "a cloudily unknown future" (42). For Shpet "the individual is not a means and a path to an abstract scheme, but is at every instant of history an end in himself" (49). The article concludes with a veritable paean to the individual person in which Shpet's voice becomes a powerful amplification of Herzen's: "The individual for Herzen is not a 'future,' spectral person but a living, flesh-and-blood individual of the actual, present day, a *real* individual . . . The individual is not a toy or a puppet, and not a means for the attainment of ends cut off from the present . . . He is an end in himself, an end for another, the highest real end for both church and state" (52). And in his own voice Shpet adds: "Not man for the Sabbath, but the Sabbath for man. There are no altars to which human sacrifices can be brought, no idols before which human sacrifices can be justified" (53).

Shpet's works in the history of philosophy, although taking the past as their immediate subject, were written at a critical time in the life of Russian society and were addressed in part to grave concerns of the day. Shpet wrote that we must study the past development of philosophy so that we will know "what we may wish and seek in the future" ("Ocherk" 270). As a philosopher he tried to present a vision of philosophy as a perfectly free and creative quest for knowledge, untrammeled by any extrinsic or utilitarian concerns—a vision that in its purity excluded the great bulk of the philosophical thought of his own homeland. But he also tried to show from a practical point of view what Russian philosophical life required in order to become genuine and productive. If his strict conception of philosophy devalued much in his own heritage, it also allowed him to mount a passionate and courageous defense of a free and creative Russian culture against the threats to it that he saw in his surroundings.

Thus Shpet was not so much demeaning the Russian spirit as fighting against the destructive influences that imperiled it—and never more menacingly than during the decades in which he wrote and died. His close analysis of the subjection of Russian philosophy to successive masters throughout its history may thus be read as one long campaign for its future freedom.

Works Cited

Emel'ianov, B.V., and K.N. Liubutin. "Russkaia filosofiia na putiakh samopoznaniia: stranitsy istorii." *Ocherki istorii russkoi filosofii.* By A.I. Vvedenskii, A.F. Losev, E.L. Radlov, and G.G. Shpet. Ed. B.V. Emel'ianov and K.N. Liubutin. Sverdlovsk: Izdatel'stvo Ural'skogo universiteta, 1991. 3-25.

Emel'ianov, B.V. and V.L. Livshits. "Neizdannaia rukopis' G.G. Shpeta 'Istochniki dissertatsii Chernyshevskogo'." *Shpetovskie chteniia v Tomske, 1991.* Ed. O.G. Mazaeva. Tomsk: Izdatel'stvo Tomskogo universiteta, 1991. 40-42.

Kline, George L. "Gustav G. Shpet as Interpreter of Hegel." *Archiwum historii filozofii i myśli społecznej* 44 (1999): 181-90.

Lossky, N.O. *History of Russian Philosophy*. London: George Allen, 1952.

Polivanov, M.K. "Zhizn' i trudy G.G. Shpeta." *Shpet v Sibiri: ssylka i gibel'*. Ed. N.V. Serebrennikov. Tomsk: Vodolei, 1995. 5-15.

Shchedrina, T.G. "*Ia pishu kak ekho drugogo . . .*" *Ocherki intellektual'noi biografii Gustava Shpeta*. Moscow: Progress-Traditsiia, 2004.

Shpet, Gustav. "Antropologizm Lavrova v svete istorii filosofii." *P.L. Lavrov: Stat'i, vospominaniia, materialy*. Peterburg: Kolos, 1922. 73-138.

Shpet, Gustav. *Filosofskoe mirovozzrenie Gertsena*. Petrograd: Kolos, 1921.

Shpet, Gustav. "Filosofskoe nasledstvo P.D. Iurkevicha." *Voprosy filosofii i psikhologii*. 125 (1914): 653-727.

Shpet, Gustav. "Istochniki disertatsii [sic] Chernyshevskogo." Ed. L.V. Fedorova. *Novoe literaturnoe obozrenie* 53 (2002): 6-48.

Shpet, Gustav. "K voprosu o gegel'ianstve Belinskogo." *Voprosy filosofii* 7 (1991): 115-76.

Shpet, Gustav. *Ocherk razvitiia russkoi filosofii. Pervaia chast'*. Petrograd: Kolos, 1922.

Shpet, Gustav. "Ocherk razvitiia russkoi filosofii. Pervaia chast'." *Sochineniia*. By Gustav Shpet. Moscow: Pravda, 1989. 9-342.

Zenkovsky, V.V. *A History of Russian Philosophy*. Trans. George L. Kline. Vol. 2. London: Routledge, 1953.

Gustav Shpet and Phenomenology in an Orthodox Key

Steven Cassedy

Gustav Shpet was one of a number of Husserl's disciples who took some of phenomenology's central principles and applied them to language theory and aesthetics. Much of the value of Shpet's contribution to philosophy derives from his introduction of phenomenology into his own country. But even though he knowingly proposed certain significant modifications to Husserl's thought, an examination of some of his major writings on language and aesthetics leads one to suspect that Shpet, apparently without knowing it, gave his own slant to those parts that he thought he was merely interpreting and passing on. Both the witting and the unwitting modifications show a thinker who is thoroughly grounded in Russian religious thought of the late nineteenth and early twentieth centuries. The result is a philosophy that combines Husserl's analysis of the structure of consciousness with the fundamental Platonism of Orthodoxy, the doctrine of incarnation, and the related notion that matter is to be venerated.

To the extent that he incorporates the Platonism of Russian Orthodoxy into his philosophy, Shpet sets himself apart not only from Husserl but also from Husserl's other, non-Russian disciples who attempted to found aesthetics on phenomenology. For Shpet, as for other early phenomenological aestheticians, the study of art is a science of essences. But *essence* has a different meaning for Shpet from what it has for Husserl's other followers, and the direction Shpet takes from his initial assumptions is quite different from what we find in the others.

An Earlier Phenomenological Approach to Aesthetics and Language

The first significant attempt to apply Husserl's methods to the field of aesthetics was a study by Waldemar Conrad titled "Der ästhetische Gegenstand. Eine phänomenologische Studie" ("The aesthetic object. A phenomenological study"). Conrad (1878-1915), one of Husserl's earliest pupils, published his study in 1908-1909, that is, after the appearance of Husserl's *Logical Investigations* (1900-1901), but before the appearance of *Ideas* (first volume, 1913). In his article Conrad sets out the principles that will govern most phenomenological approaches to aesthetics from that time on (see Haardt, *Husserl* 45-53).

If Husserl was not an aesthetician, what can we take from his work that might help us to understand the world of art? The very way Conrad defines the problem shows his indebtedness to his master. The basic material of investigation will be not only artworks, but the human subject's attitude (*Verhalten*) towards them as compared with the human subject's attitude towards human-made objects that are designed for practical uses (Conrad 71). Like Husserl, Conrad is interested in the moment of contact—and the immediate environment of that moment of contact—between consciousness and what is external to it. Taking one of the most important catchwords from *Logical Investigations*, Conrad proposes for his approach a method of description that will be "presuppositionless" (*voraussetzungslos*), by which he means that all natural presuppositions about the existence of the world and its things, all of what Husserl refers to as "transcendent" (that is, lying beyond acts of consciousness and thus transcendent relative to it), will be left to one side (Conrad 75). The consequence of adopting the presuppositionless method is that objects appear no longer as mere things, as mere objects in nature, but now as ideal objects to which essential properties (*Wesenseigenschaften*) can be attributed (Conrad 76).

Phenomenologically oriented aestheticians will thus be committed to seeing essences in the objects of their investigation. Or, to put it more generally, they are going to be committed to employing a kind of vision that penetrates through the object on its concrete level to discover something behind it: an essence, an object of a nonconcrete nature, a quality of some sort. Conrad's title, the reader quickly finds out, is evidence of this vision. "Aesthetic object" is not another phrase for "artwork." It does not mean the poem we are reading, the statue we are admiring, or the symphony we are listening to; it means something essential within the artwork, something that phenomenological analysis can discover. Hence Conrad's otherwise baffling subtitles: "The aesthetic object of music," "The aesthetic object of poetry." The aesthetic object, Conrad concludes, in contrast both to the artwork in particular and to other sorts of objects in general, is a purely ideal object whose fundamental nature is that it is realizable, the "realization" in question giving the object a "sensuous animation" (*sinnliche Lebendigkeit*), rather than the character of reality. The aesthetic object exists in its own peculiar space, one that is different from "real" space (Conrad 453-54). This and similar remarks led Husserl's much better known pupil, Roman Ingarden, to characterize Conrad's study as the first ontological investigation of artworks (Ingarden 406n40).

The same type of vision carries over to a rudimentary theory of language that Conrad finds himself developing when it comes time to discuss literary art. The word in general, poetic or not, he says, possesses an "essential core." That core is the meaning (*Bedeutung*), which is carried by an acoustic symbol and which intends (*meint*) an object (Conrad 481). The word is thus a sort of fleshly envelope for an insubstantial inner essence. That inner essence is the meaning, which, like the aesthetic object in its work of art, is realized on the concrete (acoustic) level of the word. The chief point here, as in other aspects of the phenomenological approach to aesthetics, is to avoid the principal danger of a naively descriptive method, namely, the danger of seeing objects only superficially, instead of "bringing their essence to self-givenness [*Selbstgegebenheit*]" (Conrad 86, 487).

Shpet: The Basics

Gustav Shpet, like Conrad, had been a loyal student of Husserl. Shpet had shown his familiarity with the basic texts of Husserlian phenomenology in his own first phenomenological work, *Appearance and Sense* (*Iavlenie i smysl*), which he managed to write and publish within a year after the publication of the work on which it relies most heavily, the first volume of Husserl's *Ideas*.

Much of this work is little more than an exposition, to Russian readers, of the new movement in German philosophy that Shpet had recently discovered. In fact, the basic organization of *Appearance and Sense* is based on that of Husserl's *Ideas*. Early on, Shpet introduces the concept that for him lies at the heart of phenomenology and that will lie at the heart of his own system. It is the fundamental distinction between the empirical and the eidetic, between fact and essence, a distinction that leads to the conclusion that phenomenology must be a "science of essences" (Shpet, *Iavlenie* 21).

The notion of the "eidetic" refers to a number of related concepts in Husserl, most from the period following the *Logical Investigations*. The idea common to all is that of the "reduction" a philosopher performs in order to abstract away any extraneous factors in experience and thus arrive at something essential, an idea or *eidos* (hence the term "eidetic"). The extraneous factors can be those associated with the natural or, to use Conrad's phrase, naively descriptive way of seeing things; or they can be those elements of a given phenomenon that are part of the circumstances of a particular act of apprehending that phenomenon, as, say, the way a thing appears at a particular moment in a particular light. The something essential can be what does not change in a particular object (as one commentator puts it, what has made the White House continue to be the White House even though the structure looks different from different angles and even though British troops once burned it; cf. Natanson 14). Or it can be a certain quality considered *in specie*, to use Husserl's term: the color red, for example, which, owing to shading and perspective, we almost never truly see in its purity but nonetheless "see" in a red object.

The distinction between empirical and eidetic, fact and essence is taken straight from the first chapter of *Ideas*, which is titled "Fact and Essence" ("Tatsache und Wesen"). There Husserl had insisted that every object has its essence (*Wesen*) or *eidos* (idea, form, shape, class), its own "in itself" (*in sich selbst*) or "What," and he had distinguished between two types of seeing: essential insight (*Wesenserschauung*) and individual intuition (*individuelle Anschauung*; Husserl 13-16). Essential insight is what gives us the pure essence or *eidos* of an object, while individual intuition, also called empirical intuition, gives us the object as merely something in the natural world. Shpet assimilates the *Erschauung* of *Wesenserschauung* and the *Anschauung* of *individuelle Anschauung* and uses the word *intuitsiia* for both, but this has little impact on the Husserlian scheme he is setting out. The important thing for him is the notion of essences. He quotes Husserl: "Essence [*eidos*] is a new sort of object. Just as a datum [*dannoe*] of individual or experiencing intuition is an individual object, so a datum of the intuition of essence is a pure essence" (Shpet, *Iavlenie* 25).

From these initial observations Shpet follows Husserl into a discussion of pure consciousness, distinguishing between the immanence of the cogito (the fact of our being conscious is immanent in consciousness, therefore beyond doubt for consciousness) and the transcendence of the world of reality (because objects outside consciousness are not immanent in consciousness and are therefore, strictly speaking, transcendent relative to it). In a slight modification of Husserl's theory, Shpet says that every immanent perception, by which he means every act of perception that is directed at consciousness itself (therefore immanent), is not an empirical intuition but the intuition of an essence (Shpet, *Iavlenie* 47). Shpet's topic is pure consciousness, and he follows Husserl in claiming the indubitability of the positing of one's own ego. This leads to Shpet's statement of the primary question that phenomenology must answer: "In what does the being [*bytie*] of pure consciousness consist, how can it be studied as such, and what is its content?" (Shpet, *Iavlenie* 55).

All this is a fairly routine review of Husserl's *Ideas*. Where Shpet truly betrays his own peculiar angle on phenomenology, however, is in a passage that introduces one of Husserl's most stirring and remarkable statements in the *Ideas*. Shpet is explaining the difference between transcendent being (the being of "reality") and the absolute being of consciousness. Here is what Husserl says: "Between consciousness and reality yawns a veritable abyss of meaning. On the one side a Being that exists in shadings, that gives itself fundamentally only with presumptive horizons and not absolutely, that is merely contingent and relative to consciousness; on the other side a necessary and absolute Being, fundamentally incapable of giving itself through shadings and appearance" (Husserl 117). And here is how Shpet introduces it: "What we have here is truly two worlds, two kingdoms, as in Plato, except that the kingdom of ideas stands in opposition to the world of the real not [i.e., the kingdom of ideas stands not] as reality, but as something that is in principle absolute" (Shpet, *Iavlenie* 57). Admittedly, Husserl once or twice in the *Ideas* takes up the notion of "other worlds," that is, ideal worlds like the world of geometry and imagined worlds beyond ours, but nowhere does he use the language Shpet employs here to describe the basic opposition between the natural world and the world of consciousness.

When he speaks of two kingdoms and uses Plato's name, there are several passages in Plato that Shpet could have in mind. One is certainly the famous passage in the *Phaedo* where Socrates speaks of two kinds of being, one visible and the other invisible, saying that the invisible is changeless, while the visible is ever changing, that the soul belongs to the invisible, while the body belongs to the visible (*Phaedo*

79 A-D). Another is Book VII of the *Republic*, where Socrates and his companions develop the image of the cave, the intelligible world, and the known or visible world (*Republic* 517 B-C).

Shpet might also be thinking of the passage at the end of Book IX of the same work, where the participants in the dialogue describe the way of life of a wise man. After noting that such a man will take part in only those civic activities that make him a better man, they agree that this condition can certainly be met not in the true city of the man's birth, but in "a city established only in words," the ideal city, that is, that the participants have been discussing throughout the dialogue. Socrates then says, "Perhaps in heaven there lies a model [of this city] for anyone who wishes to look at it or for anyone who, looking at it, wishes to settle there" (*Republic* 592 A-B). This passage is one source of the Christian notion of the City of God, and the city that Socrates and his companions envision is often referred to, in a spirit of retrospective Christian revisionism, as the "Kingdom of Heaven."

But in none of these passages does Plato ever use the word "kingdom" (*basileia* in Greek), nor, apart from the passage concerning the city in heaven, does he use anything similar. Instead, he uses either the word *topos* (place) or simply adjectives and participles as substantives in relatively colorless expressions like "that which is pure, eternal, and immortal." It is Plato's translators—and scholars like Shpet—who have added such words as "realm" and "kingdom."

Shpet is thus using a language that draws on both Platonism and the Christian appropriation of Platonism. Husserl certainly does not invoke Plato's name in the context of his remarks on the abyss between consciousness and reality, nor does he use the image of kingdoms, as Shpet does. In fact, the Platonic and neo-Platonic terminology is rather out of place in a discussion of this passage in *Ideas*, since Husserl's aim is to contrast the indubitability of the subjective world with the contingency of the objective world, not to claim the existence of an absolute world of ideas whose emanations we see in this world. But Shpet's impulse was clearly to impose a Platonic structure on Husserl's argument, and his language begins to take off on its own. Shpet, incidentally, was not alone among Russians in giving Husserl a Platonist, Orthodox reading. His contemporary, Sergei Bulgakov, who wrote his *Filosofiia imeni* (*Philosophy of the name*) between the time that *Appearance and Sense* and Shpet's later works on language and aesthetics appeared, had been exposed to Husserlianism, had devised an Orthodox theory of language, and had thrust a Platonic *eidos* to the forefront of that theory (Bulgakov 21). The entire phenomenological movement in Russia, in fact, has been characterized as a rereading of Husserl from a Platonist perspective (see Haardt, *Husserl* 32-34, 85-89).

The expression "two worlds" has an additional resonance, since it had recently served as the title of the opening chapter in a work Shpet quotes in *Appearance and Sense*. "Dva mira" is the title of the first "letter" in Pavel Florenskii's *The Pillar and Foundation of Truth* (*Stolp i utverzhdenie istiny*), which was published the same year as Shpet's book. It is precisely from this chapter that Shpet quotes Florenskii towards the end of *Appearance and Sense*, and the passage he quotes is precisely from a discussion of the illusory and ephemeral nature of this world as opposed to the solid pillar (*stolp*) of God's Truth (*istina* in Russian, *aletheia* in the Greek that Florenskii cites from the New Testament as the source of his title; Shpet, *Iavlenie* 212-13; Florenskii, *Stolp* 12). The phrases "kingdom of ideas" and "kingdom of the real," too, are less the choices of a Husserlian (a non-Russian one, that is) than those of a Christian religious thinker.

There is another point on which Shpet differs from Husserl, this time openly. In chapter 5, Shpet mentions Husserl's discussion of various types of being, each with its own "modes of givenness" and "method of cognition," and reproaches Husserl for failing to include social being (*sotsial'noe bytie*) in that discussion (*Iavlenie* 128-29). The notion of social being then opens up for Shpet the possibility of a challenge to the entire dualistic edifice of Husserl's system, particularly the distinction between empirical and essential intuition. Though social being quickly gets lost in the ensuing presentation of this challenge, it resurfaces briefly towards the end of *Appearance and Sense*. Shpet introduces the possibility of a third type of intuition to add to Husserl's two types and calls it "intelligible intuition," one that has to do with a type of comprehension (*urazumenie*) that appears to be tied to our position in a social world. The concept of intelligible intuition leads to this reflection: "*Absolute social solitude, the 'solitary confinement cell,' is the lot not of the individual as such but only of the madman*; to lose the capacity for intelligible intuition, for comprehension [*urazumenie*], even when the empirical and the ideal intuition exist in a state of complete perfection, means to lose one's mind, which is the sole way out of the social union" (Shpet, *Iavlenie* 207-08).

There is something terribly odd in Shpet's proposal that we consider what he had called a "third something" (*nechto tret'e*) to break up the duality of the two Husserlian intuitions (a proposal that he actually takes from Husserl himself), when he has elsewhere adopted the dualistic language of a Platonic idealist (see Shpet, *Iavlenie* 130). But here, too, he is following a tradition recently given expression in Florenskii's *Pillar and Foundation of Truth*. For the opening sections of that enormous work are devoted to exposing how we get from the "two worlds," described in the first letter, to the Christian concept of the Trinity. And Shpet's discussion of the intelligible intuition as the third member of a newly established trinity that includes Husserl's empirical and ideal intuitions immediately precedes a discussion that is really Christian doctrine in only the most thinly disguised form.

He is discussing the third type of intuition and the comprehension (*urazumenie*) associated with it, showing that a comprehension of this sort is necessary for an understanding of things that operate in a social structure. Even the concept of *expression*, one that Husserl had explored in both *Logical Investigations* and *Ideas*, takes on a new coloring in this context, he says. There are two forms of expression: a purely logical, rational one and one having to do with interpretation and comprehension (*urazumenie*). He then speaks of a "spirit of the object," saying that this spirit "finds its characterization in *logos*, 'expression,' which pervades the object and forms an appearance, a 'disclosure,' an 'incarnation' of the spirit. Its 'objectivization'

. . . is the organizing directedness for various forms of spirit in their social essence: language, religious cults, art, technology, law" (Shpet, *Iavlenie* 209-10). From here he moves on to speak of mystical comprehension, the "comprehended Spirit," and philosophy in general, which leads to the passage where he quotes Florenskii.

Shpet's discussion initially calls to mind Hegel and his notion of the manifestation of Spirit in human institutions, a notion that cannot be separated from his interest in the Christian doctrine of incarnation, or Becoming-Man (*Menschwerdung*). For Hegel, this doctrine represents a pinnacle in the development of religion because it expresses the connection between infinite being and the finite form in which that being is manifested. Shpet's reference to *logos*, too, contains an echo from Hegel, who in an analysis of the Christian Trinity, associated logos with expression (*sich äußern*) and articulation (*aussprechen*; Hegel, *Vorlesungen* 234, 239).

There is no doubt that Hegel's understanding of the incarnation had an impact on the Russian understanding of the same concept in the nineteenth and early twentieth centuries. Nowhere is this impact clearer than in Vladimir Solov'ev, who integrates into the concept of the Incarnation—and the Logos—a Hegelian notion of rational, historical process. This is how he puts it in the *Lectures on Godmanhood*:

> The incarnation of the Divinity is not something miraculous in the proper sense, that is, it is not something *alien* to the general order of being, but is instead essentially connected with the entire history of the world and of mankind, is something prepared for, something that logically follows from this history. It is not the transcendent God who is incarnated in Jesus, not the absolute plenitude of being, closed in itself (which would be impossible); it is God who is incarnated—the Word, that is, the principle that manifests itself externally and acts on the periphery of being, and its *personal* incarnation in an individual man is merely the final link in a long series of other physical and historical incarnations. (Solov'ev 165)

The emphasis is certainly different here from what it was in Hegel, who, as he surveys the world's religions, regards the *concept* of the Incarnation in Christianity as the result of an historical process (other religions had presented lesser versions of the same concept before Christianity presented its supreme version), while Solov'ev sees the *fact* of the Incarnation in an historical process (the actual Incarnation of the divinity in Jesus was the result of an historical process). We might say that Solov'ev treats the idea of the Incarnation from the point of view of faith, while Hegel treats it from the ambiguous point of view on which his readers have disagreed since his writings were published. But there can be no doubt that, by the time Shpet wrote *Appearance and Sense*, the idea of the Incarnation, complete with the Hegelian motifs it had incorporated, was largely religious in character, and this is the character it has in Shpet.

When Shpet says there is a spirit that dwells in an object and that this spirit is disclosed by being incarnate, he is using the sort of terminology used to describe icons, which allow a kind of disclosure by incarnating something immaterial. Shpet has effectively taken the world of human conscious endeavor, represented it as incarnate spirit, and claimed that, just as this world is the result of a special type of expression, it must be grasped with a special type of comprehension. Hegel, too, saw the world of human endeavor as the incarnation of spirit, but he spoke of spirit (*Geist*) in the broad sense of the term that served as the foundation for his entire philosophical system from the *Phenomenology of Spirit* on. Shpet, on the other hand, speaks of a specific "spirit of the object" and a specific type of comprehension, something that calls to mind the vision we employ when we look at an icon, "seeing" not the physical object but the invisible essence that serves as its prototype (the Mother of God, for example).

One of the items in Shpet's list of human institutions and activities is language. We know that Shpet did not choose this item purely at random, since he was later to devote so much effort to analyzing language in general and artistic language in particular. It is especially fitting that he should mention language here, though, since the context announces the guiding themes of Shpet's otherwise "phenomenological" approach to language and literary aesthetics: Platonic dualism, the view that human institutions are incarnate spirit, and the related view that social being is a necessary component of language. Philosophy of language presents especially fertile terrain for the religious element that lurks just beneath the surface in Shpet's writing, largely because of the ease with which he and other Russian thinkers conflated the notions of *word*, in the sense of a unit of ordinary language, and *Word*, in the sense of the Word of God. It thus appears that Shpet drew on earlier sources than Husserl, many of them Russian, for some of the fundamental principles of his theories of language and art, that Husserlian phenomenology provided a close fit for certain features of these principles, but that other features conflicted more or less with the recently founded "science of essences" (see Haardt, *Husserl* 31).

Shpet on Aesthetics

Shpet's most extended writing on aesthetics is his *Esteticheskie fragmenty* (*Aesthetic Fragments*), written early in 1922. These fragments, often fanciful in spirit, show the mix of phenomenology and Russian religious thought I have just described. They also establish clearly the fundamental link Shpet saw between art and language. In fact, much of the discussion in *Esteticheskie fragmenty* is given over to language.

Like many Russian critics of his generation, Shpet saw the word as a kind of formal analogy for art, and like many of the same critics, he appears to have found a basis for this belief in religious thought. As far back as Aleksandr Potebnia, Russian philosophy of language had operated on the often unsubstantiated notion that words and artworks are somehow structurally analogous to one another. And the Platonic quest for essences that always characterized philosophy of language in Russia, leading to the tenacious, metaphysical belief in a distinction between the inherent quality of poetic language and that of prose language, was itself fundamentally religious in nature.

In Potebnia the mark of Platonic essentialism was the concept of inner form, which he borrowed from the German language philosopher Wilhelm von Humboldt and modified (see Cassedy, *Flight* 39-46). For Potebnia's successors it was similar qualities. Belyi, for example, constructed an entire symbolist theory of meaning in his long essay, "The Emblematics of Meaning," that is really nothing more than a Russian Orthodox theory of icons with some of the terms changed. For Belyi the symbol is almost anything that carries creative meaning. The secret to its function is *value*, a term he had borrowed from a branch of neo-Kantian epistemology that sought to incorporate a purposive, ethical element (the recognition of value) into ordinary knowledge. Symbols carry out their function by incarnating value and presenting it to the perceiver in an accessible, concrete form. But value in Belyi's system also has the character of an ineffable, Platonic essence, which the symbol incarnates just as an icon incarnates a divine essence and presents it to the worshiper in an accessible, concrete form (see Cassedy, *Flight* 108-11; *Selected* 18-52).

Many contemporaries of Belyi and Shpet showed the same fondness for essences. Viktor Shklovskii, in his attempt to discover the difference between poetic and prosaic language, speaks mystically of images that dwell in words in their primeval (*pervonachal'nyi*) state. This is in an essay significantly titled "The Resurrection of the Word." Roman Jakobson, who spent his entire career pondering the distinction between poetic language and prosaic language, also had an abiding faith in the existence of an indwelling essence in poetic language that intrinsically set it apart from prosaic language. Like Shpet, Jakobson was a follower of phenomenology, which contributed to his search for essences in language. His famous essay on Khlebnikov, "The Newest Russian Poetry" ("Noveishaia russkaia poeziia," originally written 1919), presents the notion of *literaturnost'*, an ill-defined, essentialist term that is meant to capture the quality in literary language that distinguishes it from ordinary language.

As Shpet puts it, the word is "the prototype [*proobraz*] of all art" (Shpet, "Esteticheskie" 358). *Prototype* is not an innocently chosen word. In the theology of icons, it is customary to speak of how the honor one gives to an icon is transferred to its prototype, meaning the "original," the divine essence that is incarnate in the icon (Saint John of Damascus 1269). So it is not surprising that Shpet should quickly turn the discussion to the notion of incarnation. In art and the various forms of culture, he says, it is spirit (*dukh*) that is incarnated ("Esteticheskie" 359). This leads to a discussion of what he calls the "new realism," by which he means a realism that will be an expression of "that which *is* and not of that which *seems*" (360). The spirit that is incarnate in cultural forms is not metaphysical, Shpet says. It is something that is created but that is real only in our recognition of it, which means only in its realization, or incarnation, in an apprehensible form.

It makes sense that the word should be the prototype of all art and that art, as a cultural form, should be the result of a process of incarnation, since the word itself in Shpet's view is a form of incarnation. "The word is the archetype [*arkhetip*] of culture; culture is the cult of understanding [*razumenie*], words the incarnation of reason [*razum*]" (Shpet, "Esteticheskie" 380). It is unlikely that Shpet had systematically thought through the implications of making the word be the incarnation of reason while cultural forms are the incarnation of spirit. If we work through the details of this proposition we get the following confused picture: the word is the prototype of cultural forms, which means that it is the essence that lies behind their incarnate nature, but cultural forms incarnate spirit, and the word incarnates reason. Still, this confusion is undoubtedly not important. What is important is the general principle that language is somehow fundamental to culture and that both language and culture are strongly identified with the notion of incarnation.

And both are susceptible of phenomenological analysis. This thought immediately follows the thought that words are the incarnation of reason, since the discussion of words turns on the question of their "ontic" status. The word is both a phenomenon (*iavlenie*) of nature and a principle of culture, and this raises the issue of how our perception of natural things differs from our perception of signs (Shpet, "Esteticheskie" 380). Only a strict phenomenological analysis can resolve this issue, Shpet says, because an issue like this belongs to formal ontology, and, by implication, formal ontology is the province of phenomenological analysis (381).

And so what immediately follows these observations returns to the basic phenomenological distinction that lay at the foundation of *Appearance and Sense*. The question of the nature of the word, Shpet argues, is not one that traditional linguistic disciplines are competent to answer. It is an organic question, he says, and it has to do with how we get from an object that is sensibly perceived to a formal-ideal, which is to say an eidetic object (Shpet, "Esteticheskie" 382). The key to this distinction appears to lie in the dual status of the word: the word is both an object in nature and a fact of a particular cultural-social world. When a speaker N pronounces a word, Shpet says, we perceive that word as an indication of "the belongingness of N to some more or less narrowly recognizable [*soznavaemyi*] circle of human culture and human community, held together by the unity of language" (Shpet, "Esteticheskie" 384-85). It is in the very nature of words that we always understand them in a certain context, even at the most rudimentary level, where that context has to do only with naming things, individuals, properties, and so on (385).

Shpet now introduces a curious set of terms to describe the dual nature of words. Since there can be no meaning (*znachenie*) without a context, he says, we must distinguish between the sound of the word taken together with its intelligible meaning (*osmyslennoe znachenie*), on the one hand, and the articulate sound (*chlenorazdel'nyi zvuk*), on the other. The first he calls *logos*, and the second he calls *lexis*. Both sides of the duality show Shpet's reliance on a prephenomenological conceptual apparatus. The term *chlenorazdel'nyi zvuk* is the one Potebnia had used to describe the sound of a word considered apart from its meaning and its essential "inner form." And of course, *logos*, in addition to bearing the weight of a tradition that extends back to Heraclitus and includes, among others, Plato and Aristotle, carries the more obvious burden of the Johannine doctrine, according to which it is the second member of the Trinity, the Word made Flesh.

What seems to emerge from this analysis is an approach that confuses the duality of Husserlian eidetic analysis with the duality of Platonic idealism, drawing a correlation between the empirical of phenomenology and the material of Platonism, on the one hand, and the eidetic of phenomenology and the ideal of Platonism, on the other. Shpet asks the Husserlian question, "How can an object mean?" responds by referring to essences, and then goes on to construct a Platonic-iconological system based on the principle of the incarnation of essences.

The same fusion of systems operates in another of Shpet's writings on aesthetics, a lecture that he gave in 1922 and that was subsequently published under the title "Problemy sovremennoi estetiki" ("Problems of contemporary aesthetics"). Shpet devotes much of his discussion to a critique of aesthetic theories he disagrees with. By the time he comes to present his own views, we see that, like Waldemar Conrad before him, he has settled on the notion that the nature of a philosophical inquiry into art must be ontological, that the aesthetic object has a mode of being that merits its own peculiar type of investigation (see Haardt, *Husserl* 152).

Much of the discussion sounds like traditional phenomenological approaches to aesthetics. Shpet uses the term *aesthetic ontology* and speaks of the ontological categories of aesthetics. He analyzes the nature of the aesthetic object using a distinction similar to the Husserlian distinction he had so vigorously criticized in *Appearance and Sense*. The aesthetic object, he says, is neither an empirical-sensible object nor an ideal-thought (*ideal'no-myslimyi*) object, but lies somewhere between the two types. It has what Shpet calls *otreshennoe bytie*, an expression that one commentator has translated as "detached being" (Haardt, *Husserl* 154-55). The word *otreshennoe*, Shpet explains, is meant "to underscore [the object's] inclination to escape from pragmatic reality and its 'idealization'" (Shpet, "Problemy" 71).

Shpet then talks about the process by which detached being comes about, and the model that immediately presents itself to him is that of Plato's Demiurge, the mythic deity in the *Timaeus* who creates the real universe by using the ideal universe as a model. The creation of detached being, Shpet says, is a kind of imitation, just as the Demiurge's creation of the universe was a kind of imitation. But imitation must not be understood simplistically as mere copying. The Demiurge "reproduces, reflects [*otobrazhaet*], transmits the idea; without this the idea has neither real nor detached being. In other words," he says, "'imitation' is *incarnation*. . . . And detached being without incarnation, without transmission," Shpet goes on to say, "is not being, but nothingness." Artistic fantasy thus detaches being from its reality and "incarnates it in 'transmissible,' intelligibly expressible forms" ("Problemy" 72).

Shpet now returns to language, since what he says about art he expands to the category of signs. This allows him to introduce the notion of social being. Signs in general and cultural objects in particular are social objects. But a social object must not be understood as being a mere implement. "Signs," Shpet says, "as 'expressions' are 'imitations,' 'incarnations,' 'impressions [*zapechatleniia*]', etc., of genuine spirituality [*dukhovnost'*]." If we abstract from this spirituality we will be left with a mere thing: a canvas, a piece of paper, paints, and so on. It is in this sense that the aesthetic object must be understood as a cultural object, a sign, an expression. Because it is cultural and therefore social, it has a being that is detached, but not self-sufficient. Shpet calls this type of being "significative" (*signifikativnoe*; "Problemy" 75-76).

This is a crucial point for Shpet, because with it he revives his earlier dream of a third type of intuition, the one that took account of a set of meanings attached to a social context. Here he expands his scheme and introduces a distinction between the implements (*orudiia*) of life that are simply social and those that are cultural, claiming that the cultural possess a level of "spirituality" that the simply social lack. The implements of culture, he says, "like the implements of fundamentally spiritual being or—what is the same—the being of spiritual creation, can thus have no being apart from a spiritual being" (Shpet, "Problemy" 75). And yet the fundamental property of all "implements," social and cultural, is their incarnate nature. If cultural objects possess spirituality, that spirituality has nonetheless been expressed, incarnated in something objective. And though such objects have a peculiar mode of being, they nonetheless enter the world and dwell side by side with other objects. As Shpet points out, this is why the possibility of confusion arises: we could very well take Tolstoi's letters and use them to fuel a stove or take one of Rubens's canvases and use it as a tarpaulin ("Problemy" 75-76). It is the spirituality incarnate in these objects that sets them apart and that makes any assault on them so barbaric.

What is the status of cultural objects? One can reason to the conclusion that cultural objects are isolated and removed from the world of social reality, or one can reason to the conclusion that, while these objects enjoy a different mode of being, they still take up residence in the social world. The first conclusion would represent a Platonism that stressed the divorce of essence or idea from the world of human experience. The second represents a reconciliation between the two, and this is the one that Shpet adopts.

In arriving at this conclusion Shpet is showing his indebtedness to a tradition of Christian thought that goes back at least as far as the eighth-century church father, Saint John of Damascus, and that in Shpet's time had already grown to prominence in Russian religious thought. It is the tradition that takes the incarnation and focuses on the fleshly side of it, deriving joy from the sacred origin of matter instead of regarding matter as something that is removed from the sacred and that is therefore base and profane.

This is what Saint John had done in his celebrated work in defense of holy icons. Icons, Saint John had argued, incarnate a prototype that is immaterial, namely God. When we venerate icons, it is not the physical picture we honor, but the prototype, and yet we celebrate the fact of that prototype's taking on a material form that is apprehensible to us. What is true of icons is true of matter in general, Saint John had said. God made matter and dwells in it; for this reason we must not despise it but must honor it as the work of God. Matter includes not only physical substance, but the whole world of human social institutions, which, too, we must honor as the work of God (see Saint John of Damascus).

By the time of Shpet, the notion that matter and human institutions are to be venerated had already long enjoyed considerable favor in Russian Orthodox thought. The eleventh-century founder of Russian monasticism, Saint Theodosius, made a point of locating his cloister at the margins of urban life in Kiev, in order that the monks might participate in the affairs of the world, and he actively involved himself in social life. Theodosius's rejection of asceticism in favor of "going into the world" was a reflection of his view that the world was something estimable, something that was not beyond the concern of a religious man (Fedotov 110-31). In more recent times, the same attitude had found literary expression in Dostoevskii's *The Brothers Karamazov,* where Alesha Karamazov, on the advice of the *starets* Zosima, decides to bridge the gap between the spiritual and the worldly by leaving his monastery to "dwell in the world" (*prebyvat' v miru*).

At the end of the nineteenth century the veneration of matter finds expression in a term that an obscure Russian theologian appropriated from nineteenth-century German Protestant theology. The theologian was Mikhail Mikhailovich Tareev, a professor at the Moscow Theological Academy, and the term was *kenosis. Kenôsis* (Greek for "emptying") refers to the act, described in Philippians 2:7, by which Christ humbled himself (literally, emptied himself of divinity) in order to take the form of a man. The kenotic tradition in Germany stressed the human, historical Christ and spawned many historical-biographical treatments of Christ, of which the best known is undoubtedly David Friedrich Strauss's *Das Leben Jesu* (1835-1836). But while the Germans used the fact of Christ's kenosis to construct an anthropology of the Son of God, Tareev and other Russian religious thinkers, making of kenosis a sort of corollary to the Incarnation, used it to construct a theology of human experience, to see the converse of what the Germans saw, namely the penetration of the divine into the human. Here Tareev drew on a concept that would dominate all subsequent Russian religious thought, namely Solov'ev's Godmanhood (see Valliere 60-77).

Florenskii used *kenosis* in the same way, seeing the humiliation of God and his dwelling among the creatures he made as a sign that the world of God's creatures must be venerated. In submitting to the laws of the created world, Florenskii says in one place, God has modestly, humbly shown his creatures his light, but without dazzling them (*Stolp* 289). But, as Florenskii says elsewhere, that created world is itself a miracle, a revelation of divinity (*Stolp* 317). This belief apparently works its way into his view of language. Here, as in the case of the kenosis, it is the world, specifically the world of social institutions, that attracts his attention. In the same year that Shpet read "Problemy sovremennoi estetiki" as a lecture, Florenskii wrote an essay on language in which he referred to the rootedness of all language in a specific lived context. Florenskii rejects a more strictly Platonic view of words as containing fixed, ahistorical essences. This is the view that had been around in Russian philosophy of language since Potebnia, who identified the "inner form" of the word with its etymological root and assigned to that root a sort of timeless, mythic status (see Cassedy, *Flight* 39-42). For Florenskii, the inner core of the word "constantly wavers, it breathes, it is iridescent and has no independent meaning that exists separately from this speech of mine, spoken right here and now, in the whole context of lived experience and also in the present place of this speech" ("Stroenie" 352).

So when Shpet insists on the social dimension of language and art and uses that insistence to assert a departure from Husserl, he is returning to a tradition of long standing in the religious thought of his own culture but whose application to the philosophy of art and language was relatively recent. When he squarely places cultural objects in the social world while claiming a distinct status for them, he is likening them to the kenotic Christ (in the Russian, not the German sense) and to icons, that is, to objects that contain an otherworldly essence, dwell in this world, and thereby point to the miraculous origin of this world.

Shpet and the Inner Form of the Word

The work for which Shpet is best known is devoted almost entirely to language. It is *The Inner Form of the Word* (*Vnutrenniaia forma slova*), whimsically subtitled *Études and Variations on Themes of Humboldt*. *Variations* is the important word in the subtitle, because Shpet's approach to language in this work shows a substantial reinterpretation of his German predecessor in a way that is consistent with his own Platonism (fused, as we have seen, with doctrinal elements derived from Russian Christian iconology), on the one hand, and his emphasis on the human, social world as a primary factor in language, on the other. Shpet accomplishes much of his reinterpretation in the way he translates Humboldt's original into Russian. For example, in the chapter in which he introduces Humboldt's ideas on language, he refers to an essay by Humboldt on the writing of history and repeatedly insists on the term *incarnation* (*voploshchenie*), claiming to find it in Humboldt's essay. In Shpet's rendition, Humboldt says that "in every human individuality one can see the form of the incarnation of an idea, just as one can in every nationality." He also attributes to Humboldt the thought that language is the incarnation of spirit and idea. In fact, Humboldt never uses any of the customary German words for incarnation (*Verkörperung*, *Menschwerdung*, *Inkarnation*) in the passages to which Shpet refers. The word *voploshchenie* is entirely Shpet's contribution. On individuality and the nation, what Humboldt actually says is this: "Every human individuality is an idea grounded in appearance [*Erscheinung*], and from some [individualities] this idea shines forth so radiantly that it appears to have taken on the form of the individual only so as to be able to reveal itself in that form. . . . It is no different with the individuality of nations." And on language, what Humboldt actually says, after pointing out that languages are "ideal forms" and that the "spirit of the nation" is reflected (*sich spiegelt*) in every language, is this: "Its own essence and its inner coherence are so powerful and determining . . . that every important language appears to be the peculiar form of the generation and communication of ideas" (Shpet, *Vnutrenniaia* 33; Humboldt, "Über die Aufgabe" 603-04).

In the same section of *The Inner Form of the Word,* Shpet mentions Hegel, crediting him with the notion of the "fatal necessity of the material incarnation of spiritual culture in its historical development" (*Vnutrenniaia* 33). He goes on to say that the same notion appears in Humboldt, and he paraphrases Humboldt: "The eternal original ideas of all that can be thought [*vsego myslimogo*] find for themselves an incarnation: beauty in corporal and spiritual images, truth in the immutable action of forces according to laws inherent in those forces; law in the inexorable movement [*khod*] of events that eternally condemn and punish themselves" (*Vnutrenniaia* 34). Once again, Shpet has inserted the notion of incarnation in a place where it was at most only suggested. What Humboldt actually says is slightly different. He has just finished claiming that language is "the peculiar form of the generation and communication of ideas. . . . The eternal original ideas [*Urideen*] of all that can be thought [*alles Denkbaren*]," he continues, "even more purely and fully [than in the case of language] obtain for themselves existence and validity [*Geltung*]: beauty in all corporeal and spiritual forms [*Gestalten*], truth in the immutable action of every force according to the law [*Gesetz*] that dwells in that force, law [*das Recht*] in the inexorable movement [*Gang*] of events that eternally condemn and punish themselves" (Humboldt, "Über die Aufgabe" 604).

There is no doubt that Humboldt's thought in his essay on the writing of history contains what might sound like elements of Platonism and Christian neo-Platonism. The notion of the individual and the nation as "an idea grounded in appearance" that reveals itself could pass for a doctrine of history as Christian revelation, though it probably has its source in Schelling. But there is very little in Humboldt's thoughts on language in this essay that could be mistaken for Incarnation theology or for the sort of Platonism that Shpet reads into it. Here, as elsewhere in Humboldt, the essence of language has to do with its ability to mediate between subjective inwardness and objective reality, and subjective inwardness is connected with concerns—above all, national concerns—that transcend the individual. Language for Humboldt is constantly creating and regenerating itself through time, and this, not a theory of incarnation, is the reason for the assertion that language reflects the spirit of the nation (see Cassedy, *Flight* 35-38). In Humboldt, the features of language that transcend the bounds of individual experience are creative, fluid, always changing. The way Shpet puts it, one would think Humboldt had seen language as mediating between the material world and a world of fixed, religious truth.

Later in *The Inner Form of the Word* Shpet returns to the terminology of both iconology and phenomenology, saying that the word in its formal structure is "the ontological prototype of every cultural-social 'thing'" (*Vnutrenniaia* 140). Several pages after this remark Shpet makes roughly the same statement about language in general: it is "the prototype of every cultural-social phenomenon [*fenomenon*]" (143). The context is a discussion of art and a distinction that by now had become time worn in Russian thought, namely the one between the language of poetry and the language of prose. Since the time of Potebnia this distinction had been bound up with the question of inner form, because for Potebnia poetic language was language in which inner form was in evidence, while prosaic language was language characterized by the "oblivion of inner form" (Potebnia 134). Words function successfully, Potebnia had said, when the inner form (equivalent to the etymological root) is recognizably joined to the outer form, which he identifies with the sound of the word. When this happens, the word has what Potebnia calls "objective" meaning. In this view of inner form, then, words function iconically, that is, they take an unchanging essence like the etymological root of a word and incarnate it, make it objective (see Cassedy, *Flight* 39-46; Potebnia 77).

The doctrine of inner form and the poetry-prose distinction in Russian thought had thus by tradition been iconic and essentialist in nature. As in his earlier writings on aesthetics, Shpet shows that Platonic essentialism and iconicity are tied to a rootedness in the social and cultural world. This is because for him the important factor in incarnation is the material condition in which the incarnate quality ends up. Invoking the name of Humboldt, he repeatedly insists on the social and cultural context both for language in general and for art—which includes artistic language—in particular: art is a "social fact," and language is a "social thing" (*Vnutrenniaia* 141, 175).

Conclusion

Husserlian phenomenology had taught Shpet the distinction between two types of intuition, one empirical, the other eidetic. It had taught him the "reduction" by which we eliminate all natural presuppositions about the world or all specific features of an object in order to arrive at an essence: the essence of pure consciousness or the essence of an object. That is because for phenomenology the important thing was the subject's or the philosopher's ability to arrive at an *eidos*, or essence.

For Shpet the important thing is how the essence arrives at *us*. Russian religious thinkers are interested in the miracle by which an essence from the realm of the divine takes on material form, since the incarnation of divinity, by allowing fleshly beings to share indirectly in the experience of that divinity, creates the possibility of an earthly brotherhood in Christ. Shpet is interested in the process by which essences from the realm of meanings take on material form, since the incarnation of these essences—by allowing social creatures to share in the exchange of meanings—creates the possibility of a social-cultural structure. Phenomenology thus provided Shpet with a model of a modern, seemingly secular "science" of meanings and essences, but because of its dualism and its essentialism, it also satisfied the Platonist in him. It was a fairly easy step from the eidetic intuition of Husserl and his followers to the iconic vision that Shpet shared with so many of his overtly religious contemporaries. And, just as it had been for a whole line of Russian and non-Russian theologians in the Orthodox tradition going all the way back to Saint John of Damascus, it was an easy step from the iconic vision to the celebration of matter and the modern belief in the rootedness of human experience in a social-cultural context.

Note

The permission of Springer Verlag to reprint here an updated version of Steven Cassedy's article is gratefully acknowledged.

Works Cited

Bulgakov, Sergei. *Filosofiia imeni*. Paris: YMCA, 1953.

Cassedy, Steven. *Flight from Eden: The Origins of Modern Literary Criticism and Theory*. Berkeley: U of California P, 1990.

Cassedy, Steven, ed. *Selected Essays of Andrey Bely*. Berkeley: U of California P, 1985.

Conrad, Waldemar. "Der ästhetische Gegenstand. Eine phänomenologische Studie." *Zeitschrift für Ästhetik und allgemeine Kunstwissenschaft* 3 (1908): 71-118, 469-511; 4 (1909): 400-55.

Fedotov, George. *The Russian Religious Mind (I): Kievan Christianity. The 10th to the 13th Centuries*. Belmont: Nordland, 1975.

Florenskii, Pavel. *Stolp i utverzhdenie istiny: Opyt pravoslavnoi feoditsei v dvenadtsati pis'makh* 1914. Westmead: Gregg, 1970.

Florenskii, Pavel. "Stroenie slova." *Kontekst 1972*. Moscow: Nauka, 1973. 344-75.

Haardt, Alexander. *Husserl in Rußland: Phänomenologie der Sprache und Kunst bei Gustav Špet und Aleksej Losev*. Munich: Fink, 1993.

Hegel, Georg Wilhelm Friedrich. *Vorlesungen über die Philosophie der Religion. Werke*. Vol. 16-17. Ed. Eva Moldenhauer and Karl Markus. Frankfurt am Main: Suhrkamp, 1969.

Humboldt, Wilhelm. "Über die Aufgabe des Geschichtschreibers." *Werke*. Vol. 1. Stuttgart: Cotta, 1960-81. 585-606.

Husserl, Edmund. *Ideen zu einer reinen Phänomenologie und phänomenologischen Philosophie. Buch 1: Allgemeine Einführung in die reine Phänomenologie*. The Hague: Martinus Nijhoff, 1950.

Ingarden, Roman. *Vom Erkennen des literarischen Kunstwerks*. Tübingen: Max Niemeyer, 1968.

John of Damascus, Saint. "Pro sacris imaginibus." *Patrologiae Cursus Completus: Series Graeca*. Vol. 94. Ed. J.-P. Migne. Paris, 1857-1866. 1227-1419.

Natanson, Maurice. *Edmund Husserl: Philosopher of Infinite Tasks*. Evanston, IL: Northwestern UP, 1973.

Potebnia, Aleksandr. *Mysl' i iazyk*. Kiev: Gosudarstvennoe Izdatel'stvo Ukrainy, 1926.

Shpet, Gustav. "Esteticheskie fragmenty." *Sochineniia*. Moscow: Pravda, 1989. 343-472.

Shpet, Gustav. *Iavlenie i smysl. Fenomenologiia kak osnovnaia nauka i ee problemy*. Moscow: Germes, 1914.

Shpet, Gustav. "Problemy sovremennoi estetiki." *Iskusstvo* 1 (1923): 43-78.

Shpet, Gustav. *Vnutrenniaia forma slova (etiudy i variatsii na temy Gumbol'ta)*. Moscow: Gosudarstvennaia Akademiia khudozhestvennykh nauk, 1927.

Solov'ev, Vladimir. "Chteniia o bogochelovechestve." *Sobranie sochinenii*. Vol. 3. Brussels: Foyer Oriental Chrétien, 1966. 1-181.

Valliere, Paul. "M.M. Tareev." Dissertation. Columbia University, 1974.

Vladimir Solov'ev and the Legacy of Russian Religious Thought in the Works of Gustav Shpet

Maryse Dennes

The task of studying Vladimir Solov'ev's legacy as well as that of Russian religious thought in the works of Gustav Shpet should come as no surprise since the publication of Tatiana Shchedrina's book on the intellectual biography of Gustav Shpet in 2004. So far only a few papers have been devoted to this topic (see Boiko; Cassedy; Noskov; Epina, "G.G. Shpet," "Tvorchestvo"). The approach I use here will shed further light on this subject. I attempt to demonstrate that such a legacy is not only present in Shpet's works, but also has a pivotal role, insofar as it allows the Russian philosopher to take an active part in developing classical philosophy, thanks to the introduction of elements from the Russian religious tradition. It is indeed surprising to find Gustav Shpet—commonly considered a nonreligious philosopher—standing on the borderline between Russian religious thought and classical Western philosophy. In philosophy, according to Shpet, questions—in the way they are formulated—are invested with a national specificity, whereas scientifically accurate answers must reveal a universal meaning "for all people and for all languages" ("Ocherk" 12). Does that mean that Gustav Shpet, when using concepts from the tradition of Russian religious thought, does so because he has not yet answered with enough scientific precision the questions he has asked? In fact, Shpet's use of such concepts is his way of signalling questions that cannot receive their answers in the rationally delineated manner characteristic of the Western tradition.

What remains a philosophical problem for Shpet is the "I," its limits and social significance. And this is the reason why when trying to define the specificity of the "I"—without succeeding in getting a "scientific" answer—Shpet keeps on using a concept borrowed from Russian religious thought, that is, not quite liberated from its national specificity. This concept is *sobornost'*. It allows the philosopher to distinguish himself from all the Western philosophers, who—since Kant and Fichte, and, in particular, within the framework of Protestantism—have set the "I" as the starting point of philosophy and thus have defended subjectivism. This also allows Shpet to discover traces of subjectivism even in philosophers who criticized this trend (Natorp, Husserl). By referring to several Russian philosophers, Shpet was indeed able to put forward the concept of *sobornost'* which allowed him to open new vistas in research concerning the essence of the "I"—and thus to indicate what we must understand when talking about *consciousness*. These Russian philosophers mentioned by Shpet in his 1914 book, *Appearance and Sense*, and later, in 1916, in "Consciousness and Its Owner," are among the most conspicuous representatives of Russian philosophical-religious thought: Pavel Florenskii (qtd. in *Appearance and Sense*), as well as Sergei Trubetskoi and Vladimir Solov'ev (qtd. in "Consciousness and Its Owner").

Shpet seldom referred to Solov'ev in his texts. Indeed, the references are almost exclusively concentrated in "Consciousness and Its Owner" and they apparently do not seem—at first sight, at least—to concern the main theme of the treatise. They are rather like corns strewn in the text in order to strengthen Shpet's philosophical approach and hypotheses. Above all, Shpet refers to Solov'ev to enlist his help in raising the question about the essence of consciousness. It is instructive to quote this short text:

> I will only recall V. Solov'ev's warning: "As a matter of fact, not only should every answer be checked through precise thinking, but this is also demanded of every question. In daily life, one can ask, without much thought, 'Whose overcoat is this?,' or 'whose *galoshes* are those?'" But, in philosophy, are we really entitled to ask "whose consciousness is it?" . . . This very question is a philosophically unacceptable expression of a dogmatic certainty about the unrelated [*bezotnositel'nom*] and self-identical being of individual existences. But it is exactly this certainty that needs to be examined and justified by indisputable logical conclusions [drawn] from self-evident data . . . In the present state of things, to the question "whose consciousness is it?" . . . one can and must reply: *that's unknown* [*neizvestno*]." ("Soznanie" 76-77)

Here ends, in Shpet's text, the first reference to Solov'ev's article published in 1897 and dealing with the first principle of theoretical philosophy. It may be interesting to note that, after this quotation, Shpet asserts that "the 'I' is really a problem and in no case is it a base or a principle" ("Soznanie" 77). It means that if Shpet refers to Solov'ev it is because he looks for a confirmation, in Russian thought, of the fact that he has posed a question, to which there has been as yet no answer. Solov'ev also allows Shpet to confirm the meaning of his own question: with regard to the problem of the "I" and of consciousness, the so called scientific answer, put forward by the majority of Western philosophers, does not tally—according to Shpet—with self-evident data. Consequently, that question has no universal, or scientific, value. It must be subject to renewed doubt and sobriety, and it thus can and should be asked again within the framework of Russian thought. For Shpet, drawing support from Solov'ev, it means that we must turn to a deeper understanding of Being, that we must look for new principles, and also that such a search can be carried out only from the premises of a nationally specific and concrete experience.

The second mention of Solov'ev by Shpet is another approving reference to the above-mentioned text: "Solov'ev was profondly right when he juxtaposed this question ["whose consciousness is it?"] to the questions 'whose overcoat, whose *galoshes*?' If under 'consciousness' and 'unity of consciousness' we understand an *ideal* object, i.e., if we consider it in its essence, it is then meaningless to ask *whose* consciousness it is" ("Soznanie" 108). It is clear from this passage that for Shpet, consciousness does not belong to a personal and distinct "I." If consciousness is a whole, it then corresponds to an ideal object, and for that reason, as a whole, it concerns not only one subject but a plurality of subjects. Consciousness is thus a "gathering" (*kollektiv i sobranie*; "Soznanie" 108).

In a note added to the first of these quotations, Shpet recalls the fact that Solov'ev did not finish the work from which he now quotes and expresses his wish to draw "all the conclusions which can be drawn from the presuppositions of this unfinished work" ("Soznanie" 77). In other words, Shpet feels that there are in Solov'ev's thinking presuppositions that, owing to the way in which he presented his thoughts, remained hidden and are yet to be uncovered. References to other Russian religious thinkers, heirs to Solov'ev, could thus contain what Shpet was unable to find directly in Solov'ev's works; such references could therefore be used to throw light on what was left hidden in Solov'ev's writings.

It is interesting to note that at the close of the last chapter of *Appearance and Sense*, Shpet turns precisely to one of the representatives of the Russian religious tradition. But he mentions him in passing (in a footnote), on the fringes of the main discussion, and by way of digressing from his purely philosophical reflexions. Yet if we try to approach this enigmatic text, we may begin to understand how and why the rigorous philosophical analysis intermingles with elements from Russian religious thought. One should emphasize that the allusion to mystical experience, although remaining on the fringe, has a close, and yet hidden, link with the main discussion. The allusion in question refers to that capacity of human nature which enables man to alter his relation to the world. In the context of Shpet's thought, it is related to his reflexions on the possibility for man to participate, through what is called "neutrality modification," in the construction of reality. Here lies hidden an allusion to the fundamental freedom of each "I" which recognizes itself through the modifications produced by man's activities in the surrounding world. In that sense, the reference to "the mystical perception" does not tally with any criterion of rational comprehension: "The mystical comprehension of experience"—Shpet writes—implies "a satisfaction of the demand for its *acceptance* by the comprehensible Spirit itself" (*Appearance* 163). The expression here is cryptic but can be clarified. It leads us to the concept of *Spirit*, which can be understood precisely through a certain requirement inherent in mystical experience and in the comprehension of this experience. However, such a requirement assumes that there is no human solitude ; rather, for Shpet this requirement indicates the capacity of man to penetrate the depth of Being and to take root in the realm of culture that essentially keeps humans together. Spirit enables everyone to discover the roots of the "rational" (163), that is, to find oneself in primary communion with the others. Shpet writes: "The elimination of 'solitude' through the common feature of birth and the consanguinity of all that is 'rational' in an all-encompassing social union and in the motivation of Its Objectivations is, in this sense, the pillar of the Spirit itself" (163).

For the first time Shpet alludes here to *sobornost'*, although not explicitly. In that sentence, also the word "pillar" (*stolp*) appears: "the pillar of the Spirit itself." Shpet's allusion to Pavel Florenskii and his main work, *The Pillar and Ground of the Truth,* is made explicit later in the text when Shpet quotes from the Russian philosopher and furnishes a footnote with a lengthy comment on Florenskii's words. In that footnote Shpet cites a brief sentence from *The Pillar and Ground of the Truth*: "From the depths of the soul, however, arises an irrepressible need to rely upon 'The Pillar and Ground of the Truth'" (*Appearance* 165; translation modified). On the one hand, Shpet expresses his agreement with Florenskii: "It is not difficult to see that in a 'peculiar' comprehension, what Florenskii holds is an idea to which we also adhere." But he is also questioning Florenskii's stance: "But why must this 'need' be satisfied, and why must it turn away from the place where 'everything shakes'?" (165).

Shpet criticizes Florenskii for understanding "mystical experience" as a dismissal of this world, whereas for him, Shpet, the mystical experience—or the mystical perception—is the highest form of comprehension and of man's presence in the world, made possible by the sharp intuition of the senses. According to Shpet's interpretation of Florenskii, this mystical experience is firmly rooted in Divine life, but it comes true only after man had "eaten of the tree of knowledge of good and evil," that is, after having placed oneself on an equal footing with God, thus penetrating the so-called world of Sin (*Appearance* 166). The questions put to Florenskii by Shpet could be reduced to this: should we move away from that original Sin? The point is that the so-called Sin is a crime, "lawlessness," "a transgression [*prestuplenie*] over the border" (166), in the sense we mean when speaking about "*over*-wise" (*pre-mudryi*), "*over*-good" (*pre-blagii*), "*over*-beautiful" (*pre-krasnyi*; 166). For Shpet, the situation of man in the world (if we take into account what constitutes the essence of that "Being-within-the-world," i.e., the link between Being and Logos), is what makes *trans*-gression possible. In other words, what does make *trans*-gression possible is man's knowledge of "the Comforter, *qua Hypostasis*" (166), of the "Holy Spirit." If knowledge is comprehension, it then engenders sin while still surpassing it. That is why it might be better to say, as Shpet does, that from the point of view of philosophy, there is no sin. Indeed, Shpet stresses the fact that Florenskii considers the problem from a theological point of view, whereas Shpet's perspective is strictly philosophical. That does not mean there is no mystical perception for Shpet. That perception exists. Being the deepest form of man's presence in the world, it is thereby distinct from the religious attitude that considers this world as the world of sin and turns away from it. For Shpet, to sum up, sin, if it nonetheless exists, does so as a "transgression" embodied in the acts of comprehension. At the bottom of these acts of transgression there lies the "need" of man to surmount "the essential antinomical character, the contradiction, that penetrates each one and everything without exception" (*Appearance* 165), the desire to *be* in what brings us together. This desire manifests itself through the act of comprehension. Such an act, which in *Appearance and Sense* Shpet calls "hermeneutic," enables man to determine the basic elements that make up the structure of the world (i.e. the Logos, i.e. the Being). For Shpet, that act of *comprehension* (an essentially hermeneutic act), appears also to be an act of "mystical perception". Just as the reference to "mystical perception" in Florenskii's writings, "mystical perception" is also a philosophical "*transgression,*" although it is a constituent part of philosophy itself. But the reference to Florenskii plays another role as well. In Shpet's work, it acts as a *trans*-gression *sui* generis, propelling the philosopher forward, beyond the limits of the "*comprehensible,*" and *compelling* him to take into account the legacy of the Russian religious thinkers who developed the concept of *sobornost'* –which seemed necessary in order to express that mystically-transgressive experience of true comprehension. The concept of *sobornost'* draws attention to that level of reality where everyone takes root in what is one's essence and *entelechy* (see Shpet's treatment of entelechy in *Appearance* 150).

   "Consciousness and Its Owner," as we have seen, is Shpet's work in which the philosopher clearly addresses the Russian religious tradition, and in which the philosophical reflections developed in *Appearance and Sense* remain in the background. Yet it is interesting to examine how the two fields intersect, and how the questions that are asked on the basis of Russian religious thought remain problematic, whereas when approached from the perspective of philosophical thinking, they begin to receive an answer (in particular, when Shpet, in the last two chapters of *Appearance and Sense*, outlines the basic elements of the structure of the word). The reference to Solov'ev in "Consciousness and Its Owner" enabled Shpet to strengthen the premises of his questions and his criticism of subjectivism. But these references are pushed to the background when Shpet begins to look for the possibility of developing and formulating his views on the priority of supra-individual consciousness. He then turns to Sergei Trubetskoi and, referring to his "On the nature of human consciousness" (1889), writes: "in his afore-mentioned article, S.N. Trubetskoi adduced a plethora of empirical arguments in favour of the collectivity or *sobornost'* of consciousness." Significantly, Trubetskoi's findings are confirmed for Shpet by a French psychologist who cannot be suspected of any sympathy for Russian religious thought. Quoting at length from the Introduction to Lévy-Bruhl's *Les Fonctions mentales*, Shpet asserts: "We have a science—whatever we call it—whose object is consciousness [from Lévy-Bruhl:], a consciousness, whose existence does not depend on the individual. Not because the data of that consciousness presuppose a collective subject [*un sujet collectif*], different from the individuals forming a social group, but because those data are characterized by features that one cannot derive by just considering the individuals as such" ("Soznanie" 110-11). Thus a Western thinker becomes for Shpet the ally of his home intellectual tradition, in which important impulses came from religious thinkers such as Solov'ev and Trubetskoi. In order to translate their idea of *sobornost'* into the universal (dominant) language of Western philosophy, Shpet resorts once again to Lévy-Bruhl: we perceive constantly "images of action, thought and feeling,

whose remarkable specificity is their existence outside individual consciousnesses"
("Soznanie" 111). This is why the question, "whose" is no more than purely rhetorical
when addressed to consciousness. Thus for the Russian philosopher there is a non-
individual consciousness that has its own thoughts and its own feelings; he submits
that people are essentially determined by being part of that form of consciousness.
For Shpet, consciousness is both an instrument and an embodiment of the "principle
of entelechy" that works successfully within it. In this dual capacity, "consciousness
itself works as something already apprehended by consciousness" ("Soznanie" 113).

Shpet terms those who realise the passage from the act of consciousness to
what is apprehended by consciousness *first names*. First names stands for the so-
called *imreki* (i.e., individual persons), which no analysis can completely comprehend. They can be identified by the traces they leave in the surrounding world, but
also through a description of the various spheres of reality and the modifications
generated by their actions within these spheres. Comprehension of this fact is itself
already a participation in a higher and unifying consciousness, destroying no "I," but
on the contrary: allowing each "I" to fulfill itself.

At the end of "Consciousness and Its Owner," Shpet comes closer to an explanation of the experience to which he has alluded at the end of *Appearance and Sense*
when he referred to Pavel Florenskii: "*Sobornoe* [what is brought together] in its essence and its essential types is an independent sphere of research" ("Soznanie" 114).
For Shpet, it is only through experience, and not by drawing on the field of previously established knowledge, that one can discover collective (*sobornoe*) consciousness. This is the reason why collective consciousness is not an area of generalization
(*obobshchenie*), but an area of interconnection (*obshchenie*). One has access to it,
Shpet writes, through common participation (*souchastie*), communion (*soprichas-
tie*), and complicity (*soprichastnost'*). Here the allusion to religious mystery is quite
clear. It echoes the interpretation of the prayer "Our Father, who art in Heaven,"
which Shpet puts forward a little further in the text ("Soznanie" 109-10). Thus it is
no wonder that, at the end of that passage, Shpet again turns more specifically to religious consciousness: "Consciousness, e.g. religious consciousness, can be considered not only as general [*obshchee*] but as collective [*obshchnoe*]" ("Soznanie" 115).
For Shpet, the realm of the general is the realm of form. Every type of consciousness
(whether religious, aesthetic, or scientific) has its own form and its own categories
and criteria of emergence and evolution. Yet this is not what Shpet wants to show.
Instead, he attempts to determine the meaning of each type of consciousness. He
tries to discover what, in *Appearance and Sense*, was already implied in the expression "hermeneutic act." He considers in particular religious consciousness because
it reveals itself in concrete experience which allows a unity of "[necessary] prereq-
uisites" and liberty, that is, of what already "is" and of what can be created anew. He
also turns to religious consciousness in so far as it permits the recovery of the utmost
profoundness of human experience, of that which, through the action of each *imrek,*
inclines this *imrek* to commune with the others. Shpet had already alluded to that
when he dismissed the Aristotelian two-dimensional logic ("Soznanie" 29-30) and

proposed in its place another logic, one that makes it possible "to leave the level of rational thought and to fathom the depth, the innermost being of the subject through a comprehension of this innermostness [*intimnosti*]" ("Soznanie" 29). He had suggested the limitations of such logic (of such a science of Logos) in *Appearance and Sense,* where he used the term *entelechy* to bring together and unite "significance" and "sense" within the same act of comprehension. This theme runs through "Consciousness and Its Owner" as well: "Significance and sense are 'disturbing' for logic and darkening its formal purity" ("Soznanie" 30).

The question, then, invites itself: Does Shpet's interpretation of consciousness mean that the *imrek* can be fully defined by his participation in the *sobor* (community)? Things are a little more complicated than that. At the end of the text, after Shpet has for the last time referred to Sergei Trubetskoi, he objects to *sobornost'* as a simple solution to the problem of consciousness: "The cunning thing is not to 'keep communion [*sobor*] with everybody,' but to find *oneself* next to the community [*mimo sobora*], to find oneself in one's own, personal [*imiarekovaia*] freedom, not in the communal [*sobornaia*] one" ("Soznanie" 116). But then, one could wonder, where is the so called "freedom of the *imrek*" (*imiarekovaia svoboda*)? Shpet himself notes that it would be unreasonable to assume it existed. In a barely veiled reference to Chekhov's story, "Chamber No. 6," he asserts that absolute personal consciousness, and therefore freedom, remains an unresolved issue: "Not because it is unlikely, but because it is irrational, i. e., ineffable. On the ground of reason and comprehension [*urazumenie*], such a 'personal [being]' is no longer 'mine,' because it is no longer I who is 'possessed' [*oderzhimyi*], not the *imrek*, but "Chamber No. N . . . ." ("Soznanie" 116).

Russian religious tradition, through such representatives as Solov'ev, Florenskii, and Trubetskoi, gave Shpet the possibility to point to the concrete experience of Being, which he believed should serve as a foundation of one's act of comprehension. Does this mean that in spite of his attempt at a scientific approach, Shpet implied in his pre-1917 works that he himself belonged to a community with its own (Russian) experience of Being? He hints as much, though he doesn't say so explicitly. Maybe because this "belonging" is, for the philosopher, "irrational," that is, "ineffable," it is his "madness," his being "possessed" and, in some way, his "transgression," his "lawlessness." But in that transgression are the conditions of his existence as *imrek*. Thus one can understand why the extracts that end *Appearance and Sense* and "Consciousness and Its Owner" and that have busied us here at some length are totally enigmatic. They signal Shpet's deep and personal experience, his powerful inner sense of individual freedom, which no philosophical text can apprehend to the end, but which justifies his entire philosophical work.

Works Cited

Boiko, V.A. "Kontseptual'no-stilisticheskoe edinstvo 'Ocherka razvitiia russkoi filosofii' G.G. Shpeta." *G.G. Shpet/Comprehensio. Vtorye Shpetovskie chteniia.* Ed. O.G. Mazaeva. Tomsk: Vodolei, 1997. 195-98.

Cassedy, Steven. "Gustav Shpet and Phenomenology in an Orthodox Key." *Studies in East European Thought* 49 (1997): 81-108.

Epina, L. "G.G. Shpet i problema ponimaniia russkoi filosofii XIX v." *G.G. Shpet/ Comprehensio. Tret'i Shpetovskie chteniia.* Ed. O.G. Mazaeva. Tomsk: Vodolei, 1999. 180-87.

Epina, L. "Tvorchestvo G.G. Shpeta i problemy metodologii istoriko-filosofskikh issledovanii." *G.G. Shpet/Comprehensio. Chetvertye Shpetovskie chteniia.* Ed. O.G. Mazaeva. Tomsk: Izdatel'stvo Tomskogo universiteta, 2003. 486-90.

Noskov, A. "G.G. Shpet o russkoi filosofii." *G.G. Shpet/Comprehensio. Tret'i Shpetovskie chteniia.* Ed. O.G. Mazaeva. Tomsk: Vodolei, 1999. 174-80.

Shchedrina, T.G. *"Ia pishu kak ekho drugogo . . ." Ocherki intellektual'noi biografii Gustava Shpeta.* Moscow: Progress-Traditsiia, 2004.

Shpet, Gustav. *Appearance and Sense. Phenomenology as the Fundamental Science and Its Problems.* Trans. Thomas Nemeth. Dordrecht: Kluwer, 1991.

Shpet, Gustav. "Ocherk razvitiia russkoi filosofii." *Sochineniia.* By Gustav Shpet Moscow: Pravda, 1989. 9-342.

Shpet, Gustav. "Soznanie i ego sobstvennik" ["Consciousness and Its Owner"]. *Filosofskie etiudy.* By Gustav Shpet. Moscow: Progress, 1994. 20-116.

Part Three

Phenomenology

Shpet's Departure from Husserl

Thomas Nemeth

Already in the early 1900s, we find references to Husserl in Russian philosophical literature. N.O. Losskii mentioned him in his 1906 work *Obosnovanie intuitivizma*, where in the context of a discussion of the structure of judgmental acts Losskii quoted from the former's *Logical Investigations*. Shpet's mentor in Kiev and later Moscow, G.I. Chelpanov, a keen observer of contemporary developments abroad in philosophy and psychology, had already presented in 1900 a relatively brief synopsis of Husserl's 1891 treatise *Philosophy of Arithmetic*. Translations were soon to follow: the original first volume of the *Logical Investigations*, the "Prolegomena to Pure Logic," appeared in a Russian edition in 1909 and that of the essay "Philosophy as Rigorous Science" in 1911 (the same year as the original German publication). Until the end of World War I, Russia was arguably the most receptive country to phenomenology outside its homeland (in France, e.g., Husserl's philosophy did not begin to claim wider attention until the mid-1920s). That at least one Russian scholar should return from his *de rigueur* study abroad imbued with the ideas and concepts of the latest philosophical "star" should not surprise us. In this essay, I trace the evolution of Shpet's philosophical stand towards Husserl, particularly the transcendental idealism of the latter's 1913 *Ideas I*, and examine the additions, modifications and oversights (at times the result of sheer misunderstanding) that Husserl's phenomenology experienced at the hands of its most prominent Russian follower.

The Germination of Shpet's Phenomenology

Shpet's acquaintance with Husserl took place, more likely than not, in October or November 1912 in Göttingen (Shchedrina 53). Shpet arrived there at the beginning of April to research and write the second part of his dissertation. After spending two summer months in Moscow, Shpet returned to Göttingen to continue his writing and matriculated at the University, where Husserl taught at the time (Haardt 55-56). Certainly during this period, Shpet drew closer to Husserl both intellectually and personally. The degree to which Shpet had already become a "Husserlian" before this crucial stay in Göttingen is contentious, simply for the reason that the meager evidence is ambiguous. Around 1912 Shpet viewed psychologism as an epitome of philosophical skepticism and relativism. Just as logic needed to be purged of psychology, so too psychology needed to be purged of logic, that is, of any form of reductionism and of all category mistakes. True to its name, psychology is a study of the psyche, not of something else. Instead, modern psychology had become with its divorce from philosophy in the nineteenth century a science of psychic phenomena. It had, in Shpet's eyes, substituted empty schemata and abstractions for concrete facts. The way back for psychology lay in unprejudiced self-observation, in an analysis of immediately given mental processes (*Erlebnisse*).

Of particular interest for my discussion is that in the spring of 1913, with the publication of *Ideas I*, Husserl revealed a turn of his own to a transcendental idealism. Exactly when Shpet conceived the idea of writing a book on Husserl's new approach is unknown. On the basis of a letter, however, to Husserl dated 23 November of that year, he must have acquainted himself with the latter's new work rather quickly, despite its opaqueness, for he there remarks that he has already prepared a draft of his own work. For its publication, Shpet added a short lecture delivered in Moscow in early 1914 outlining his conception of phenomenological philosophy and a preface dated at the end of May—just one month before the start of World War I, which dramatically shattered relations between Germany and Russia. Purporting to be, at least by its original design, a primer into Husserlian transcendental phenomenology for a Russian audience, *Appearance and Sense* often expresses striking sympathy with the overall thrust of Husserl's position while nevertheless engaging in a critical assessment of those ideas. What the reader immediately recognizes is Shpet's fundamentally different concerns. Whereas Husserl combats reductionism of any sort in order to defend the objectivity of cognition, a defense that is necessary in order to establish philosophy as rigorous science, Shpet fears reductionism entails an omission of at least some forms and types of what exists. For example, Kant recognized that the cognizing subject was a non-empirical being, but he turned away from a study of this being per se, directing his attention instead solely to its functions. Assuredly, Shpet did not reject Husserl's clarion call to make philosophy into a rigorous science. It is just that in Shpet's eyes phenomenology, with its scientific rigor, provides the foundation from which his own ontological inquiries can advance. We should not be surprised, then, that Shpet devotes an entire chapter of his slim treatise to "pure consciousness," even though it is largely a summary of three chapters from *Ideas I*. Most importantly, however, Husserl's predominant concern is with delineating the essential sense-bestowing structures of consciousness that explain how the intentionality of consciousness is achieved. Shpet, on the other hand, is not ready to sunder so much of classic philosophy. While recognizing the value, even need, of Husserl's exploration of consciousness, the ultimate goal is broader: a delineation of all that actually exists, proceeding both descriptively and discursively (*Appearance* 10, 97).

Shpet manifestly accepts the phenomenological reduction, but his account of it is disquieting. That he introduces it already in the chapter preceding the one specifically entitled "The Phenomenological Reduction," contra Savin (Savin 25), should not be thought strange when we consider that Husserl himself did much the same. Nonetheless, whereas for Husserl the reduction involves the methodic exclusion of nature and, concomitantly, of all intellectual and cultural formations that presuppose the natural attitude, for Shpet the reduction is the exclusion of relative individuals, leaving the entire eidetic realm to be studied (Husserl, *Ideas* 131; *Appearance* 11, 27). In other words, in leaving the natural attitude we, nevertheless, retain the eidetic realm, the "world as eidos." All too often, Shpet speaks of the phenomenological reduction as equivalent to the eidetic reduction. To be sure, even in his "Fundamental Consideration" Husserl refers repeatedly to essences, but his point is to disentangle phenomenology, as the science of the essential structures of consciousness, from mundane psychology, that is, a psychology which presupposes, and is undertaken in, the natural attitude along with its associated contingencies.

In light of Shpet's later intellectual development, we should note his acceptance at this time of the Husserlian transcendental ego. In fact, clearly recognizing the importance of the topic, he devoted almost half of a chapter to it. In *Ideas I*, Husserl holds that the pure ego belongs to every mental process (*Erlebnis*), but it is not a residuum within the flux of such processes. Although it seems to be continually present and necessarily identical throughout every change in the mental processes, the pure ego is, in no way, a part of these processes. Consequently, the ego cannot become an object of investigation. It has neither content nor any essential components (see Husserl, *Ideas* 191). Likewise for Shpet, the ego is constant, identical and is that to which all mental processes belong. Nevertheless, despite its necessity, we cannot find it within the stream of those processes. Along with Husserl, Shpet characterizes the pure ego as a peculiar "transcendency within immanency" (*Appearance* 58; Husserl, *Ideas* 133). Thus, Shpet grants that both the object of consciousness and the pure ego are transcendent. However, a failure to recognize the *essential* difference between these transcendencies can lead to: 1) a denial of the ego, and therewith an abandonment of positive philosophy; 2) subjectivism, which explains nothing; or 3) the endowment of the object with purported properties of the ego, or vice versa (*Appearance* 61-63). In the third case, we risk lapsing into the metaphysics of materialism and spiritualism.

Shpet accedes to phenomenology studying consciousness essentially, and he recognizes that its object is acquired in another attitude involving a suspension or "bracketing" of all naturalistic assumptions. There are only two sorts of intuition: experiencing intuition, which yields individual objects, and ideal intuition, whose object is pure essences. Phenomenology, being a study of essences (*Appearances* 101) can employ only ideal intuitions. How, then, can phenomenology deal with the individual? How can we, as phenomenologists, conceptually capture the actual? Although willing to accept the notion of a purely individual essence, Shpet is evidently uncomfortable with dropping the specific "hic et nunc" of any individuation (*Appearance* 90; Husserl, *Ideas* 168). This should not be surprising if we bear in mind that his ultimate concern is with "What is?" and not with a conceptual scheme for a transcendental reality as in Kant (*Appearance* 99). In the same vein, Shpet has misgivings concerning Husserl's central theme of the sense-bestowing function of consciousness. The former certainly affirms that the essential character of consciousness is intentionality. Yet, Husserl additionally claims that the sensuous moments in a concrete mental process, moments that in themselves are not intentional, are bestowed, or "animated," with a sense. Consciousness relates to its object through sense, and it is this that has Shpet puzzled. What is there within consciousness that allows it to perform this function? Husserl's position, as Shpet understands it, is that consciousness not only synthesizes psychical contents but also introduces sense, including that of objectivity. However, in that case how do we account for the specificity of the object? Finally, if we grant that the bestowed sense includes specificity, do we not have to include sensuous material as a component of consciousness? Shpet's concern is that Husserl's position entails—whether surreptitiously or not—an intrusion of Kantianism where the actual thing recedes from view.

The role of the reduction itself remains contentious. For Husserl, it is not a tool to be eventually dropped or discarded upon reaching some independent goal. No, the reduction makes genuine philosophy possible. Although we have excluded the whole world, we have really lost nothing but have acquired the whole of absolute being which contains within itself all worldly transcendencies (Husserl, *Ideas* 113). Shpet, on the other hand, situates himself closer to Husserl's earlier position in the *Logical Investigations*, where a reflection on consciousness was seen as an interruption of our natural attitude towards an object. Throughout, Shpet's ultimate goal is to return to the actual, which is in danger of being abandoned in the reduction. For Husserl a thorough phenomenological description of the manner in which a transcendent object is constituted in consciousness leaves nothing more to be explained. Shpet, however, believes that even if the mode in which an object is given motivates a positing of the object as actual, we still need to explain what this motivation is like. If the motivation lies in the evidence, how can that givenness provide rational motivation? Nonetheless, the rational motivation for the positing of actuality is something that Husserl himself regards as misguided from the outset. There is no object behind the noemata; rather, the object is in the noemata. From a Husserlian perspective, it is Shpet who is in danger of introducing a Kantian "transcendentness" or of lapsing into metaphysical naturalism.

Another difference in the respective positions of Shpet and Husserl stems from their divergence on the "authentic sense" of the concrete object in the noemata. To see where this difference lies, let us briefly summarize one aspect of Husserl's position. Husserl remarks that the "matter" of a psychic act is its "noematic core," or simply "sense" (*Ideas* 310, 317). This sense, for example, is the "perceived apple tree as such," that is, the sense of that tree and not the physical tree that can die or be struck by lightning (*Ideas* 216). Coupled with this sense, or noematic core, are thetic components, that is, the properties of the correlated object that distinguish an act of remembering, for example, from that of imagining or of actually perceiving. The noematic core and the thetic components together comprise the full noema. One concept that results from this analysis is that of the intended object that remains unaltered despite its changing modes of appearance. For example, I can move closer to the apple tree or go around it, seeing it from different perspectives. Even though the properties of what I perceive may change, there remains a unity or identity to the sense of the object, a "pure X," that stays the same. This "X" can be looked upon as an abstract form. Indeed, it is the object abstracted from its particular properties (*Ideas* 315-16). It is this notion that arouses consternation in Shpet. For, he asks, how can an abstract form make up the content of an object (*Appearance* 148)? Are not these two notions, form and content, mutually exclusive? For Shpet, the authentic, or internal, sense of an object lies within the object. It does lie within at least those objects that we would characterize as objects of the social world.

That Shpet's position already in 1913-14 straddled the Husserl of the *Logical Investigations* and the Husserl of the *Ideas* is evident enough from the former's reservations. We know from his correspondence with Husserl at this time that he was deeply affected by the newly reprinted *Investigations* and reworked his "entire presentation" in light of the book (*Briefwechsel* 529). In a letter to Husserl in March 1914, Shpet himself raised the issue of "how 'sense' can merely be an abstract form, while being at the same time the 'content' of the noema" (*Briefwechsel* 535). Judging from a subsequent letter from May, Shpet was entirely satisfied with Husserl's reply: "I believe the question of the concrete or abstract nature of the sense in the noema is clearer to me now, because I see the source of my misunderstanding. I came to the question *from the other angle*. Certainly, the entire noema is already an abstraction, just as anything 'left over' from the whole is also an abstraction (a 'dependent something')" (*Briefwechsel* 541). Thus, assuming no disingenuousness on Shpet's part, his consternation on this point in *Appearance and Sense* was meant to serve merely as a heuristic device to emphasize his position that the sense must concern the object's concrete nature.

Returning to the main line of our narrative, although we may take any object in abstraction and find in it its concrete noema, the "object in the How of its determinations," we do not find at this level its "authentic sense." To find the latter, we must penetrate into the (social) object's "internal something," which, using Husserlian terminology from the *Logical Investigations*, is "intimated" (*Appearance* 148; Husserl, *Logical* 277). The "internal something" lies as a deeper stratum than the noematic core, for the "internal something" is revealed only in the description of the object in the How of its determinations, but is not a property of any of the predicative determinations (*Appearance* 149). Again alluding to Husserl's first "Logical Investigation," Shpet says that an object's sense as content is a sign of its "internal something." Clearly, Shpet's "internal something" is a revival of the classic (metaphysical) notion of essence which a concrete object possesses and which makes that object what it is, albeit not physically but for others. As a precaution, Shpet warns against confusing the classic notion of essence with Husserl's respective notion, that is, with the eidetic. At this point, Shpet's concern is with avoiding a collapse of the classic notion into the eidetic, resulting in a blindness toward teleology (*Appearance* 151). Indeed, if we focus on the "Hows" of the object—on what is originarily given—we will over-look the "internal something," that is, its entelechy. Phenomenologically, both an object of the social world and one purely of the natural world have determinations. However, an object of the social world has something else, entelechy, that can be seen even in the natural attitude. Passing into the phenomenological attitude, though, according to Shpet, allows us to see the situation more clearly. In particular, we can see that any object, even if it is purely natural, can, with the help of a corresponding intentional act, be made to appear as if it possessed entelechy. That is, any object can be endowed with a quasi-entelechy.

The correlation between an object of experience and its modes of givenness, that, for example, the perceptual act has a corresponding actually existing object, is a basic phenomenological tenet. Shpet wholeheartedly agrees with this Husserlian claim that each species of being essentially must have its own mode of givenness and, thereby, calls for a specific cognitive method. Thus for each species of being we can determine the respective correlative cognitive method and mode of givenness. Shpet believes, however, that Husserl has not accorded social being its due as such a pecu-liar species with its own peculiar mode of givenness. Additionally, Shpet questions whether the intuitive viewing of the other's mental processes does not present those processes originarily (*Appearance* 100; Husserl, *Ideas* 6). Manifestly, were Shpet cor-rect, the entire complexion of the problem of intersubjectivity that so plagued Husserl would be radically altered. More to the point, for the entelechy of the object there must be a correlative noesis and intuition. However, the admission of such an originariness would entail the admission of a new attitude alongside that of the natural and the phe-nomenological (eidetic). Shpet rejects this logical possibility (*Appearance* 158). Using his own example, to see that an axe chops does not, after all, require a new attitude or a third genus of intuition. Nevertheless, although we do "see" the presence of an object's entelechy in its originary givenness, it is not given directly, but by means of signs.

For Shpet, an object's entelechy lies within the core of the noematic content. Thus, the corresponding entelechic noesis forms a stratum of a positional act. As the internal core of an object, entelechy requires a distinctive act that motivates the doxa, that is, the positing of belief, but this act *lies* within a positional act and is not itself one (cf. Husserl, *Ideas* 331). Such an act that "sees" the noematic sense as a sign for entelechy, and therefore, as motivating the positional act, is hermeneutic (*Appearance* 153). In other words, the entelechic noesis is a hermeneutic act, and just as the noesis serves the function of sense-bestowal, so too does the hermeneutic act, the fulfilled expression of which is an interpretation (*Appearance* 158). Unlike with an empirical or an eidetic intuition, we cannot identify or isolate the presenta-tive moments in a mental process that reveal entelechy. We know that an axe is for chopping, but there is no property, or even properties, that show this to me. I, as a human individual, know the respective entelechies of many objects, because I was told or read about them. For example, I know the entelechy of an axe, because when I was a child my father told me about it before using the axe to clear trees in the field. In this case, the entelechy was communicated to me. By itself, this is not a breach of the phenomenological program requiring that the attribution of a sense, entelechy, be rule governed and describable. Communication itself, in fact, can be an intentional object whose essence is to be comprehensible. In *Appearance and Sense*, Shpet does provide further, specific reflections on the role of comprehension and of those objects whose essence is to be comprehensible. For us here, however, the question is the status of these thoughts vis-à-vis Husserlian phenomenology. Shpet recognizes that his discussion of entelechy, hermeneutic acts, and comprehension is absent from Husserl's own work. Yet at least for now, Shpet earnestly believes he is working within the phenomenological framework. By his own admission, he returns repeatedly to a "phenomenological analysis," saying how and what it shows (*Appearance* 156, 158, 159, 160). Two questions, therefore, arise: 1) Has Shpet revealed a genuine lacuna in transcendental phenomenology; and 2) Is this lacuna compatible with the overall framework of that phenomenology? If the answer to the first question is a "no," then, assuming Husserl is himself true to phenomenology, the answer to the second question should be in the affirmative. However, it is also possible that Shpet's own elaborations are incompatible with phenomenology.

The complexity of the Husserlian response to the first question forbids a thorough and detailed response here. It is certainly to Shpet's credit that at such an early date he already saw so much that would later lead Heidegger in *Being and Time* also to part ways with Husserl. This does not entail, though, that either Shpet or Heidegger were correct or uncovered problems Husserl could not, at least in principle, solve. All we can hope to show here is that, regardless of their cogency, Husserl was not oblivious to Shpet's concerns and their importance. To a large degree, they led Husserl from the static analysis of *Ideas* to the genetic one introduced in his subsequent writings. As he saw the matter in these writings, the task of phenomenology lies in uncovering a "sedimented '*history*'" implicit in sense constitution (Husserl, *Formal* 250). This does not mean that the phenomenologist becomes a factual historian of sense-bestowal. Rather, phenomenology contains a regressive inquiry into the structure of "the pregiven world with all of its sedimentations of sense . . . to the original life-world" (Husserl, *Experience* 50). Husserl recognized that an actual noema contains, among other things, a set of "sedimented" senses that can be unraveled. Already in *Ideas II* Husserl raised many of Shpet's concerns. Husserl there explicitly recognized that to overlook the human sciences, whose objects are personal or "cultural" accomplishments, is a form of blindness. We live in a common world with other egos. Each individual ego becomes a complete person only through a "comprehension" of our relation to the surrounding world. Through mutual determination based on comprehension, the common world acquires new senses (Husserl, *Studies* 201). In this work, Husserl also speaks explicitly of communication and of communicative acts. Was it purely coincidental, then, that many of the themes, with which Shpet concerned himself in *Appearance and Sense* and which in subsequent years would be the focus of his attention, were addressed by Husserl in *Ideas II*, an early draft of which Husserl read to a class in 1913 that we can, with some confidence, presume Shpet attended (Weiler xxviii)?

First Fruits of the New Harvest

Shpet's enormous dissertation of 1916, *Istoriia kak problema logiki*, an outstanding monument of Russian scholarship, had little to do with overt phenomenological
themes. We should not forget that he had already chosen his thesis topic before he
became familiar with *Ideas I*. Based on the lack of overt references and the paucity
of implicit ones to phenomenology in this thesis, one might conclude that already by
this time Husserl's influence was diminishing, indeed that Shpet had, for all intents
and purposes, separated himself from phenomenology. Such a judgment would be
decidedly premature. With minor reservations, most notably the lack of any hints
of transcendental idealism, Shpet remains within his earlier framework. In the first
portion of his thesis, published in his lifetime, Shpet speaks of the analysis of comprehension as a means to approach the originary given in social and historical phenomena (*Istoriia* 63). As an enterprise, history deals with documents and artifacts
that serve as signs, whose signification (*znachenie*) needs to be comprehended. As a
discipline, history is a hermeneutic science.

However, in the only recently published second portion of his work, Shpet not
only elaborates many of these points, but also shows how close he remains to his
earlier, 1913-14 stance. Phenomenology is still termed the "fundamental philosophical science," though it is not a "theory of cognition," but a "theory of the object"
(*Istoriia* 563). In a marginal note in his manuscript copy, Shpet notably adds that, in
terms of its tasks, phenomenology is an "ontology" (*Istoriia* 1158). As such, as the
fundamental science, it is a descriptive, nontheoretical study of objects with respect
to both their concrete and their abstract character. Owing to his concern with the social sciences in general, and history in particular, Shpet asks for the signification of
the concept *social*. What lies in the originary given intuition of, say, an ashtray, that
makes us recognize it as a "social thing" (*Istoriia* 1012)? In his lengthy discussion,
Shpet retains his earlier stand substantially unaltered. Suffice it to say, he mentions
eidetic intuition, though he clearly prefers the expression *intellectual intuition*. What
is given in the sensuous intuition of a social thing serves as a sign that needs understanding. As such, how we are to understand the given is "a matter of interpretation,"
the "science" of which is hermeneutics. However, "only after a phenomenological
investigation of the 'social' is a correct solution to these problems possible" (*Istoriia* 1039). Even here, in 1916, Shpet does not entirely reject the phenomenological reduction, albeit as he understood it, although he clearly implies its irrelevance
with regard to the givenness of the historical. In the "'natural understanding' of the
world"—Husserl's "natural attitude"—we find ourselves confronted with all manner
of objects, all of which are naively viewed as homogeneous. To observe the fundamental difference between the factual and the eidetic, or ideal, a separate approach,
or attitude (i.e., the phenomenological attitude) is necessary. However, with regard
to the problems of historical methodology, the phenomenological reduction is unnecessary, since "hardly anyone would think of denying the empirical givenness of
the historical and of ascribing it to ideal objects" (*Istoriia* 1082).

Only when Shpet turned once again to a topic of mutual interest did his divergence from Husserl clearly emerge. In his *Logical Investigations*, the latter stated that the "phenomenological ego" reduces a "real experiential complex" to a unity of consciousness (541). It is not, however, above experience, nor does this ego have any unity beyond that given to it by the unity of its experiences. For the contents of the ego have "their own law-bound ways of coming together . . . and, in so far as they thus become and are one, the phenomenological ego or unity of consciousness is already constituted, without need of an additional, peculiar ego-principle which supports all contents and unites them all once again" (541-42). In the intervening years before the appearance of *Ideas I*, Husserl reversed his position. By 1913, he declared he had found the phenomenological ego. Shpet, on the other hand, who also had seen it at this time, had, so to speak, lost it by 1916. Without commenting on his earlier agreement with Husserl's 1913 stand, Shpet, in his 1916 essay "Consciousness and Its Owner" reverted, as it were, to Husserl's earlier position in the *Logical Investigations*. According to Shpet, a major source of confusion in dealing with the ego is that we tend to seek a common meaning for homonyms, one of them being the word "I," or ego, which can be used in a number of senses. In saying that I live on a particular street and have certain possessions, each of us conceives of oneself as a single psychophysical organism. By ever enlarging the surroundings to which the "I," or ego, is contrasted and concomitantly narrowing the sphere of the "I," we come to an "I" that is situated within personal consciousness itself, that is, an "I" of consciousness. This last "I" is understood as the source of conscious activity analogous to the way we see our individual physical selves as the agents of our actions in the world ("Soznanie" 157). Taken alone, such a practice is, for Shpet, understandable. A difficulty arises, though, when this "I" of consciousness is interpreted on the basis of a philosophical subjectivism that we find prominent in recent (neo-Kantian) idealism. Nevertheless, the question remains whether, after we effect the phenomenological reduction, we find in the stream of our mental processes a residuum that can serve as an object. On the face of it, there is much even in *Ideas II* that mirrors Shpet's reflections. Husserl there agrees that the concepts of the ego and the surrounding world are inseparable: he recognizes that each of us has his own world, whereas in communicating with others we have a common surrounding world (*Studies* 195). The world is a world not "in itself" but a world "for me." It is posited in mental processes with a sense-content.

Shpet recognizes that for Husserl the phenomenological ego is not itself a mental process (Husserl, *Ideas* 132). Nevertheless, that ego belongs to every flowing mental process. In spite of all the changes in such processes, the ego is absolutely identical throughout. On what basis, then, does Husserl come to his conclusion, Shpet asks. According to Husserl's own "principle of all principles," a theory can draw its truth only from originary data, but Husserl does not provide such data. If we carry out the phenomenological reduction, we thereby exclude the empirical ego but keep the eidetic ego, though now only as an object, not a subject of consciousness. In turning its attention to this "residuum," phenomenology does indeed find a pure consciousness, a "unity of consciousness," but, importantly, it is no one's ("Soznanie" 195, 205). In other words, if we take the ego essentially, that is, as an ideal object, an object within the phenomenological attitude as Shpet understands it, the question "Whose consciousness?" makes no sense. For it presupposes sociality, that is, the possibility that another empirical individual, at a particular time and place, could possess in some unexplained manner this particular consciousness, in much the same way that someone could ask whose shoes these are.

To avoid any possible misunderstanding, Shpet, pace Zinchenko (Zinchenko 37), does not deny that there is any pure consciousness, any phenomenological ego. The ego of the *Logical Investigations*, however, is not the one we find in *Ideas I*. We saw that in 1914 Shpet equated the phenomenological reduction with the eidetic reduction. This remains the case into early 1916. His phenomenology is an eidetic phenomenology, but not a transcendental one in Husserl's sense. That Shpet failed to recognize that the two reductions are not equivalent, that the phenomenological domain, which results from a suspension of belief in existence, is not the same as the eidetic, lies at the root of his failure to find the phenomenological ego of *Ideas I*.

Contrary to Shpet's claim, Husserl did believe he showed that the ego is to be found in every mental process. Granted it does not unreservedly appear as a "residuum" after effecting the reduction. Nevertheless, the ego performs the acts that we recognize as the cogito, though it comes and goes along with these acts (Husserl, *Ideas* 190). The ego remains numerically identical throughout the changes in mental processes. In the phenomenological attitude, we see that intentionality is like a ray emanating from the ego. Although the ego is always present, it can never be made the object of a special study. This is precisely why Husserl calls it a "transcendency of a peculiar kind—one which is not constituted" (Husserl, *Ideas* 133). The domain revealed by the eidetic reduction, which Shpet focuses on, is ontological (essences), whereas that revealed by the transcendental-phenomenological reduction concerns senses and their constitution. Shpet's failure to see the latter—as we saw at the outset, his concern was expressly ontological—led him to overlook the phenomenological ego's role in sense-constitution. Shpet's manifest eagerness to avoid introducing "theory" may well have had its origins in Husserl's remark that he himself had earlier rejected the ego partly in order not to be led astray by "corrupt forms of ego-metaphysic" (Husserl, *Logical* 549n).

Surely that the role of the phenomenological ego received only a brief treatment in *Ideas I* could not have escaped Shpet's attention. There Husserl remarked that all theories concerning the ego that venture beyond its uniqueness and givenness are to be excluded, though he promised to return to the problems associated with the ego in a second volume (Husserl, *Ideas I* 133). Thus, in his eyes the absence of a definitive treatment of the issues should not, and indeed need not, obstruct further progress into "the free vista of 'transcendentally' purified phenomena" (*Ideas* xix). Likewise, for Shpet "the ego is precisely a problem, and in no way is it either a foundation or a principle. On the contrary, taken as the starting point of philosophy, concern with the ego can only distort an analysis of consciousness, forestalling a pure description of the facts by means of preconceived theories" ("Soznanie" 188). He asks, rhetorically, whether it is essentially impossible for there to be a super-personal ego, a multi-personal ego, even an individual ego. We see that even in the nonphenomenological, natural attitude, we come to problems with talk of an owner of consciousness. For Shpet, we can meaningfully talk of a collective consciousness, which has features that cannot be obtained from an examination of individuals alone ("Soznanie" 207). The ego, in its concrete sense, is a social "thing," a definite object, and can be immediately experienced as such ("Soznanie" 202).

There can be no doubt that Husserl did not offer an analysis of the constitution of social consciousness with the care and detail that he gave to other, lower levels, particularly in the works with which Shpet could have been familiar. However, Husserl does not deny that the personal ego lives in a communal world with other egos. Indeed, for Husserl, only if each ego comprehends the common surrounding world—note the terminological similarity between Husserl and Shpet—do we become persons for others (Husserl, *Studies* 201). However, unlike Husserl, Shpet fails to investigate the phenomenological origin of the sense of the acts that make up his study. The latter's concern is with the object of the intentional act, not, as in Husserl, with the intentional act itself from which the sense derives. In reflection, in the phenomenological attitude, the intentional act is made the object. The ego is thereby revealed neither as an act nor as an object but rather as a "pole," the "ego-pole," out of which all intentional acts emanate (*Studies* 104). Husserl adds that the pure ego itself can be made an object of reflection, that is, it can posit itself as an object. In doing so, we must distinguish the objectified pure ego from the nonobjectified one. Nonetheless, the two are "in truth one and the same" (*Studies* 108).

Regrettably, "Consciousness and Its Owner" was to be Shpet's last technical piece on a topic resonant with Husserl's concerns. Nevertheless, Shpet continued to combat the "scientific philosophy" of positivism, contrasting it with what, in a piece entitled "Wisdom or Reason?" from January 1917, he termed "philosophy as pure knowledge." In it, Shpet often used the locution "philosophy as knowledge" and traced its origin back to Parmenides. Whether in doing so Shpet sought to cast aside the Husserlian call for "philosophy as rigorous science" (Haardt 90-91) is unclear. On the one hand, he simply does not mention Husserl's own expression "philosophy as rigorous science." Nor, as Haardt correctly observes, does Shpet portray Husserl as the completion or pinnacle of European philosophy (Haardt 115). On the other hand, he writes that "philosophy, understood as knowledge, is the 'fundamental' science in the most direct and originary sense" ("Mudrost'" 15-16). On one occasion, he even writes that "philosophy, as pure science, is distinguished from mathematics and the formal-ontological disciplines" (52). Above all, philosophy, as it should be, as pure knowledge, takes nothing for granted (20). Shpet's lucubration here continues the single line of thought espoused earlier, a general eidetic phenomenology, however far this may be from Husserl's own transcendental phenomenology with its independent eidetic reduction. What remains unaltered throughout is Shpet's concern with "what is": "The object of philosophy as knowledge is, therefore, truth, i.e., what is, being. It is not this or that sort of being in particular, but being as such, its essence, i.e. being as opposed to non-being" ("Mudrost'" 7). Certainly, Shpet's continuing ontological concerns effectively eliminate any attempt at a rapprochement with transcendental phenomenology. Nevertheless, we cannot help but notice Shpet's unremitting belief that philosophy deals with essences, not facts, and as such yields eidetic knowledge ("Mudrost'" 16). Each of the two kinds of objects has a rigorously corresponding mode of givenness and a corresponding form or attitude of consciousness. When we recognize this and also that the essential characteristic of consciousness is its directedness, its intentionality, we are at the threshold of philosophy as pure knowledge ("Mudrost'" 28). In order to get to philosophy as pure knowledge, that is, to the "fundamental science" in principle—and remember Shpet in 1917 is using that expression to characterize phenomenology—our eidetic judgments must concern consciousness itself in its essence: "For this, we must stop examining experience itself as a 'dogmatically' given thing of the actual world, but instead must look at it *through* consciousness as it is given in eidetic intuition essentially, originarily, immediately and adequately"("Mudrost'" 36-37). The intentional object can be presented to us with either factual or essential content depending on our attitude, that is, depending on whether we take that content as the data of sense intuition or essential intuition.

The Withering Vine in Increasingly Arid Soil

Despite the agony and tension of the war years and with it a lapse in his correspondence, Shpet wrote to Husserl in June 1918: "However, I may say with confidence that what has happened could not change my estimation of German philosophy, and there is not a thing in the world that could shake my inner devotion to you personally. Not a day has passed during these four long years that I have not thought about phenomenology and enjoyed a meeting of the minds with its creator" (Husserl, *Briefwechsel* 542). However, as the years passed Shpet devoted himself increasingly to issues far removed from Husserl's major concerns. We find but scant references to Husserl in Shpet's publications from the 1920s. All of these references are, as it were, in passing—for example, a mention of Husserl's name in a footnote (*Vvedenie* 81), an allusion to "contemporary phenomenology" ("Problemy" 70). Hardly any of these, though, are to specific issues found in *Ideas I*, and none are to the variety of transcendental idealism he, Shpet, himself once espoused.

On the one hand, his isolation within Soviet Russia took its toll on Shpet's already subsiding passion for Husserlian phenomenology. On the other hand, Shpet devoted his last seminar at Moscow University, before the closing of its philosophy department in the early 1920s, to Husserl's "Philosophy as Rigorous Science" (Severtseva 175). Despite their fundamental differences, Husserl's influence lingered through the 1920s and beyond. Husserl's name is not mentioned so much as even once in his 1927 *Inner Form of the Word*, but Shpet there does explicitly reaffirm the general conclusion given in "Consciousness and Its Owner" and uses the expression "phenomenological description" (*Vnutrenniaia* 189).

As Shpet saw it in the 1920s, his chief divergence from Husserl concerned the role of social consciousness and of language. In addition to Husserl's dichotomy of empirical, or experiencing, intuition and the intuition of essences, or ideation, there is language, which in the form of words is a material bearer of concepts, of thought, of sense: "Thought is born in a word and along with it" (*Esteticheskie* 43). Words present a distinctive form of intellectual, not sense, givenness, but the sense in the structure of a word is objective. Although an idea, a sense, can "get into our head," its being is independent of our existence (96). Through sense intuition, we see our finger pointing to a physical thing; through intellectual intuition a word points to something. In the one case, my finger serves as a sign that needs to be understood; in the other, words are that which needs to be understood. Shpet spent much of the 1920s developing his philosophy of language which, ostensibly concerned with social being, had little room for phenomenological reduction, however the latter was to be construed. Indeed, he criticized "the phenomenologists" who, "in searching for the immediate givenness of perceptible reality, greatly simplify the problem of reality, treating it as merely 'natural.' In fact, the reality surrounding us prima facie is not 'natural,' but 'social,' 'historical,' 'cultural'" ("Problemy" 74). All that is around us, even the apples on the table, are part of our sociocultural reality, and to abstract them from that reality would be to yield to a metaphysical temptation.

In the last brief statement of his overall philosophical position, an encyclopedia entry published in 1932, Shpet revealed that although he had traveled some distance down a different path, Husserl's influence had not quite disappeared. He reaffirmed his allegiance to the direction of Brentano and Husserl and held, just as he had a decade and a half earlier, that philosophy dialectically passed through three stages, moving from wisdom through metaphysics to rigorous science. Still combating positivism and neo-Kantianism—but possibly also alluding to the by then discredited "Marxist" Mechanists of the 1920s—Shpet viewed philosophy, properly conceived, as founding the natural sciences, not vice versa. The epistemological problem indicated by Kant can with the help of reflection and the method of reduction—which Shpet regrettably does not further elaborate—advance to a critique of consciousness, as Husserl indicated, starting from immediate experience. However, "we must take this experience in the concrete fullness of cultural-social experience, and not in the abstract form of the perception of a 'thing'" (G. G-n [Shpet], "Shpet, G.G." 379). Far from being uncritical with regard to Husserl's philosophy, Shpet returns to it in all seriousness in this final summary of his own credo.

Concluding Observations

Despite his differences with Husserl on specific issues, Shpet believed he was true to the principles and the original intention of phenomenology. Shpet noted every explicit departure from Husserl's thought with caution and qualification. While today we may fault his understanding of the phenomenological reduction, there were few, if any, among Husserl's contemporaries in Göttingen who did understand it. In later years, Shpet believed his concern with higher-level issues, specifically aesthetics and linguistics, did not necessitate the reduction, not that he rejected it or its possibility. His overall judgment of phenomenology is thus ambiguous. However, into at least the early 1920s, Shpet remained, in his own eyes, a practicing phenomenologist.

Works Cited

Haardt, Alexander. *Husserl in Rußland: Phänomenologie der Sprache und Kunst bei Gustav Špet und Aleksej Losev*. München: Fink, 1993.

Husserl, Edmund. *Briefwechsel*. Ed. Karl Schuhmann. Vol. 3. *Die Göttinger Schule*. Dordrecht: Kluwer, 1994.

Husserl, Edmund. *Experience and Judgment: Investigations in a Genealogy of Logic*. Trans. James S. Churchill and Karl Ameriks. Evanston: Northwestern UP, 1973.

Husserl, Edmund. *Formal and Transcendental Logic*. Trans. Dorion Cairns. The Hague: Martinus Nijhoff, 1969.

Husserl, Edmund. *Ideas Pertaining to a Pure Phenomenology and to a Phenomenological Philosophy*. Trans. F. Kersten. The Hague: Martinus Nijhoff, 1982.

Husserl, Edmund. *Logical Investigations*. Trans. J.N. Findlay. 2 vols. New York: Humanities P, 1970.

Husserl, Edmund. *Studies in the Phenomenology of Constitution*. Trans. Richard Rojcewicz and Andre Schuwer. Dordrecht: Kluwer, 1989.

Savin, A. E. "Interpretatsiia i kritika G. G. Shpetom filosofii Ed. Gusserlia." *G.G. Shpet/Comprehensio: Vtorye Shpetovskie chteniia*. Ed. O.G. Mazaeva. Tomsk: Vodolei, 1997. 24-27.

Severtseva, O.S. "G.G. Shpet: fragmenty biografii." *Gustav Gustavovich Shpet. Arkhivnye materialy. Vospominaniia. Stat'i*. Ed. T.D. Martsinkovskaia. Moscow: Smysl, 2000. 170-82.

Shchedrina, T.G. *"Ia pishu kak ekho drugogo . . ." Ocherki intellektual'noi biografii Gustava Shpeta*. Moscow: Progress-Traditsiia, 2004.

Shpet, Gustav. *Appearance and Sense: Phenomenology as the Fundamental Science and Its Problems*. Trans. Thomas Nemeth. Dordrecht: Kluwer, 1991.

Shpet, Gustav. *Esteticheskie fragmenty*. Vol. 2. Petrograd: Kolos, 1923.

Shpet, Gustav. *Istoriia kak problema logiki*. Ed. V.S. Miasnikov. Moscow: Pamiatniki istoricheskoi mysli, 2002.

Shpet, Gustav. "Mudrost' ili razum?" *Mysl' i slovo* 1 (1917): 1-69.

Shpet, Gustav. "Problemy sovremennoi estetiki." *Iskusstvo* 1 (1923): 43-78.

Shpet, Gustav. "Soznanie i ego sobstvennik." *Georgiiu Ivanovichu Chelpanovu ot uchastnikov ego seminariev v Kieve i Moskve, 1891-1916. Stat'i po filosofii i psikhologii*. Moscow: n.p., 1916. 156-210.

Shpet, Gustav [G.G-n]. "Shpet, G.G." *Entsiklopedicheskii slovar' Granat*. Vol. 50. Moscow: Russkii bibliograficheskii Institut Granat, 1932. 378-80.

Shpet, Gustav. *Vnutronniaia forma slova*. Moscow: Gosudarstvennaia akademiia khudozhestvennykh nauk, 1927.

Shpet, Gustav. *Vvedenie v etnicheskuiu psikhologiiu*. Moscow: Gosudarstvennaia akademiia khudozhestvennykh nauk, 1927.

Weiler, Michael. "Einleitung des Herausgebers." *Natur und Geist: Vorlesungen, Sommersemester 1927*. By Edmund Husserl. Dordrecht: Kluwer, 2001. xi-li.

Zinchenko, Vladimir. "Shpet protiv ego-logii Gusserlia." *G.G. Shpet/Comprehensio: Tret'i Shpetovskie chteniia*. Ed. O.G. Mazaeva. Tomsk: Vodolei, 1999. 35-38.

Shpet as Translator of Hegel's *Phänomenologie des Geistes*

George L. Kline

Introduction

Gustav Shpet published five books during the 1920s. The first three—*Filosofskoe mirovozzrenie Gertsena* (*Herzen's Philosophical World-View*; 1921), *Ocherk razvitiia russkoi filosofii* (*An Outline of the Development of Russian Philosophy*; 1922), and *Esteticheskie fragmenty* (*Aesthetic Fragments*; 1922-1923)—were published by Kolos in Petrograd, a private publishing house. This was during the period of the New Economic Policy (1921-1928), when limited small-scale enterprises were tolerated in the Soviet Union; however, the publishing houses were subject to government censorship, which resulted in the removal of certain politically sensitive passages in *Aesthetic Fragments*, omissions restored in the 1990 reprint, although, even under glasnost, certain other cuts were made by the Soviet censors.

By the time Shpet's last two books appeared, in 1927, he was being published by the Gosudarstvennaia Akademiia khudozhestvennykh nauk (GAKhN, State Academy of Artistic Sciences) in Moscow. This was the penultimate year of the New Economic Policy. In 1928 Stalin's first five-year plan got underway, which resulted in the closing down of all private enterprises, including publishers. The Academy, although it had the word "State" in its title, was more like a private research institute; its members were serious non-party scholars. As a result, it was subjected to a brutal purge and then shut down. For the next half-dozen years, until his arrest in March 1935, Shpet was permitted to publish none of his own work, only translations of foreign works in philosophy and literature, some of which were published without the name of the translator, for example, Berkeley's *Three Dialogues between Hylas and Philonous*, 1937 (see Serebrennikov 144 n. 5). He translated works of Dickens and Byron, wrote an extensive commentary on the Russian translation of *The Pickwick Papers*, and revised some of the translations in the Soviet edition of Shakespeare published by Academia. He was co-editor of the Soviet edition of Constance Garnett's English translation of Tolstoi's *Anna Karenina* published in 1933.

Shpet's Final Scholarly Project

Shpet was an exceptional linguist. He took Edmund Husserl's philosophy seminars at the University of Göttingen in 1912-1913 and carried on an extensive correspondence, in German, with Husserl between 1913 and 1918 (Kline, "Meditations" 144). In a letter to the Public Prosecutor's Office (4 June 1937), requesting that he be allowed to "work on the front of our [i.e., Soviet] cultural construction," he listed several areas of his scholarly competence and the thirteen ancient and modern languages that he could read freely (Serebrennikov 190). In the draft of an unsent letter to Stalin, written in Eniseisk in November 1935, attempting to justify his claim to take part in the preparation of the Soviet edition of Shakespeare's works then in progress, he mentioned that three major Russian poets—Pasternak, Kuzmin, and Antokolskii—would be willing to attest to his abilities as a verse translator (Serebrennikov 73-74). Judging from the version of Tennyson's narrative poem, *Enoch Arden* (1864), that he dictated to his daughter Marina in Eniseisk in 1935, he was a gifted if minor poet: his generally accurate version, in the blank verse of the original, is impressive for the power and dignity of its language (this translation was first published in Serebrennikov 17-38).

During the 1930s and 1940s such major Russian poets as Akhmatova and Pasternak, barred from publishing their own poetry, were reduced to verse translation. Both of them translated from languages they knew well: Akhmatova from Italian, Pasternak from German and English. But they also translated from languages they didn't know: Akhmatova from Serbo-Croatian and Korean, Pasternak from Georgian. In contrast, Shpet translated only from languages he knew well, making no use of the scholars and linguists who provided Akhmatova and Pasternak with literal interlinear versions of poems in such languages as Korean and Georgian. In all such cases, the motivation of the translator for doing what Akhmatova once called "slave labor," was twofold: 1) they wished to remain active in the cultural life of their country at a time when their own original work had been banned as ideologically unacceptable and 2) they needed to make a living, even though in most cases it was a meager one. Shpet complained in a letter to his wife, written in Tomsk (11 June 1936), that his advance for the Hegel translation was supposed to last him for a full year, but would in fact be exhausted long before that (Serebrennikov 143). In a letter to his teen-age son Sergei (8 October 1936), after referring to his work on the Hegel translation, he added that he was earning barely enough to live on and that Sergei might have to sell most of Shpet's Moscow library, rent out a room in the family apartment, and so on (Serebrennikov 164).

With the publication in 1995 of many of Shpet's letters written in Siberia to his wife, children, and friends in Moscow, we now know a good deal about how Shpet obtained the contract, how and when he did the work, who typed his manuscript and where. Before going into some of those details, I pause to consider Shpet's choice of a translation of Hegel's *Phänomenologie des Geistes* (1807) as what he rightly sensed would be his final scholarly project. Given his personal and philosophical closeness to Husserl, he would presumably have preferred to translate a major un-translated work of Husserl's such as *Ideen I* (1913), which he had already brilliantly discussed and commented on in his *Appearance and Sense* (*Iavlenie i smysl*; 1914). But he realized that, because of the implacable hostility toward Husserl's philosophy of Soviet Marxist-Leninists, there was no chance that such a translation would be published in the Soviet Union. On the other hand, Shpet had always admired Hegel's thought and was well aware that seven volumes of the Soviet edition of Hegel's Works (*Sochineniia*) had already been published between 1929 and 1934. So there were reasonable grounds for assuming that his new translation of such a key text as the *Phänomenologie* would eventually be published. He also knew that there had been a 1913 Russian translation of this work (in fact he held a copy of it in his Moscow library), but did not consider this a problem. He presumably also knew that the Soviet Hegel edition had already included, as volumes 1 (1929) and 2 (1934), the first two parts of the *Encyclopedia of Philosophical Sciences*, which had been published in Russian translation in 1861 and 1868.

In fact, after Shpet's death five more volumes of the Hegel edition were pub-lished, which contained works that had already been translated once in the past: both volumes of the *Science of Logic* (first translated in 1916 by N.G. Debolskii. 2nd ed. Moscow, 1929) and all three volumes of the *Lectures on Aesthetics* (first translated in 1847-1860). An interesting question that I have not been able to pursue here is whether all, or even many, of the seven volumes of the Soviet edition were as derivative, in the wording of sustained passages, from their nineteenth- and early twentieth-century predecessors as Shpet's translation was from the 1913 edition. On 13 April 1936, Shpet signed a contract with the State Socio-Economic Publishing House (Sotsekgiz) to produce a Russian translation of Hegel's *Phänomenologie*. Many of Shpet's friends helped him get the contract, in some cases by turning down the offer of a contract themselves, insisting that Shpet was the only person who could do this challenging assignment justice (see the reminiscences of Shpet's daughter Marina; Serebrennikov 224). The contract specified the length of the work as thirty printer's signatures (16 pages each), to be paid for at the rate of 225 rubles per signa-ture, or a total of 6,750 rubles. On 25 September 1936, the publisher dissolved the contract unceremoniously without informing Shpet or his family. As of 20 August 1937, when he had already completed the translation, Shpet still assumed that the contract was valid (Serebrennikov 199-200). He apparently went to his death believ-ing this.

After charges against Shpet were officially dropped on 27 January 1956, Sotsekgiz offered Nataliia Konstantinovna, Shpet's widow, a contract on condition that the translation be published without the name of the translator. She refused. After her death in the fall of that year, Shpet's children continued to try to get the work published, finally receiving a contract on 8 June 1959, with the publishing House of the Institute of Philosophy of the Soviet Academy of Sciences. The text was sent to the printer on 20 June 1959, approved for publication on 2 October, and appeared later that year in a print-run of 15,000 copies. The Shpet archive contains copious evidence of the way the translation was done. Shpet used 26-page school notebooks, and filled 57 of them with his handwritten text, for a total of 1,485 pages. He sent this, in small increments, to his wife and daughter Marina in Moscow, who typed it and sent it back, keeping a copy. The typescript is 706 pages long ("Typed Listing of Contents of Shpet Archive" 13). Shpet started the translation on 1 April 1936 and completed it in mid-August 1937. Its progress is documented for the period April to October 1936 and July to August 1937. Shpet and his wife tried to write every day and during these two periods there are letters from Shpet to her or to one of his children almost every day. But the correspondence during the winter of 1936-1937, when most of the work was completed, appears to be missing.

Shpet reported to his wife that the translation was moving rapidly: between 1 to 18 April he had completed 207 pages, filling seven school notebooks. He estimated that he had been averaging 8 ¾ German pages per day (Serebrennikov 99). The actual figure is 11½ pages! Later he estimated that, by doing two German pages a day, he could finish in February 1937, well ahead of the 1 April deadline (Serebrennikov 112). Still later he said that by doing 2½ German pages a day (at least eight hours' work) he would be able to finish in January 1937, leaving three months for careful checking (Serebrennikov 152, 154). As we know, it actually took him until mid-August. Shpet lamented not having a typewriter, mainly because— having no way to make copies of what he had written in his school notebooks—he had to send his one and only copy to Moscow without being able to keep a copy to refer to (Serebrennikov 99). In her memoirs Marina fills in many details of the Tomsk-Moscow-Tomsk transactions. Mail during the 1930s took only five or six days to arrive, in contrast to 1990 when it took two or three weeks. Shpet sent the notebooks to Moscow by registered mail. His wife, a skilled typist, or Marina, would type up these texts and send one copy back to Tomsk by registered mail. Shpet corrected typing errors, revised certain passages, and sent the corrected typescript back to Moscow. Marina reports that in all this time, with what must have been scores of mailings in both directions, no manuscript or typescript was ever lost in the mail (Serebrennikov 243).

In order to translate such a long, difficult, and in many ways puzzling work, Shpet obviously needed many books: the German text of the *Phänomenologie*, various dictionaries, commentaries, as well as general reference works in philosophy, mostly in German (occasionally also in Russian). We know that the NKVD forbade him to have any contact with Tomsk University and its library. So how did he get the needed books to his tiny office-bedroom in Tomsk? The correspondence provides a number of clues. Shpet had a magnificent library in his Moscow apartment, where his wife, daughter Marina, and son Sergei lived during his exile. Marina estimated its holdings at more than 30,000 volumes. Art historian A.A. Sidorov, who often visited Shpet during the 1920s, remembered the library as occupying an entire floor of the cooperative apartment building where Shpet lived and as containing more than 100,000 volumes (Petritskii 25). I assume that Marina's figure is closer to the mark. Shpet had numbered the individual stacks or bookcases, of which there were at least 17, probably many more, and in various letters asked his wife or daughter to find and send a given book in, for example, No. 17, 2nd shelf, or No. 12, 7th shelf (Serebren-nikov 102, 121). In other cases, Shpet requested books to be brought to Tomsk by the next visitor. He was permitted to receive a number of extended visits from friends and family members; in all cases the visitors came from Moscow. His wife was with him in Tomsk for three weeks (March-April 1936), for more than ten weeks later that year (2 July to 29 September), and for eleven weeks in 1937 (10 July to 21 October). His three adult daughters also visited him in Tomsk, as did his son Sergei.

Among the specific titles that Shpet requested are Debolskii's three-volume Russian translation (1916) of Hegel's two-volume *Science of Logic*, the Radlov trans-lation of the *Phänomenologie* (1913), Hegel's three-volume *Geschichte der Philoso-phie*, the two-volume Ivan Il'in commentary on Hegel (1918), and Rudolf Eisler's "three-volume *Philosophisches Lexikon*" (it appears that Shpet meant rather Eisler's three-volume *Wörterbuch der philosophischen Begriffe* [1927]; Eisler's *Philosophen-Lexikon* [1912] was published in one large volume). He also asked for the manuscript of the Russian translation of Hegel's "Introduction to Aesthetics," made by his former student, Nikolai Volkov, with Shpet's corrections and comments, including explana-tions of many of Hegel's terms. On 16 May 1936, he asked his wife to try to borrow, from friends or acquaintances, the German text of Hegel's *Wissenschaft der Logik* and mail it or bring it along on her next visit (Serebrennikov 133-34, 125).

Shpet and Radlov's 1913 Translation

When I said that Shpet had requested, among many other books to be brought by visitors from Moscow, the 1913 Russian translation of Hegel's *Phänomenologie*, edited by Ernest Radlov (Hegel, *Fenomenologiia*), I was filling out what in Shpet's letter to his wife (5 May 1936) was sparse and elliptical. Shpet in fact referred to the book in question simply as "Hegel's 'Phenomenology'" ("*Fenomenologiia' Gege-lia*"), but he went on to describe its binding in close detail that entirely corresponds, judging by a copy held by the Bundesarchiv in Berlin (information kindly confirmed by Bernd Knabe, 21 October 2004), to the appearance of the Radlov version. Shpet mentions the book nowhere else in his Siberian correspondence, nor does he refer to Radlov by name at any point. It is clear, in any case, that for a period of more than thirteen months—from 2 July 1936, when his wife brought the Radlov translation with her from Moscow, until mid-August, when he completed his own version—Shpet had that translation beside him as he worked. I have been able to compare, in close detail, nearly sixty pages—texts from widely separated portions of Hegel's work—of Shpet's version with that of Radlov. There is a great deal of verbatim and near-verbatim repetition. A fraction of this may be of the sort that happens even in in-dependently done translations, but most of it appears rather to be the result of Shpet's deliberate decision, knowing how desperately little time he had, to repeat Radlov's version—especially in the passages with relatively few technical terms—either mak-ing no change or changing a word or two in the shorter passages, a few more in the longer ones. He sometimes adds or deletes a word, and occasionally changes singular verbs to plural or the reverse. He also introduces occasional trifling shifts in word order, easy to do in a highly inflected language like Russian. I have identified twenty-five passages, ranging in length from 13 to 99 words, in which more than 90% of Shpet's text is a verbatim reproduction of the Radlov text.

In judging Shpet's heavy reliance on the Radlov version of Hegel's *Phänom-enologie*, we must keep in mind that during his exile in Tomsk (1935-1937) he had a powerful premonition that he did not have long to live. He gave voice to this sense of imminent death in at least three letters, two to his wife (15 September 1935 and 17 May 1936) and one to Sergei (27 September 1935; Serebrennikov 62, 127, 65).

There seem to have been two distinct, though not unrelated, reasons for Shpet's premonition. The precarious state of his health, which he detailed in several places in his letters home, was an issue; and quite apart from his health problems, Shpet must have sensed, during his time in Tomsk, that his life was under constant threat from the Soviet authorities. Several of his friends and acquaintances among the politi-cal prisoners exiled there simply disappeared. Arrests of alleged conspirators in the monarchist "Union for the Salvation of Russia," an organization wholly fabricated by the NKVD, began in March 1937, at a time when Shpet—who was himself to be arrested on 27 October, convicted as a conspirator, and executed on 16 Novem-ber—was hard at work on his Hegel translation. The poet Nikolai Kliuev was ar-rested on 3 June 1937 (and executed in October of the same year); M.A. Petrovskii, a former GAKhN colleague, was arrested on 21 October 1937 and executed ten days later (Serebrennikov 322-24). Furthermore, it appears that in mid-May Shpet him-self was called in for interrogation by the NKVD, apparently for four days. He uses Aesopian language to report this to Sergei (May 27), saying that he had been "really, really sick" (*zdorovo pobolel*) and unable to work for ten days—using a prison-slang expression that meant "detained for some time" (Serebrennikov 188, 323-24).

Having pointed out Shpet's debt to Radlov, I must also say that the passages in which Shpet's versions do differ from Radlov's are superior in every way (Shpet sometimes quietly corrects errors: Radlov, for example, had *sluchainoe* ["the con-tingent"] for Hegel's *das Besondere*; Shpet puts the correct *osobennoe* ["the particu-lar"]). I have noticed only one case in which Radlov's term is preferable to Shpet's: Radlov had *mgnovenie* ("instant") for Hegel's *Augenblick*; Shpet puts *moment* (Hegel, *Fenomenologiia* 1959 104), which blurs Hegel's key distinction between, on the one hand, his much-used technical term *das Moment* ("non-temporal phase or aspect") and, on the other, the less frequently used *der Moment* ("brief interval of time") and—as here—*Augenblick* ("instant"). In any case, Shpet's principal, and major, contribu-tion lies in two areas: his splendid rendering of a great many key passages in Hegel's text and his innovative renderings of certain of Hegel's terminological distinctions.

A Critical Assessment of Shpet's Translation

The extraordinary skill, sensitivity, and inventiveness that Shpet has brought to the rendering into Russian of Hegel's text is perhaps most adequately conveyed by a series of examples—brief texts drawn from various parts of the *Phänomenologie*. I group those under three headings: 1) three passages which exhibit key points of Hegelian doctrine; 2) a passage which exhibits a striking beauty and lyricism—perhaps unexpected in so technical and systematic a thinker; and 3) three passages that exhibit Hegel's famous irony as well as his mordant wit.

1) Passages that exhibit key points of Hegelian doctrine. First, from the celebrated dialectic of master and slave:

> Desire [in the master's consciousness] has reserved to itself the pure negating of the object and thereby its unalloyed feeling of self. But . . . this satisfaction is itself only a fleeting one, for it lacks the side of *objectivity* and *permanence*. [The slave's] work, on the other hand, is desire *held in check*, fleetingness *staved off*; in other words, work *forms and shapes* the thing. . . . It is in this way . . . that consciousness, *qua* worker, comes to see in the independent being [of the object] its *own* independence. (Hegel, *Phenomenology of Spirit* 118, para. 195; italics added to conform to Hegel's [*Phänomenologie*] usage)

In Hegel's words:

> Die Begierde hat sich das reine Negieren des Gegenstandes und dadurch das unvermischte Selbstgefühl vorbehalten. Diese Befriedigung ist aber ... selbst nur ein Verschwinden, denn es fehlt ihr die *gegenständliche* Seite oder das *Bestehen*. Die Arbeit hingegen ist *gehemmte* Begierde, *aufgehaltenes* Verschwinden, oder sie *bildet* . . . Das arbeitende Bewusstsein kommt ... hiedurch zur Anschauung des selbständigen Seins *als seiner selbst*. (Hegel, *Phänomenologie des Geistes* 148-49)

Shpet renders this cleanly and accurately:

> Vozhdelenie uderzhalo za soboi . . . chistuiu negatsiiu predmeta, a vsledstvie etogo i besprimesnoe chuvstvovanie sebia. No . . . dannoe udovletvorenie samo est' tol'ko ischeznovenie, ibo emu nedostaet *predmetnoi* storony ili *ustoichivogo sushchestvovaniia*. Trud, naprotiv togo, est' *zatormozhennoe* vozhdelenie, *zaderzhannoe* . . . ischeznovenie, drugimi slovami, on *obrazuet*.... Rabotaiushchee soznanie prikhodit . . . etim putem k sozertsaniiu samostoiatel'nogo bytiia *kak sebia samogo*. (Hegel, *Fenomenologiia* 1959 105)

In another passage, in the section on "Active [or "Practical"] Reason," Hegel expresses a key doctrinal point in a formulation which is, at least on the surface, paradoxical:

> Action is simply the coming-to-be of Spirit as *consciousness* . . . Accordingly, an individual cannot know what he [really] is until he has made himself a reality through action. However, this seems to imply that he cannot

determine the *End* of his action until he has carried it out; but at the same time, since he is a *conscious* individual, he must have the action in front of him beforehand as *entirely his own*, i.e., as an *End*. (Hegel, *Phenomenology of Spirit* 240, para. 401)

The German text reads:

> Das Handeln ist . . . das Werden des Geistes *als Bewusstsein*. . . . Das Individuum kann daher nicht wissen, was *es ist*, eh es sich durch das Tun zur Wirklichkeit gebracht hat.—Es scheint aber . . . den *Zweck* seines Tuns nicht bestimmen zu können, eh es getan hat; aber zugleich muss es, indem es Bewusstsein ist, die Handlung vorher als die *ganz seinige*, d.h. als *Zweck* vor sich haben. (Hegel, *Phänomenologie des Geistes* 287-88)

Shpet captures nicely both the doctrine and the paradox:

> Deiatel'nost' . . . est' stanovlenie dukha *kak soznaniia*. . . . Individ poetomu ne mozhet znat', chtò *est' on*, poka on deistvovaniem ne pretvoril sebia v deistvitel'nost'.—No tem samym on . . . ne mozhet opredelit' *tsel'* svoego deistvovaniia, poka on ne deistvoval; no v to zhe vremia, buduchi soznaniem, on dolzhen napered imet' pered soboiu postupok *kak tselikom svoi* postupok, t.e. kak *tsel'*. (Hegel, *Fenomenologiia* 1959 212-13; italics modified to conform to Hegel's usage in this passage)

The spiritual, cultural, and intersubjective dimensions and functions of language are concisely formulated in the following passage:

> Here . . . we see *language* as the existence of Spirit. Language is self-consciousness existing *for others*, self-consciousness which *as such* is immediately *present*, and as *this* self-consciousness is universal. It is the self that separates itself from itself, which . . . becomes objective to itself, which in this objectivity equally preserves itself as *this* self, just as it coalesces immediately with other selves and is *their* self-consciousness. It perceives itself just as it is perceived by others, and the perceiving is just *existence which has become a self.* (Hegel, *Phenomenology of Spirit* 395, para. 652; trans. revised, italics modified to conform to Hegel's usage)

Hegel puts it this way:

> Wir sehen hiemit . . . die *Sprache* als das Dasein des Geistes. Sie ist das *für andre* seiende Selbstbewusstsein, welches unmittelbar *als solches vorhanden* und als *dieses* allgemeines ist. Sie ist das sich von sich selbst abtrennende Selbst, das . . . sich gegenständlich wird, in dieser Gegenständlichkeit sich ebenso als *dieses* Selbst erhält, wie es unmittelbar mit den andern zusammenfliesst und *ihr* Selbstbewusstsein ist; es vernimmt ebenso sich, als es von den Andern vernommen wird, und das Vernehmen ist eben das *zum Selbst gewordne Dasein.* (Hegel, *Phänomenologie des Geistes* 458)

Shpet's version is both eloquent and accurate, except for the use—in which he follows the Radlov version—of *nalichnoe bytie* for *Dasein* ("existence"):

> Tem samym my . . . vstrechaemsia s *iazykom* kak nalichnym bytiem dukha. On est' sushchee *dlia drugikh* samosoznanie, kotoroe neposredstvenno *kak takovoe imeetsia nalitso* i, buduchi "*etim*," vseobshche. On est' otdeliaiush-chaiasia ot sebia samoi samost', kotoraia stanovitsia dlia sebia predmetom . . . i v etoi predmetnosti v takoi zhe mere sokhraniaet sebia v kachestve *etoi* samosti, kak i slivaetsia neposredstvenno s drugimi i est' *ikh* samosoz-nanie: ona tochno tak zhe prinimaet sebia na slukh, kak i ee prinimaiut na slukh drugie, i eto prinimanie na slukh . . . i est' *nalichnoe bytie, stavshee samost'iu.* (Hegel, *Fenomenologiia* 1959 350)

2) I offer as an example of the occasional beauty and lyricism of Hegel's prose just one, somewhat more extensive, passage. In this passage Hegel is contrasting the vitality and immediacy of Greek religion and art as these were experienced by the Greeks themselves with the dead and distanced way in which the Romans later experienced that religion and that art. It is Hegel's acerb corollary that his contemporaries among classical scholars were, in this respect, much closer to the Romans than to the Greeks:

> The works of the Muse now lack the power of the Spirit. . . . They have become what they are for us now—beautiful fruit already picked from the tree, which a friendly Fate has offered us, as a girl might set the fruit before us. It cannot give us the actual life in which they existed, not the tree that bore them, not the earth and the elements which constituted their substance. . . . So Fate does not restore their world to us along with the works of antique Art, it gives not the spring and summer of the ethical life in which they blossomed and ripened, but only the veiled recollection of that actual world. (Hegel, *Phenomenology of Spirit* 455, para. 753)

Here is Hegel's text:

> Den Werken der Muse fehlt die Kraft des Geistes. . . . Sie sind nun das, was sie für uns sind—vom Baume gebrochne schöne Früchte, ein freundliches Schicksal reichte sie uns dar, wie ein Mädchen jene Früchte präsentiert; es gibt nicht das wirkliche Leben ihres Daseins, nicht den Baum, der sie trug, nicht die Erde und die Elemente, die ihre Substanz . . . ausmachte. . . . So gibt das Schicksal uns mit den Werken jener Kunst nicht ihre Welt, nicht den Frühling und Sommer des sittlichen Lebens, worin sie blühten und reif-ten, sondern allein die eingehüllte Erinnerung dieser Wirklichkeit. (Hegel, *Phänomenologie des Geistes* 523-24)

Shpet renders this passage in a Russian whose classical *gravitas* is no less striking than its tender lyricism and gentle melancholy. But this is one of those non-technical passages, mentioned above, in which Shpet took over major portions from the Radlov version, here including some of his most eloquent phrases (Boris Groys, a native speaker of Russian, finds such passages reminiscent of the early nineteenth-century prose of the senior Slavophiles Khomiakov and Kireevskii, with just a whiff of the twentieth-century prose of Andrei Belyi):

> Proizvedeniiam muzy nedostaet sily dukha. . . . Oni teper' to, chto oni sut' dlia nas,—sorvannye s dereva prekrasnye plody, blagoskonnaia sud'ba predostavila ikh nam, kak devushka predlagaet takie plody; sud'ba ne daet deistvitel'noi zhizni ikh nalichnogo bytiia, togo dereva, kotoroe ikh pri-nosilo, toi zemli i tekh stikhii, kotorye sostavliali ikh substantsiiu. . . . Takim obrazom, s proizvedeniiami etogo iskusstva sud'ba ne daet nam ikh mira, ne daet vesny i leta nravstvennoi zhizni, v kotoroi oni tsveli i zreli, a daet lish' tumannoe vospominanie ob etoi deistvitel'nosti. (Hegel, *Fenomenologiia* 1959 401)

3) We turn now to three passages that display Hegel's well-known irony and mordant wit. In an early critique of what he calls "monotonous formalism," and we might call simple-minded and reductionist schematism, Hegel declares:

> The instrument of this monotonous formalism is no more difficult to handle than a painter's palette having only two colours, say red and green. . . . It would be hard to decide which is greater in all this, the casual ease with which everything . . . is coated with this broth of colour, or the conceit regarding the excellence of this universal recipe: each supports the other. (Hegel, *Phenomenology of Spirit* 30-31, para. 51)

Hegel's German text reads:

> Das Instrument dieses gleichtönigen Formalismus ist nicht schwerer zu handhaben als die Palette eines Malers, auf der sich nur zwei Farben befinden würden, etwa Rot und Grün. . . . Es würde schwer zu entscheiden sein, was dabei grösser ist, die Behaglichkeit, mit der alles . . . mit solcher Farbenbrühe angetüncht wird, oder die Einbildung auf die Vortrefflichkeit dieses Universalmittels; die eine unterstützt die andere. (Hegel, *Phänomenologie des Geistes* 43)

Shpet's translation is deft, accurate, and no less ironic in tone than Hegel's text:

> Ovladet' instrumentom etogo odnoobraznogo formalizma ne trudnee, chem palitroi zhivopistsa, na kotoroi vsego lish' dve kraski—skazhem, krasnaia i zelenaia. . . . Trudno bylo by reshit', chego pri etom bol'she —chuvstva udovol'stviia, s kotorym takoi kraskoi zamazyvaetsia vse . . . ili vnushennoi sebe mysli o prevoskhodstve etogo universal'nogo sredstva; odno podkrepliaet drugoe. (Hegel, *Fenomenologiia* 1959 27)

In another passage Hegel makes fun of highfaluting but uninformative terminology:

> Something which perception takes to be an "animal with strong muscles" is defined as an "animal organism of high irritability," or what perception takes to be a "condition of great weakness" is defined as "a condition of

high sensitivity," or . . . as an "abnormal affection" and a "raising of it to a higher potency"—expressions which translate sensuous facts into a Germanized Latin instead of into the concept. (Hegel, *Phenomenology of Spirit* 169, para. 282; trans. revised [putting "Germanized Latin" for Hegel's *Deutschlatein*])

So wird etwa etwas, das für die Wahrnehmung ein Tier von starken Muskeln ist, als tierischer Organismus von hoher Irritabilität, oder was für die Wahrnehmung ein Zustand grosser Schwäche ist, als Zustand hoher Sensibilität oder . . . als eine innormale Affection, und zwar eine Potenzierung derselben (Ausdrücke, welche das Sinnliche, statt in den Begriff, in ein Deutschlatein übersetzen) bestimmt. (Hegel, *Phänomenologie des Geistes* 209)

Shpet's version:

Nechto, chto dlia vospriiatiia est' zhivotnoe s krepkimi myshtsami, opredeliaetsia kak zhivotnyi organizm s vysokoi stepen'iu razdrazhimosti, ili to, chto dlia vospriiatiia est' sostoianie bol'shoi slabosti, opredeliaetsia kak sostoianie vysokoi stepeni chuvstvitel'nosti . . . ili kak nenormal'naia "affektsiia," a imenno nekotoroe "potentsirovanie" ee (vyrazheniia, kotorye vmesto togo, chtoby perevesti chuvstvennoe v poniatie, pervodiat ego na onemechennuiu latyn'). (Hegel, *Fenomenologiia* 1959 151)

Here Shpet's *chuvstvennoe* is measurably closer to Hegel's *das Sinnliche* than is Miller's "sensuous facts," largely because Russian, like German—in contrast to English—regularly uses neuter adjectives as substantives.

One final example. Sharply criticizing the self-proclaimed purity and perfection of the *schöne Seele* and its "conscience," Hegel declares: "Conscience . . . in the majesty of its elevation above specific law and every content of duty . . . is the moral genius which knows the inner voice of what it immediately knows to be a divine voice . . . It is in its own self divine worship, for its action is the contemplation of its own divinity" (Hegel, *Phenomenology of Spirit* 397, para. 655). Here is Hegel's text: "Das Gewissen . . . in der Majestät seiner Erhabenheit über das bestimmte Gesetz und jeden Inhalt der Pflicht . . . ist die moralische Genialität, welche die innere Stimme ihres unmittelbaren Wissens als göttliche Stimme weiss. . . . Sie ist ebenso der Gottesdienst in sich selbst; denn ihr Handeln ist das Anschauen dieser ihrer eignen Göttlichkeit" (Hegel, *Phänomenologie des Geistes* 460). In this passage too Shpet's version owes a good deal to Radlov's, although all of his changes strike me as improvements, for example, the "Biblical" inversion (typical of the Russian and Old Church Slavonic Bibles) *golos bozhestvennyi*, with which Shpet replaces Radlov's more pedestrian *bozhestvennyi golos* and Shpet's *vsiakim* for "every" (*jeden*), which strikes me as more direct and effective than Radlov's over-elaborate *kakim by to ni bylo* (Hegel, *Fenomenologiia* 1913 297).

Shpet's Handling of Hegel's Technical Terms and Distinctions

In this section I discuss key details of Shpet's choices for translating a number of Hegel's terms as well as his striking terminological innovations.

Ding and *Sache* can both mean "thing," but in Hegel the latter has a special sense, particularly in his notorious expression *die Sache selbst*, rendered in a wide variety of ways, almost all of them misleading, by such English translators as Baillie, who used "main concern," "main intent," "objectified intent," "real intent," "object in mind," and "fact of the matter" (*Phenomenology of Mind* 430, 431, 432, 433, 434, 436, 437, 438), and Miller, who used "matter in hand" and "very heart of the matter" (*Phenomenology of Spirit* 246, 247, 410-12). Shpet's renderings of *die Sache selbst* as *sama sut' dela* (Hegel, *Fenomenologiia* 1959 15, 218-23) and *samoe sut' dela* (219, 220, 222) are better than any of these. A closer English equivalent would be "essential cause." Shpet translates *Sache* ("cause") adequately as *delo*, and *Dingheit* ("thinghood") as *veshchnost'*, a simpler and more effective term than Radlov's rather cumbersome *veshchestvennost'*.

The text of the *Phenomenology* includes many philosophical puns (see Kline, "Philosophical Puns" esp. 214-15, 217, 219-20, 222-25, 228, 230-32, 234). Shpet comes up with effective Russian counterparts for some of them. Thus in the "Don Quixote" passage, "empty, ineffectual words . . . which edify, but raise no edifice" (Hegel, *Phenomenology of Spirit* 234, para. 390) for Hegel's *leere Worte . . . welche . . . erbauen, aber nichts aufbauen* (Hegel, *Phänomenologie des Geistes* 28) is nicely rendered as *pustye slova . . . kotorye . . . nazidaiut, no nichego ne sozidaiut* (*Fenomenologiia* 1959 207). Hegel's *Stellungen und Verstellungen* ("attitudes and dissemblances") is transformed, quite deftly, into *ustanovok i perestanovok* (*Fenomenologiia* 1959 342). But in many other cases, as Shpet explains (*Fenomenologiia* 1959 xlviii), he does not attempt to provide a punning Russian counterpart of the original, but simply gives a straightforward rendering and inserts the relevant punning German terms. Thus Hegel's famous "pathway of doubt" (*Weg des Zweifels*) that is actually a "way of despair" (*Weg der Verzweiflung*) is rendered unpretentiously as a *put' somneniia* (*Zweifel*) which is a *put' otchaianiia* (*Verzweiflung*) (*Fenomenologiia* 1959 44).

There is an important verbal distinction, involving a distinction of substance, which Hegel's genius, in combination with the genius of the German language, first made current in the *Phänomenologie des Geistes* and later developed more systematically in works such as his *Wissenschaft der Logik*. German nouns which end in *-ung* have the same kind of ambiguity as English nouns which end in "-tion" or "-sion." The word *decision*, for example, can mean either the act or process of deciding or the state or condition of having been decided. An example of the former (the process sense of the word) would be: "The decision I am now making is a difficult one." An example of the latter (the product sense of the word) would be: "I now regret the decision I made last week." Hegel was careful—certainly more careful than any of his predecessors and most of his successors in the nineteenth century—to disambiguate his *-ung* terms. For example, *Vorstellung* ("representation") can mean either (*das*) *Vorstellen* ("the act or process of representing") or (*ein*) *Vorgestelltes* ("what has been represented"), or, more abstractly, (*das*) *Vorgestelltsein* ("the state or condition of having been represented"). Similarly, *Vermittlung* ("mediation") can mean either (*das*) *Vermitteln* ("the act or process of mediating") or (*ein*) *Vermitteltes* ("what has been mediated").

The generally fluent, readable, and accurate Radlov version makes almost no attempt to reproduce such distinctions. So far as I know, Shpet was the first translator of Hegel to make such an attempt. His effort, although not entirely consistent, was strikingly successful when compared not only to the Radlov translation but to most of the earlier and later translations of the *Phänomenologie* into the major European languages.

Shpet employs two quite different devices to render the dynamism of *-en* forms: 1) the "process" formulation, for which he could find inspiration in the philosophical writings of Vladimir Solov'ev, who as early as the 1870s spoke of *protsess myshleniia* ("thought process") and *protsess integratsii* ("process of integration") (Solov'ev 1: 828; 2: 544, 546). Thus Shpet renders the nominal infinitive (*das*) *Wahrnehmen* ("act or process of perceiving") as *protsess vospriiatiia* (e.g., *Fenomenologiia* 1959 60, 63, 129) and 2) in other cases he renders the *-en* form by using the imperfective verbal noun: *vosprinimanie* for *Wahrnehmen* (e.g., *Fenomenologiia* 1959 64, 65, 66) in contrast to the perfective verbal noun *vospriiatie* for the noun *Wahrnehmung* (e.g., *Fenomenologiia* 1959 60, 61, 62). Shpet renders the past participle (*ein*) *Wahrgenommenes* ("what has been perceived") as *vosprinimaemoe* (e.g., *Fenomenologiia* 1959 60, 74, 79). I have found only one instance in Radlov's version of the long form—*poznavanie*, contrasted with *poznanie*—and no cases of the *protsess . . .* formulation as a rendering of the nominal infinitive.

Shpet renders the term *Vorstellung* ("representation"), as Radlov did, in the standard way, by *predstavlenie*; but Shpet consistently renders *Vorstellen* (as Radlov had not) as *protsess predstavleniia* (e.g., Hegel, *Fenomenologiia* 1959 49, 51, 82) and (*ein*) *Vorgestelltes* ("what has been represented") as *predstavlennoe* (e.g., Hegel, *Fenomenologiia* 1959 17, 107, 328), and occasionally as *predstavliaemoe* (Hegel, *Fenomenologiia* 1959 87, 297).

Hegel's key term *Vermittlung* ("mediation") is regularly rendered, again as in Radlov, as *oposredstvovanie*, but *Vermitteln* ("act of mediating") as *protsess oposredstvovaniia* (*Fenomenologiia* 1959 10). The term (*ein*) *Vermitteltes* ("what has been mediated") is cleanly rendered as *oposredstvovannoe* (*Fenomenologiia* 1959 52). *Veränderung* ("alteration") is standardly translated— again as in Radlov—as *izmenenie*, but *Verändern* as *protsess izmeneniia* (*Fenomenologiia* 1959 118) and once as the odd coinage *pereinachivanie* (*Fenomenologiia* 1959 303).

On the whole, Shpet uses the imperfective form, such as *vosprinimanie*, more frequently than the *protsess . . .* formulation. Examples are the translation of *Anerkennung* ("recognition") as *priznanie* and *Anerkennen* ("act of recognizing") as *priznavanie* (*Fenomenologiia* 1959 99, 100), with an occasional confusing use of *priznanie* for *Anerkennen* as well (*Fenomenologiia* 1959 252, 343). (*Ein*) *Aner-kanntes* ("what has been recognized") is generally rendered as *priznannoe*, but also in certain other ways. The more abstract term (*das*) *Anerkanntsein* ("state or condition of having been recognized") is rendered, adequately, I think, as *priznannost'* (e.g., *Fenomenologiia* 1959 102, 103, 242). Shpet preserves Hegel's distinction between *Annerkanntsein* and *Annerkanntwerden* ("condition of becoming recognized") by translating the latter, at least twice, as *priznavaemost'* (343).

The celebrated *Aufhebung* ("sublation," i.e., "cancelling, preserving, and raising to a higher dialectical level") is rendered as *sniatie*, a term not only used throughout the Radlov translation but current, at least since the early 1840s, in Russian philosophical discourse. Shpet generally follows Radlov in also using *sniatie* to render *Aufheben* ("act of sublating") (e.g., *Fenomenologiia* 1959 16, 18, 56), which obscures Hegel's distinction. At least once Shpet renders *Aufheben* by the more adequate *snimanie* (*Fenomenologiia* 1959 150). The term (*ein*) *Aufgehobenes* ("what has been sublated") is generally translated as *sniatoe* and the more abstract *Aufgehobensein* ("state or condition of having been sublated") as *sniatost'*, although Bykova would prefer the more elaborate *bytie v kachestve sniatogo* (see her remark in Hegel, *Fenomenologiia* 2000 427n.68). Shpet renders *Aufgehobenwerden* ("the process of having become sublated") as *snimaemost'* (*Fenomenologiia* 1959 102). Other terms for which the imperfective verbal noun rather than the *protsess . . .* formulation is used include: *uslovie* ("condition"; e.g., Hegel, *Fenomenologiia* 1959 34, 136, 278) for *Bedingung* and *obuslovlivanie* (36) for *Bedingen* ("act of conditioning"), and *razdvoenie* (e.g., *Fenomenologiia* 1959 9, 75, 90) for *Entzweiung* ("bifurcation"), reserving *razdvaivanie* (e.g., *Fenomenologiia* 1959 89, 90, 96) for *Entzweien* ("act or process of bifurcating").

Anschauung ("intuition"), rendered as *sozertsanie*, *vozzrenie*, and *intuitsiia*, has as its counterpart *Anschauen* ("act of intuiting"), rendered, confusingly, as *sozertsanie* (e.g., *Fenomenologiia* 1959 23, 31, 35), *intuitsiia* (*Fenomenologiia* 1959 9) and as *protsess sozertsaniia* at least once (*Fenomenologiia* 1959 431). Shpet uses *postizhenie* to render both *Auffassung* ("apprehension") and *Auffassen* ("process of apprehending"), but in half a dozen places he uses the imperfective form *postiganie* (e.g., *Fenomenologiia* 1959 32, 66, 74) for *Auffassen* and in another place he uses *protsess postizheniia* (*Fenomenologiia* 1959 69). He frequently uses the same term, *nabliudenie*, to translate both *Beobachtung* ("observation") and *Beobachten* ("act of observing"). But in a few cases he puts *protsess nabliudeniia* for *Beobachten* (*Fenomenologiia* 1959 130, 132, 161).

The term *Empfindung* ("sensation") is sometimes rendered as *chuvstvo* (e.g., *Fenomenologiia* 1959 193, 226, 238), less often as *oshchushchenie* (e.g., *Fenom-enologiia* 1959 26, 128, 367). Shpet does not translate *Empfinden* ("act of sensing") as *chuvstvo*, but sometimes as *oshchushchenie* (*Fenomenologiia* 1959 131) and at least once as the preferable *protsess oshchushcheniia* (*Fenomenologiia* 1959 128). Shpet, like Radlov, sometimes (e.g., 33, 310) uses *dvizhenie* for both *Bewegung* ("motion") and *Bewegen* ("act of moving"), but he also employs the dynamic expressions *privedenie v dvizhenie* (*Fenomenologiia* 1959 230) and *protsess dvizheniia* (*Fenomenologiia* 1959 419) for *Bewegen*. In one place *Bewegen* is left untranslated (*Fenomenologiia* 1959 232). The case of *Handlung* ("action") and *Handeln* ("process of acting") is complex. The first term is most often rendered as *postupok*, but twice as *deiatel'nost'* (*Fenomenologiia* 1959 174, 218); the second term is translated as both *postupok* (about a dozen times) and *deiatel'nost'* (five times). I have not found the *protsess . . .* formulation for *Handeln*, but two equally dynamic expressions—*sovershenie postupkov* and *sovershat' postupki* (e.g., *Fenomenologiia* 1959 213, 236, 250)—occur frequently, and the expressions *sovershenie deistvii* and *sovershat' deistviia* occur at least three times (*Fenomenologiia* 1959 389, 391). Shpet, like Radlov, regularly uses *proverka* to render both *Prüfung* ("examination") and *Prüfen* ("act of examining"). But the expression *protsess proverki* appears as the rendering of *Prüfen* on a page where *proverka* alone is twice used to render the same German term (*Fenomenologiia* 1959 228).

Perhaps because his time for work on, and revision of, the translation was so severely limited, Shpet often makes no perceptible advance over Radlov, using the same Russian term to translate both Hegel's *-ung* and *-en* terms. Thus, he uses *vozniknovenie* for both *Entstehung* ("origination") and *Entstehen* ("originative act or process"), *opyt* for both *Erfahrung* ("experience") and *Erfahren* ("act of experiencing"); *ob'iasnenie* for both *Erklärung* ("explanation") and *Erklären* ("act of explaining"); *porozhdenie* for both *Erzeugung* ("procreation") and *Erzeugen* ("act of procreating"); *opisanie* for both *Beschreibung* ("description") and *Beschreiben* ("act of describing"); *opredelenie* for both *Bestimmung* ("determination") and (*das*) *Bestimmen* ("act of determining'), although he rightly uses the term *naznachenie* to render a different sense of *Bestimmung* ("vocation" or "destiny"; *Fenomenologiia* 1959 278). Certain German nouns that do not end in *-ung* are paired with nouns ending in *-en*, for example, *Arbeit* ("work")/(*das*) *Arbeiten* ("process of labor"), *Erkenntnis* ("knowledge")/*Erkennen* ("cognitive process"), and *Genuss* ("enjoyment")/*Geniessen* ("act of enjoying"). Unlike Radlov, Shpet sometimes uses the *protsess . . .* formulation to convey this distinction as well, for example, *protsess truda* (*Fenomenologiia* 1959 118, 119).

In most cases Shpet follows Radlov in rendering both *Kampf* ("struggle") and *Kämpfen* ("act of struggling") by the same word, *bor'ba*. But in at least one place he translates *Kämpfen* as *protsess bor'by* (*Fenomenologiia* 1959 206). He chooses the Latinate *negatsiia* to render Hegel's *Negation* ("negation") in preference to Radlov's Slavic *otritsanie*, but, like Radlov, he mostly fails to use a different term to translate (*das*) *Negieren*. However, in a passage in which both terms occur, he does preserve Hegel's distinction (as Radlov does not), putting *protsess negatsii* for *Negieren* (*Fenomenologiia* 1959 61). Hegel frequently uses the term *Übergang* ("transition"), the counterpart (*das*) *Übergehen* ("process of transition") less frequently. In most cases Shpet renders both terms by the same Russian word, *perekhod*. But in at least two places he uses *protsess perekhoda* to translate *Übergehen*, thus preserving Hegel's distinction (*Fenomenologiia* 1959 210, 242). Shpet generally translates *Ar-*

beit ("work") as *trud*, but sometimes as *rabota*, the term used almost exclusively by Radlov. As in Radlov, (*das*) *Arbeiten* ("process of labor") is sometimes rendered as *rabota*. But in at least two places Shpet uses the expression *protsess truda* to render *Arbeiten* (*Fenomenologiia* 1959 118, 119). He also uses the different, but equally dynamic expression *vypolnenie raboty* for this purpose (*Fenomenologiia* 1959 316). In other cases Shpet preserves Hegel's distinction by using variant forms of the Russian term used to translate the first German word of the pair. Thus *Begriff* ("concept"), standardly rendered as *poniatie*, is contrasted with (*das*) *Begreifen* ("act of conceiving") by the use of either *postizhenie v poniatii* (*Fenomenologiia* 1959 313) or the preferable imperfective form *postiganie v poniatii* (*Fenomenologiia* 1959 23, 418, 428). Shpet usually translates both (*das*) *Urteil* ("judgement") and (*das*) *Urteilen* ("act of judging") as *suzhdenie*. But at least twice, he renders (*das*) *Urteilen* as (the somewhat awkward) *sostavlenie suzhdenii*, thus still maintaining Hegel's distinction (*Fenomenologiia* 1959 269).

Conclusion

We have no way of knowing how Shpet would have changed his translation if he had been granted the leisure to revise it and see it through the press. Would he have reduced the verbatim overlap with the Radlov version? Would he have made his use of the *protsess . . .* formulation and the imperfective forms (like *poznavanie*) to distinguish Hegel's *-en* forms from his *-ung* and other forms more consistent and far-reaching? There is reason to think that he would have done both, and that he would have made a number of other changes, to improve his already hugely impressive translation, one of the very best in any European language.

I entirely agree with the praise lavished on Shpet's translation of Hegel's *Phänomenolie des Geistes* by such knowledgeable commentators as Marina Bykova, a noted Hegel scholar, and Tat'iana Shchedrina, a serious Shpet biographer. This translation, in Bykova's words, "was executed in a way that was truly brilliant" (*Misteriia* 184). Shchedrina adds: "He translated this work as only he could do it, with complete knowledge of the tradition of the school of philosophical translation" (76). As Shpet's wife had reported earlier, "He used a variety of different dictionaries in his search for the necessary meaning, unique in context, of the word he was translating" (qtd. in Shchedrina 44). The work, even in its present imperfect and, in a sense, unfinished form—despite its closeness in many of the less technical passages to the earlier Radlov version—stands as a towering achievement, one which puts, and will put, every Russian reader of Hegel's profound, rich, and brilliant treatise permanently in Shpet's debt.

Works Cited

Bykova, Marina F. *Misteriia logiki i taina sub"ektivnosti v filosofii Gegelia*. Moscow: Nauka, 1996.

Hegel, G.W.F. *Phänomenologie des Geistes*. Ed. J. Hoffmeister. Leipzig: Meiner, 1949.

Hegel, G.W.F. *The Phenomenology of Mind*. Trans. J.B. Baillie. New York: Macmillan, 1910.

Hegel, G.W.F. *Phenomenology of Spirit*. Trans. A.V. Miller. New York: Oxford UP, 1977.

Hegel, G.W.F. *Fenomenologiia dukha*. Trans. Ekaterina Amenitskaia, Nina Anikieva, Zinaida Efimovskaia, Kseniia Miloradovich, and Natal'ia Muretova. Ed. Ernest Radlov. St. Petersburg: Trudy S.-Peterburgskogo Filosofskogo Obshchestva, 1913.

Hegel, G.W.F. *Fenomenologiia dukha*. Trans. G.G. Shpet. Moscow: Akademiia Nauk SSSR, Institut Filosofii, 1959.

Hegel, G.W.F. *Fenomenologiia dukha*. Trans. G. Shpet. Ed. M.F. Bykova. Moscow: Nauka, 2000.

Kline, George L. "Philosophical Puns." *Philosophy and the Civilizing Arts: Essays Presented to Herbert W. Schneider on his Eightieth Birthday*. Ed. John Anton and Craig Walton. Athens: Ohio UP, 1974. 213-35.

Kline, George L. "Meditations of a Russian Neo-Husserlian: Gustav Shpet's 'The Skeptic and His Soul.'" *Phenomenology and Skepticism: Essays in Honor of James M. Edie*. Ed. Brice R. Wachterhauser. Evanston: Northwestern UP, 1996. 144-63, 249-54.

Petritskii, V.A. "K tvorcheskoi biografii G.G. Shpeta (po materialam ekzempliara 'Vvedeniia v etnicheskuiu psikhologiiu' s inskriptom filosofa)." *Shpetovskie chteniia v Tomske, 1991*. Ed. O.G. Mazaeva. Tomsk: Izdatel'stvo Tomskogo Universiteta, 1991. 21-26.

Shchedrina, Tat'iana G. "*Ia pishu kak ekho drugogo . . .*" *Ocherki intellektual'noi biografii Gustava Shpeta*. Moscow: Progress-Traditsiia, 2004.

Serebrennikov, N.V., ed. *Shpet v Sibiri: ssylka i gibel'*. Tomsk: Vodolei, 1995.

Solov'ev, Vladimir S. *Sochineniia v dvukh tomakh*. Ed. A.F. Losev and A.V. Gulyga. Moscow: Mysl' and Akademiia Nauk SSSR, Institut Filosofii, 1988.

The Objective Sense of History: Shpet's Synthesis of Hegel, Cieszkowski, Herzen, and Husserl

Ulrich Schmid

Gustav Shpet is well known for his strong opinions. He relentlessly searches for objective truth—and truth is only acceptable to him if it represents life (Shpet, *Istoriia kak problema* 53). Mere formalistic thinking is highly suspicious to him (Eismann 219). For all his inclination towards rigorous scientific categorization Shpet always ties theory to practice. Even pure logic is in his view not without subject matter: the laws of logic are applicable to logical thinking itself. His philosophy is never autotelic; he unremittingly strives to explain the objective phenomena of the world. In his *Outline of the Development of Russian Philosophy* Shpet justifies his own methodological approach and insists on the objective quality of his research: "If I only made observations, reacted impulsively in an act of self-protection on the visible and transferred my 'state of mind' into the book, I would succumb to a subjective moment. But if I step aside and try to look from a distance at the historical surrounding as an objective reality . . . I proceed methodologically correctly" ("Ocherk" 220).

Shpet followed Husserl in his ambition for strict scientific objectivity and fought against psychologism and subjectivism. After his "phenomenological turn" (Haardt, *Husserl* 83), Shpet grew increasingly sceptical towards Kant and especially the Neo-Kantians. The introduction to the second part of *History as a Problem of Logic* begins with a diatribe against Kant's reduction of philosophy to a critique of the human apparatus of cognition. Shpet criticizes Kant's simplistic assumption that all experience is empirical (*Istoriia kak problema* 558-61). He finds rather harsh words for Kant, calling him a "sophist" (550) whose "doctrine is based on falsity" (557). Kant is reproached for his formalistic understanding of philosophy which does not consider "real life." Already in the first part of *History as a Problem of Logic* Shpet had turned down Kant, pointing out his blindness towards the possibility of a philosophy of history. Since all reality for Kant is exclusively empirical, Shpet argues, Kantian philosophy is not able to deal with the given reality, but only with possibilities. The same holds true for the problem of history: Kantian philosophy describes merely the "conditions of the possibility" of interpreting the historical process, but not the process itself (*Istoriia kak problema* 421).

157

I argue in this paper that Shpet draws in his own philosophy of history on other thinkers (mainly Hegel), with whom he shares a tacit unanimity throughout *History as a Problem of Logic*. However, Shpet's take on the philosophy of history should not be hastily identified with orthodox Hegelianism. Shpet adds significant corrections to Hegel's views on history—he integrates August Cieszkowski's "philosophy of the deed," Herzen's preoccupation with the social dimension of history and Husserl's understanding of history as an objective reality. Finally, Shpet insists, independently of all these thinkers, on a hermeneutic approach to history, which could lend justification to seeing him as an early predecessor of Hayden White (see also Steiner, "Shpet's Philosophy") or Hans-Georg Gadamer (Schmid 269).

Hegel

In Shpet's *opus magnum* on the philosophy of history, one thinker is significantly absent: Hegel. On more than 1000 pages of his book, Shpet dwells at length on Hume, Bacon, Bolingbroke, Montesquieu, Voltaire, Rousseau, Turgot, d'Alembert, Wolff, Kant, Bernheim, Chladenius, Iselin, Adelung, Schelling, Mill, Wundt, Sigwart, Dilthey, and Rickert. The few approving remarks which Shpet makes about Hegel in the course of his argumentation prove that Shpet omits Hegel neither by negligence nor because he disagreed with him. Why then, we should ask, does Shpet give Hegel a wide berth?

Shpet's taciturnity towards Hegel has to be seen in the context of his own philosophical project and its methodological premises. Shpet wants to establish the philosophy of history as a "rigorous science." Although he embraced Hegel's philosophy of history, he could not find in Hegel the strong ally he needed in his struggle against subjectivism and psychologism. In a short essay written probably around 1914-1916, Shpet formulates his ambivalent stance toward Hegel. He follows Hegel's critique of Kant's "confused" epistemology as formulated in paragraph 10 of Hegel's *Encyclopaedia of the Philosophical Sciences*: "The attempt to perceive before any perception is as absurd as the wise intention of a scholastic to learn to swim before he even goes into the water". But then, while praising Hegel for his good intentions, Shpet goes on to accuse him of not taking his criticism of Kant to its logical end:

> Hegel did not listen to Kant and threw himself into the water; but still he was deceived by Kant, because he firmly believed that he will find in the plains of Prussia—after having returned to himself—the treasure of truth. He was at the threshold of the kingdom of ideas; the revelation reached him that he wasn't the legislator, and all that was real became for him penetrated with reason, he saw that the rational [*razumnoe*] was not a spectre and not an "als ob," but was actually real; yet its reality garbed in flesh bowed to Kant's enthusiasm for the familiar [*rodnogo*] article of faith [*deviza*]: "Submit!" . . . Hegel threw himself into the water but when he got out he found only himself—the absolute idealism remained a subject-centered philosophy. ("Rabota" 223)

The same reproach is repeated in the draft of a review of I.A. Il'in's 1918 book on Hegel. Hegel appears as a serious philosopher who overcame Kant's fixation on epistemology but who limited himself to a *"subjective* logic" (Shpet, "Opyt" 287). The only aspect in Hegel's philosophy that Shpet exempts from this critique is Hegel's philosophy of history. Here—according to Shpet—Hegel really jumped into the water and managed not to give in to the temptations of subjectivism. Shpet demanded from history a minimum of rationality, otherwise it would be impossible for the philosophical mind to interpret history at all. Hegel's conceptualization of history could of course supply this much needed rationality.

Hegel advocates a historical optimism—the first part of his lectures on the philosophy of history bears the programmatic title "The Reason in History." For Hegel, history is nothing but the unfolding of spirit in time, and its ultimate goal is freedom. In his view, theory necessarily entails practice. If freedom is known theoretically, then it will also be realized in practice: "The Orientals do not know that the spirit or man as such is free. Because they do not know [this], they are not [free]. They only know that *one* is free . . . But this one is only a despot, not a man . . . The Greeks and Romans knew that *some* are free . . . But only the Germanic nations became within Christianity aware that Man as Man is free, that Freedom of the spirit constitutes his innermost nature" (62). In Hegel's conception there are even hints at a possible "end of history"—in European Christianity spirit has come to full consciousness of itself and thus history is completed, and it would be senseless for it to continue its course. A similar, albeit more reserved, strain of optimism can be perceived in Shpet's postrevolutionary works. In the introduction to his *Outline of the Development of Russian Philosophy*, there is a distinct sense of a historical progress—Shpet explicitly mentions that maybe he would not have written this work without the revolution. Shpet was by no means a Bolshevik, but it is quite possible that he misinterpreted the Russian revolution in Hegelian terms as a decisive stage in the general movement of history towards freedom: "As the revolution itself is an antithesis, an antechamber [leading] to the synthesis, so dusk . . . promises a new daybreak . . . All *Weltanschauung*, all understanding of life, all 'ideology' have to be principally new. All this being true, it is clear that the revolution is a recapitulation which can be a criterion and a completion in whose light it is entirely acceptable to consider any aspect . . . of our history" ("Ocherk" 221-22). These sentences (published in 1922) were written after the civil war and the consolidation of Lenin's government. Shpet rejects the upheavals of the power struggles, but he accepts the revolution as an antithesis to the deficient tsarist rule. The revolution is seen as a plough that eliminates culture from the Russian soil but makes it at the same time ready to conceive a new seed (Lektorskii 130). Shpet sighs ironically that he wished he was a Marxist: in this case he could have easily adopted the position of a chronicler who looks back on history as following a higher necessity. But Shpet prefers a Hegelian interpretation: history progresses, yet not along entirely predictable lines. Nations have a biography, and this biography is governed by rationality rather than necessity. Already in a letter to Husserl from 10 June 1918, Shpet takes recourse to the Hegelian notion that mankind—like man—comes of age: "The madness of the aging mankind seems to be far from coming to an end, and we don't know what the near future will bring" (Husserl 542).

Sphet justifies the revolution by making a very Hegelian distinction between *existence* and *reality*. This allows him to see behind the cruel everyday life under the Bolshevist regime a certain historical sense which is allocated on a higher level of reality. Shpet begins with an elaborate explication of Hegel's famous formula "Everything rational is real, and everything real is rational": "If we want to understand the notion of 'reality' we have to keep in mind Hegel's gradation of being on which consciousness dialectically rises from the dim immediate sensual givenness to the last speculative rational givenness of spirit and the absolute . . . In a strict sense real is only the absolute, and in this sense it can be identified with the reason; and it is the exclusive and true reality" ("K voprosu" 123-24). Hegel's concept of a rational reality runs like a red thread through Shpet's philosophical work. Shpet adds several modifications to this basic idea, but Hegel is often implicitly present in his arguments. In his review of Il'in's book on Hegel, Shpet praises Hegel enthusiastically for his conceptualization of reality as the result of history which endows reality with a specific sense. The blind forces of nature would not be able to guarantee a rational reality: "This is Hegel's major achievement: to show reality as historical reality! In his person 'history' won over 'nature'" (Shpet, "Opyt" 294).

Cieszkowski

Altough Shpet defends Hegel's conception of the mutual penetration, indeed the identity, of reason and reality, he obviously did not want to confine himself to an apology of right-Hegelian philosophy of history. It is not by chance that Shpet turned in this situation to the Polish thinker August Cieszkowski who published in 1838—seven years after Hegel's death—a small book written in German under the title *Prolegomena zur Historiosophie*. Cieszkowski criticizes Hegel's conception of history for dealing exclusively with the past. Against Hegel's thesis that history is coming to an end in the present, Cieszkowski claims that any philosophy of history has to respect the future. Cieszkowski agrees that philosophy has reached its culmination point in Hegel's encyclopaedic system of sciences, but he does not share Hegel's belief that reality will adapt itself automatically to the progress of theory. Cieszkowski calls for a "philosophy of the deed" which will accommodate reality to the insights of philosophy: "The discovery of method is in fact the discovery of the philosopher's stone; now we have to create the miracles which lay in the powers of this stone" (131).

Shpet appreciates Cieszkowski's position as the "only link" (*Filosofskoe* 79) between Hegel and left Hegelianism: Cieszkowski tried to conceptualize the urgent social problems as a lack of practical rationality, a state which has to be overcome by implementing rationality in everyday reality. Cieszkowski thus corrected Hegel's optimistic view of the power of theoretical thought to unfold automatically in reality and maintained that human action has to complement the insights of philosophy. For Cieszkowski, there were very concrete historical reasons for such a correction: the Polish uprising against the Russian occupation in 1830 had just failed, and the Polish intelligentsia was not prepared to accept the status quo as rational. A "philosophy of the deed" could justify the preparations for a new strike against the Russian enemy. This position is very close to Shpet's own modification of Hegelianism. For Shpet, too, the ideal identity of rationality and reality is far from obvious. He conceives of history as an ongoing process with a past, a present and a future: "Historical Reality is—as we said—a continuous movement which was realized, realizes itself and has to be realized. It is not a mechanical movement but a *creative* one: it creates, embodies and realizes an idea" (Shpet, *Die Hermeneutik* 280). Both Cieszkowski and Shpet assume, against Hegel, that the historical process has not yet come to an end—and prevailing for both is the notion of a future which has to be created according to the rational insights of the present. Shpet underlines the dialectic nature of Cieszkowski's amendment to Hegel's philosophy of history: Cieszkowski formulates a simple and convincing approach to the unsolved problem of the relationship between theory and practice. Action is conceived of as an antithesis to the thesis of philosophical thought—and action and thought together will push mankind towards a new synthesis.

Shpet deals with Cieszkowski in his book on Herzen. The "philosophy of the deed" is presented here as a decisive mediating influence that turned Hegel's philosophy of history into a base for Herzen's *Weltanschauung*. Cieszkowski's transformation of Hegel provided a solution not only for Herzen but also for Shpet himself. Alexandre Koyré states that Shpet "exaggerated Cieszkowski's influence on Herzen" (190). This is likely to be true and may indicate that Shpet does speak here also *pro domo sua*. Cieszkowski is granted a chapter of his own in Shpet's book on Herzen—not so much because Herzen's philosophy of history cannot be understood without Cieszkowski, but because Shpet's own Hegelian conception needs a practical extension which is readily provided by the "philosophy of the deed."

Herzen

In his longish essay "Herzen's philosophical Weltanschauung," Shpet tries to free Herzen from the bonds of socialist and Marxist philosophy (Paperno 127). Shpet's new interpretation of Herzen can at the same time be read as an explication of the genealogy of his own thinking: "Herzen was attracted, firstly, by the scientific quality [*nauchnost'*] of Hegel's philosophy, and, secondly, by the fact that the ultimate goal of this philosophy was reality itself" (Shpet, *Filosofskoe* 12). These two aspects correspond at the same time to the main criteria that Shpet had established for his own critical appreciation of any philosophical system. The early Herzen—Shpet quotes his *Letters about the Inquiry into Nature*—claimed that rationality is omnipresent but sometimes hidden. A person's task consists in the disclosure of the secret rationality in the real world that surrounds him or her. Shpet emphasizes that Herzen rules out any subjective moment in this process and quotes approvingly from the *Letters*: "Man does not discover his rationality everywhere because he is rational and projects his rationality onto everything, but on the contrary: he is rational because everything is rational" (Shpet, *Filosofskoe* 15).

After 1848, Herzen's Hegelianism suffered a severe blow. The failed revolutions and his own family drama led Herzen to a very pragmatic view of historical reality. According to Herzen, history is driven by the will and energy of the individual personality, and not by itself, not by some unalterable laws—be they those of God or Nature. This is a clear departure from Hegelianism, but Shpet nevertheless tries to save Hegel for Herzen: he underlines the Hegelian notion in Herzen's late thinking that every individual has to fulfil a historical task and that the history of nations can be likened to the biographies of individuals (*Filosofskoe* 38). Shpet makes use of Cieszkowski's skepticism regarding Hegel's trust in the practical power of theory and points to the fact that Herzen had read and approved of Cieszkowski's book on historiosophy (*Filosofskoe* 76). But still, Shpet insists on the Hegelian nature of Herzen's late conception of the role of the intellectual in society: according to Herzen, man is not completely free in his actions; he is a "continuation of nature" and, like nature, subordinated to the laws of logic. Being himself part of nature, by creating history, man links nature with logic. For Herzen, history does not follow blindly a providential plan; it provides space for human action. History is "improvisation," it is closely linked to human freedom. Shpet thus sees the difference between Hegel and Herzen in Herzen's rejection of Hegel's vision of history moving by design towards freedom—he wants human action to be credited for historical rationality (*Filosofskoe* 40).

Shpet stresses that teleology is generally suspect for Herzen: if one looks at life under a teleological aspect, the goal is always death. Shpet discovers Herzen's solution of this dilemma in the latter's orientation towards the present. Only the present can justify human endeavor in history: "The last dualism, the dualism between the ideal goal of man and his real behaviour, is being resolved in his own reality in the present which deletes all antinomies and turns all ideal goals of history into real tasks of an actual agenda in all its richness, with the inheritance of the past and the seeds of the future" (*Filosofskoe* 52). For Shpet, the distance between thought and reality is not only a question of historical creativity. It is above all a question of rationally overcoming all dualisms and bringing them together into a unity: "Herzen unterstood the task of the epoch as follows: it was about time to remove the last emerging dualism between practice and theory, the antinomy of reality and reason which manifests itself in the fact. If the fact itself shows that our cruel and petty reality is not reasonable, then the task of the epoch lies precisely in the transformation of the theoretical understanding into practical reality, in the creation of a reasonable reality. If it is not reasonable, it has to become reasonable" (*Filosofskoe* 20). Shpet thus maintains that the task of philosophy is to show that every dualism is a state of alienation. It is by discursive work that the philosopher can resolve all precarious dualisms. The worst dualism is the alleged nonidentity of the objective sense of life and its various possible subjective interpretations: "With the resolution of the problem about the relation between the universal and the particular we ascertain or, more accurately, once again see the immediate unity between them, that unity in which we live and act. The content of life is animated not only through the significations that we discover in it but also through that inner sense thanks to which there arises in us a feeling of our own place in the world and of everything in it" (*Appearance* 171).

It should be noted that Herzen's and Shpet's ideal unity of theory and practice in history is not Hegelian. Hegel asserted that periods of "happiness" are "empty sheets in world history" because they are periods of consent, of lacking opposites (Hegel 92). Furthermore, Herzen and Shpet rule out Hegel's idea of a teleological historical process: both Russian thinkers maintain that history has to be created by mankind. While they agree with Hegel that there is rationality in the historical process, they part ways with him in believing that it has to be completed by responsible and creative human action. In "Hermeneutics and Its Problems," Shpet writes: "I do not think that we could learn from [existing] knowledge of the realization of history and its rationality how we should realize history in the future. I even believe the opposite—if we tried to realize history according to this knowledge we would commit an evil deed: we would put an end to our free and unlimited creativity. We would furthermore deprive history of the possibility to realize itself. We would end history" (281).

Husserl

Shpet's *History as a Problem of Logic* was written in a phase of growing skepticism towards pure phenomenology. Already in a letter to Husserl from November 23, 1913 Shpet had expressed some reservations about phenomenology: "The magic of phenomenology makes me blind in some directions, but for the time being I do not want to know if this is bad or not!" (Husserl 529). Perhaps as a direct consequence of this self-imposed blindness Shpet praised phenomenology in *Appearance and Sense* (1914) as the basic science for all philosophy:

> The corner-stone of the entire edifice of phenomenology is that it firmly establishes a presentativism of everything that exists in all of its species and forms of our consciousness. It strikes a blow equally against both phenomenalism and Kantian dualism . . . One of the greatest contributions of phenomenology is the fact that it transferred the old dispute about universals and particulars, about realism and nominalism, from the sphere of anemic abstractions to the living depths of intuitive experience, which within the entire mental process forms the "beginning" and the "source" of any philosophizing at all. (170)

Later on, Shpet moved away from the pure logic of phenomenology and tried to establish a new basic science which encompasses both semiotics and semasiology. Not only the sign-based constitution of meaning is central to Shpet, but also the connection between the objective reality of life and the inventory of semiotic representations which can be ascribed to historical phenomena. Shpet does not immerse himself into the description of human cognition, which could for him easily present a step back to Kantianism; he tries instead to clarify the interconnections between historical events and their interpretation, between the logic of objects and hermeneutics—or as he would have it, between appearance and sense.

Shpet identifies the sign as the missing link between those terms. Only the sign can bridge the gap between subjective thinking and objective reality. Shpet proposes to look at the sign not from the point of view of its function as iconic representation of a thing, but—on the contrary—as a part of reality itself. In an essay with the title "Sign-Signification as a Relation Sui Generis and Its System," probably written between 1921 and 1925, Shpet explains his definition of the sign: "If we look at the sign in its role as an objective go-between, we see that—in spite of its ideal signification—it denominates any item of a given class or of a given extension. Thus it becomes a kind of realization and brings the ideal exemplarily into existence. In this sense it can be said that the sign is nothing else but a historical fact" ("Znak-znachenie" 84).

Most importantly, the sign embodies historical reality. In an essay with the title "History as the Subject of Logic," written in 1917 but published only five years later, Shpet accepts reality only insofar as it can be represented semiotically: "History as a science knows only one source of knowledge: the word [*slovo*]. The word is the form in which the historian finds the content of reality which is the basis of his scientific knowledge, and the word is the sign from which the historian comes to his subject with its specific content which constitutes the significance or sense of this sign" ("Istoriia, kak predmet" 15-16). History thus must be read as a text. The historian's task consists not only in understanding the text of the historical signs, but in rewriting this text anew. As a consequence, history is basically a philological science (35). Shpet even maintains that the logical structure of history may be demonstrated through fictional examples. The borderline between literature and history is not relevant for a logical analysis of history. Shpet declares that the logical analysis of history has nothing to do with the actual historical process: "History as a science has to do with the *word* as a sign which interests the historian first of all and almost exclusively in its meaning, i.e. in the content about which the word speaks. It tells the historian about different social events, relations, states, changes etc. But precisely the real content of history does not interest the logician, he is not able to do anything with this kind of content" (23)

Shpet draws attention to the various modes of narration and interpretation that can be applied to historical reality. He calls for a special kind of epistemology for the historical sciences—and this task can only be performed by hermeneutics ("Filosofiia i istoriia" 437; "Istoriia, kak predmet" 35).

Shpet's Hermeneutic Dimension

Shpet adds a hermeneutic dimension to his conceptual synthesis of Hegel, Cieszkowski, Herzen, and Husserl. He appreciates all these predecessors as representatives of a "positive philosophy" as opposed to "negative philosophy," which he condemns as blind and empty. In Shpet's understanding, positive philosophy stands in Plato's tradition and is oriented towards an inquiry into the first principles of science ("Filosofiia i istoriia" 428-30). According to this positive point of view, following the Platonian concept of *methexis* ("participation"), truth can be perceived in the real world. Negative philosophy refers to Kant and eventually leads to a complete relativism: all knowledge depends on the forms of subjective perception, and objectivity is reduced to mere intersubjectivity (Kuznetsov 202-03). From early on, Shpet rejects this kind of "negativism." Andrei Belyi—in the first decade of the twentieth century himself a follower of Neo-Kantianism—describes in his memoirs Shpet's brave fight: "The Kantians entered the battle in heavy armours and looked from afar like Goliaths; but Shpet came out in the nakedness of scepticism and threw the skittles ball energetically like David: 'trakh'—Goliath's forehead was smashed" (Belyi 277).

Shpet's choice of history as a topic for his dissertation is not just an example of the application of positive philosophy. For Shpet, history is the most important repository of reality and the first source for philosophical analysis: "History is finally the reality which surrounds us, and philosophy has to start with its analysis. Solely in history does this reality present itself in its unconditional and singular [*edinstvennoi*] fullness—in comparison with history, any other reality has to be considered as 'part' or abstraction" (*Istoriia kak problema* 61; see also"Filosofiia i istoriia" 432).

Shpet insists on the presence of reason in reality. The historical reality consists of signs and provides thus an objective significance; Shpet's wording in *History as a Problem of Logic* sounds definitely Hegelian: "The task of positive philosophy lies . . . in the disclosure of the sense of that which exists, of rationality in reality" (56). Shpet also adopts the Hegelian notion that history moves towards freedom. Only this assumption can in his view guarantee that history has an objective sense and is not merely a chaotic heap of individual actions: "The philosophical study of the historical . . . has to concentrate exclusively on the connection and inner unity in the absolute itself or in freedom as the only form of the activity of the absolute. As history would lack unity and wholeness if it consisted only of 'fragments,' of arbitrary individual decisions, so philosophy, too, needs for its creativity an absolute source of unity: freedom" (64).

At this point, Cieszkowski comes into play. Shpet shares Cieszkowski's doubts about Hegel's ideal identity of theory and practice. The most famous formula for this assumption can be found in Hegel's letter to Niethammer of 28 October 1808: "Theoretical work . . . achieves more in the world than practical [work]; if a revolution has only permeated the kingdom of imagination, reality [still] won't be able to withstand" (Hoffmeister 253). Shpet believes just like Cieszkowski that human action—based on the rational analysis of reality—is necessary to push history forward. In this context, Herzen, too, becomes important for Shpet, and for two reasons. On the one hand, Herzen interpreted Russian history in a dialectic way which corresponds very much to Shpet's own view: every stage of history is succeeded by its opposite. Once a system becomes outdated, it is no longer rational and therefore has no longer any legitimate claim on continuous existence. Revolution on this interpretation is nothing but the reinforcement of the rationality of reality (Zimmermann 6). On the other hand, Herzen insisted on the social nature of history. Not individuals, but the educated public was in his eyes the main actor in the drama of history. Shpet adopts a similar stance: the individual is not a "prisoner in solitary confinement" (*History as a Problem* 62) but an organic part of a social entity (Fedorova 201).

Because for Shpet reality is given only in signs, the writing of history is an understanding in the second degree: historical documents already represent a certain interpretation of a situation—the historian has to find a common denominator for all interpretations of a given historical event; he has to understand what others have understood. This is why Shpet does not confine himself to a phenomenological solution of his epistemological problem: "History cannot confine itself to 'outsideness' because it starts from the assertion that everything which is given is only a sign. The explanation of this sign is history's only task. Documents and chronicles are signs which ask for an understanding of some actions which themselves are only signs of hidden historical factors . . . History is in its core not a technical but a *hermeneutic* science" (*Istoriia kak problema* 63).

Stressing the hermeneutic essence of history, Shpet tries to avoid any subjectivism. The fact that historical evidence is given as a sign does not mean that all results of historiography are compromised by the narrator's subjective point of view. It is of the utmost importance that the title of Shpets investigation is not "History as a problem of hermeneutics": in no way does Shpet in his anti-psychological and anti-subjectivist abandon the link between the sign and the logic of the objects that exist in reality. The understanding of a sign refers to an objective logical order which constitutes life. Shpet's solution of the problem is, again, basically Hegelian. In his book "Hermeneutics and Its Problems" he writes: "The problem of understanding is nothing but the problem of spirit itself; spirit and understanding correspond to each other, as an object corresponds to the act which is directed at it. . . . Understanding can be directed exclusively at reason. Spirit as an object of understanding is rational spirit" (279).

It is indicative that Husserl is mentioned only *en passant* in Shpet's "Hermeneutics and Its Problems": Husserl's phenomenology was of use only for the logic of history, not for its hermeneutics. Shpet underlines the figurativeness not only of poetic, but also of scientific language (Haardt, "Shpet, Gustav" 757). Understanding always works through and behind the hidden figurative wording of a sense. The task of a philosophical hermeneutics lies in the explication of the structure of understanding which is directed towards an objective sense. Shpet stresses, however, that the significance of an utterance, a text, or an event does not depend on our thoughts about them (Kuznetsov 205). Shpet insists on a single, objective sense also for the historical interpretation. He warns, though, against identifying thought and the object of thought as Hegel does. For Shpet, the objective sense has to be laid bare in an intentional act that "fills the object with thought and makes it thus thinkable" ("Opyt" 304). However, Shpet overshoots the mark by ruling out the possibility that hermeneutics could yield more than one sense. Biblical interpretation is for him nothing but a "lie" since it allows for several interpretations: "Hermeneutics has to assume that every given sign has only one signification. The basic lie of biblical hermeneutics consists precisely in accepting the premise of a dual sense in every expression: a human and a God-inspired sense" (*Die Hermeneutik* 60). In Shpet's study of Humboldt's philosophy of language, a similar assertion can be found:

> Only in novels can *any* possibility be made rational; in reality only the one possibility which realized itself and became reality is rational, because reality itself is the *reason* [*razum*] of the one and only of the possible senses which has been realized. The realized reality contains in itself its reason as its ratio, i.e., the notion which explains why it is precisely as it is and nothing else. This last explication [*urazumenie*] links *immediately* the concept [*poniatie*] and its subject in a single valid sense. (*Vnutrenniaia* 116)

Such a reduction of history to only one—objective and rational—sense testifies to the high standards of logic which Shpet adopted for his own philosophical thinking. But at the same time, Shpet's trust in the semiotic transparency of the historical process led him to an optimistic interpretation of the Russian Revolution which proved fatal for him. In 1922, he was already on Lenin's list of intellectuals to be expelled from the country. Shpet opposed this verdict with his entire determination and was allowed to stay. In hindsight, this permission has to be considered the beginning of his end. Shpet never received a chance to revise his unbending views on the objective sense and the rationality of history; months before he was shot in Tomsk in 1937, he was still busy translating Hegel's *Phenomenology*.

Works Cited

Belyi, Andrei. *Mezhdu dvukh revoliutsii*. Moscow: Khudozhestvennaia literatura, 1990.

Cieszkowski, August von. *Prolegomena zur Historiosophie*. Hamburg: Meiner, 1981.

Eismann, Wolfgang. *Von der Volkskunst zur proletarischen Kunst. Theorien zur Sprache der Literatur in Russland und der Sowjetunion*. Munich: Sagner, 1986.

Fedorova, L.V. "G. Shpet i A. Gertsen ob istokakh istorizma i realizma." *G.G. Shpet/ Comprehensio. Vtorye shpetovskie chteniia*. Tomsk: Vodolei. 1997. 198-201.

Haardt, Alexander. *Husserl in Rußland. Phänomenologie der Sprache und Kunst bei Gustav Špet und Aleksej Losev*. Munich: Fink, 1993.

Haardt, Alexander. "Shpet, Gustav Gustavovich." *Routledge Encyclopaedia of Philosophy*. Ed. Edward Craig. Vol. 8. London: Routledge, 1998. 754-58.

Hegel, Georg Wilhelm Friedrich. *Vorlesungen über die Weltgeschichte*. Vol. 1. *Die Vernunft in der Geschichte*. Hamburg: Meiner, 1994.

Hoffmeister, Johannes, ed. *Briefe von und an Hegel*. Vol. 1. Hamburg: Meiner 1961.

Husserl, Edmund. *Briefwechsel.* Vol. 3. *Die Göttinger Schule.* Dordrecht: Kluwer, 1994.

Koyré, Alexandre. *Etudes sur l'histoire de la pensée philosophique en Russie.* Paris: Vrin, 1950.

Kuznetsov, V.G. "Germenevticheskaia fenomenologiia v kontekste filosofskikh vozzrenii Gustava Gustavovicha Shpeta." *Logos* 2 (1991): 199-214.

Lektorskii, V.A. "Nemetskaia filosofiia i rossiiskaia gumanitarnaia mysl': S.L. Rubinshtein i G.G. Shpet." *Voprosy filosofii* 10 (2001): 129-39.

Paperno, Irina. "Sovetskii opyt, avtobiograficheskoe pis'mo i istoricheskoe soznanie: Ginzburg, Gertsen, Gegel.'" *Novoe literaturnoe obozrenie* 63 (2004): 102-27.

Schmid, Ulrich. "Gustav Špet." *Russische Religionsphilosophen des 20. Jahrhunderts.* Ed. Ulrich Schmid. Freiburg: Herder, 2003. 265-69.

Shpet, Gustav. *Appearance and Sense: Phenomenology as the Fundamental Science and Its Problems.* Trans. Thomas Nemeth. Dordrecht: Kluwer, 1991.

Shpet, Gustav. *Die Hermeneutik und ihre Probleme (Moskau 1918).* Freiburg: Alber, 1993.

Shpet, Gustav. "Filosofiia i istoriia." *Voprosy filosofii i psikhologii* 134 (1916): 427-39.

Shpet, Gustav. *Filosofskoe mirovozzrenie Gertsena.* Petrograd: Kolos, 1921.

Shpet, Gustav. "Istoriia, kak predmet logiki." *Nauchnye izvestiia. Sbornik 2. Filosofiia, literatura, iskusstvo.* Moscow: Akademicheskii tsentr Narkomprosa, 1922. 1-35.

Shpet, Gustav. *Istoriia kak problema logiki.* Ed. V.S. Miasnikov. Moscow: Pamiatniki istoricheskoi mysli.

Shpet, Gustav . "K voprosu o gegelianstve Belinskogo." *Voprosy filosofii* 7 (1991): 115-76.

Shpet, Gustav. "Ocherk razvitiia russkoi filosofii." *Ocherki istorii russkoi filosofii.* By A.I. Vvedenskii, A.F. Losev, E.L. Radlov and G.G. Shpet. Ed. B.V. Emel'ianov, and K. N. Liubutin. Sverdlovsk: Izdatel'stvo Ural'skogo universiteta, 1991. 217-578.

Shpet, Gustav. "Opyt populiarizatsii filosofii Gegelia." *"Ia pishu kak ekho drugogo . . ." Ocherki intellektual'noi biografii Gustava Shpeta.* By T.G. Shchedrina. Moscow: Progress-Traditsiia, 2004. 281-322.

Shpet, Gustav. "Rabota po filosofii." *Logos* 2 (1991): 213-33.

Shpet, Gustav. *Vnutrenniaia forma slova (Etiudy i variatsii na temy Gumbol'ta).* Moscow: Gosudarstvennaia akademiia khudozhestvennykh nauk, 1927.

Shpet, Gustav. "Znak-znachenie kak otnoshenie sui generis i ego sistema (glava iz rukopisi "Iazyk i smysl." Ch. I)." *Voprosy filosofii* 12 (2002): 79-92.

Steiner, Peter. "*Tropos Logikos*: Gustav Shpet's Philosophy of History." *Slavic Review* 62 (2003): 343-58.

Zimmermann, Judith E. *Midpassage: Alexander Herzen and the European Revolution. 1847-1852.* Pittsburgh: U of Pittsburgh P, 1989.

Shpet's *Aesthetic Fragments* and Sartre's Literary Theory

Alexander Haardt

Translated from the German by Graham Bartram

At the very latest by the time of his 1927 Humboldt interpretation, *Vnutrenniaia*, Shpet's phenomenological descriptions of eidetic structures take on a dialectical dimension derived from Hegel's *Phenomenology of Spirit*. Every description that attempts to grasp the essence of the object lying before it proves to be one sided, and points to alternative descriptions that go beyond itself: "The contradiction, which arises between the posited [*zadannoiu*] fullness of a concrete object and its present [*nalichnuiu*] incompleteness at any given moment, dissolves in its own process of becoming" (Shpet, *Vnutrenniaia* 39). In relation to "culture as the object of linguistic awareness and every kind of cultural awareness" this means that "it [culture] bears within itself the contradiction we have identified, but within culture too, in its own movement, its life and its history, lies the overcoming of the contradiction. The method of the movement of consciousness that is prescribed by an object of this kind, is the dialectical method" (39).

I apply this method of "dialectical interpretation" (Shpet, *Vnutrenniaia* 31) of linguistic and other cultural constructs, as sketched by Shpet, to his own poetics, as laid out in his *Aesthetic Fragments* (written in January-February 1922, published in 1922-23). The characterization offered there of the essential features of poetry or poetic discourse—a characterization that is informed by Shpet's Platonist interpretation of Edmund Husserl's phenomenology, and by predispositions deriving from the intellectual milieu of Russia and the Soviet Union in the late 1910s and early 1920s—is analyzed in its one-sidedness and is juxtaposed with an alternative descriptive model of poetry or literature, which sets other priorities and which historically came into being in a quite different sociocultural context. The model in question is that of Jean-Paul Sartre's essays *What is Literature?*, published in France immediately after the Second World War. Sartre is ultimately bound to a Cartesian interpretation of Edmund Husserl, and both in his understanding of phenomenological method and equally in his selection of literary material sets priorities quite different from those of the author of the *Aesthetic Fragments*. It is precisely because the Russian phenomenologist's and the French phenomenologist's theories of literature are so opposed to each other on the most diverse levels of their analyses that they can be brought into a dialogic relationship with each other with the aid of Shpet's own method of a "dialectical interpretation."

I begin by showing that Husserl's phenomenology is itself susceptible to a dual interpretation that connects it on the one hand with the Russian reception context of Gustav Shpet, orientated to classical Platonism, and on the other with the modern Cartesian understanding of phenomenology dominant in France and shared by Jean-Paul Sartre. Accordingly, Shpet's *Aesthetic Fragments* are shaped by an approach that is oriented to the idea or the structure of the literary work, whereas Sartre in the above-mentioned essays takes the subjectivity of the activity of writing as the starting-point of his analysis. Further reasons for the divergence of the two equally justified—and mutually complementary—attempts to describe literature will be discussed in the course of the comparative analysis itself.

Cartesian and Platonist Phenomenology

Husserl's demand that attention be directed "to things themselves," precisely as they appear does not mean a simple return to the familiar objects of everyday consciousness. For to focus on how a thing appears involves precisely turning one's attention away from the thing itself and towards its mode of appearance, towards the way in which it is given to a subject. Phenomenology admittedly encompasses all the phenomena occurring in everyday life and in the sciences—but from a new point of view. Instead of perceiving and observing things and events of the natural and the social world, detecting patterns or laws in them, the phenomenologist reflects on the processes of perception and observation in which those objects and events are given, as well as on the thought and speech acts through which they are described and explained.

The turning to things thus takes place through a turn back to the consciousness that every individual has of these things. Through the description of those acts of consciousness in which objects are intended, the objects themselves are simultaneously described in the manner of their intendedness. The purpose is to work out, on the basis of individual intentional experiences, the general structures of such experiences. From a single perception of red, for example, the characteristics specific to any and every perception of color are to be determined. This attempt to characterize the key idea and the method of phenomenology—an attempt that essentially corresponds to the procedure in Book 1 of Husserl's *Ideas* (1913)—belongs in the context of the modern philosophy of consciousness: the turn to the things themselves in the precise form in which they appear proves to be a turning away from things and a turning back to the consciousness of them, a consciousness through whose transcendental workings they are to be made comprehensible. While Descartes, in his *Meditations*, had shown in his experiment of radical doubt that for the reflecting subject the whole world becomes doubtful, and that it is completely certain only of itself through the performance of its cogitations, Husserl emphasizes the idea that for the individual who turns away from the world and back to his intentional experiences, this whole world becomes accessible once more in a transfigured form—as the intentional correlate of his consciousness. Alongside this Cartesian version of the path to phenomenology—the version adopted by Husserl himself from his middle phase onwards (*Krisis* 157-58)—phenomenology can also be understood as the continuation of a classical Platonic line of thought. In this version, what is foregrounded is the idea of the particular thing, and it is this idea that has to be determined before questions can be asked about the mode of appearance and consciousness peculiar to this thing. This is also the procedure of the early Husserl, who in his *Logical Investigations* of 1900-01 first set out the ideality of logical constructs, before he enquired into those acts of consciousness through which they achieve reality.

The fact that phenomenology can be interpreted in this dual fashion, both as a resumption of classical Platonism and as a radicalization of the modern philosophy of subjectivity deriving from Descartes, is a crucial reason for there being more than one kind of description in phenomenology. There are at least two descriptions of a thing's mode of appearance, one of which, grounded in classical Platonism, foregrounds the idea of the thing that is manifesting itself, while the other in modern Cartesian fashion reflects the constitutive activity of the consciousness of the transcendental subject. The opposition of a "Cartesian" and a "Platonic" way into phenomenology that will be used in what follows is undoubtedly only an ideal-typical simplification, but it is one that enables us to make sense of wide areas of the history of the reception of Husserl's phenomenological thought.

Because of the different philosophical traditions that were predominant in France, on the one hand, and in Russia, on the other, the two phenomenological movements were each shaped by a different one of the two ways. For the phenomenology of literature that is the focus of our discussion here, this means that in Shpet's Plato-oriented aesthetic, the structure of the literary text occupies a central place, while the relationship of author and reader to the text recedes into the background, in contrast to the "Cartesian" Sartre, for whom it is precisely the subjectivity of the creator and that of the receiver, as well as their relationship to one another, that form the horizon for the analysis of the literary text.

Gustav Shpet's Description of the "Poetic Word"

Shpet's phenomenological description of language and literature is to be found—as already mentioned—in the 1922-23 *Aesthetic Fragments*, his contribution to the contemporary literary-theoretical discussion that was taking place within and in the immediate orbit of the Russian formalist movement (Haardt 136-39). Here he is particularly concerned to establish the specific character of poetic language as distinct from other kinds of language, be they scientific, rhetorical, or everyday. His answer to this question takes the Platonic path of phenomenology, in that under the title "The

Structure of the Word in Usum Aestheticae" he first analyzes the structure of the poetic word, before proceeding to the analysis of the aesthetic reception of poetry. By
"structure" Shpet here understands "a concrete construct whose individual parts may
change in their 'size' and even in their quality but where no single part of the whole
in potentia can be removed without destroying the whole" (*Esteticheskie* 11). The
phrase "whole *in potentia*" refers to the fact that individual parts of a structure may
be found in a purely potential state, without this modifying the structure's pattern. A
structure can furthermore be split up into new, self-enclosed structures, whose own
structuration is representative of that of the whole.

By "structure of the word," the Russian author understands "not its morphological, syntactic or stylistic disposition [*raspolozhenie*], its disposition 'on one level'
[*ploskostnoe*], but, on the contrary, the organic, vertical [*vglub'*] disposition— from
the audible [word] to the formal-ideal (eidetic) object" (Shpet, *Esteticheskie* 11). According to this, the structure of a word includes not only the relationships between
the word's sound and its meaning, but also those between meaning and "object," with
the latter *qua* ideal object being ontologically distinguished from concrete individual
things and their properties. Shpet's repeated references to the structure of the word
are meant in the broad sense of the Russian expression for "word," namely, *slovo*.
Slovo can refer not only to words but also to clauses and complex sentences, even to
literary texts and the totality of a natural language. Shpet too uses the Russian *slovo*
in these manifold ways, but his main concern in his central linguistic-philosophical
analyzes is the "communicating" word, that is, meaningful speech that is capable of
making something known to another person. Here the Russian phenomenologist is
ultimately going back to Plato's definition (in his dialogue *The Sophist*) of the predicative statement as the "shortest and simplest *logos*" (262c).

The structure of this is presented by Shpet as follows. In a simple predicative
statement the expression in the subject-position is the naming of a concrete individual object; the predicate denotes a quality that this object exhibits. Via a user-oriented
analysis of these expressions Shpet shows how such a sentence, formed from proper
noun (or identifying expression) and predicate expression, can have a meaning, and
through that meaning can refer to objects. In the act of naming the speaker refers to a
thing (or to a feature of it), in the predication he says something about it. What can be
said about a particular thing and what predications are excluded from the outset, is
determined by the species that the thing falls under. For this reason, the intending of
this species, which Shpet also terms the "eidetic object," plays a constitutive role in
the formation of a meaningful statement (*Esteticheskie* 34-36). These features define
for Shpet the "structure of the word" that is common to the three kinds of discourse:
the factually communicative or scientific, the rhetorical, and the poetic. The key
to the specifying of this general structure in the literary-artistic use and shaping of
words, clauses and complex sentences lies in Shpet's theory of linguistic functions.
His starting point is the three different functions of language which are fulfilled by
every type of speech, but with a different function dominating the two others in each
case. These are the factually communicative (*soobshchaiushchaia funktsiia*), the ex-

pressive, and the poetic, that is, the creatively language-forming function. The fact that in speech language, as a system of predetermined means of expression, can be reshaped, can be seen, for example, in the formation of new metaphors, but also in the turning of everyday expressions into scientific concepts. According to which of the three language functions just mentioned becomes dominant, we are confronted either with a scientific mode of speech geared to factual communication, with a rhetorical mode of speech concerned above all to influence the listener emotionally, or with poetic speech, whose primary aim is the forming of linguistic expressions as such. The predominance of one or other of the three language functions determines a different interrelationship of the elements of the word structure. Whereas in the language of everyday communication the shaping of the expressive level is aimed primarily at the structuring of the meaning that is being articulated, and within this at the objective communication of facts, in poetic speech each linguistic level acquires a relatively independent significance. The rhythmical forms and syntactical peculiarities of speech, together with the creation of new patterns of meaning, are to be foregrounded for their own sakes. What matters here is not the representation of existing states of affairs, but the adequate realization of the chosen theme or subject. At the same time, the meaning expressed in sentences of poetic speech becomes more greatly dependent on those outward forms of language. Whilst the meaning of a factual communication—especially in the case of scientific discourse—is not affected by every change of wording and of syntactic structure, "poetic meaning," Shpet avers, reacts much more sensitively to such changes. What is formulated in scientific and everyday speech can also be expressed in another way. In contrast, the meaning that is conveyed poetically can only be articulated in one particular way.

With the phenomenological description of poetic speech that we have briefly outlined here Shpet was intent, completely in accordance with the Platonic version of phenomenology, on first of all clarifying the idea of literature, conceived as the textual structure that was peculiar to it, before investigating its aesthetic mode of reception. At this point, however, the question arises whether the notion of the poetic function, whose effectiveness is what constitutes the specifically literary, does not already presuppose a particular view of that attitude of the reader in and through which literature constitutes itself as an aesthetic object. The dominance of the poetic function in a given utterance can after all only be identified by the fact that the latter's structure diverts the reader's attention away from what is said, and directs it towards itself. Only with reference to an aesthetic attitude, which detaches certain phenomena from their pragmatic contexts in order to contemplate them in and for themselves, and which thus also views particular utterances as something other than simple means of factual communication or practical persuasion, can we determine what the poetic function of language consists of. Shpet's analyses of the structure of the aesthetic consciousness are thus not—as he intended—a subsequent addition to the structural analysis of the literary text; they are on the contrary a vital necessity for the explication of the central concept of that analysis, that is, the concept of the poetic function.

This simple thought has a far-reaching methodological consequence: namely, that in the phenomenology of literature, the Platonic way, based on the idea or structure of the literary text, is no longer independent from the Cartesian way, in which the mode of reception of literature is described, but is instead dialectically sublated (*aufgehoben*) in it. There is another sense in which the analyses of the Russian phenomenologist point to something beyond themselves. As is always the case with reflections on the phenomenon of literature, his thoughts are grounded in a particular literary genre and movement, and this is reflected in the make-up of the concept of literature that results. The supreme example of literature for Shpet is modern Russian lyric poetry, especially that of the Symbolist movement, which he includes in his own *Aesthetic Fragments* in the form of interpretations of poems by Aleksandr Blok and Andrei Belyi. What is also important is the fact that he develops his theory of literature and art in a debate with representatives of Russian Formalism, who in turn are oriented to the poetry of the Futurists. The manifestos of the Futurist movement proclaim that intrinsic value of the word (Erlich 46-57) which for Shpet, too, constitutes the very essence of poetic speech. For him, literature (that is first and foremost poetry) is the shaping of language, not the interpretation of the world. This also remains the case when the Russian philosopher is defending the thesis—essential to every Platonic aesthetic of representation—that art is the representation of ideas. For unlike traditional Platonists, he does not mean by this that art establishes a relationship to reality by giving expression to ideas that are also realized—in imperfect form—in the world outside art. Rather, for Shpet the idea in art means simply a formal structure such as the plot in literature, whose function is to subordinate the realm of artistic creativity to certain rules.

Sartre's Definition of Literature as Appeal to the Reader

If one searches in the history of the phenomenological movement for an alternative description of literature, which is not based like Shpet's on lyric poetry but on prose literature, and which methodologically places not the structure of the literary text but the subjectivity of the writer and reader at the centre of attention, one soon comes across the above-mentioned essays of Sartre from 1947, *What is Literature?* Under the headings "What is Writing?" "Why Write?" and "For Whom Does One Write?," Sartre attempts to explain the fundamental objectives of the writer, which are decisive for the structure of the literary text, on the basis of the constitution of human subjectivity. In what follows, this train of thought will be briefly recapitulated, to a large extent using Sartre's own language.

It is a feature of human existence that the things, events, and persons that surround it appear to it in the horizon of a world in a way such that the subject, from the perspective of its concrete situation, actively makes the things appear (45). In this the subject is led by practical interests: things present themselves as useful, harmful, enjoyable, and so on. This means that in the revelation of reality, the latter is always already interpreted with reference to human possibilities, and to that extent transcended in the sense of its own changeability. Speaking and writing in general, and the activity of the prose writer in particular, are thus presented as a specific form of this world-revealing activity of the subject, in which one's own revelation of the world is communicated to another (25-30). Sartre here defines the specific nature of literary prose by differentiating it from two other things: from the production of artistic constructs with which no revelation of the world is intended (Sartre discusses poetic creation as a prime example), and from forms of prose which are not artistic.

The starting-point of artistic creation in general and of the decision to become a writer in particular is seen by Sartre to lie in the experience of the limitedness of everyday consciousness, a limitedness which consists in the fact that the subject in its projection of the world is dependent on predetermined things (45-46). As an alternative to this, artistic creativity is chosen as a form of heightened activity which essentially involves the creation of new constructs. Art springs from a dissatisfaction with the everyday situation of man, who experiences his "inessentiality" vis-à-vis the world he is confronted with, and who tries to overcome it in the creation of a work. For Sartre art is consequently not imitation of nature, but a transformation of preformed materials into autonomous works, which are set over and against nature as its equals. In the sphere of artistic literature in the broadest sense this tendency is manifested most markedly in poetry, insofar as the words that are its material do not function as signs pointing beyond themselves to a pre-existent reality, but are perceived and shaped by the poet as constructs with a value of their own, as "things." Words—conceived as entities made up of sound and meaning—are transmuted in poetry into ambiguously shimmering constructs that lack any precise counterparts in the world of everyday consciousness (17-22).

A peculiar feature of Sartre's definition of the specifically literary is the fact that he assigns prose literature—as the, as it were, least artistic of the literary arts—a midway place between poetry and the nonliterary use of language. The (prose) writer uses words as a simple means of denoting things and thereby opening up a world-horizon for the reader, whereas for the poet the shaping of language is an end in itself and does not serve either the interpretation of the world or the communication of this interpretation to a reading public. At the same time the literary-artistic form of world-revelation is distinguished from those of everyday and scientific discourse insofar as it is mediated by the construction of imaginary objects. Via individual events, characters invented by the writer and the world-horizon of a time and a society (or class) are communicated to the reader.

Sartre tries to show that the central position he gives in his literary-phenomenological analyses to the communication between author and reader is a necessary consequence of taking the subjectivity of the author as his starting point. As an artist the latter seeks to overcome his "inessentiality" vis-à-vis the world, a world that in his everyday awareness he experiences as pre-existent and determining him. He creates a work with the intention of becoming essential vis-à-vis the world, as the person who brought that work into being. But he is forced to discover that what has been produced in this way is, in its mode of creation and the methods he has used, too transparent to him for it to be able to confront him as an independent work. According to Sartre, this is only possible if it is constituted from the distance of aesthetic contemplation as an "aesthetic object." For that to happen, the joint efforts of author and reader are needed: "The creative act is merely an incomplete and abstract moment in the production of a work; if the author exists alone, he could write as much as he wanted, and the work would still never see the light of day as object . . . It is the joint efforts of author and reader that bring into being this concrete and imaginary object that is a work of the mind. Art exists only for and through the Other" (49-50). Sartre appeals to the freedom of the reader to "give objective existence" to the "revelation of the world that he has undertaken by means of language" (53). This appeal to the reader addresses the mode of reception that is required for literary texts, and in which Sartre distinguishes three dimensions:

1) The reading process is a projection of "imaginary objects" on the basis of a "guided creation" (*création dirigée*) steered by the signs on the page. In this process, the understanding of the signs is at the same time shaped by the culturally and socially specific pre-existing knowledge of the particular readership.

2) The imaginary objects created under these conditions in the reader's consciousness appear as "open windows on the world" (63) and refer the reader to that "life-horizon" on the basis of which the narrative is to be understood. Seen in this way, the "aesthetic object is in fact the world, insofar as it is sighted through the medium of the imaginary" (66).

3) For Sartre, the freedom of the reader is ultimately realized in the application of the understanding thus gained of the text to his or her own (personal and social) situation, which, in the horizon of the world revealed through the narrative, can be experienced anew, and thus also changed.

Shpet and Sartre in Dialogue

If one compares Sartre's attempt to give a phenomenological definition of artistic literature to that of Shpet, the results of the two analyses seem diametrically opposed to each other. Whereas the Russian phenomenologist with links to Russian Formalism sees the essence of literature as lying in the formation of autonomous linguistic constructs, for the French existential phenomenologist the shaping of language is only a medium that allows the reader to reconstruct a particular interpretation of the world. The two descriptions diverge not only in the content of their respective concepts of literature, but equally in their methodological approaches to the specificity of literary texts, which is to be grasped on the one hand through a structural description of those texts, on the other by taking the text-producing subjectivity of the author as starting point. It is thus all the more astonishing that these diverging paths finally attain convergence, insofar as they both open up a way into the same phenomenon, namely, the mode of reception of literature in the reader's consciousness. Thus Shpet, when he describes the "structure of the word in usum aestheticae" and to this end introduces the concept of the poetic function, ultimately has to have recourse to the aesthetic attitude of the reader which receives a text as poetic. And Sartre's concept of literature as an appeal to the reader to lend an "objective existence" to his world-revelation, likewise leads to the definition of the mode of reception peculiar to literary texts, insofar as it is precisely this mode of reception that the author "calls upon" the reader to realize.

"Shaping of language" and "interpretation of the world" are the contrasting focuses of the two approaches to literature, a divergence that is already contained in their different points of departure and in the expressions chosen to denote their respective objects of investigation. While Shpet refers to "poetic speech" (*poeticheskaia rech'*) and accordingly selects his examples primarily from the realm of (modern) lyric poetry, Sartre is centrally concerned with "literature," which he expressly wishes to differentiate from lyric poetry. His examples are logically enough taken from the sphere of narrative prose. In so doing, he defines the "poetry" thus excluded in a way that is strongly reminiscent of the characterization of poetic speech by Shpet and Russian Formalism. Roman Jakobson's dictum—typical of Russian Formalism—that poetic speech is "utterance orientated towards expression" and indifferent in relation to its objects (Jakobson 30) would have been fully accepted by Sartre for his understanding of poetry. Only as a characterization of artistic literature in general would that formula be unacceptable to him. This, however, gives rise to the suspicion that the two descriptions under the headings "poetic speech" and "literature" are simply not talking about the same thing, but are referring to two different areas of artistic literature in the broadest sense, and that the impression of a contradiction only arises if one assumes that each of these two descriptions is meant as an all-encompassing concept of literature. This suspicion is seemingly confirmed by the fact that Shpet anachronistically sees the novel as a merely rhetorical-didactic genre that cannot be assigned to the category of poetic speech (*Vnutrenniaia* 167n1), which means that he would have excluded most of Sartre's examples of artistic literature from his analysis. But this attempt to explain the divergence of the two descriptions by assuming two different objects of investigation is doomed to failure. For Shpet, "poetic speech"—in his sense of the phrase—manifests itself not only in lyric poetry, but also in the two other principal literary genres, the epic and the drama, and Sartre clearly also subsumes dramas such as those of Corneille (95) under his concept of literature. Consequently the extensions of the two concepts "poetic speech" and "literature" overlap insofar as they both include drama, but remain distinct inasmuch as the lyric poetry that Sartre excludes from his concept of literature forms the prime example of Shpet's "poetic speech," while the novel-literature favored by Sartre is assigned by Shpet to the category of rhetorical discourse.

Each of these two descriptions of literature is, when viewed in its own sociocultural context, meaningful and fully justified. Insofar as they also conflict with each other in essential respects, neither of the two conceptions of literature can really do justice to its object. "The contradiction which arises between the posited fullness of a concrete object and its present incompleteness at any given moment" (Shpet, *Vnutrenniaia* 39) is manifest in the dialogue that has here been set up between Shpet's and Sartre's understanding of literature, without being brought to a definitive resolution (or reconciliation). Admittedly, Shpet's Platonic path, taking the structural analysis of the literary text as its point of departure, and Sartre's Cartesian approach, based on the subjectivity of the writer or reader, point to each other, so that they can be brought together in a dialectical relationship of mutual complementarity. But the attempt to modify the divergent views and steer them into a comprehensive dialectical synthesis seems to me neither meaningful nor practicable. The whole point of Shpet's method of a "dialectical interpretation" of cultural constructs and their associated theories is, after all, to make apparent the ultimate incomprehensibility of the given object of investigation, in an open and never-ending dialogue of mutually conflicting attempts to describe it.

Works Cited

Erlich, Victor. *Russischer Formalismus*. Trans. M. Lohner. Munich: Hanser, 1964.

Haardt, Alexander. *Husserl in Rußland. Phänomenologie der Sprache und Kunst bei Gustav Špet und Aleksej Losev*. Munich: Fink, 1993.

Husserl Edmund. *Die Krisis der europäischen Wissenschaften und die transzendentale Phänomenologie*. Ed. W. Biemel. The Hague: Nijhoff, 1954.

Husserl, Edmund. *Logische Untersuchungen*. Vol. 1. *Prolegomena zur reinen Logik*. Vol. 2-1. *Untersuchungen zur Phänomenologie und Theorie der Erkenntnis*. Vol. 2-2: *Elemente einer phänomenologischen Aufklärung der Erkenntnis*. Tübingen: Niemeyer, 1968.

Jakobson, Roman. "Die neueste russische Poesie." *Texte der russischen Formalisten*. Vol. 2. *Texte zur Theorie des Verses und der poetischen Sprache*. Ed. Wolf-Dieter Stempel. Munich: Fink, 1972. 18-235.

Plato. *Der Sophist*. Ed. Helmut Meinhardt. Stuttgart: Reclam, 1990.

Sartre, Jean-Paul. *Qu'est-ce que la littérature?* Paris: Gallimard, 1985.

Shpet, Gustav. *Esteticheskie fragmenty [Aesthetic Fragments]*. Vol. 2. Petrograd: Kolos, 1922-23.

Shpet, Gustav. *Vnutrenniaia forma slova (Etiudy i variatsii na temy Gumbol'ta) [The Inner Form of the Word]*. Ivanovo: Ivanovskii gosudarstvennyi universitet, 1999.

Part Four

Semiotics and Philosophy of Language

Sign and/vs. Essence in Shpet

Thomas Seifrid

What I mean to indicate by my somewhat cryptic title is a certain tension or distance, perhaps introduced by our retrospective gaze but possibly present in Shpet's thought itself, between two different kinds of philosophical projects that unfold within his works: between, on the one hand, Shpet's several insightful theorizations on the nature of semiotic phenomena and their role in human culture; and, on the other, a project that is present throughout but less evident, which I would briefly summarize as an attempt to elaborate a model of selfhood that is grounded in linguistic consciousness and to establish its ontological security against a variety of perceived threats ranging from materialism to Neo-Kantianism, epistemological skepticism, and relativism. Shpet was arguably the most conscientiously "professional" philosopher in the Russia of his day, markedly different in philosophical persona from such wilder, "disheveled," more "Russian" types as Rozanov, Losev, or even Florenskii. But one of the things that makes him such an interesting figure is that the former project, on which his reputation as a forerunner of semiotics deservedly rests, in fact represents the derivative (if careful) surface of his work; while the latter is more innovative and links him up with an array of Russian (rather than European) thinkers of the early twentieth century.

The starting point for any consideration of Shpet's thought is, of course, his Husserlian phenomenology. Much of *Iavlenie i smysl* (*Appearance and Sense*, 1914; English trans. 1991)—first fruit of the time Shpet spent with Husserl in Göttingen in 1912-13, and the beginning of productive extensions of Husserlian thought in Russia (Haardt, *Husserl* 68)—is devoted to reiterating Husserl's explication in the first volume of *Ideas Pertaining to a Pure Phenomenology and to a Phenomenological Philosophy* of phenomenology as a science of essences knowable via intuition. Following Husserl, Shpet urges philosophy to turn its attention away from the empirical realm of "being in the world" and direct it instead toward the eidetic realm of "being in an idea" (Shpet, *Iavlenie* 25). Philosophers must develop a "presuppositionless" science of essence by taking the "natural" attitude toward the world out of action, so that what remains is "the entire 'world as *eidos*'" (41). Skepticism of the kind espoused by the likes of Hume arises out of concentration on the "accidental" factors of the object's appearances to us, while phenomenology proposes to deal with the non-accidental and the necessary components of its essence (*nesluchainost'*, *neobkhodimost'*; 58-59), which the object retains throughout changing contexts and which enable us to recognize it as the same object "in spite of all the changes of the intentive mental processes and in spite of the fluctuation of the attentional acts of the pure Ego" (122). "Physical things" are given to us only empirically, through "adumbrations in appearances," whereas immanent being is apprehended as an absolute (44). As in Husserl, this absolute is apprehended by the inner eye. Phenomenology attains its aim, Shpet asserts, not through any mechanical process of abstraction but through an "advertence of vision" (26): the philosophical gaze or "regard" refuses to stop with the "experientially given" but penetrates through to essence (28). Eidetic intuition is fulfilled when "the contemplated itself" (*usmatrivaemoe samo*) stands before us as "ob-ject" ("pred-met," i.e., "placed before us," an etymological play Florenskii was later to dwell on), when it gives itself to us in its originary givenness ("gde ono daetsia nam v svoei pervichnoi dannosti"; 88).

One trait already separating this seemingly slavish paraphrase from its Husserlian model, however, is the greater emphasis Shpet places on what might be called ontological security (as Savich points out, Shpet's professed desire in *Iavlenie i smysl* merely to acquaint the reader with Husserl's thought is disingenuous, as Russian translations of Husserl's works already existed; Shpet's purpose, rather, was subtle revision and redirection; Savich 24). Husserl had been concerned to assert that the eidetic contents of consciousness *exist* and constitute objects in their own right—he claimed that phenomenology had "opened up a new region of *being* never before delineated in its peculiarity, that of the world as *Eidos*" (*Ideas* 63)—but the need to establish the being of consciousness becomes an even more pressing issue in Shpet, who I think for this reason "ontologizes" and "Platonizes" Husserl (Haardt; *Husserl* 90, 63, 33; see also Savich 26-27). There is a certain ontological anxiety running through Shpet's works, which I think also explains, for example, his efforts to establish the collective nature of consciousness, of which much has been made as a supposedly "Russian" versus "Western" aspect of his thought (see especially "Soznanie i ego sobstvennik"). It is true that Shpet draws on S.N. Trubetskoi's *O prirode chelovecheskogo soznaniia* (*On the Nature of Human Consciousness*) and its notion of the "collective consciousness" that arises within a cohesive community or nation, but in the larger context of his works one senses that it is less anti-individualism or the ethics of community that drive him than it is the anxiety that the self becomes too fragile, too ephemeral, if it is not secured in some more stable (in this case collective) form. One notes that Shpet's historical moment was one of a "crisis" of idealism, which was only exacerbated in the Soviet era; but whatever the underlying cause the effort to ensure the existence of eidetic phenomena is pronounced in his works.

Another way in which Shpet departs from Husserl is the relatively greater attention he devotes to language, and in a sense the theme of this article is how these two concerns—ontological anxiety and an interest in the structure of language—

come together in Shpet's thought. For his part, Husserl never really provides a definitive statement on the relation of thought to speech. On the whole he treats them as
closely linked but takes care to limit the nature of the link to "a certain parallelism
between thinking and speaking" within which there is no assurance of a perfect,
a priori correspondence (Husserl, *Logical* 257). Yet in other passages he accords
linguistic phenomena a privileged role in his account of noema and noesis. What
we know about judgments, he observes, is that they always take verbal form; the
objects of pure logic come embedded in concrete mental states that function as the
"meaning fulfillment" of certain verbal expressions (Husserl, *Logical* 250). In *Ideas*
he speaks of "expressive act-strata," which take linguistic form, being woven into
the other strata of the noema/noesis. If our perception is "This is white," he argues,
even if we have not expressed this perception linguistically, if we have thought or
asserted "This is white" "then a new [i.e., linguistic] stratum is co-present" (Husserl,
Ideas 295). In other words, to hold in mental regard, which is the essence of the
phenomenological act, is to invoke linguistic or language-like forms, while the function of words themselves is to awaken within us corresponding "sense-conferring
acts" (Husserl, *Logical* 282). Moreover, even if he will not quite define it, Husserl
suggests that there is something essential in the relation between such "expressive"
forms or strata and their eidetic sense. The meaning combinations we find in the
expressive strata are governed by nothing less than "*a priori* laws of essence," he
states (*Logical* 510), and in *Ideas* he describes "the act-stratum of expressing" as
a distinctive form to which all other strata of the noema conform (i.e., they are pat-
terned or modelled after it) and which raises the given sense "to the realm of 'logos,'
of the conceptual and, on that account, the universal" (*Ideas* 295). In this passage
Husserl in fact states quite explicitly that what he has done is to take the language-
based notion of "expressing" and in "an important cognitive step . . . appl[ied] [it]
to the whole noetic-noematic sphere" (*Ideas* 294; on language issues in Husserl see
especially *Logical Investigations* IV; see also Lamarque 489).

In *Iavlenie i smysl* Shpet points out this very application by Husserl of a linguistic term to the whole of the noematic-noetic sphere (120), and makes language
or language-like phenomena unequivocally central to his version of phenomenology
(see Haardt, *"Appearance and Sense"* xxi). Although one can approach *eidos* as a
point of unity, as "simply the object" (*Iavlenie* 124), Shpet argues, on closer examination one perceives it as a complex, multilayered structure: the "sense" (*smysl*) of
an object is not the whole of its noema, but a "moment of sense-endowing" at its
core (its *moment osmysleniia* or *predmet v svoei opredelitel'noi kvalifikatsii*; Shpet,
Iavlenie 117, 124). The full noema consists of various other layers grouped around
this core as well. These other layers form a "logical" stratum of the noema which
serves to "express" its core of sense. Shpet terms the relation between the two that
of sense to meaning (*smysl/znachenie* [Shpet, *Iavlenie* 158]; i.e., "meaning" is the
mechanism through which the logical layer expresses the sense of the noema). In
different but synonymous terms Shpet observes toward the end of *Iavlenie i smysl*
that within the act of "positing" there are certain subordinate acts which are directed

not to the sense itself—they are not the "doxic" act as such—but to its expressive layers or meaning. These acts perceive the contents of the noema to be (only) a sign for its inner side or sense: "We can call these acts which enliven every positing hermeneutic acts," he states, "and we can consider 'positing' not only as a unity of sense and certain thetic moments, but as their unity together with the unity of the entelechy and of hermeneutic moments, which unity constitutes the unity of the object with its living intimate sense" (*Iavlenie* 164-65). In other words essences are susceptible to but also, and it is of equal importance, demand hermeneutic acts for their realization ("enlivening"). Shpet explores at some length the problematic of distinguishing "sense" as such from the expressive structures that attend it, but what is clear is that, like Husserl, he has invoked a concept of very long lineage which holds that essence exists first and foremost as articulable form. Husserl places his "form-theory of meanings" (*Logical* 313) within a philosophical tradition assuming an essential relation between the forms of language and those of sense that reaches as far back as ancient Greek concepts of *logos* and their treatment by Aristotle (on whose *Organon*, with its doctrine of complex vs. uncomplex signs, Husserl draws directly in elaborating the distinction between categorematic and syncategorematic forms in *Logical Investigations*); that was handed down through the middle ages, where *inter alia* it influenced Augustine's theory of signs in *De doctrina christiana* and *De trinitate* (the latter of which makes the important assertion that "concepts are words at heart") and the neoplatonic tradition represented in Boethius's theological treatises; and that resurfaced in Locke and Leibnitz (Husserl mentions "the undoubted soundness of the idea of a universal grammar conceived by the rationalists of the seventeenth and eighteenth centuries"; *Logical* 524). In the case of Shpet it takes the form of one of his central tenets: that essence is structured like a sign.

What this shift in emphasis from sense to meaning, from *eidos* as such to its expressive forms, gives rise to in Shpet is his "hermeneutic turn," the prolific interest in semasiological systems that generated such studies of his as "Germenevtika i ee problemy" ("Hermeneutics and its Problems"); although we always have to bear in mind that "hermeneutics" for Shpet means an eidetic operation, interpretation as an eidetic seeing or reading) and *Vvedenie v etnicheskuiu psikhologiiu* (*Introduction to the Psychology of Ethnos*). For such systems language serves as prototype. "To a certain—profound—degree," he remarks in another work, "language is the natural and the closest prototype and representation of any expression which harbors meaning" ("Vvedenie" 515); and, Shpet notes, it is contemporary linguistics that has given hermeneutics its philosophically productive interest in "semasiology" ("Germenevtika" 1993 275). Indeed Shpet often seems to identify language as that very "expressive" layer of the noema that bears its sense to us. When experience causes our regard to pause on it, he says, we have to do not with a naked datum but one "vested in a word" (*oblechennoe v slovo*), which is the very *principium cognescendi* of our knowledge (Shpet, "Mudrost' ili razum" 293-94). It is through language that we communicate with one another; it is in the words of language that meaning, in the form of ideas, has its existence.

What one ends up with as the focus of Shpet's philosophy is the "word-concept," or the "hermeneutic *eidos*," as one could call it, which is also his specifying
revision of the Husserlian noema (although one interesting ambiguity Shpet's formula fails to remove has to do with whether signs, or more precisely signs in relation
to their correlative meanings, are to be regarded as analogs for eidetic objects—as
when Shpet talks about the parallelism between speech and understanding, *rech' i
ponimanie* [Shpet, "Germenevtika" 1989 243]—or as ontologically coextensive with
them, indeed, prototypes of any such object). Given our insight into the structured
and sign-like nature of reality, Shpet announces, we "now place on *eidos* the same
demand we place on 'the word': we regard essence itself as a sign . . . the semasiological approach to essence itself forces one *eo ipso* to search in it, as in a 'foundation' [*nachale*], for sense, which opens up before us as the rational basis [*razumnoe
osnovanie*] deposited in essence itself; here essence in its content proceeds out of
reason [*razuma*] as out of its founding principle" ("Mudrost' ili razum" 315). Or, as
he puts it in a particularly revealing passage, "Thus for us the word-concept is not
just a 'volume' or 'class' but also a sign demanding understanding, i.e., penetration
into a certain meaning, as if into something intimate, into the 'living soul' of the
word-concept. Put another way, the word-concept, the word as term [*terminirovan-
noe slovo*], demands interpretation" ("Mudrost' ili razum" 310).

This "hermeneutic" turn in Shpet's thought, so productive within his philosophical career, however, represents not a reversal of the celebrated "transcendental" turn in Husserl's thought which perplexed many of his followers (and which is
represented in the differing concerns of *Ideas I* over the earlier *Logical Investigations*)—not, or not only, a diversification into the more "accessible," "hyletic" realm
of studies in social and cultural phenomena, but in fact an intensification of his interest in consciousness and in particular the self. Obviously, as a form of consciousness
an entity such as the "word-concept" is contiguous with the self, but there is a difference between examining some element of selfhood and mapping onto that element
the essential features of the self as a whole, so that it becomes a replica of that self in
miniature. But this is precisely what Shpet does: he projects onto the "word-concept"
selflike qualities which are by no means necessarily foreseen in Husserl, suggesting
both that our selves are structured like this "word-concept" and that it *is* a kind of self
in its own right. For example, in describing this hermeneutically structured *eidos*
he readily resorts to perhaps the most fundamental spatial metaphor in European
conceptions of the self, that of opposition between an inner (ideal, spiritual) core and
outer (material) shell. In both phenomenology and hermeneutics as Shpet defines
them one moves from the structured, empirically available, and often literally material givenness of external form to the noncontingent, *a priori*, and transcendant inner
core. It is in this sense that signs resemble, or are, eidetic objects, and in this way that
working with signs serves as a "prototype" for the cognizing of essence.

Moreover, it is from language in particular that we learn what the relation is
between external (acoustic, graphic) and inner (meaning-bearing) form: "in relation
to things this form reveals itself as idea, i.e., as inner form with respect to outer

form, the difference being that inner form is free from matter while outer is linked to it. It is in this quality of inner form . . . that the specific being of ideas consists" ("Germenevtika" 1989 260). The hermeneutic act that constitutes understanding then turns out to be a penetration into something intimate, as into the "soul"—so that the metaphor Shpet offers in the passage I quoted above, to the effect that eidetic understanding involves penetration into meaning, as if into something intimate, into the "living soul" of the word-concept—turns out not to be casual. As a privileged analogy for this aspect of sign/essence Shpet offers some remarks Dilthey makes on the possibility of "scientific" cognizing the self of the other: "The being of the other [*chuzhoe bytie*]," Shpet paraphrases, "is not exhausted by the sensually-given phenomena we have as evidence for it, because it is an inner reality which inhabits sensory facts such as sounds, gestures [which function as signs of this inwardness]— i.e., signs of various sorts." For Dilthey, understanding (*ponimanie*, Shpet's act of hermeneutic deciphering) is the process by which "through external, sensory signs we come to know [*poznaem*] that which is inner." Shpet then makes a remarkable (but characteristic) shift: instead of stating that the word ends up looking something like a self, he suggests that selfhood inhabits this structure that is language. "Only in language does human 'inwardness' find its completely exhaustive and objectively comprehensible expression" (Shpet, "Germenevtika" 1991 252). Or, as he outlines the tasks facing a phenomenologically reconceived hermeneutics in the conclusion of "Germenevtika," "the problem of understanding is nothing less than that of spirit [*dukh*]" (Shpet 1993 278).

One finds a similar logic at work when Shpet discusses the unity characteristic of the eidetic word-concept. As the core of the noema, sense belongs first of all to "that which constantly abides in the object and which remains identical in spite of all the changes of the attentive mental processes and in spite of the fluctuation of the attentional acts of the pure Ego" (Shpet, *Iavlenie* 122). The unity of "thetic" moments and sense in the object arises out of its "the same thing" (*to zhe*), that element of it which is constant from perception to perception, a "certain X as the bearer" of sense (Shpet, *Iavlenie* 137; on these matters in Husserl see Investigation VI in *Logical Investigations*). But from this understanding of noematic unity for us (that is, as that constant X which we must recognize as stable from attentional act to attentional act, and which we must separate from everything changing and therefore non-eidetic), Shpet then subtly shifts to one of noematic unity for the object itself. To perceive the sense of an object fully and adequately, Shpet asserts, we must go beyond regarding it as pure abstraction and penetrate into its "inner intimate [space]" (*vnutrennee intimnoe*), which requires perceiving it in its "rational motivation" (*Iavlenie* 138). As a "useful analogy" for how this is done he again offers the example of how we unite all the threads of our perception when we regard the whole constituted by another *self* ("*chuzhoi individual'nosti*," here citing the Danish philosopher G. Finnbogason; Shpet, *Iavlenie* 147).

To illustrate his point further he offers an example drawn from Aristotle. If we consider the object that is an axe, Shpet says (his Russian word is *sekira*; one would only have to say "the word 'axe'" and hypothesize about its etymology to turn this into the kind of argument Shpet's predecessor Aleksandr Potebnia used to advance about the "inner form" of words), we find its inner sense in the idea "to chop" (*rubit'*; Shpet, *Iavlenie* 159), that is, in the intended use for which it exists ("or has been made" would be more accurate: Shpet somewhat dubiously sets aside objects in the natural vs. the social world as having "pure content" alone, at most a quasi-teleology; see *Iavlenie* 162-63). Where Shpet's "self-ward" turn becomes conspicuous is in the unabashedly vitalist way in which he couples this teleology of function with the Aristotelian concept of "entelechy"—that principle or mode through which the essence of a thing is fully realized, its informing spirit (Blackburn 121)—to explain this innermost core of the object. In the case of the axe, he states, "to chop" reveals itself to me as nothing less than the object's "soul" or entelechy (*Iavlenie* 160). This entelechy constitutes the "core of the very sense" of the object (*iadro samogo smysla*), and the object in its "defining qualification" exists for this entelechy as mere external sign (160). Moreover, this entelechic core comes close to constituting the object as a *sui generis* being in its own right. If we wanted to define the sense in which the noema of an object consists as abstract form, Shpet says, we would have to "turn back to Aristotle's teaching in order to trace it back to Plato and then, skipping over the centuries, encounter an analogous thought in Leibniz"—that of form understood as something which "'animates' what is dead" ("*odushevliaiushchee*" *mertvoe*; *Iavlenie* 158). He makes similar statements when rebutting the claim that the I by itself "creates" sense in the noemas it perceives: the object with its noema would remain dead, he asserts, if it did not bear in itself its own "enlivening sense" (*Iavlenie* 122). Husserl himself at one point refers to meaning as "ensouling" the sensual-linguistic side of objects (*Logical* 289), but elsewhere emphatically asserts that "being is nothing *in* the object, no part of it, no moment tenanting it" (*Logical* 780). Shpet's discussion works to suggest that, at least when we are dealing with social objects, especially with language, being does "tenant" the object.

I suspect that the concept of intentionality that Brentano develops in his seminal *Psychologie vom empirischen Standpunkt* (1874), so influential on Husserl, betrays some of the same impulses, and in a late essay Cassirer suggested similar things about structural linguistics (see Cassirer 99-120). At any rate, in the case of Shpet, given this framework, the "Humboldtian meditations" contained in *Vnutrenniaia forma slova* (*The Inner Form of the Word*, 1927), and the related comments on "inner form" in the earlier *Esteticheskie fragmenty* (*Aesthetic Fragments*, written 1922), emerge as central to his thought. In *Vnutrenniaia forma slova* Shpet aims to define "linguistic consciousness as such" (36), which he claims is archetypal for all other forms of thought and cultural activity. Following Wilhem von Humboldt, he calls language the "organ of inner being, even that being itself, as that being gradually attains inner cognition and reveals itself" (*Vnutrenniaia* 11), the "formative organ of thought" (15; both are direct quotations from Humboldt). As such, language turns out to concentrate in itself the complex, dialectical interplay between subjectivity and objectivity in general. Within language thought confronts sound in order to generate articulate sound-forms: language is generated out of this "completely inner intellectual" element of an intention to mean, of "ideas directed toward language." In his verbal activity man surrounds himself with a world of sounds in order to take up into himself (*vospriniat'*) and work over the world of objects; but the process by which this happens is imperfect and dialectical, because "the inner idea, in order to reveal itself (become manifest), must overcome a certain resistance [*zatrudnenie*] from the side of sound, which overcoming does not even always succeed" (Shpet, *Vnutrenniaia* 21; see Humboldt 77: "The making of language in general must be seen as a producing, in which the inner idea, to make itself manifest, has a difficulty to conquer"). The "spirit creates, but in that very act opposes what is created to itself, and the latter, as object, in its turn exerts influence on it" (Shpet, *Vnutrenniaia* 28). What we encounter in these passages is simultaneously an account of the metaphysical structure of language and an account of the self's interactions with the empirical world. Shpet even describes the inner form of language as inhabiting its "external" grammatical and lexical forms "in the manner of a soul" (*napodobie dushi*; *Vnutrenniaia* 26).

But in what, specifically, does this "inner form" consist? It is especially important for Shpet that this energy pulsating in the heart of language does not stop with some vague activity of spirit but yields determinate *form*, which in the end is the focus of his philosophical work as a whole. In his definition "inner form" is not just "sense" itself, in some simple undeveloped form; nor is it a visual "image," a psychological mechanism of association and apperception, or the etymological meaning of the word (Shpet, *Vnutrenniaia* 106; see also Shpet, "Esteticheskie" 443, 447). Rather, it is the "guiding law of the development of the word's sense" (Shpet, *Vnutrenniaia* 106), a "certain rule of the concept's formation which is registered [*zapechatlennoe*] within the concept as a formal moment. This rule is none other than the device, method, and principle of selection [of those moments of the sense important to the given expressed thought]—the law and basis of verbal-logical creativity in the service of expression, communication, and the transmission of sense" (Shpet, *Vnutrenniaia* 98). It represents the dialectical relation arising "between external signifying form and the objective form of [the concept's] thing-content" (*predmetnoi formy veshchnogo soderzahaniia*, Shpet, *Vnutrenniaia* 117; Shpet's concept of inner form is obviously influenced by the "*rein formale Grammatik*" which Husserl proposes in *Logical Investigations* as the central discipline in a formal theory of meaning; see Haardt; Husserl 35).

In Shpet's account the word's "inner form" thus emerges as a set of relational rules by which thought takes on expressive form and through which the objective world is adequately given in consciousness—that is, the locus in which mind encounters the objective world, which is very close to saying "the self." Although he invokes relatively little of it in the 1927 monograph, Shpet in fact had outlined a more detailed account of inner form earlier in *Esteticheskie fragmenty*. There he makes it clear that what he means by "inner form" is not to be identified directly with the grammatical or lexical elements of a given natural language but belongs to the realm of intellectual sense-expression, which makes use of these elements without being reduced to them (in *Esteticheskie fragmenty* he explicitly separates syntax and morphology from inner form, and draws a distinction between a dictionary containing mere *lexis*, a simple listing of the names found in a language and the set of *logoi* which bear meaning-sense; "Esteticheskie" 390-91). Instead, at the center of inner form stands the object (*predmet*), which Shpet defines as whatever is presupposed when N uses a word and I understand him ("Esteticheskie" 393). At the same time—and it is this next step in the argument which is so characteristic of Shpet in contrast to Husserl—its "presupposition" forms only a starting point of attention, an assigned theme which must then be developed, and it is this developing which generates "inner form," and the inner forms so generated which call for hermeneutics in order to be apperceived. Between the "ontic forms" of the object and the morphological forms of the given language there enters a new network of forms as a system of relations between the two of them ("Esteticheskie" 398). Morphological forms are "external," ontic ones are "pure," while it is these intermediary "logical" forms that Shpet identifies with Humboldtian "inner form" of speech (see Humboldt's notion of language as *Zwischenwelt* ["world in-between"] interposed between humans and the objective world; Humboldt 157).

The word as a whole thus turns out to be "a kind of absolute form, a form of forms, the highest and final in a system and structure of verbal logical forms" (Shpet, *Vnutrenniaia* 101). As such it constitutes "the only completely universal sign," capable of replacing any other sign (*Vnutrenniaia* 140) and it provides the ontological prototype for every other social or cultural artefact (for Shpet not only words as such but speech in general, books, literature, and languages also constitute "words" possessing "inner form"); social manifestations are "always homologous to verbal structure" (*Vnutrenniaia* 141). This is essentially the point behind the aesthetic explorations in *Esteticheskie fragmenty*; it represents not just an "inviolable structural unity" but nothing less than a "*sui generis* mode of being [*bytie*] of a social-cultural type" (*Vnutrenniaia* 67). Moreover, the process of its formation leads to something resembling Hegelian self-consciousness: "At its most profound level, linguistic consciousness is nothing less than the verbal-logical consciousness of the law-governed nature [*zakonomernosti*] of life and of the development of language as a whole" (*Vnutrenniaia* 128; see also Potebnia 147). The only movement left to consciousness beyond this point, Shpet declares, is toward an understanding of the very content of absolute forms.

If these claims exceed even those advanced by Humboldt on behalf of language's inner form, it is because Shpet has gone even farther than Humboldt in working out a philosophical theory that identifies selfhood with the structures of language. But Shpet has also followed the concretizing revision of Humboldt found in the works of his Russian predecessor Potebnia (see Seifrid) and transferred inner form from language in general to the integral word, just as he has promoted "the word," as I.M. Chubarov suggests, into a surrogate for the Husserlian transcendental ego (32). For Shpet the word harbors the algorithm for the being of consciousness in the world

(*Vnutrenniaia* 141)—not the activity or product of the individual psychological subject, but "the spontaneous process of sense itself in its movement" (*Vnutrenniaia*
128). As he puts it in a passage of *Esteticheskie fragmenty* that discusses the hermeneutics of the literary work, when we read literature—it is hard to imagine he is not
thinking of novels—we begin to discern behind every word a secondary sense that
serves as an index to nothing less than the author's self: "on the whole the author's
selfhood [*lichnost'*] emerges as the analog of a word," Shpet comments. "Selfhood
is a word and demands its own [form of] understanding" ("Esteticheskie" 471; in
Vnutrenniaia forma slova he also refers to poetic forms as "objectified subject,"
186). How very like Bakhtin such remarks are. But this is because in this effort to
make language out to be a form of self, and to anchor the self in language, Shpet was
not alone, but was continuing a project begun in Russia by Potebnia and carried on
by Aleksei Losev, Pavel Florenskii, Sergei Bulgakov, and Mikhail Bakhtin—among
others.

Note

The permission of Cornell University Press to reprint here an updated version of
Thomas Seifrid's text is gratefully acknowledged.

Works Cited

Blackburn, Simon, ed. *Oxford Dictionary of Philosophy*. Oxford: Oxford UP, 1994.

Cassirer, Ernst. "Structuralism in Modern Linguistics." *Word* 1 (1945): 99-120.

Chubarov, I.M. "Modifikatsiia fenomenologicheskoi paradigmy ponimaniia soznaniia v proekte germenevticheskoi dialektiki G.G. Shpeta." *G.G. Shpet/
Comprehensio. Vtorye shpetovskie chteniia*. Ed. O.G. Mazaeva. Tomsk: Vodolei,
1997. 27-33.

Haardt, Alexander. "*Appearance and Sense* and Phenomenology in Russia."
*Appearance and Sense. Phenomenology as the Fundamental Science and its
Problems*. By Gustav Shpet. Trans. Thomas Nemeth. Dordrecht: Kluwer, 1991.
i-xxxi.

Haardt, Alexander. *Husserl in Russland. Phänomenologie der Sprache und Kunst
bei Gustav Špet und Aleksej Losev*. Munich: Fink, 1993.

Humboldt, Wilhelm. *On Language: The Diversity of Human Language-Structure
and its Influence on the Mental Development of Mankind*. Trans. Peter Heath.
Cambridge: Cambridge UP, 1988.

Husserl, Edmund. *Ideas Pertaining to a Pure Phenomenology and to a
Phenomenological Philosophy. First Book*. Trans. F. Kersten. The Hague:
Martinus Nijhoff, 1983.

Husserl, Edmund. *Logical Investigations*. 2 vols. Trans. J.N. Findlay. New York:
Humanities P, 1970.

Lamarque, Peter V., ed. *Concise Dictionary of the Philosophy of Language*. New
York: Pergamon, 1997.

Potebnia, A.A. "Mysl' i iazyk." *Estetika i poetika*. Moscow: Iskusstvo, 1976. 3-220.

Savich, A.E. "Interpretatsiia i kritika G.G. Shpetom filosofii Ed. Gusserlia." *G.G. Shpet/Comprehensio. Vtorye shpetovskie chteniia*. Ed. O.G. Mazaeva. Tomsk: Vodolei, 1997. 24-27.

Seifrid, Thomas. "The Structure of the Self: Potebnia and Russian Philosophy of Language, 1860-1930." *American Contributions to the Twelfth International Congress of Slavists*. Ed. Robert A. Maguire and Alan Timberlake. Columbus: Slavica, 1998. 169-81.

Shpet, Gustav. "Esteticheskie fragmenty." *Sochineniia*. Moscow: Pravda, 1989. 345-474.

Shpet, Gustav. "Germenevtika i ee problemy." *Kontekst 1989*. Moscow: Nauka, 1989. 231-67; *Kontekst 1990*. Moscow: Nauka, 1990. 219-59; *Kontekst 1991*. Moscow: Nauka, 1991. 215-55; *Kontekst 1992*. Moscow: Nauka, 1993. 251-84.

Shpet, Gustav. *Iavlenie i smysl. Fenomenologiia kak osnovnaia nauka i ee problemy*. Tomsk: Vodolei, 1996.

Shpet, Gustav. "Mudrost' ili razum?" *Filosofskie etiudy*. Moscow: Progress, 1994. 222-336.

Shpet, Gustav. "Soznanie i ego sobstvennik." *Filosofskie etiudy*. Moscow: Progress, 1994. 20-116.

Shpet, Gustav. *Vnutrenniaia forma slova (etiudy i variatsii na temy Gumbol'ta)*. Moscow: Gosudarstvennaia akademiia khudozhestvennykh nauk, 1927.

Shpet, Gustav. "Vvedenie v etnicheskuiu psikhologiiu." *Sochineniia*. Moscow: Pravda, 1989. 475-574.

Problems of Sense, Significance, and Validity in the Work of Shpet and the Bakhtin Circle

Craig Brandist

The works of Gustav Shpet and the Bakhtin Circle (most notably Mikhail Bakhtin and Valentin Voloshinov) represent two of the most important episodes in the Russian reception of the so-called linguistic turn in philosophy. Each recognized the paucity of systematized thought in Russian philosophy of the period and was dissatisfied with the intuitive, even mystical manner with which language was understood. While nineteenth-century Russian philology reached considerable heights, philosophical reflections on language had developed largely within the bounds of Orthodox theology and this continued to shape the spirit of secular debates on language in the twentieth century and to endow linguistic terms with metaphysical connotations. This, combined with the strong ethical leanings of Russian philosophy, helped the seeds of German idealist philosophy find fertile ground. The result was that Russian philosophy of language often developed impressionistically and was always devoid of an elaborated theory of reference. However, the strong ontological impulses of Russian thought, which partly derived from Orthodoxy, often pulled discussions of cognition away from the identification of metaphysics and the theory of knowledge that constituted the neo-Kantian legacy and pushed Russian thinkers in a direction usually associated with Austrian philosophy. Instead of the neo-Kantian "consciousness in general," the Brentanian intentional consciousness became a central point of orientation for both Shpet and the Bakhtin Circle, but each sought to develop this phenomenological notion in different ways, the former remaining close to the Orthodox heritage while the latter sought a hybrid of phenomenology and neo-Kantian idealism.

Personal relations between members of the Bakhtin Circle and Shpet are limited to the mid-1920s when the initiator of the Circle, Matvei Kagan, worked in the Philosophy Section of the State Academy of the Artistic Sciences (GAKhN: Gosudarstvennaia Akademiia khudozhestvennykh nauk) that Shpet directed. A champion of Marburg School Neo-Kantianism, Kagan regularly attended the section's research seminars (RGALI, f. 941 [GAKhN], op. 14, d. 14. l. 69) where he was allied with

Boris A. Fokht in frequent disagreements with the more "Orthodox" Aleksei Losev (see, for example, the exchange between Kagan and Losev following Fokht's paper on "The Problems of Philosophical Aesthetics in Paul Natorp's Work" in May 1925; cf. the records at RGALI, f. 941 [GAKhN], op. 14, d. 14, l. 55). These discussions continued at least until 1928; see, for example, Losev's and Kagan's interventions following Fokht's paper about Ernst Cassirer's *Philosophy of Symbolic Forms* in December 1927 (RGALI, f. 941 [GAKhN], op. 14, d. 32, l. 15-16). Relations between Kagan and Shpet were always respectful, though from the outset the latter was clear that he disagreed with the former's adherence to Neo-Kantianism (Shpet, "G.G. Shpet M. I. Kaganu" 629). Shpet's familiarity with the work of Voloshinov and Bakhtin is unknown, but both were clearly familiar with Shpet, whose profile was then significant. There are several references to Shpet in publications by the Circle and while there are many points of disagreement, Shpet is generally treated seriously (for an overview, see Bakhtin, *Sobranie* 388-96). An understanding of Shpet's and the Circle's respective developments of phenomenology requires, however, an examination of the types of German thought that influenced them.

Neo-Kantianism, Phenomenology, and Psychology

Although influenced decisively by neo-Kantian philosophy, in the 1920s Voloshinov and Bakhtin were also influenced, as recent scholarship on Bakhtin has demonstrated, by such contemporary trends as *Lebensphilosophie* (Dilthey, Simmel, Bergson), Marxism (Bukharin, Lukács) and the intersubjective phenomenology of Max Scheler. It is also now widely accepted that in the 1930s Bakhtin himself also followed the neo-Hegelian evolution of the Marburg philosophers, particularly as represented by Cassirer. Shpet, meanwhile, flirted with both Marxism and Neo-Kantianism before his conversion to phenomenology (Shpet, "Soznanie" 68, 86; Shpet, "Vvedenie" 554-56), but his enthusiasm for Husserl was complicated by the ontological concerns of the München "realist" phenomenologists and the lingering influence of Orthodox Christianity. Shpet's subsequent ideas developed in a distinctly hermeneutic direction, which included important encounters with Dilthey and Hegelianism. The Circle and Shpet both engaged with Humboldt's philosophy of language, particularly the notion of the inner form of language, although this was mediated by contemporary philosophies of language. In this, both trends engaged with the Brentano School philosopher Anton Marty as well as the so-called Vossler School of neo-philology.

The Circle's and Shpet's excursions into philosophy and literary studies were also matched by serious engagements with the psychology of the period. From 1898 Shpet studied under the philosopher-psychologist G.I. Chelpanov at Kiev University and in 1907 followed his former teacher to work at the newly established and lavishly equipped Moscow Institute of Psychology, which Chelpanov headed. Although flirting with neo-Kantianism at the time, Shpet shared Chelpanov's insistence on the necessity of retaining *das Ding an sich* ("thing in itself") as the basis of the "evocation" of a particular representation of the object. This led him to resist the neo-Kantian idea that the object of perception was fully "produced" by and in thought and to draw close to the ideas of Brentano and his followers, especially Karl Stumpf, whose "guiding principles" were an "allegiance to the 'immediately given' as the source of psychological knowledge, with measurement used only to specify the given more precisely; and opposition to Neo-Kantian critiques of knowledge, with the intention of establishing a realist worldview based on empirical research" (Ash, *Gestalt* 41; on the reception of Stumpf's work in Russia at the time see Balmaton and Grinbaum). Chelpanov was especially influenced by Stumpf's studies of the perception of space and in 1906 he submitted a dissertation to Moscow University on precisely this topic. Considering this work, Losev characterized Chelpanov as a "representative of the realist point of view based on the Kantian theory of knowledge" who also "participated in the struggle against materialism" ("Russkaia" 92). In 1910, Chelpanov and Shpet spent time working with Stumpf and Oswald Külpe, the teacher of Karl Bühler, further reinforcing their belief in the interdependence of philosophy and psychology: philosophy needed expertise in empirical psychology while experimentation needed a grounding in epistemology to rise above mere "artisanry" (see Kozulin; Ash, "Academic Politics"; Shpet, "Odin put'").

Several members of the Bakhtin Circle were interested in contemporary psychology in the mid-1920s, but only Voloshinov published work specifically dedicated to psychology, with an article hostile to Russian psychoanalysis (1925) and a book on Freud (1927). By 1928 we know that Voloshinov was seriously engaging with Bühler's ideas, having translated the German's essay on syntax (1922) into Russian ("Lichnoe delo" 75). Bühler's work had been discussed at GAKhN, with A.A. Buslaev, one of the founders of the Moscow Linguistic Circle, reporting on the new conception of the utterance found in Bühler's work in November 1924 (RGALI, f. 941 [GAKhN], op. 14, d. 10, l. 24-25; see also Freiberger-Sheikholeslami). Even before the World War I, Losev, who also later worked at GAKhN, had been in Berlin, preparing a monograph on the Würzburg School, with particular attention being paid to Bühler. Research was curtailed by the war, but a manuscript was prepared by 1919 (Losev, "Issledovaniia"). The discussions undoubtedly filtered through to the Leningrad Institute (ILIaZV) where Voloshinov studied in the late 1920s. Voloshinov displays a familiarity with different contemporary trends in psychology and linguistics, including the work of Brentano, Stumpf, Meinong and Bühler in his chief work *Marxism and the Philosophy of Language*.

The Brentano tradition was thus clearly a major influence of the Circle and Shpet. This thought was based on an Aristotelian and anti-Kantian epistemology in which the mind "feeds" on objects that it encounters and derives formal categories from this encounter rather than imposing those categories a priori. This took the well-known if frequently misunderstood form of intentional mental acts:

> Each psychical phenomenon is characterised by . . . the intentional (or mental) in-existence of an object . . . the reference [*Beziehung*] to a content, the directedness [*Richtung*] toward an object (which in this context is not to be understood as something real) or the immanent object-quality [*immanente*

Gegenständlichkeit]. Each contains something as its object, though not each in the same manner. In the representation [*Vorstellung*] something is represented, in the judgement something is acknowledged or rejected, in desiring it is desired, etc. (Brentano qtd. in Spiegelberg 36)

The category of intentionality is found throughout the work of the Circle and of Shpet, in the case of the former mediated by the ethics of Max Scheler and "functional psychology," and in the latter by Stumpf and Husserl. Neo-Kantianism was in some ways the diametrical opposite of Brentanian thought in that it attempted to reconstruct all cognition exclusively in terms of "subjective spontaneity." Objects of representation are constituted from transcendental forms and categories dwelling in "pure consciousness" or "consciousness in general." This was most succinctly stated in the Marburg School slogan: "nothing is given [*gegeben*] everything is set as a task [*aufgegeben*]." The stratospherically abstract philosophy that resulted undoubtedly contributed to the phenomenological demand "to the things themselves." The terms of the divergence is clear in Husserl's criticism of the philosophy of science of the Baden School neo-Kantian Heinrich Rickert, for being "so much a 'theory from above' that not a single example is to be found . . . and nor does this absence makes itself felt." Husserl argued that "a fruitful theory of concept formation in the natural sciences can . . . only be a theory 'from below', a theory that has grown out of the work of the natural sciences themselves" (qtd. in Mulligan and Smith, "Mach and Ehrenfels" section 5). This observation is generalizable, but the opposition is not quite as total as the sloganeering suggests. As Ernst Cassirer recognized, the fact that Brentano's intentional object is "immanent" to the mind makes its relation to putative objects problematic. In his *Ideas* Husserl deals with this by introducing the theory of noemata that constitute an intermediate realm of meanings between the mental or linguistic act and its putative object. Cassirer applauded this solution since it opened the way to a fully fledged neo-Kantian idealism similar to his own "self-contained" dimension of the "pure 'image'" in which the human spirit "weaves itself into a world of its own, a world of signs, symbols and of meanings" (*Philosophy* 196-98; "'Spirit' and 'Life'" 869). This is because although Husserl suggested that every act has its corresponding noema, even when there is no external object, there is no guaranteed link to any external objects at all. Though neo-Kantianism and phenomenology converged, significant differences remained. While from *Ideas I* onward Husserl accepted Natorp's concept of Pure Ego, unlike that of the latter Husserl's own version is "individual in character and not identical with the pure unity of objective thought represented by 'pure apperception,'" that is, the "ideal subject as such [*Subjekt überhaupt*]" (Kaufmann 823, 842-43). The rapprochement between neo-Kantianism and phenomenology continued from the neo-Kantian side with Cassirer's description of the "essential forms" of human culture in his *Philosophy of Symbolic Forms.* Even here, however, while Cassirer is concerned with the indefinite extension of the objectifying processes of the universal subject, Husserl's "transcendental ego" remains a single ego even while not being essentially finite.

When Shpet visited Göttingen in 1912-13 he came under the influence of Husserl as the latter was drawing closer to neo-Kantianism and developing his noema theory, which severed all necessary links to external objects. However, like Chelpanov, Shpet retained the "thing in itself" as the basis of the "evocation" of a particular representation of the object. The Bakhtin Circle, meanwhile, sought to overcome the "theoretism" of neo-Kantian philosophy through a turn to the intersubjective phenomenology of Scheler (pioneered by Bakhtin) on the one hand and a distinctly Brentanian account of the concrete discursive act (pioneered by Voloshinov) on the other. Scheler's influence was, however, limited to certain areas and did not extend to accepting his neo-Platonic notion of "material value essences" or his critique of the Marburg School on the basis of a quasi-ontological *Urgrund* ("primal ground"), which he derived from Jakob Böhme. In this regard it is easy to appreciate Voloshinov's comment that relations between neo-Kantianism and phenomenology in the philosophy of language are marked by a "vital struggle" between "conceptualism" and "medieval realism" ("Archival Materials" 232-33). Furthermore, Voloshinov continued, Russian philosophy of language, including that of Shpet, had become mixed with less scientific modes of thought that had derived from ascendant literary modernism, so that phenomenology had been combined with the Symbolists' "cult of the word." Losev's *Philosophy of the Name,* which is "isolated from all strictly philosophical traditions" is cited as an extreme example of this feature (240-41).

Phenomenology

The phenomenology of Shpet and Bakhtin diverge in their respective emphases: the former focuses on relations between subject and object and the latter on intersubjectivity. Much of Shpet's 1914 *Appearance and Sense* is little more than an exposition of Husserl's noema theory of meaning but Shpet transforms Husserl's distinction between the transcendental being of reality and the absolute being of consciousness into Christian and neo-Platonic "Kingdoms" (Cassedy 85-87). Contra Husserl, and translating the Orthodox notion of incarnation into Aristotelian terminology, Shpet also argues that the sense of an object is immanent to the object itself as its "entelechy," and he presents Husserl's phenomenology as a pre-theoretical "first philosophy" (*Appearance* 3-20, 69). For Shpet, sense derives from the aspects of the object in cognition and the noema is considered what Lichkovakh calls a "thing-sign" (Lichkovakh 73). The noema becomes a stratified ontology of consciousness the core of which is "objective sense" and around which are grouped various predicative layers and doxical modalities. The rational conceptualisation of sense occurs by means of the logical act of "positing" (*polaganie*). However, again unlike Husserl, Shpet is interested in the object as a *social* object and so the transferral, or translation, from the ontological to the logical dimension is a matter of rendering the object social through "signification" (*znachenie*) (see, especially, chapter 7 of *Appearance and Sense*). This is the "hermeneutic act." Shpet exploits the Russian *znachenie,* which means both signification and significance, and is linguistically connected to *znachimost'*, meaning validity. The realization of sense in signs (*znak*) renders the former simultaneously valid and significant in social being and there is a "strict correlation" between these spheres. The subject objectifies an object's social sense and renders this as a cultural meaning (*znachenie*), making it socioculturally valid (unlike the neo-Kantian *Geltung*, this validity is the rendering of the object of cognition as a part of social *being* in the full, ontological sense).

The early Bakhtin also turns to phenomenology in search of a "first philosophy" that deals with "unitary and once-occurrent Being-as-event" (Bakhtin, *Toward* 19). Such a philosophy must relate the content/sense aspect of an "objectivised product" to the "once-occurrent" act/deed of its "author" as "theoretically thinking, aesthetically contemplating, ethically acting" (*Toward* 27-28). Neo-Kantianism is incapable of being such a philosophy, according to Bakhtin, because "it can only be a specialised philosophy. It is a philosophy of the regions of culture and their unity in the form of a theoretical transcription from within the objects of cultural creation themselves and the immanent law of their development" (*Toward* 19). Bakhtin suggests that Neo-Kantianism has theorized the ethical act by separating these two "moments." Such a reservation is precisely the point at which Husserl's later phenomenology and neo-Kantianism diverge: the nature of the constitution of "cognised being." Bakhtin wishes to maintain the neo-Kantian categories that are applied in acts of subjective spontaneity, as is clear from his endorsement of the Marburg nomination of jurisprudence as the "logic of ethics" ("Lectures" 208), but he wants to combine this with the unrepeatable act of their realization through a single ego that one finds in phenomenology.

As a neo-Kantian, Bakhtin treats the world as an "ethical reality" that is eternally being "produced" in the encounter between the "I" and the "other," but he also adopts the Simmelian argument that objective culture has become alienated from the sphere of life. Bakhtin's project is to establish a way to overcome the resulting "tragedy of culture" by re-establishing, or rather disclosing the link between the product of culture and the ethical act of its production. This is discussed in terms of making an element of the "eternal" realm of sense (*smysl*), or the (objectively valid) cultural meanings delineated by neo-Kantian thought, valid (*znachimyi*) in life by realizing it in a specific intersubjective context (Bakhtin, *Toward* 58-59). Recent research, in particular by Brian Poole, has shown that different modalities of producing and bestowing relevance were explored by Bakhtin in his long (unfinished) essay "Author and Hero in Aesthetic Activity," in which Scheler's subtle typology of intersubjective relations was applied to aesthetic forms. Bakhtin calls the phenomenological distance discussed by Scheler "outsideness" (*vnenakhodimost'*), and he inventively applies this to relations between author and hero. The former, enmeshed in the "open event of being," is engaged in *ethical* activity, while the latter, viewing the activity from without as a determined whole is engaged in *aesthetic* activity. Aesthetic activity removes the act from the open "event of being" and subjects it to an aesthetic logic while ethical activity remains within the open event.

The Linguistic Turn

Like their German predecessors, both Shpet and the Circle moved from discussing intentional and meaning-bestowing acts in general to discursive acts in particular. The mutual point of departure therefore was Husserl's theory of linguistic acts in the *Logical Investigations*, which Shpet addressed in chapters 5 and 6 of *Appearance and Sense*, despite the book's overt focus on the *Ideas*. In the *Investigations* Husserl had argued that meaning is bestowed on language in intentional acts that comprise reciprocally dependent moments of quality (modes of "directedness") and immanent content (manner of objectual presentation). These meaning-bestowing acts are either nominal (directed toward objects) or judgemental (directed toward states of affairs [*Sachverhalte*]). As I have argued elsewhere, the Bakhtin Circle could not accept this model, since for Neo-Kantianism, judgement is the judgement of being (not of states of affairs) and being is the being of thinking (see Brandist, "Law"). This divergence lies behind Voloshinov's objection to Shpet's and Marty's distinctions between perception and evaluation. However, neither could accept Husserl's downgrading of the communicative dimension of language use. It is only for Shpet, however, that the meaning-bestowing act itself assumes the transmission of some objective sense between speakers acquiring social being. Shpet recasts the hermeneutic circle to argue that the word (part) only exists in a cultural context (whole) and makes up culture itself, but it is only in the communicative context of a society and social relations that sense is realized objectively. In an argument that echoes some of the concerns of such "realist" phenomenologists as Adolf Reinach, Shpet argues that a theory of the word is a task of formal ontology, for the word is not only a sign but also a "thing" or referent in its own right. The word has both a significative and an ontological nature with the consequence that the study of syntax is simultaneously both a logical and an ontological study. Shpet's is a fundamentally different ontology to the München phenomenologists, however, since the Russian's version bears a theological charge. The word itself takes on flesh and is incarnated, consecrating being as social being. Where Reinach outlined an ontology of social acts such as promises, obligations, orders and the like (see Mulligan), Shpet treated such phenomena as the incarnation of spirit.

Shpet identifies three different dimensions of sense: 1) the inner content-sense of the object, or its objective sense as defined above; 2) the "methodological" sense, which is a regulative criterion that organizes, formulates and directs human thought toward a specific goal; and 3) axiological sense which is the basis of more intimate and personal motivations, the cultural expression of subjective reality (for a discussion see Elentukh). The subject's conception of the noema is guided by the selection of object domains which is, in turn, motivated by certain axiological foundations that are not amenable to objectivization but which appear only as the expression of the subject's relationship to the world. Rendered linguistically, the intentional object becomes a social reality. All objectively given sociocultural phenomena are the products of linguistic consciousness and they are revealed to the percipient by means of intellectual-hermeneutic reflection. In this the true sense, the pure *eidos*, the entelechy of the object itself is revealed. In a move that Bakhtin would have undoubtedly described as "theoretism," Shpet distinguishes between the signifying function of the word and its expressive function so that the first case deals with the communication of the objective sense in intersubjective interaction as "pure logic," in isolation from all ethical and historical processes. Hermeneutic accounts such as those of Lipps, Dilthey, and Simmel, which revolve around notions of empathy and co-experiencing are capable of only uncovering the doxa rather than the logical core, the *eidos*, of sense. However, Shpet seeks to incorporate a wider hermeneutic perspective with the purely logical aspects by depsychologizing Dilthey's method and lending it a "rigorous" character.

Voloshinov opposes the ontological thrust of Shpet's work, remaining faithful to the neo-Kantian principle, derived ultimately from Lotze (Lotze 2: 209), that what has validity cannot be. Significance is defined as a *linguistic* function awaiting sense-bestowal, "the expression of a relationship of a sign, one instance of actuality, toward another actuality that it stands in for, represents, depicts. Significance is a function of a sign, therefore it cannot present significance to itself (being pure relation, function) as existing outside a sign, as some particular, independent thing." A little later on he notes that "by significance . . . we understand all those moments of the utterance which are repeatable and self-idententical in all repetitions" (Voloshinov, *Marxism* 28, 100) and "The sense [*smysl*] of a word is entirely defined by its context. In essence, there are as many meanings [*znachenie*] of a given word as there are contexts of usage" (Voloshinov, *Marxism* 79). Every utterance has a unitary sense, that is, a theme: "Theme is the upper, real [*real'nyi*] limit [*predel*] of linguistic validity [*znachimost'*]; in essence, only theme means [*znachit*] something definite. Significance is the lower limit [*predel*] of linguistic validity [*znachimost'*]. Significance, in essence, means [*znachit*] nothing, but possesses only potentiality—the possibility of meaning [*znachenie*] within a concrete theme" (Voloshinov, *Marxism* 101). The echoes of Shpet in Voloshinov's work are palpable at such times. In Shpet, too, one finds the notion that in being rendered as significance sense becomes valid, but for Shpet social validity equals ontological positivity: "sense has an insuperable demand to be materially embodied, which is why the idealists also say that it is embodied in the things of nature. But . . . sense also thirsts for creative embodiment, which its material bearer finds if not exclusively then preferably in the word" (Shpet, "Vnutrenniaia" 88). A little later he notes that "if we understand the significance of the word as the real sense of a word, grasped by us from the context of discourse [*rech'*] about a definite order, a definite sphere of things, that is not an abuse of the term," before going on to note that the meanings of the word "significance" in Russian include a plethora of nuances: "importance" (*vazhnost'*), "role" (*rol'*), value (*tsennost'*), "actuality" (*deistvitel'nost'*), "force" (*sila*), and so on (Shpet, "Vnutrenniaia" 118).

The Circle adopted Shpet's terminology here, but their focus is on intersubjectivity rather than discursive relations with objects of knowledge. Voloshinov transforms the intersubjective relations described in Bakhtin's early work into dialogue, which gains a definite philosophical charge in the process. Bakhtin's typology of author-hero relations is developed into the "history of forms of utterance" in the final part of *Marxism and the Philosophy of Language* and is simultaneously turned into a typology of forms of discursive interaction in the final chapter of Bakhtin's 1929 study of Dostoevskii. This relates to the creation of the world of culture as a moral reality, but that reality is fundamentally different to Shpet's social consecration of being as such.

Mediating Figures

While there is a direct line of influence from Husserl to Shpet and on to Voloshinov, it is crucial to recognize the influence of two specific mediating figures: Anton Marty and Karl Bühler. Marty is now a largely forgotten figure, but as Voloshinov noted in 1928, his work had been massively influential in shaping the discussion of both language and literature in the first part of the twentieth century ("Archival Materials" 233-34). Marty's 1908 book, *Untersuchungen zur Grundlegung der allgemeinen Grammatik und Sprachphilosophie,* was responsible for foregrounding the communicative function of triggering (*Auslösung*) in language in opposition to Husserl's *Darstellungstheorie* (*Theory of Representation*). While, like Husserl, Marty presents an act-based theory of linguistic meaning, the latter upheld Brentano's division of mental phenomena into presentations, judgments, and emotive phenomena. In Marty's hands this became a division of linguistic phenomena into names, statements and "emotives," or "utterances calling forth an interest." In opposition to both Wilhelm Wundt's *Kundgabetheorie* and Husserl's *Darstellungstheorie*, Marty argued that what is "primarily intended" by a speaker is "a certain influencing or controlling of the alien psychic life of the hearer. Deliberate speaking is a special kind of acting whose proper goal is to call forth special psychic phenomena in other beings. In relation to this intention the announcement of processes within oneself appears merely as a side-effect." According to Marty, the speaker strives to "generate a judgement in the hearer that is analogous to that which is as a rule expressed by the statement uttered" (qtd. in Smith 42). Marty discusses language use in "asking questions, in issuing complaints, reprimands, requests, commands, recommendations, threats, in giving comfort, encouragement, praise" and even raises the ethical dimension of "emotives," but always does so at the level of psychology (Smith 43, see also Schuhmann).

    Bühler admired Marty's work and shared much of his critique of Husserl, but insisted on amending the account of "triggering" so that what emotives relate to is not so much the hearer's "mental processes" but the "acts" the hearer may perform, discursive or otherwise. Triggering was an element of the "mutual steering of the meaningful behaviour of members of a community," while representation includes "purely symbolic" representations, making language a crucial aspect of "objective spirit" and thus an object of *geisteswissenschaftliche* psychology (Bühler, *Die Krise* 21-23). Thus modified, Bühler argued that the speech event (*Sprechereignis*) is a gestalt-unit, with the three functions identified by his predecessors, intimation (*Kundgabe*), representation (*Darstellung*), and triggering (*Auslösung*) merely abstract moments read off it. As I have shown elsewhere (Brandist, "Voloshinov's Dilemma") Bühler's "organon model'"of the speech event and his crucial distinction between the symbol and deictic fields against which all utterances are made and understood became the foundations of Voloshinov's theory of the utterance. The extent to which Shpet engaged with the ideas of Marty has recently been clarified through the publication in 2005 of Shpet's 1921-25 manuscript "Language and Sense" ("*Iazyk i smysl*"). Marty features in the text prominently (see Shpet, "Iazyk i smysl"), while in the second of his 1922 *Aesthetic Fragments* Shpet outlined a theory of the word (*slovo*) in terms distinctly reminiscent of Marty and Bühler. The word is above all a means of communication, the meanings of which can refer to "things" and to "signs," and an exact interpretive method must discern each aspect.

The "Inner Form" of the Word

Shpet's most sustained work on language is his 1927 book *The Inner Form of the Word: Études and Variations on Humboldt's Themes*. While Humboldt appeared in the title, the notion of inner form had been developed by several theorists, the most significant of which were Marty, Cassirer, and Aleksandr Potebnia. Shpet's conception of inner form owes most to Marty, whose work was much more conducive to an ontological reworking: the discursive rendering of a given object of reference. Shpet's point of departure is Marty's account of "figurative inner form of language" in which an inner meaning (*Bedeutung*) is rendered in a sentence or word (*Sprachmittel*) in a way that deviates from the etymon (ideal content) of the word. The inner language form itself is neither meaning nor sentence/word. The etymon, for Marty, is crucial in drawing the attention of the hearer to the intended meaning, but this link is distorted in some way when the usage is figurative. Thus, to borrow an example (from Funke 26), the word "lion" is a sign for the inner concept "lion," but when the former is used by Marcius in Shakespeare's *Coriolanus* to mean "brave warrior" figuratively, then the concept "lion" can be said to be the figurative inner language form of the concept "brave warrior." The concept "brave warrior" is related to the word "lion" as an outer language form through the concept "lion" as an inner language form (see Kuroda). When the relationship is one of subject and predicate, for example, "the coal is black," then the relationship is termed the "constructive inner language form." In each case, however, the inner form serves as a "means of association between sound and meaning," enabling "the creator of phrases to group an immense variety of semantic contents with the help of a rather small number of signs that are understandable by themselves or have become understandable as a result of unsophisticated linguistic habits" (qtd. in Kiesow 56). Over time the inner form fades into the background and metaphors are likely to be taken literally so that, for example, few recall the religious metaphor behind the term "disgrace" (dis-grace, absence of divine blessing).

Although Shpet is critical of Marty, he draws much from him. Like the Brentanians, of which Marty was a fairly orthodox representative, Shpet distinguishes between the (real) "thing" and the (ideal) "object," with the latter approximating Brentano's "in-existing" intentional object. While contending that he remains faithful to Husserl's noema theory, Shpet actually undermines it by arguing that the object bears meaning and that like a gestalt it requires both objective form and subjective apprehension. The noema now becomes the content of thought and the inner form is consciousness's relation to this content, a notion that echoes Potebnia's definition of inner form as "the relation of thought's content to consciousness" (Potebnia 77). The result is that while Shpet repeatedly asserts the dependence of the object on the thing he never establishes exactly what the link between them really is, and it seems the existence of the thing must be taken as a matter of faith. The logical or poetic form is the inner (intersubjective) form of the word and the outer form is the ontological being of the word. The empirical world essentially remains an unknown thing-in-itself that mysteriously evokes a sense. Despite some bluster, Shpet's calling the inner forms "poetic" and "logical" respectively is a direct borrowing from Marty ("Esteticheskie" 410). The logical form for Shpet is a "relationship between things and objects placed in the common context of such a relationship which in the final analysis is the world, all actuality" ("Esteticheskie" 412). It strives for the exhaustion of the sense of a concrete concept, to explain all its possible uses for the subject. While dependent on logical form, the poetic form abstracts from objective connections and establishes more or less arbitrary and fantastic connections. In this duality, inner form is presented as an energy that drives toward the limits of a sense through a dialectic of real and realized cultural sense, serving the aim of comprehending the world. In and through this process of linguistic combination and systematization, the unity of the social object is fixed in the flow of changing impressions: the thing becomes a social object. Thus, "the theory of the sign in its objective aspect is nothing other than the theory of the social object" (Shpet, "Germenevtika" 1989 256), a specific level of being in the process of becoming according to the dialectical laws of the inner language form.

Conclusion

It seems that ultimately while the Bakhtin Circle remains on the side of the idealist "conceptualists," Shpet's ontology strives to be a realism without actually becoming one in the modern, philosophical sense. He strives to establish a link between thing and object but fails to establish that link and compensates by ontologising the realm of culture. As he puts it at one stage, the "new realism" that he advocates is an "expressive realism, and not a realism of being," for it expresses "what actually is rather than what seems" ("Esteticheskie" 360). Shpet is here seeking a link based on a neo-Platonic incarnation of essence rather than a correspondence theory of truth. While Bakhtin prepared to sever links between the sign and a given extra-discursive reality, Voloshinov holds fast to the notion that the sign "refracts" something that is given to consciousness rather than producing a totally detached world of culture. Voloshinov and Shpet thus converge in their unresolved equivocation between realism and idealism, but their respective directions are divergent. Criticizing Shpet for separating objective significance and evaluative connotation, and ignoring the revaluation that is central to changing word meanings, Voloshinov claims such an approach ontologizes the word and separates it from sociohistorical becoming (Voloshinov, *Marxism* 105). Thus, while both trends interpenetrate, the difference in approach comes down to the principles that divided neo-Kantianism from phenomenology: for all their excursions into phenomenology, the Bakhtin Circle remained faithful to their neo-Kantian principles. Where Shpet, like Husserl, argued for the fundamental distinction between the acts that make up the realm of experience as such and the objects given intentionally in those acts, the Circle insisted on the fundamental constitution, or reconstitution, of objects from the "world of transcendental, a priori, formal being." Bakhtinian dialogism is the ongoing and endless process of constituting the world of consciousness in intersubjective interaction (life) from the categories of objective validity: ethics, aesthetics, science and so on, but at the same time building up those categories. The subject occupies a sociospecific point of view from which the "unknown X" of "empirical actuality" is transformed into a plurality of aspects that bear meaning with the world consisting of the systematic totality of these aspects. The notion of meaning being totally determined by context flows directly from this. Shpet, on the other hand, maintains a phenomenological adherence to the ontological positivity of the objects of perception and judgement and thus must insist on the duality of the given thing or state of affairs and the object of consciousness. This is reflected in his commitment to the distinction between objective and evaluative meaning that Voloshinov found inadmissible. The subject now bestows meaning on the given manifold of experience (hyletic data) in discursive acts, with the realm of consciousness granted an ontological self-sufficiency. In the Bakhtinian scheme such metaphysics dissolves into the theory of knowledge, and so despite pursuing mediations between neo-Kantianism and phenomenology, the Circle and Shpet remained in separate camps.

Note

This article was produced as part of the project "The Rise of Sociological Linguistics in the USSR, 1917-1938: Institutions, Ideas and Agendas" at the Bakhtin Centre in the Department of Russian and Slavonic Studies at the University of Sheffield, UK, funded by the AHRC.

Works Cited

Ash, Mitchell G. "Academic Politics in the History of Science: Experimental Psychology in Germany 1979-1941." *Central European History* 13 (1980): 255-86.

Ash, Mitchell G. *Gestalt Psychology in German Culture 1890-1967: Holism and the Quest for Objectivity*. Cambridge: Cambridge UP, 1998.

Bakhtin, M.M. "Lectures and Comments of 1924-1925." [From the Notebooks of L. V. Pumpianskii]. *Bakhtin and Religion: A Feeling for Faith*. Ed. S.M. Felch and P.J. Contino. Evanston: Northwestern UP, 2001. 193-237.

Bakhtin, M.M. *Sobranie sochinenii*. Vol. 5. Moscow: Russkie slovari, 1996.

Bakhtin, M. M. *Toward a Philosophy of the Act*. Trans. Vadim Liapunov. Austin: U of Texas P, 1993.

Balmaton, Ts.P. "Opyty Karla Stumpfa i ego shkoly." *Voprosy filosofii i psikhologii* 68 (1903): 377-417.

Brandist, Craig. "Voloshinov's Dilemma: On the Philosophical Roots of the Dialogic Theory of the Utterance." *The Bakhtin Circle: In the Master's Absence*. Ed. Craig Brandist, David Shepherd, and Galin Tihanov. Manchester: Manchester UP, 2004. 97-124.

Brandist, Craig. "Law and the Genres of Discourse: The Bakhtin Circle's Theory of Language and the Phenomenology of Right." *Bakhtinian Perspectives on Language and Culture*. Ed. F. Bostad et al. Houndmills: Palgrave, 2004. 21-45.

Bühler, Karl. *Die Krise der Psychologie*. Jena: G. Fischer, 1927.

Cassedy, S. "Gustav Shpet and Phenomenology in an Orthodox Key." *Studies in East European Thought* 49 (1997): 81-108.

Cassirer, Ernst. "'Spirit' and 'Life' in Contemporary Philosophy." *The Philosophy of Ernst Cassirer*. Ed. P.A. Schlipp. Evanston: Library of Living Philosophers, 1949. 857-80.

Cassirer, Ernst. *The Philosophy of Symbolic Forms*. Vol. 3. *The Phenomenology of Knowledge*. Trans. R. Mannheim. New Haven: Yale UP, 1957.

Elentukh, I.P. "Kategoriia smysla: problema sootnosheniia semioticheskogo i aksiologicheskogo." *Shpetovskie chteniia v Tomske 1991*. Ed. O.G. Mazaeva. Tomsk: Izdatel'stvo Tomskogo universiteta, 1991. 61-65.

Freiberger-Sheikholeslami, E. "Forgotten Pioneers of Soviet Semiotics." *Semiotics 1980*. Ed. M. Herzfeld and M. Lenhart. New York: Plenum, 1980. 155-65.

Funke, Otto. *Innere Sprachform. Eine Einführung in A. Martys Sprachphilosophie*. Reichenberg: Sudetendeutscher Verlag Franz Kaus, 1924.

Grinbaum, A. "Funktsional'naia psikhologiia (po povodu sochineniia Stumpfa: Erscheinungen und psychische Funktionen, 1907)." *Voprosy filosofii i psikhologii* 97 (1909): 192-203.

Kagan, Matvei. "German Kogen." *O khode istorii*. Moscow: Iazyki slavianskoi kul'tury 2004. 33-44.

Kaufmann, F. "Cassirer, Neo-Kantianism and Phenomenology." *The Philosophy of Ernst Cassirer*. Ed. P.A. Schlipp. Evanston: Library of Living Philosophers, 1949. 799-854.

Kiesow, Karl-Friedrich. "Marty on Form and Content in Language." *Mind, Meaning and Metaphysics: The Philosophy of Anton Marty*. Ed. K. Mulligan. Dordrecht: Kluwer, 1990. 51-65.

Kozulin, A. "Georgy Chelpanov and the Establishment of the Moscow Institute of Psychology." *Journal of the History of the Behavioral Sciences* 21 (1985): 23-32.

Kuroda, S.-Y. "Anton Marty and the Transformational Theory of Grammar." *Foundations of Language* 9 (1972): 1-37.

Lichkovakh, V.A. "Veshch′ kak znak: kontseptsia evokativnosti predmetnykh form kul′tury." *Shpetovskie chteniia v Tomske 1991*. Ed. O.G. Mazaeva. Tomsk: Izdatel'stvo Tomskogo universiteta, 1991. 72-74.

Losev, A.F. "Russkaia filosofiia." *Ocherki istorii russkoi filosofii*. By A.I. Vvedenskii, A.F. Losev, E.L. Radlov, and G.G. Shpet. Ed. B. V. Emel'ianov and K.N. Liubutin. Sverdlovsk: Izdatel'stvo Ural′skogo universiteta, 1991. 67-95.

Losev, A.F. "Issledovaniia po filosofii i psikhologii myshleniia." *Lichnost′ i absoliut*. Moscow: Mysl′, 1999. 5-224.

Lotze, R.H. *Logic in Three Books: of Thought, of Investigation and of Knowledge*. 2 vols. Trans. B. Bosanquet. Oxford: Clarendon, 1888.

Mulligan, Kevin, and Barry Smith. "Mach and Ehrenfels: The Foundation of Gestalt Theory." *The Foundations of Gestalt Theory*. Ed. Barry Smith. München: Philosophia, 1988. 124-57.

Mulligan, Kevin, ed. *Speech Act and Sachverhalt: Reinach and the Foundations of Realist Phenomenology*. Dordrecht: M. Nijhoff. 1987.

Potebnia, A.A. *Mysl i iazyk*. Kiev: SINTO, 1926.

Rossiiskii gosudarstvennyi arkhiv literatury i iskusstv (RGALI). Moscow. Fond 941 (Gosudarstvennaia akademiia khudozhestvennykh nauk (GAKhN) 1921-31).

Schuhmann, Karl. "Contents of Consciousness and States of Affairs: Daubert and Marty." *Mind, Meaning and Metaphysics: The Philosophy of Anton Marty*. Ed. K. Mulligan. Dordrecht: Kluwer, 1990. 197-214.

Shpet, Gustav. *Appearance and Sense: Phenomenology as the Fundamental Science and Its Problems*. Trans. Thomas Nemeth. Dordrecht: Kluwer, 1991.

Shpet, Gustav. "Esteticheskie fragmenty." *Sochineniia*. Moscow: Pravda, 1989. 345-475.

Shpet, Gustav. "Germenevtika i ee problemy." *Kontekst 1989*. Moscow: Nauka, 1989. 231-67; *Kontekst 1990*. Moscow: Nauka, 1990. 219-59; *Kontekst 1991*. Moscow: Nauka, 1991. 215-55; *Kontekst 1992*. Moscow: Nauka, 1993. 251-84.

Shpet, Gustav. "G.G. Shpet M.I. Kaganu, 20.02.1920." *O khode istorii*. By M.I. Kagan. Moscow: Iazyki slavianskoi kul′tury, 2004. 629.

Shpet, Gustav. "Iazyk i smysl." *Mysl′ i Slovo. Izbrannye trudy*. Ed. T.G. Shchedrina. Moscow: ROSSPEN, 2005. 470-668.

Shpet, Gustav. "Odin put psikhologii i kuda on vedet." *Psikologiia sotsial′nogo by-tiia. Izbrannye psikhologicheskie trudy*. Ed. T.D. Martsinkovskaia. Moscow and Voronezh: Institut prakticheskoi psikhologii and MODEK. 1996. 28-48.

Shpet, Gustav. "Soznanie i ego sobstvennik." *Filosofskie etiudy*. Moscow: Progress, 1994. 20-116.

Shpet, Gustav. "Vnutrenniaia forma slova." *Psikologiia sotsial′nogo bytiia. Izbrannye psikhologicheskie trudy*. Ed. T.D. Martsinkovskaia. Moscow and Voronezh: Institut prakticheskoi psikhologii and MODEK. 1996. 49-260.

Shpet, Gustav. "Vvedenie v etnicheskuiu psikhologiiu." *Sochineniia*. Moscow: Pravda, 1989. 475-574.

Smith, B. "Towards a History of Speech Act Theory." *Speech Acts, Meanings and Intentions: Critical Approaches to the Philosophy of John R. Searle*. Ed. A. Burkhardt. Berlin: de Gruyter, 1990. 26-61.

Spiegelberg, Herbert. *The Phenomenological Movement: A Historical Introduction*. The Hague: Nijhoff, 1982.

Voloshinov, Valentin. *Marxism and the Philosophy of Language*. Trans. L. Matejka and R. Titunik. Cambridge: Harvard UP, 1973.

Voloshinov, Valentin. "Lichnoe delo V.N. Voloshinova." Ed. Nikolai Pan'kov. *Dialog Karnaval Khronotop* 2 (1995): 70-99.

Voloshinov, Valentin. "Archival Materials." *The Bakhtin Circle: In the Master's Absence*. Ed. Craig Brandist, David Shepherd, and Galin Tihanov. Manchester: Manchester UP, 2004. 223-50.

Semiotics in Voloshinov and Shpet

Dušan Radunović

The conceptual foundations of Gustav Shpet's general semasiology and Valentin Voloshinov's principle of dialogic speech interaction have rarely been considered from a comparative perspective. This article purports to draw critical attention to the partly convergent, partly divergent trajectories that these two thinkers followed in their approach to language. Whereas the two methodologies and discursive practices may not appear commensurable on the surface, there emerge beneath important philosophical convergences between Shpet and Voloshinov. Notwithstanding the fact that the two thinkers developed their views on language in different directions, coextensive philosophical concerns and common intellectual backgrounds provide a certain justification for a concise comparative study of their ideas. Shpet inherited a remarkably diverse intellectual baggage that comprised German classical idealism, Wilhelm von Humboldt's post-Romantic ideas of language, and Husserl's phenomenology. In Shpet's works of the 1920s, most notably in his 1927 study *The Inner Form of the Word*, the author developed a complex theory of the mechanisms that generate meaning in language. Curiously, in his struggle against the objectivist concept of meaning that he had inherited from his philosophical predecessors, Shpet advocated in his general semasiology, tacitly rather than in an elaborate fashion, the outer, extra-linguistic (in Shpet's words, *cultural*) constitution of verbal meaning.

Unlike Shpet's, Voloshinov's contribution to twentieth-century philosophy of language has been more widely acknowledged. Influenced by a similar intellectual tradition—the turn-of-the-century German philosophy of language and aesthetics, in the first place—Voloshinov promotes an approach to the phenomenon of verbal communication that takes into consideration the social reality of the speaking subject. Distancing himself from the European linguistic tradition, Voloshinov idiosyncratically defines discourse (an active, living word, rather than a dictionary entry) as a real *social event*, the unity of the speaking subject, the listener (who is, in fact, another speaking subject, a constituent of the chain of verbal interaction), and the object ("Discourse" 11).

I examine Shpet's and Voloshinov's theories with reference to their contribution to the articulation of certain issues that shaped the agenda of philosophy of language in Europe. Particular attention will be paid to the problem of meaning, which served as a benchmark in the study of language in the late nineteenth and the early twentieth century. In conclusion, on the grounds of certain explicit, but more often implicit, correlations between the two theoretical orientations, I raise the question of the commensurability of Shpet's and Voloshinov's philosophical projects.

Shpet on the Notion of Meaning and Its Philosophical Requisites

Although captivated by Edmund Husserl's redefinition of philosophy as a strict science, Shpet did not adhere uncritically to all aspects and spheres of application of Göttingen phenomenology (epistemology, semantics, axiology, and formal ontology). The problem of sense (*Sinn*) that reverberates most forcefully in Husserl's philosophy was significantly modified in its early Russian reception. Moreover, even in his initial appropriation of Husserl's ideas, in *Appearance and Sense* (finished in October 1913, in the midst of productive intellectual exchanges with Husserl), Shpet criticized Husserl's concept of intentionality as well as his view of noematic sense as the final objective of eidetic reduction. More precisely, Shpet argued that noematic sense—defined not only as the actual meaning, but as the only sense of an object that concerns phenomenological philosophy—appears to be the property of both the subject and the object. The noema is subjective inasmuch as it is achieved by the noetic act of the subject's consciousness; however, noematic sense is also objective, as the transcendental consciousness of the subject refers to, or intends, the ideal meaning of an object or a state of affairs. In Husserl's own words, "the Eidos of the noema points to the Eidos of the noetic consciousness" (241). Thus, we have an ambivalent situation in which the sense-bestowing act comes from the subject's consciousness, but the sense of the object, or the state of affairs, remains the primary property of that object. As he principally maintained that "the object is only possible as the unity of a noematic composition," that is, in the unity of the mind (noetic) and the object (noematic), Husserl had to find his way out of this overlap and bridge the chasm between the contents of the eidetic consciousness and the (ideal) sense. The crucial instrument that Husserl's phenomenology provided for bridging this dichotomy was found in eidetic intuition. Termed aptly the "principle of all principles," intuition is in *Ideas I* not only a mediating instance between the two realms, but "*the legitimizing source of cognition*" (Husserl 44) of transcendental subjectivity.

Shpet did not accept Husserl's transcendental subjectivism in its entirety. He was particularly uneasy about the Platonic traits of Husserl's philosophy, for example, about the claim of a fundamental structural identity between the intellect and the world of the objects. Therefore, the question of the teleological aspect of the phenomenological method, the transcendental position of the phenomenological subject that originates in the analogous structure of the noetic-noematic sphere in which the essence of an object corresponds to the noematic structure of the intellect, became an important point of disagreement in Shpet's reception of Hussserl's philosophy. In addition, the teleological function of the eidetic reduction, which is made possible through the subject's faculty of eidetic intuition, entails principally the exclusion of subjective (historical, psychological, and other) contingencies in the subject's pursuit of "noematic sense." In spite of this rigorous methodological reduction, it still does not enable one to fully grasp the essence of an object. Rather, the purpose of the eidetic reduction is to arrive at a certain "intentional essence" of the object that is experienced in the "actional consciousness."

The thetic structure of the sense-bestowing act is inextricably tied to the position the subject holds in Husserl's analysis. Paradoxically, as Shpet notices in his *Appearance and Sense*, thetic acts were conceived of in *Ideas* as sense-bestowing acts, but it remained unclear from where the sense-bestowing capacity of these acts comes, as they are "empty" and the sense always resides in the object itself (Shpet, *Mysl'* 148). This moment is of particular importance for our understanding of certain features of Shpet's thought in a more general key: by bringing to critical attention one of the underlying dilemmas of Husserl's entire philosophical endeavor, namely, the question of the identity, or the inextricable "correlation between mind/reason and reality" (*Mysl'* 148), Shpet undoubtedly anticipated but, as we shall see, never fully accomplished his fundamental critique of the main postulates of European idealism.

Although Shpet never questioned Husserl's argument that meaning is determined principally by the noematic features of the object, he was aware that the semantic field is a more complex, multifaceted realm that, importantly, has to do with the subject's consciousness. Unlike Husserl, whose early discussions of semantic issues were criticized as psychologism (see Gottlob Frege's critique of Husserl's *Origins of Arithmetic*), it seemed initially that Shpet was less apprehensive about the inclusion of the attributes of subjective existence in the theory of meaning. If phenomenology is about an acting consciousness, the Russian philosopher argued, how can we rule out those features that constitute, guide, and affect both the consciousness and the processes related to its activities? Being equally indebted to the philosophical legacy of Wilhelm Dilthey's hermeneutics, Shpet was well aware that dealing with semantic issues from the premises of transcendental subjectivism simply does not do justice to the subject, that is, fails to acknowledge the other aspects of the subject's consciousness that affect his/her cognitive faculties. Thus, in his account of the positional acts, that is, the acts that would meet the entelechy of the objects, Shpet insisted that the real unity of meaning can only be achieved as the "unity of the entelechy and the moments of hermeneutical character" (*Appearance* 153). Without its transcendental supplement (i.e., the notion of eidetic intuition), the binary structure of the phenomenological reduction, which aimed to overcome the chasm between cognition and the objective world, remains not only paradoxical but also incapable of exhausting the complex and heterogeneous realm of meaning.

Questioning the structural equation between the mind and the world, and thus the transcendental foundations of Husserl's philosophy, Shpet went on to reconcile the contradictions by refiguring the original principles of Husserl's theory. For Shpet, sense (*smysl*) is inextricably linked to the process of cognition (*urazumenie*), in the same way as the act of judgement is inseparable from the process of understanding (*ponimanie*). Here one should not fail to notice the common denominator of Shpet's interventions—his focus on the productive role of the concrete empirical subject; it is precisely due to this new focus that his departure from Husserl appears to be more than simply cosmetic and becomes more substantive.

The idiosyncratic methodological path Shpet chose to critique the phenomenological notion of the transcendental subject and traditional semantics is emblematic of his eclectic treatment of the philosophical sources. Shpet was no doubt dissatisfied with the binary-coded practices of European Modernity (noematic sense vs. real sense; or, in his later debates with Humboldt's legacy, the rift between the realm of the idea and the sphere of its sensuous manifestation). On the other hand, it was perhaps his belonging to the tradition of European idealist philosophy that made him refrain from radical steps and, even when expanding beyond the limits of a single disciplinary practice, remain faithful to the philosophical master narrative that had enshrined and perpetuated these binary oppositions. With this in mind, Shpet's subsequent evolution as a thinker becomes more readily comprehensible. Although by the mid-1910s the focus of his philosophical concerns was drifting away from phenomenology as a strict science, the question of meaning, while taking on a different form, remained one of his vital philosophical concerns. The specific philosophical concept, which Shpet utilized in his attempt to build another nexus that would bridge the two disparate areas of philosophy of language, was the concept of inner form. As in the case of his account of linguistic pragmatics and phenomenological practice, the diversity of Shpet's approaches to the problem of inner form will emerge more clearly against the wider background of the nineteenth and early twentieth century continental tradition of philosophy of language, particularly the philosophical practices of Wilhelm von Humboldt and Anton Marty.

From Humboldt Shpet adopted the understanding of language as *energeia*, a dynamic structure in becoming that mediates between the realm of meaningful ideas and their physical manifestation in sound. One of Humboldt's crucial tenets was that the origin of language was to be found in the maieutic attempt of an inner idea to manifest itself, to surmount the impenetrability it encounters in the sound material (see Shpet, *Vnutrenniaia* 20): the essence of language, its "purely intellectual side," argued the German thinker, is concealed in this inner form. As Marty pointed out, followed here closely by Shpet, it was precisely this idealist (Hegelian, but in essence Platonic) conception of language that was responsible for the crucial limitations of Humboldt's entire theory: 1) Humboldt in his approach operates with a presupposed opposition between the principal realm of ideas and, on the other side, the secondary realm of appearance and 2) more importantly, in such a constellation, language, exemplified in its physical aspect, or pure sound, inevitably becomes axiologically and ontologically subordinated to man's mental (*geistige*) faculties.

Although aware of the problems of the Humboldtian idealist legacy, Shpet did not completely refute the German philosopher's views on language; rather, he made an effort to reconcile the opposites by postulating that "the forces that initiate language and thought are one and the same" (*Vnutrenniaia* 24). Nonetheless, this seemingly cosmetic correction of Humboldt's philosophy of language suggested the main concerns of Shpet's own approach to language in the 1920s. Without Humboldt's "grand divide," Shpet conceived of language as the "formative instrument [or *organon*] of thought" (*Vnutrenniaia* 15). The inner form of language then naturally appears as the "formative principle" by virtue of which language practically manages to translate the intellectual activity of the mind into an external form. As the definition implies, the constitutive moments of language are 1) its inner sense ([der] *innere Sprachsinn*) and 2) its sound, or pure matter. This dual disposition of language necessitates what Shpet, following Humboldt, calls the high synthesis, whose final objective is the marriage between sound and meaning.

This general mechanism of language is the grand paradigm according to which the small-scale productive mechanisms of meaning are activated in the real language in use. However, Shpet claims that Humboldt ruled out the possibility that any other act of consciousness, apart from the high synthesis, has relevance for the generation of meaning. The additional mechanisms that Shpet summons here as possible examples are the acts of apperception and association. For Shpet, Humboldt's immanentism with regard to the production of meaning testifies to the strong conceptual influence of Kant's treatment of the categories of pure reason: analogous to Kant's famous argument that the categories of the natural sciences actually constitute (the concept of) nature, Humboldt's dynamics of the generation of meaning presupposes that purely linguistic categories (such as flexion and affixes, for example) would suffice to constitute meaning (Shpet, *Vnutrenniaia* 42-44).

What Shpet proposes instead of this immanent mechanism is a more unpredictable process in which the conceptual unity of linguistic consciousness is achieved through the contribution of the subject. The principal correlation between this argument and Shpet's 1914 discord with Husserl's understanding of meaning is obvious: whereas the corrective to Husserl's notion of noematic sense and the supplement for the notion of eidetic intuition was found in a crypto-hermeneutic activity of the subject, the criticism of Humboldt's immanentism of language production is lodged in Shpet's argument for the existence of a substratum of linguistic consciousness. In contrast to the eidetic sense produced in the noetic-noematic field, Shpet here advocates a socially constructed foundation realized through the multiple efforts and—being part of a complex social network, not normally accountable—work of a multitude of individual consciousnesses. The productive mechanisms of language, Shpet proceeds to argue, are neither determinate by *a priori* patterns (as was argued by Humboldt), nor are they absolutely arbitrary (as claimed by Saussure, for example). In concurrence with his previous argument, their role as mechanisms for the generation of meaning may well be indisputable, but the process itself is never fully calculable in its entirety.

On these grounds Shpet also critiques Humboldt's notion of a "pure articulation sense" as yet another trace of the Kantian interference in Humboldt's philosophy of language. The Russian thinker did accept that *a priori* forms of perception are embedded in each speaking subject (see his previous argument for the existence of a substratum of linguistic consciousness), but he refused to conform to Humboldt's stance that these are solely dependent on subjective and psychological features. Rather, as we have just suggested, certain aspects of the individual subject's language (and thus, of his or her production of meaning) are, to a considerable extent, modeled by his or her concrete cultural-cum-social disposition. Marty, on the other hand, advanced the theory of the spontaneous, a-logical emergence of language (in this respect Marty stands as a strong opponent to Humboldt's theory). However, he did not rule out the existence of an initial tie between sound and meaning. In the distant past of language, he argued, the ideal nomination (*prima appellata*) had indeed taken place, that is, the "root signs" had really existed. But it was the historical development of language, corroborated by the processes of metaphorization and "metonymyzation," that inevitably brought about both the distance between words and the sphere of sensorial experience, on the one hand, and the further dissemination of the originary nominations, on the other. The latter often did not follow any logical principles, and it is for this reason that logically similar "names" are often assigned to dissimilar objects. As a result, every language contains words that maintain their connection with a "primary" content, but it is also abundant in morphologically allied terms of completely a-logical or distant semantic relations. The latter phenomenon is the consequence of the unplanned, spontaneous process of the emergence of language, of the process of the metaphorization of root signs. According to Marty, the significance of these initial nominations is immense: the initial creative mechanisms that brought forth the *prima apellata* became the foundation, or inner forms, of creation, the linguistic embodiments of causal, temporal, and other more complex sets of relationships. But despite this, by taking into account the reality of the historical development of language, Marty rejected any conflation of the notions of meaning and inner form (the most notable example of which we find in Humboldt's philosophy), arguing that the former (sense, *Sinn*) can never be reduced to the latter.

It is exactly at this point that Shpet himself departs from Humboldt. Hence, I am convinced that, even though frequently critical of Marty, it was from him that Shpet actually adopted the main tools for his critique of Humboldt's reduction of meaning to inner form. Differentiating between the concepts of inner form and meaning, Shpet did allow that the two notions correspond to some extent, but he insisted the "initial" character and the givenness of the former could never exhaust the complex realm of meaning. For Shpet, forms (and thus also inner forms) are no more than "vessels" that allow meaning to occur. The meaning itself is then conceived as a kind of surplus, which can only be accomplished through the act of understanding. The fact that in his working notes for the study on inner form Shpet seems to equate the concepts of meaning and understanding (*Mysl'* 620) only proves how vital, but eventually undecided, his struggle against objectivist approaches to language was in the early 1920s.

To sum up, Shpet was attempting in various ways to negotiate the radical incongruity of the two philosophical traditions epitomized here by Humboldt's and

Husserl's philosophical projects. In both cases, the Russian thinker recognized that the way out of the *cul-de-sac* is in affirmation of the productive role of the subject, but he was nevertheless unready for the radical theoretical ramifications of this insight, and thus he failed to take the appropriate methodological steps. Although setting the ground for a fundamental reappraisal of the subject-object dichotomy, he never fully rejected the idealist presumption of a structural correlation between consciousness and the world of the objects. Therefore, both his critique of immanentism and that of objectivism remained limited in their scope.

Voloshinov's Social Linguistics

In the case of Voloshinov's social linguistics, we witness the author's radical endeavor to situate the linguistic debate beyond the ill-fated framework of the subject-object relationship, by way of transcending the limits of both the individual subjectivism and the abstract objectivism characteristic of the early twentieth-century studies of language (e.g., the traditional legacy of historical linguistics and the recent synchronic linguistics, respectively). Although we can recognize here the central problem that Shpet was struggling to solve within the phenomenological tradition—how to posit a linguistic or a philosophical subject—Voloshinov's philosophical intentions move away not only from Shpet but also from the Russian intellectual milieu of the time. I argue that the differences between Shpet and Voloshinov become vivid precisely in the way their linguistic-philosophical projects managed, or failed, to define how the subject copes with the otherness of the outer world.

The way in which Voloshinov attempted to resolve the grand dichotomy between the subject and the world is indeed worthy of attention. Rather than working out the solution within the boundaries of a given model, Voloshinov's idiosyncratic *Weltanschauung* actually dissolved the initial constituents of the dichotomy, both the subject and the world. According to Voloshinov, instead of the world as a given set of data, it is the world in becoming that is the real object of linguistic consciousness. He thus sees no contradiction in defining the individual consciousness as inner word, a realm he believes to be essential for any philosopher of language. Quite unlike the Humboldtian tradition, Voloshinov's notion of inner word does not presuppose the subject's interiorization of his or her sensations of the world; for him, the inner word only testifies to the fact that discourse, understood as the verbal refraction of the world in becoming, emerges precisely in the dynamic verbal interspace between the subject and the world.

The way Voloshinov deals with the dichotomy between "inner" and "outer" is a good example of his master strategy of inverting and reassessing the dichotomized values of the European intellectual legacy. In the same vain, Voloshinov's strategy of inversion is revealed in his dual understanding of discourse as both the semiotic material of the inner life of consciousness and the ideological sign *par excellence* (*Marxism* 9, 14). Thus when he asserts that language is the expressive exponent of human consciousness, Voloshinov only seemingly echoes the main postulate of Wilhelm Wundt's expressive theory of language: in fact, he is out to highlight the fundamental situatedness of the linguistic consciousness (the individual subject) in the concrete social environment. This tie between the subject and the social sphere appears as a dominant factor in the construction of the subject (therefore, Voloshinov's notion of refraction leaves no space for the mimetic theory of reflection); furthermore, it presupposes a permanent interaction, an exchange between the two realms, a process of fundamental, constitutive relevance to both of them.

As a consequence of the former argument, the subject of an utterance is not given the choice whether or not he or she will enter the verbal interaction; rather, Voloshinov's subject is always already exposed to it as part of the continuous chain of speech performances. Consequently, as the universe of verbal interaction is the subject's inescapable necessity, no speaker is ever a primordial speaker, no more than he or she is the creator of an original discursive situation. In a constellation in which the subject is from the very beginning exteriorized and placed in the network of discursive intercourse, everything subjective is instantaneously objectified at the very moment of becoming, and the subjective-objective dichotomy loses its sense. However, it should be the subject of a separate debate to what extent Voloshinov's aphorism that "individual consciousness" is nothing but a contradiction in terms can lead to its cancellation. On the one hand, it is important to praise the Russian thinker's daring reassessment of the traditional categories of philosophy of language, including his attempted break with the tradition of subject-object dichotomy, but on the other, as I will subsequently come to assert, it is highly questionable whether his radical social ontologization of all constituents of the verbal interaction can really work. Ostensibly calling upon the Humboldtian legacy, Voloshinov maintained that individual consciousness has developed in close connection with the word/discourse. Nevertheless, as I have already argued, Voloshinov's important departure from the Humboldtian model (as well as other contemporary traditions) originates in the fact that the products of the individual speaking consciousness are only seemingly "individual," as they emerge in the subject's reaction to the "being in becoming."

Voloshinov's concept of the subject, as well as his model of dialogic interaction, should not be separated from the fundamental principle of his social ontology that the world (the concrete social world) and the subject (the concrete social subject) permeate each other in the two-faced process in which they are both the creators and the created. Accordingly, being constituted in the interaction with the social sphere, the subject's consciousness is not a passive intellect, or *tabula rasa*. Utilizing this argument Voloshinov made the case for the notion of "life ideology" (*zhiznennaia ideologiia*). Life ideology is not only the "organizing centre of every utterance" but also presents the organizing force of experience, a "consistent line of social orientation" that is fundamental to the constitution of the subject (Voloshinov, *Marxism* 93; for more on this important notion, see Tihanov, "Voloshinov"). Life ideology consists of two registers, the primary that is generated in the social sphere, and the secondary one that comprises the "phylogenetic" (psychological and other individual) features of the subject. While Voloshonov grants an entirely privileged position to the former register, his circular argumentation does not give a clear answer to the question how and by what means it is constituted. He rather implies that the constitutive elements of life ideology are the human acts, deeds, thoughts and discourses, which seems to suggest that the subject (the linguistic consciousness) is at the same time founded by and the founder of this super-imposed body.

The way in which Voloshinov applied the overarching framework of life ideology in the determination of the linguistic subject calls for a structural juxtaposition with the constitution of the transcendental subject in phenomenology. As I have demonstrated, Husserl utilized the notion of ideal intuition in order to create a *sui generis* transcendental, objectivizing gateway for his subject. Notwithstanding Voloshinov's pathos of sociality, the position of his subject in principle resembles Husserl's objectivizing strategy: not unlike the interplay between the noetic faculties of the subject and transcendental intuition, Voloshinov's individual subject undergoes a specific objectivization conditioned by a super-imposed social structure. In other words, in Voloshinov's case, the ideologically (i.e., intellectual, cultural, ethical) contaminated social environment plays a role comparable with that of the transcendental instance in Husserl's phenomenology: to provide the consciousness with an uninterrupted resource of ideologically articulated (and this also means, meaningful) contents. Given the fundamental role of the social nexus in Voloshionov's conception of language, the fact that the pragmatic framework of discourse is placed, almost without remainder, in the social horizon in which the three constitutive factors of the utterance (speaker, listener and object/state of affairs) coalesce, appears to be a logical consequence. This horizon (the real social context) comprises various extra-linguistic factors (e.g., a concrete spatial purview, shared knowledge of the circumstances and a common axiological stance); we see that, even though Voloshinov's model basically emerges from traditional semantics, it completely reassesses the constitutive elements of the pragmatic field, in that these elements are selected exclusively from the extra-linguistic realm ("Discourse" 11).

No wonder then that Voloshinov's assessment of Shpet's philosophy of language, at least judging from his accounts in *Marxism and the Philosophy of Language*, was ambiguously critical. Although the two thinkers essentially agreed on the discrepancy between ideal sense and real meaning, the differences between them became visible exactly in the semantic domain. Voloshinov's main objection to Shpet's doctrine was addressed to Shpet's neglect of the role of evaluative overtones in the production of meaning. Notwithstanding Voloshinov's unjustified equation of meaning and the axiological stance of the subject, his critical remark is important and epitomizes the point at which the difference between him and Shpet become fundamental. Disapproving of Shpet's radical distinction between referential denotation and evaluative connotation, Voloshinov argued that this flaw in Shpet's discussion of meaning stems from his failing to assign evaluation a greater significance (*Marxism* 105). Undeniably, Voloshinov's criticism is appropriate. Shpet, following on this count Marty and Husserl, wished to demarcate the realm of meaning, protecting it, as it were, from unwanted subjective, primarily psychological, contents. It is perhaps for this reason that Shpet's reconsideration of Husserl's transcendental subject proved so incomplete: after rejecting the Husserlian notion of the subject, Shpet became dimly aware of the importance of the subject's social disposition but failed to pursue this line further. Voloshinov, on the other hand, tacitly equated meaning and evaluation by arguing that the change in meaning is "always a reassessment," or a change in evaluation. Among other sources, Voloshinov's radical corrective has its roots in Bakhtin's early ontology of the event (here I refer to the early Bakhtin's notion of act), but equally in German theories of value at the turn of the twentieth century (see Brandist 120). Just as Bakhtin, in the early 1920s, argued that every actually pronounced "word cannot avoid being intonated," that is, axiologically engaged with its object or state of affairs (32), Voloshinov contends in *Marxism and the Philosophy of Language* "that [the] separation of word meaning [semantics] from evaluation [axiology]" neglects the reality of verbal interaction and "inevitably deprives meaning of its place in the living social process" (*Marxism* 105).

Voloshinov's account of the categories of conventional semantics epitomizes his propinquity to Shpet's philosophical legacy, but it also demonstrates well the main conceptual incongruence between Voloshinov's project and the dominant Russian and European contexts. In *Marxism and the Philosophy of Language,* Voloshinov utilizes the traditional semantic dichotomy between *sense* and *meaning* in the context of his own linguistics, social ontology and value theory. Gottlob Frege's classic distinction between *Sinn* (sense, expression, mode of presentation) and *Bedeutung* (reference, meaning, denotation) was implemented by Voloshinov to exemplify the difference between the potential, abstract linguistic structure and the actual meaning of the language in use. Meaning (*znachenie*) is, for the Russian thinker, the self-identical aspect of speech communication; outside the stream of speech communication, it is a hypothetical category that exists only in the abstraction of grammatical—lexical and syntactic—forms. Detached from the real social context, without axiological stance, the semantic potential of meaning is empty. It becomes accomplished only in the concreteness of the social context: therefore its semantic potential cannot be exhausted by content, denomination, or the eidetic core of meaning. In Voloshinov's words, meaning can only be assumed to be a "technical apparatus for the implementation of theme," while theme represents the reaction of a consciousness in becoming to the being in becoming (*Marxism* 100).

It is obvious that although Voloshinov's contribution to semantics is technically indebted to the Fregean tradition, the Russian philosopher is opposed to a logical analysis grounded in immanentism. In the dialogic verbal universe in which the subject is always prompted to act/utter, and in which every utterance entails evaluative stance, formal logic and the other intrinsic mechanisms of the production of meaning in language become inappropriate and have to give way to a methodologically impure and eclectic, but more comprehensive and plausible, socially engendered conception of meaning. On the other hand, overly general and lacking in subtler formal-ontological distinctions in the domain of pragmatics—and as a result of this equating the notions of meaning and value and arguing that every speech act, in its intonation, necessarily entails an axiological position—Voloshinov's notion of utterance (here strongly reflecting, it would seem, the ethical maximalism of Bakhtin's philosophy of the act) arrives at the radical, yet almost self-annulling argument that every speech act can and does perform the functions of a meaningful act of nomination.

Although Voloshinov's concept of utterance seems to be decisively informed by the imperatives of his ethics of practice, the latter is, in actual fact, the product of his concept of verbal interaction, that is, of the understanding of language as an uninterrupted chain of speech performances. On this view, each utterance, being part of that string of verbal acts, is in essence eventual (although not purely accidental). Triggered in a real verbal-cum-social context, every concrete utterance represents the speaker's response, and this responsive attitude of the subject, Voloshinov argues, necessarily entails his or her evaluative stance. In the multitude of discourses, every word is inherently multi-orientated, that is, potentially oriented towards different contexts. All this has a radical consequence as far as the field of pragmatics is concerned: in accord with Voloshinov's understanding of ideology and language, a word-meaning can have as many connotative senses (themes) as there are contexts for its use. If a poststructuralist take on Voloshinov be allowed, it is this multiplicity of semantic potential that in the end could construct the "wider unity of meaning."

Conclusion

As we have seen, the discontent with traditional semantics for its inability to account for, and cope with, the Protean reality of language was growing in Russia in the 1910s-1920s; the need to introduce new approaches was felt acutely. Valentin Voloshinov recognized this need more urgently than others, and his theoretical enterprise therefore anticipated in many respects a fundamentally new epistemological paradigm which fond expression in his "notorious" (from the standpoint of traditional linguistics) reorientation of linguistics towards the extra-linguistic realm, and in connection with this, his equally radical struggle against the inherited concepts of the linguistic subject, which culminated in the formulation of his theory of the dialogic subject. Voloshinov's radical assertion of the dialogically contextual nature of meaning should not prevent us from seeing that in other respects his platform was not that different from Shpet's. Shpet's semasiology too recognized the inherent polyvalence of the linguistic sign; however, his view of the mechanisms of language production being virtually inexhaustible remained inchoate and without adequate theoretical implementation. In its own way, Shpet's notion of inner form also aimed at overcoming the idealist gap between inner and outer, ideal and real. The Russian phenomenologist did acknowledge the dynamic, emerging nature of language; but, unlike Voloshinov, he was reluctant to endorse its philosophical ramifications, and it is for this reason alone that his philosophy of language remained within the ideological and cognitive confines of an idealist set of values that looks back to the nineteenth century. Thus, despite the methodological differences that separated their philosophical practices, Shpet and Voloshinov shared and pursued at least one important intellectual intuition: that it is the dynamic, ever-emerging and fluctuant reality of discursive communication, taken as an integral part of life in society, which has to set the parameters of our approach to language.

Works Cited

Bakhtin, Mikhail. *Toward a Philosophy of the Act*. Trans. Vadim Liapunov. Austin: U of Texas P, 1993.

Brandist, Craig. "Voloshinov's Dilemma: On the Philosophical Roots of the Dialogic Theory of the Utterance." *The Bakhtin Circle: In the Master's Absence*. Ed. Craig Brandist, David Shepherd, and Galin Tihanov. Manchester: Manchester UP, 2004. 97-124.

Husserl, Edmund. *Ideas Pertaining to a Pure Phenomenology and to a Phenomenological Philosophy (First Book: General Introduction to a Pure Phenomenology)*. Trans. F. Kersten. The Hague: Martinus Nijhoff, 1982.

Shpet, Gustav. *Vnutrenniaia forma slova*. Moscow: Gosudarstvennaia akademiia khudozhestvennykh nauk, 1927.

Shpet, Gustav. *Appearance and Sense: Phenomenology as the Fundamental Science and Its Problems*. Trans. Thomas Nemeth. Dordrecht: Kluwer, 1991.

Shpet, Gustav. *Mysl' i slovo. Izbrannye trudy*. Ed. T.G. Shchedrina. Moscow: ROSSPEN, 2005.

Tihanov, Galin. "Voloshinov, Ideology and Language: The Birth of Marxist Sociology from the Spirit of *Lebensphilosophie*." *South Atlantic Quarterly* 97.3-4 (1998): 599-621.

Voloshinov, Valentin. *Marxism and the Philosophy of Language*. Trans. Ladislav Matejka and I.R. Titunik. New York: Seminar, 1973.

Voloshinov, Valentin. "Discourse in Life and Discourse in Poetry." Trans. John Richmond. *Bakhtin School Papers*. Ed. Ann Shukman. Oxford: RPT, 1983. 5-30.

Part Five

Translations

Introduction to Excerpts from Shpet's "Germenevtika i ee problemy" ("Hermeneutics and Its Problems")

George L. Kline

"Hermeneutics and Its Problems"offers a concise critical history of hermeneutics—
"the general theory of understanding and interpretation," from its Greek and Hellenis-
tic origins, through the formulations, focused on Biblical interpretation, of medieval,
Renaissance, and Reformation theorists, to the British, Scottish and French thinkers
of the seventeenth and eighteenth centuries. It concludes with a close examination of
the (mainly German) hermeneutical systems of the early nineteenth century, which
culminated in the work of Schleiermacher and Boeckh, and the late nineteenth- and
early twentieth-century developments in Dilthey and Husserl. This brief outline suggests why Soviet censors did not permit the publication of Shpet's book for more
than seventy years. St. Augustine and Biblical hermeneutics were forbidden topics,
Schleiermacher was a "Protestant pastor," and such thinkers as Simmel, Dilthey,
Meinong, and Husserl were routinely dismissed as "bourgeois idealists." It was not
until 1989, at the height of Gorbachov's glasnost', that the first quarter of Shpet's text
appeared in the Moscow yearbook *Kontekst*, the other three installments following
in 1990, 1991, and 1992.

Like Shpet's earlier "Husserlian meditation," *Appearance and Sense* (Russian 1914, English translation by Thomas Nemeth 1991), "Hermeneutics and Its
Problems" focuses steadily on questions of sense (*smysl*), meaning (*znachenie*),
the sign (*znak*), the symbol, understanding, and interpretation, including the vexed
question of "equivocal" versus "univocal" interpretations of given texts, in the first
instance Biblical texts. In both books the Husserlian stress on the intentionality of
consciousness is reinterpreted to bring out the intention to communicate, to use signs
and symbols to convey an objective sense or content to another sign user, and ultimately to a historical community of sign users. On this point, as on many others,
Shpet follows Hegel rather than Husserl in seeing understanding and interpretation
as social and historical acts. Despite his impressive erudition in more than a dozen
languages, Shpet is no mere antiquarian or historian of other people's ideas. He is a

philosophically sophisticated, original, acute, and often penetrating—though never carping—critic of the positions which he scrutinizes. More than ninety years after it was written, "Hermeneutics and Its Problems" remains fresh, lively and, in a sense, without rival as a historical survey of this important field.

The translation from which these three excerpts were taken was made from the manuscript (with numerous handwritten corrections and occasional insertions) that Erika Freiberger-Sheikholeslami (1942-1993) obtained from Shpet's granddaughter, Elena V. Pasternak, in Moscow during the 1970s. Freiberger-Sheikholeslami completed the English translation, which I edited, and parts of which (on Wilhelm Dilthey) appeared in *Russian Studies in Philosophy* (1999). It is befitting at this point to remind the reader of her rich and promising career, which was cut short by cancer in her fifty-second year. Freiberger-Sheikholeslami was born and raised in Austria. She completed her doctoral work with a dissertation on Boris Pasternak at the University of Pennsylvania in 1978. She translated Shpet's "Hermeneutics and Its Problems" not only into English but also, with Alexander Haardt, into German (the German translation was published in the year of her death as *Die Hermeneutik und ihre Probleme*). Freiberger-Sheikholeslami published several articles on Shpet, including "Forgotten Pioneers of Soviet Semiotics" (1980), "Philosophical Linguistics: W. v. Humboldt and G.G. Shpet (A Semiotic Theory of Inner Form)" (1983), and "Gustav G. Shpet: Phenomenological Semiotics and Hermeneutics" (1984). She also gave several conference papers on Shpet, some of which, in addition to her published articles, were translated into Russian in the first and the second volumes of the Tomsk-based series *Shpetovskie chteniia* (1991 and 1997). The second volume of that series was dedicated to the memory of Shpet, his grandson Mikhail Polivanov, and Erika Freiberger-Sheikholeslami.

The three excerpts in the present volume were first published in Russian, as follows: the first excerpt, on St. Augustine, edited by A.A. Mitiushin, was published in *Kontekst 1989*, the second, on Simmel, and the third, on the contemporary state of hermeneutics and the work of Swoboda, both edited by E.V. Pasternak, were published in *Kontekst 1992*. The published and manuscript versions of Shpet's text have been carefully compared, and improvements, including occasional restoration of material previously omitted, have been made where necessary. The division into sections adopted here follows that of the latest Russian publication of "Germenevtika i ee problemy" by T.G. Shchedrina (2005). All three sections are translated in full; the third section fuses, for the sake of convenience but without any cuts or omissions, the last two sections, "The Contemporary Situation" and "Swoboda," from Shchedrina's 2005 edition.

Excerpts from "Germenevtika i ee problemy" ("Hermeneutics and Its Problems")

Gustav Shpet

Translated from the Russian by Erika Freiberger-Sheikholeslami and edited by George L. Kline

Augustine

St. Augustine in his *De doctrina christiana* (397 A.D.) and *De Magistro* (389 A.D.) provides us with a kind of textbook of Biblical hermeneutics, organized like a textbook of rhetoric,[1] and although, as befits a textbook, there are no analyses or justifications, but only what might be called results, nevertheless it can be seen from Augustine's divisions and definitions that he saw clearly and thought through a significant number of questions connected with the problems of sign, meaning, sense, understanding, and interpretation. But the same strong interest in the practical role of interpretation which hindered the Alexandrians also prevented Augustine from elucidating the purely scholarly, theoretical meaning of these questions.

Augustine begins his exposition in *De doctrina christiana* with a division which, in my opinion, should be placed at the basis of any classification of the sciences, but which up to now has not been thought through in all of its fundamental significance either by philosophy or, in particular, by logic. Every doctrine, he maintains, refers either to *things* or to *signs*; however, we learn about things by means of signs. That which is not used to designate something else is what he calls a "thing" in the strict sense. On the other hand, by signs (words, for example) something is designated; but it is clear that other things too, besides words, can serve as signs, so that one and the same thing can appear now as a thing in the strict sense and now as a sign.[2] Thus a *sign* is a thing which not only conveys its form or appearance to the senses but also brings something into thought besides itself.[3]

Augustine divides signs into *strict* or *proper* signs (*propria*, which are interpreted *proprie*, *historice*) and *metaphorical* signs (*translata*, which are interpreted *figurate*, *prophetice* [3.12]). Proper signs are used to designate the things for which they were devised; signs are metaphorical or "figurative when the very things which we signify by the literal term are applied to some other meaning."[4] One cannot deny that there is clarity and even a certain subtlety in this definition. But it requires conclusions which Augustine does not follow out with sufficient firmness.

First, such a definition of metaphorical signs makes it clear that in order to understand them it is necessary to know and study the real relations themselves. Augustine does draw this conclusion, stressing that in order to understand Holy Scripture one must have a knowledge of history, geography, physics, astronomy, etc. (2.28-30) and likewise of dialectic (which, although it does not teach us how to discern the truthfulness of meanings, does give us the rules for connecting truths [2.3lff]), logic (*scientia definiendi, dividendi atque partiendi,* 2.33), and arithmetic (2.38). However, in spite of the fact that even in dialectic and logic Augustine understands relations *objectively—in rerum ratione,*—in the metaphorical signs he seeks the *spiritual* meaning (3.6) and the *will of God* (*voluntas Dei,* 2.5, 3.1).

The fact that the will of God—as one would expect—also appears as the will of the Church as codified in its dogmas (2.8; 3.1, 2, and *passim*; 2.42)[5] is not of fundamental significance. As with Origen, the problem of understanding is thus eliminated without even having been properly formulated. On the one hand, understanding is reached through an acceptance of Church dogmatics;[6] on the other hand—and only with respect to the first—the divine inspiration of Scripture requires divine inspiration on the part of the reader as well (cf. 3.37).

Secondly, Augustine's definition obliges one to acknowledge the *uniqueness* of the meaning behind the sign, since the apparent multiplicity of meanings, according to his definition, springs only from the assumption that the *meaning* of the sign can function, in turn, as a sign.[7]

However, it does not follow from this that the reverse is also true. A single meaning, like a single content, cannot be expressed by different signs. This multiplicity of modes of expression (figures of speech, tropes, images, etc.) is not infrequently taken for a multiplicity of meanings. The multiplicity of expressions is a question of syntax, poetics, rhetoric, and logic. Hermeneutics, however, should begin with the assumption that every *given* sign has a single meaning. The basic falsehood of Biblical hermeneutics consists in the fact that it admits, as a premise, the duality of meaning—human and divine—in given expressions. The grounding is thus subjected to this premise: it is asserted as a matter of principle that a sign has several meanings.

So long as it is a question of the "second" meaning, the one which is divinely inspired, no matter with what show of science or scholarship the claim about the equivocity of the sign is justified—all of this remains *outside of science and scholarship*. But the stubbornly consistent pursuit of this view also touches upon science and scholarship, when this claim rests upon a new foundation which calls for recognition, at the least, of the possibility that every sign has several *literal* meanings. But such a recognition is consistent only from the standpoint of one who recognizes the first division, as Augustine did, admitting that, however many meanings may be found in Scripture, we should recognize all of them, so long as they "do not contradict the truth."

Why would it not be right to believe that Moses, the "divinely inspired writer intended all of these different truths, since through him the one God has adapted the Holy Scriptures to the understanding of the many, so that they might comprehend, in these Scriptures one and the same truth in its different aspects?"[8]

The whole theory of the understanding and interpretation of other people's words rests on this "intended" (*vidisse*); is it a question of *objective* relations, about which the author informs us, or is it a question of his *subjective* ideas about these relations? Divine inspiration can be understood quite differently in the two cases. In the first case it may refer to an especially subtle ability to "see" what is objectively there; in the second case, to an ability to fantasize in regard to what is objectively there. Augustine, contradicting his own definitions, chooses the second way of explaining the role and meaning of signs, that is, the *psychological* way. According to such a theory, the meaning of a sign or word is the idea of the communicator. It is obvious then in what the multifariousness consists and how it is possible. The schema of understanding here is extremely simplified: *A*—the thought (idea)—a sign (the word as pronounced or written)—*B*—a sign (as heard or seen)—the thought (idea).[9]

It might seem that such a theory, although it is not true in general, since it requires an understanding of objective relations, may be correct in a particular case, where it is a question of understanding the person who is communicating something about objective relations. But here one must distinguish two cases: either we understand another person through his words (signs) about himself—and such a case is not different in principle from any other understanding of objective relations; or else we understand him through *other* signs which accompany his speech (mimicry, tone of voice, emotional expressions, etc.) for which we also set up requirements as to their uniqueness of meaning. The rare case is also possible where, as it were, we take *one* sign both as an objective indication and as an indication of psychic agitation.

Without doubt, a more thorough analysis is needed, one which will reveal that what we take to be one sign with two meanings actually consists for us of two different signs. Augustine does not introduce this distinction, because his psychological theory blinds him to the fact that at the foundation of understanding—at least understanding of a person—there is neither "recollection" of something previously known, as he thought, nor "association," in the newer terminology, but something *primary*, an act which is not reducible to anything else.[10]

The theory of "recollection," which is a natural consequence of a general psychological theory of understanding, involves still another complication. The question of the *truthfulness* of what is understood does not end with correct understanding, and the latter can be established only through verification of the objective relations of that which is understood. Thus it is natural that someone who regards what is understood as a subjective idea about what is communicated gets into the greatest difficulty, being unable to find *any* criterion for establishing the objectivity of the communicated content. Augustine did not bypass this difficulty and drew the appropriate *skeptical* conclusion[11] but was not able to resolve this skepticism satisfactorily. He appeals to *mystical* experience, to the "truth which is present within our mind," to the "Christ who dwells in the inner man."[12] But this amounts to a return in principle to one's own experience and to the process of experiencing in general, that is, to the beginning of the theory of "recollection"—which means moving in a circle.

Moreover, when Augustine is expounding rather than explaining, he persistently stresses the correct idea that one who asks a question is to be answered only from the *point of view of those objects* which are designated by given words, that what is said is to be accepted or rejected from the *point of view of the object* which is designated.[13] And Augustine himself suggests a way to eliminate the apparent duality of a single sign when, for example, we understand the word *homo* both as a living being (the real interpretation) and as a noun (the grammatical interpretation).[14]

But what do these two ways of studying signs mean and what role do they play: 1) the study of a sign *qua* sign, that is, that which *has* a meaning, and 2) the study of the meaning itself, that is, that which *is* a meaning. Augustine does not know this, just as he does not know whether these two ways of studying signs exhaust such study. In any case, as compared to Origen, Augustine widens the scope of hermeneutics, adding to the problem of whether words are univocal or equivocal the further problem of *signs in general* as well as the problem of *understanding* as a transition from sign to meaning.

Notes

1. Pt. I: *Inventio*, Pt. II: *Elocutio*. "The entire treatment of the Scriptures is based upon two factors: the method of discovering what we are to understand and the method of teaching what has been understood" ("Duae sunt res quibus nititur omnis tractatio Scripturarum: modus inveniendi quae intelligenda sunt, et modus proferendi quae intellecta sunt"). Books I—III are devoted to the first part, i.e., the *modus inveniendi* or "method of discovering." Book I is "about things," Books II and III are "about signs." Book IV is devoted to the second part, i.e., the *modus proferendi* or "method of communicating or teaching." Augustine himself speaks about the relation to rhetoric in the first chapters of Book IV. *De doctrina christiana* apparently served to a certain extent as a prototype for later hermeneutical systems (in other words, these latter serve apologetic rather than cognitive ends), remaining, incidentally, free from those tedious and minute rules which are illustrated by Augustine's own example: when you are walking, don't lift one foot until you have put the other foot down (2.37).

Ed. note: Trans. in John J. Gavigan, *Writings of St. Augustine*, vol. 4 (New York, 1974): 27. Shpet is using the edition of Carl H. Bruder, *De doctrina christiana libri quatuor*, (Leipzig, 1838), 1.1; we quote the Latin text from the William H. Green edition, *De doctrine christiana libri quattuor* (Vienna, 1963).

2. *De doctrina christiana*, 1.4-5: "All teaching is concerned with either *things* or *signs*. But things are learned by means of signs. I have defined a thing in the accurate sense of the word as that which is not used to *signify* something, for example, wood, stone, animal or others of this kind. . . . There are other signs whose whole usefulness consists in signifying. Words belong to this class. . . . From this is understood what I designate as signs, namely, those things which are employed to signify something. Therefore, every sign is also a thing. For, whatever is not a thing is absolutely nothing, but not every thing is also a sign." ("Omnis doctrina vel rerum est vel signorum, sed res per signa discuntur. Proprie autem nunc res appellavi, quae non ad significandum aliquid adhibentur, sicuti est lignum, lapis, pecus atque huiusmodi cetera. . . . Sunt alia signa quorum

omnis usus in significando est, sicuti sunt verba. . . . Ex quo intelligitur quid appellem signa, res eas videlicet quae ad significandum aliquid adhibentur. Quam ob rem omne signum etiam res aliqua est; quod enim nulla res est, omnino nihil est. Non autem omnis res etiam signum est").

Ed. Note: In Bruder's edition this passage is at 1.2 but in Green's edition it is at 1.4-5.

3. *De doctrina christiana*, 2.1: "A sign is a thing which, apart from the impression that it presents to the senses, causes of itself some other thing to enter our thoughts." ("Signum est enim res, praeter speciem quam ingerit sensibus, aliud aliquid ex se faciens in cogitationem venire").

4. 2.10: "Translata sunt, quum et ipsae res quas propriis verbis significamus, ad illud aliquid significandum usurpantur . . ." Green's superior text reads: ". . . ad aliquid aliud significandum . . ." (*De doctrina christiana*, 2.33).

5. "Whatever a man has learned apart from Scripture is censured there, if it is harmful; if it is useful, he finds it there." ("Nam quidquid homo extra [i.e., extra Divinas Scripturas] didicerit, si noxium est, ibi damnatur, si utile est, ibi invenitur"; 2.151). Cf. also 2.39. Thus the Father of the Christian Church anticipated the Prophet of Islam. . . .

6. Characteristically, Augustine offers as a criterion for distinguishing in Holy Scripture between figurative and literal language the inappropriateness of the former (as we have seen, Origen saw in such inappropriateness a special indication of divine inspiration): "In general, that method [viz., of determining whether an expression is literal or figurative] is to understand as figurative anything in Holy Scripture which cannot be attributed either to an upright character or to a pure faith" (Gavigan trans. 129). ("Et iste omnino modus est, ut quidquid in Sermone Divino neque ad morum honestatem neque ad fidei veritatem proprie referri potest, figuratum esse cognoscas," 3.10 [Green's ed. 3.33]). Cf. also 3.16. As regards this "hermeneutical rule," Doedes remarks that it "necessarily opened the floodgates to the most unlimited caprice" (Jacob Doedes, *Manual of Hermeneutics for the Writings of the New Testament*, trans. from the Dutch by G. W. Stegmann [Edinburgh, 1867]: 20). However, Augustine himself permits great freedom in the transition from literal (historical) interpretation to allegorical (spiritual) interpretation. This is apparent from the example of his attitude toward the interpretation of the building of the Ark, on the one hand, where he defends the historical interpretation *to excess* (*De Civitate Dei*, 15.27), and the interpretation of the sayings of the prophets concerning the earthly and the heavenly Jerusalem on the other, where he asks: "[W]ho will not avow that these sayings of which we spoke are to have a spiritual interpretation also; who will not leave such sayings to those who can interpret them in that manner?" ("[Q]uis ea non ad intelligentiam spiritualem revocet, si possit, aut ab eo qui potest revocanda esse fateatur?") (*De Civitate Dei*, 17.3).

7. Here of course we are raising the question of the essential connection between sign and meaning or sense (the latter being individualized by a context); the contingent coincidence of meanings—equivocity—is not a rare phenomenon. Nevertheless, homonyms, in essence, not only *have* different meanings; they *are* different signs. It does not matter how identical the sound combinations may be in words derived from different roots, for example, in Russian *tri* (the number "three") and *tri* (the imperative mood of the verb *teret'*, "to rub") or in German *acht* ("eight"), *Acht* ("care"), and *Acht* ("disgrace").

8. Shpet here quotes from the Russian translation of Augustine's *Tvoreniia* (*Works*; edition of the Kiev Theological Academy), Bk. 7 and gives the Latin text: "[C]ur non illa omnia vidisse credatur, per quem unus Deus Sacras Litteras vera et diversa visuris multorum sensibus temperavit?" (*Confessions*, 12.31); cf. *De doctrina christiana* 3.27.

9. Cf. I. V. Popov, *Lichnost' i uchenie bl. Avgustina* (Sergiev Posad, 1917), Pt. II, 282. Cf. also the schema of St. Dionysius the Great in his *Works* (Russian translation by Fr. A. Druzhinin, ed. by L. Pisarev [Kazan Theological Academy, 1900], 37).

10. Augustine's theory of the understanding of signs is set forth in his work *De magistro*, which he wrote eight years before *De doctrina christiana*. Cf. esp. Ch. X. (Russian translation in Augustine's [*Tvoreniia*], Bk. 9.)

11. *De Magistro*, Ch. XIII.

12. Ibid., Ch. XI, XIV.

13. Ibid., Ch. VIII.

14. Ibid. Cf. also his classification of objects which are pointed out for study; we either indicate the objects themselves without using a sign or else by the use of signs—either signs or other things which are not themselves signs (ibid., Ch. VII).

Simmel

Recognizing the *autonomy* of "spirit,"[1] and presupposing the specificity of the method of investigation of spiritual processes, both social and historical, Dilthey ranks among the major sociologists of our time, along with Durkheim and Simmel. A general comparison of Dilthey with Simmel seems to me especially instructive, since it immediately exhibits a number of interesting themes which are connected with this kind of recognition of the autonomy of culture. The concept of *spirit* as the subject matter of the human sciences, and consequently as the object of understanding, requires a more precise definition through a delimitation of its various possible meanings. Dilthey made an attempt to set off his understanding of the concept of spirit from Hegel's speculative, *metaphysical* concept. One cannot be satisfied with this. In the first place, there is no doubt that we often use the concept "spirit" as a synonym for the concept "*soul*" or "*psyche*," that is, we take it in the psychological sense and not in the objective sense, used especially in so-called social and ethnic psychology.[2]

Thus Simmel—whose use of the term "spirit," by the way, is a modest one—tries to draw a decisive boundary line between sociology with its objective subject matter and social psychology.[3] The problem of social psychology is expressed as follows: "What modifications are experienced by the psychic process of an individual when that process takes place under determinate influences of the social milieu?" (*Soziologie* 561). As distinguished from social psychology, the subject matter of the human sciences—language, law, cultural formations, etc.—in their separation from individual processes of realization, are not products of the individual subject: either of the individual spirit, mind, or soul, or of the social spirit. "There is a third thing: the objective spiritual content, which is by no means psychological, any more than the logical sense of a proposition or judgment is something psychological, although it can come to reality in consciousness only in the dynamics of psychic processes and as their result" (ibid., 559). Thus, if the subject matters are distinguished, the methods of apprehending them should also be distinguished. And if these methods are methods of understanding and interpretation, one must also distinguish their kinds and types.

The quoted definition indicates yet another distinction which should also have an influence on the classification of the types of understanding. Dilthey, who opposes "experiencing" to Hegel's speculative spirit, by the same token implies by his concept of "spirit" a certain *reality* which is not at all of a metaphysical kind. And in this respect he should be compared not with Simmel but with Durkheim, for whom the "social fact" as the subject matter of sociology is also a special kind of reality, alongside the reality of individual—biological and psychological—life. According to Durkheim,[4] the social fact has "its own existence, which is independent of its individual manifestations," from which follows the first rule for the observation of facts of this kind: *to consider them as things* (*comme des choses*).

Simmel's position is somewhat more complex. He distinguishes the psychological from the social, and from the spiritual generally, and he is evidently not inclined to ascribe an independent reality to the latter. Nevertheless, the psychic has such a reality for him. But, as he himself declares—and he attaches extreme methodological importance to this declaration, considering it "decisive for the principles of the human sciences"—*a scientific consideration of psychic facts is not yet necessarily psychology.*[5]

Thus, leaving the particular questions of the human sciences aside, we find that with Simmel sociology as a fundamental science which studies the *forms* of social unification, has in mind not *really existing* objects but objects of an *ideal* order. But, equally, the subject matter of the particular human sciences—those which study language, the state, law, religion, and mores—as well as the sciences which study the general forms of spirit, go far beyond the boundaries of each individual soul, at least in its forms and insofar as these forms are also distinguished by their ideal character.

Thus the stock of words in a language and the forms of their connectedness, as we find them in dictionaries and grammar books; legal norms, as they are expounded in codes of law; the dogmatic content of religion—strictly speaking, all this does not have real existence, but is merely "valid," *gilt*, as the Germans say. "But this validity (*Gültigkeit*)," says Simmel, "their content, is not a psychic existence which would need some empirical carrier, any more than the Pythagorean theorem—to maintain the same distinction—would need it" (*Soziologie* 558). But how we arrive at it is for us the main question. As in mathematics, by way of intellectual intuition in terms of sensuously given examples (*exempla*), or by way of *sui generis* understanding and interpretation of signs, both verbal and material? Simmel gives us reason to think that he has answered the first of these questions affirmatively.

By the same token, Simmel shows that he does not see the universal and fundamental significance which really belongs to understanding. For him the whole problem is narrowed down to the standard limits of the question of the role of understanding in history. But while he denies the independent reality of what is social apart from the psychic, Simmel, as compared to his predecessors, does not shed much light on the question. Like them, he fails to do more than merely formulate the questions, which, moreover, as a result of his psychologistic sympathies, are surrounded by a very dense fog.[6]

History, Simmel is convinced, has as its direct object the psyche, its subject matter being the ideas, desires, and feelings of individual persons (*Die Probleme der Geschichtsphilosophie* 1). One must assume that he has Boeckh's formula in mind and that he wishes to expand it: "If the task of philology is the knowledge of what has been known, historical knowledge is only an extension of this, since it has the task of knowing, not only what has been known, i.e., theoretically represented, but also what has been desired and what has been felt."[7] But here we encounter the important qualification introduced earlier: an interest in psychic processes is not yet a psychological interest. Sociology, as we have seen, works with psychic materials and approaches them with a special kind of *method*—it is itself this method (*Soziologie* 3). Sociology, which extracts the ideal *forms* of socialization, is the science of these forms. History is not an ideal science; according to Simmel's definition, it studies the ideas, etc., of individual persons. It is concrete and studies what is singular and individual (*Probleme* 2).[8] But it is not a method: on the contrary, it itself requires a special method.

In contrast to psychology, for which a process is essential simply because it is a psychic process, history is interested in the content of the process, something toward which, conversely, psychology is indifferent. "For history the question concerns not so much the *development* of psychological contents as the psychological development of [such] *contents . . .*" (ibid. 4; cf. 47 ff.). The content, in any case, is the "point of departure" for historical consideration. But further, as interaction (*Verkehr*) between people is possible only on the assumption that at the basis of certain physical movements of the individual—gestures, mimicry, sounds—there are psychic processes which constitute for us the psychic unity of "the other [person]," and this assumption constitutes *a priori* the relation between subject and subject (7-9). Thus in historical knowledge too we need a methodological assumption about the unity of the person –whether an individual (real) or a social (fictitious) party[9]—which constitutes the *a priori* of history and makes history possible (27).

One can scarcely call an assumption of this type anything but psychological. And if history is interested in "content," it should have its own special ways of reaching that content as well as special assumptions from which we could move toward objective diversity and, in all probability, objective unity as well. Evidently Simmel too recognizes this; but things immediately begin to become unclear. At least, he himself asserts that if one presupposes a spiritual (psychological) foundation of events, the isolation of their content raises further epistemological problems. These latter problems need a "very general assumption." But, on the basis of Simmel's own words, one might think that *this* assumption should precede the others. And one who is free from psychological preconceptions could hardly think otherwise.

"Whether the psychological connecting links which the historian introduces into the events are objectively true, i.e., whether they really express (*nachzeichnen*) the psychic acts of the agents involved, would not be of any interest to us if we did not *understand* these processes in terms of their content and their flow" (27). It would seem clear that precisely this objective understanding, which is, strictly speaking, historical understanding, should be made the fundamental problem of the theory of historical knowledge. It remains only to ask the question: what is this understanding and what are its conditions?

Simmel does, in fact, raise this question (28). The general answer which he gives is interesting only in the sense that he does not reduce understanding—as was done earlier—to "clear" ideas, but takes it in a broad sense—as Dilthey did—in the sense of an integral and original act of experiencing which copies (*nachbildet*) the relevant acts of consciousness of the person who is the object of understanding in the sense that one *transports oneself* into the psyche of another person. However, this answer also constrains Simmel so that he fails to discern the other "methods" of understanding. In particular, he fails to assign an independent significance to the understanding of the *sign*. In other words, his "general" answer in fact only refers to the psychological type of understanding. Of course, a mere reference to "copying" does not reveal much about the essence or the content of understanding. In this connection Simmel is as barren as were his predecessors. Therefore, more interesting is his "answer" from the other side—the side that concerns those difficulties which Schleiermacher had already experienced when he got the idea of linking grammatical and psychological interpretation by reducing them to a single type of interpretation, that of the "individual person."

Simmel elucidates the understanding of "the speaker" and the understanding of "what has been said." For him this distinction is illustrated by the distinction between the understanding of the law of gravitation or the *chorus mysticus*, on the one hand, and the understanding of Newton and Goethe, on the other (29-30). But his elucidations of this distinction are not at all deep. In the first case, he believes, it is all about the *theoretical content of thinking*, and strangely he does not find it puzzling. It seems to him somehow self-evident. The whole thing is for the psychic processes of the speaker, expressed in words, to be elicited by these words in the listener as well. If there is an essential difference between the ideas of the two, then the words of the one will be misunderstood, or simply not understood, by the other. This is rather too simple. The real puzzle for Simmel is not understanding what is objective but precisely what is *subjective*.

"This sensation of what I, strictly speaking, do not feel, this copying of subjectivity—which once again is only possible within subjectivity but at the same time is given to it objectively—this is the puzzle of historical knowledge, a solution for which has, up to the present, hardly been attempted for our logical and psychological categories" (32). There is no doubt that this is a puzzle which up to now has not been solved;[10] but it is doubtful whether the problem of historical and objective understanding has here been solved by Simmel.

It would seem natural to look for the "subjectivity" of which Simmel speaks in the area which he separates off from sociology under the title *social psychology*, which, as we have seen, focuses on the modifications of the psychic processes of the individual under the influence of the social environment.[11] But then he should rather have focused more sharply on the question of the historical understanding of that social environment as an objective fact. Simmel does not see this. Here he wraps us in that fog of which I have already complained. Consequently, the subjectivity of the individual person still remains for him, in the last analysis, the object of historical understanding.

On the one hand, this subjectivity—as we have already seen—is its own non-communicable content, which is mysterious and hard to reach; but, on the other hand, in Simmel's account it appears simpler and not of very wide scope. He opposes the "speaker" to "what is said." The latter is objective and represents the "theoretical content of thinking." In one way or another we understand what is said. However, if we note that the speaker communicates what he has to say under the influence of a personal aim, a preconception, fear, irritation, etc., we turn to another *kind* of understanding (*die Art des Verstehens*, 29), which, it turns out, is the understanding of a "historical person," something which is also important for historical knowledge.

It is all too obvious that Simmel, by combining two different meanings of the term in the concept of "individual person," merely succeeds in reducing several problems to one. In general, Simmel does not suffer from any partiality for clarity of thought or precise definition of terms. But here he has confused different strands of thought so hopelessly, attempting to spin them into one, that he himself cannot distinguish which one of them runs which way.

The individual person is an object and a term of both psychology and history—we need not consider the other meanings of the term here. As an object of psychology the person is considered in social and historical psychology as well: the individual person, individual self-consciousness in a given social and historical setting. The individual person in this sense is always taken as something typical in the given conditions of time and place.[12] The individual person is not a historical reality in this sense; such a person is not involved with any *institution*, constitution, or other social organization. There are the social and historical categories: citizen, human being, juridical person, political subject, adult of full legal age, legally competent person, etc., etc.—but no "individual person."

It is quite a different matter when a human being, as a psychologically and psycho-physically defined individual person, is the bearer of, or one who expresses, a certain combination of objectifiable social and historical potentials, that is, is himself a sign, the interpretation of which reveals specific social and historical institutions and organizations. The individual person here speaks and acts as a social factor, a social and historical reality. As Droysen puts it: "The individual becomes a totality only within relationships. As one who understands and is understood the individual exists only as an…expression of the community of which he is a member, participating in its nature and its development" (*Historik*, §12).

Such an individual person is indeed the object of the historian's study and understanding. Simmel speaks of "historical personalities" (29-30) and depicts them very well (36-37). But then it is clear that psychological understanding contributes nothing to our understanding of *this* individual person. An individual person must be understood in terms of the "nature and development" of a *community*, that is, what is required is precisely historical rather than psychological understanding. Simmel tries to convince us that psychological understanding is genuine historical understanding.[13] But it is difficult to believe him when we know that psychologism is his basic premise and that, before he began his "epistemological study," he already knew that there is only one historical reality—the *psyche*, the ideas, desires, and feelings of "individual persons." Thus his "non-psychological" interest in psychic factors did not save the situation. Simmel sought shelter in sociology, assigning the "forms" to it, but apart from this he did not find any sources for the psychological study of psychic factors. Thus it is remarkable that, although he distinguished between the "speaker" and "what is said," he found nothing to assign to the latter except the "content of thought." He ascribed objectivity to that content.[14] But such objectivity is not empirically historical but only *logical*, that is, it is also ideal and, in a certain sense, formal.

What is the result? Simmel wanted to drive all the kinds of understanding into the single blind alley of psychology, but they all slipped away from him and flew off in different directions: ideal understanding, the fundamental significance of which Simmel failed to grasp; historical understanding, the objective significance of which he did not adequately value; psychological understanding, which he brushed aside as "copying" (*nachbilden*), closing his eyes to its hermeneutical nature in the strict sense. He did not advance the problems of interpretation; he paid no attention to the problem of the expressive sign. But, on the other hand, his separation of sociology from social psychology as well as his idea concerning the non-psychological interest in psychic factors should not be forgotten in the sequel.

Notes

1. The Russian *dukh*, like the German *Geist*, also has the sense of "culture"; similarly, the Russian *dukhovnyi* (in the next line) has the sense of both "spiritual" and "cultural."—Ed.

2. For some suggestions as to how one might delimit these meanings of the term "spirit," see my article "Predmet i zadachi etnicheskoi psikhologii," *Psikhologicheskoe obozrenie* I (1917); cf. esp. 245-51.

3. Georg Simmel, *Soziologie: Untersuchungen über die Formen der Vergesellschaftung*. Leipzig, 1908, 21 and "Exkurs über Sozialpsychologie," 556-63.

4. Émile Durkheim, *Les règles de la méthode sociologique* (1895), 6th ed. Paris, 1912, 19-20.

5. Simmel, *Soziologie* 21. Cf. his *Die Probleme der Geschichtsphilosophie*, 3rd ed. (greatly expanded as compared to the first edition of 1892). Leipzig, 1907, 4: "Allein das Interesse an einem psychischen Vorgang ist noch kein psychologisches Interesse." ("The interest in a psychic process, by itself, is not yet a psychological interest.")

6. Simmel himself has a quite different opinion of his own contribution to the theory of historical knowledge: "I recognize very well," he declares, "that this proposal for solving the psychological-epistemological problem of historical understanding is only a first attempt, and perhaps it can be justified only because it clarifies the presence of the problem generally in all its depth" (*Die Probleme der Geschichtsphilosophie* 41). Undoubtedly, from Simmel's viewpoint, his "proposal" is a first attempt but it is doubtful whether he has succeeded in clarifying the presence of the problem in all its depth.

7. This quotation is from the first edition (2). These words do not appear in the third edition. Nevertheless, that edition contains a further development of the same idea: "If the task of *history* is not only the knowledge of what has been known but also of what has been desired and what has been felt, then this task can be carried out only when, in

some mode of psychic transformation, what has been desired is co-desired, and what has been felt is felt empathetically" (30; first ed. 15).

8. However, not in its "reality"—as *naïve realism* understands this, with its formulation of the historical task as the determining of "how things really were" (42), since history is not a copy of reality (51) or a reflection of historical reality (55) but is a certain [word missing.–Ed.] of the communicated content, where the psychic processes themselves take on the "form of history" (cf. 40-41).

9. Simmel also admits "impersonal forces" as operative factors in history ("die unpersönlichen Mächte, die sich teils als Ursachen, teils als Wirkungen mit den Handlungen und Zuständen der Persönlichkeiten verflechten"): law and customs, language and ways of thinking, culture and forms of social relationship (18). It is curious that in the third edition Simmel is not prepared to call these things objective (*die objektiven Gebilde*) as he had done in the first edition (12).

10. Simmel's own "solution"—a conception of the historical as the "form" of mental processes in the spirit of Kant—is hardly acceptable. But we shall discuss this in another place.

11. On the method of an interpretive approach to this subject matter see my aforementioned article, "Predmet i zadachi etnicheskoi psikhologii," *Psikhologicheskoe obozrenie* I: 1-4.

12. See my "Predmet i zadachi etnicheskoi psikhologii."

13. He reproaches "historicism" for failing to understand just this point. Cf. 28-29n.

14. 29: "in the case of [items of] objective knowledge" ("bei objektiven Erkenntnissen"). In the first edition (14): "in the case of [items of] objective and logical knowledge" ("bei objektiven und logischen Erkenntnissen").

The Contemporary Situation

However critical our assessment of Simmel's arguments, we should not deny the significance of his attempt to reach a solution of the problem of understanding from a somewhat novel and radical point of view. When we compare him with Dilthey we are persuaded that the problem is indeed more complex and multifaceted than it seemed to Dilthey. We are persuaded that a large number of the basic problems of contemporary philosophy and methodology cluster around the fundamental principles of hermeneutics. Following in the wake of philology, and aided by history and the recognition of the universal significance of the historical method in the "human sciences," these sciences as a group have begun to place their hopes in the theory of understanding as their philosophical foundation. The theory of historical knowledge in the most comprehensive sense is beginning to emerge not as a pendant to the theory of knowledge in the natural sciences but as—to say the least—an independent division, in its own right, of the fundamental principles of our knowledge.

Moreover, Dilthey's works and, to some extent, Simmel's as well, cause us to suspect that the philosophical principles of all knowledge as they are represented in widely accepted philosophical systems, particularly in their exclusive orientation toward mathematical and natural-scientific knowledge, are not only incomplete and one-sided but in many respects simply erroneous, given the fact that they ignore the independent foundations of historical knowledge. The increased attention which for some time now philosophy has again begun to devote to the problem of history attests even more clearly to this. But the very failure and unfruitfulness of the attempts to solve this problem—insofar as they were directly connected with the ideas of natural-scientific knowledge and their philosophical foundations—should have made the investigators turn their attention to the original hermeneutical way of knowing as well. All the attempts to ground historical knowledge have proved to be equally unsuccessful: whether on the model of empirical natural science on the part of the empiricists and positivists; on the model of mathematical knowledge on the part of the Kantians; on the model of psychology among the eclectic thinkers—just as the attempts of those who had a skeptical attitude toward historical knowledge among another group of Kantians, from Schopenhauer up to and including Rickert,[1]—have turned out to be unconvincing.

All of these attempts, however, are in one respect very instructive: the very possibility of comparing historical knowledge with such widely different types of knowledge indicates that the genuine foundation of historical knowledge—understanding—should have a reciprocal influence on the philosophical foundations of both the natural sciences and psychology, and even of ideal knowledge. And insofar as the philosophical foundations of knowledge, in their objective relatedness, are motifs of reality itself, to that extent the problem of reality itself, as the ultimate root problem of philosophy, should in its very formulation undergo significant modifications. Moreover, these should evidently be in the direction of widening it and freeing it from the abstract schemata of mathematical natural science. From this point, pressure is exerted on philosophy itself in the sense, finally, of carrying out the intention present in it from the beginning, of achieving concreteness and historicity, in the deepest, most fundamental sense of those terms.

In a word, from all of this it is evident that the problem of understanding has fully matured for our time. To solve it we are faced with the solution of three subproblems of understanding: (a) an independent, psychologically empirical problem; (b) a logically methodological problem; and (c) a fundamental philosophical problem. And we can report that, at least with respect to the first two, the working out of the problem has already begun.

Swoboda

(a) It is strange, but until recently theorists did not recognize the psychology of *understanding* as an independent problem. And Hermann Swoboda was profoundly right when he began his investigation about understanding with the distinctive aphorism: "'understand' and 'grasp' are not scientific terms."[2] Psychology simply considered understanding as a function of the mind or intellect and did not pause to elucidate the specific character of this process in greater detail. Sometimes this process was identified with a clear idea, sometimes with a "concept" and its formation. Only the comparison of thinking, as a function of the mind, with speech sometimes reminded theorists of the special role of understanding, which in most cases was casually defined in terms of the psychology of association or apperception, or at best was compared to reasoning "by analogy." There was no problem. Perhaps this sprang from the general abstractly schematic tendencies of the explanatory psychology which has been prevalent until recently. But in any case one can insist that a freer approach to the concrete complexities of psychic experience, especially if the intention of such an approach is purely descriptive, should also have led investigators to the problem of understanding. This, at least as far as one can judge, was Swoboda's approach.

Finnbogason[3] approaches the problem in this way in his interesting book on sympathetic understanding—the most detailed treatment of this question to have appeared to date. Lipps also comes upon the problem constantly in his studies of *Einfühlung* ("empathy"), especially insofar as it is connected with the psychological and philosophical problem of other minds. Spranger too, as we have seen, approached understanding partly in connection with the problem of descriptive psychology and partly in connection with the problem of history itself. It is precisely this connection with the tasks of *descriptive* psychology which accounts for the possibility of formulating the psychological question of understanding, considered as an experience which is *sui generis*, as well as for the one-sidedness of this formulation, which causes the attention of these investigators to be concentrated mainly, or even exclusively, on the problem of *understanding* the *individual person*.

Elsenhans also came close to the position of the works just mentioned. His attempt to separate interpretation from understanding and even to oppose it to the latter is, as we already know from our earlier discussion, wholly legitimate—except that Elsenhans carries it out in a naïve and superficial way. His psychological appeals to "common feeling" are also elementary. Only his general idea of the significance of the problem of interpretation for the human sciences may be of some interest. To be sure, this idea is expressed very vaguely and is prompted rather by a sense of the importance of the problem than by any deep theoretical penetration of its content.

Indeed, this idea has remained, to the best of my knowledge, without further development; nevertheless, when Elsenhans characterizes the status of hermeneutical problems in contemporary philosophy, one must not pass over such remarks in silence. In a paper which he read at the Congress for Experimental Psychology in Giessen in 1904[4] he took as his point of departure the insufficiency for the human sciences of mere direct knowledge of one's own mental life and the need for an indirect investigation of the mental life of other persons as well. He went on to demand, for the sake of this latter study, a study both of one's own mental life and of the process of *interpretation* (*Deutung*) as necessary preliminary work for the human sciences. By "process of interpretation" he meant the process in the course of which, on the basis of a sensuously given sign, we come to know and reproduce something mental. On his view, such an interpretation of sensuous signs is carried out in a way analogous to one's own mental life, and presupposes that it has something in common with this life (7, 5).[5]

Such an interpretation is to be distinguished both from *empathy* by the fact that in the latter the self and the not-self merge immediately into one, which is not the case in interpretation, and from *understanding* (*Verstehen*), which, in spite of Dilthey, is not a transition from sensuous signs to something internal—that is precisely what interpretation is—but, in accordance with the meaning of the word *Verstand*, is the inclusion of the object in the connectedness of our knowledge, whether or not this object is a sensuously perceived sign. Moreover, interpretation is further distinguished from mere understanding by the fact that it reproduces the given mental content in verbal form (8, 10-11). The theory of interpretation, if it is to be helpful to the human sciences, must keep the following three points in mind: (1) the sensuous sign, which mediates our knowledge of the mental life of other persons; (2) the connection of this sensuous sign with a mental content; (3) the transmission of this mental content in verbal form (11).

The most important of these points is obviously the second one. A mere associative connection is not sufficient to explain it. In addition to the activity of the imagination, one must also have recourse to a special sense, something to which Boeckh had alluded, which makes itself known to the extent that we penetrate into the common world of representations of the whole given historical period that is under study, a sense which, following Wundt, one might call an "*integral feeling*" (ibid., 20) or a "common historical feeling" (*Lehrbuch* 344).

Benno Erdmann[6] treats this question in the same psychological way, but more broadly. Although he attempts to solve the problem by using the unoriginal means of explanatory psychology, i.e., by means of the now familiar associations, apperceptions, and inferences by analogy, nevertheless, certain aspects of his work are very revealing, precisely from the standpoint of the present status of the problem. He not only raises the problem of understanding in connection with the division of the sciences—according to both subject matter and methodology—into the natural sciences and the human sciences (1241-42); he also regards understanding as a "kind" of knowledge (1243-58, 1261, 1270), recognizing at the same time a certain universal function of understanding in knowledge (1265-66, 1268).

On the other hand, although he takes as his point of departure the assumption that knowledge of the mental life of other persons presupposes a knowledge of one's own mental life, which is possible only through introspection, and that in general feeling oneself into (*Einfühlung*), thinking oneself into (*Eindenkung*), in a word, putting oneself into (*Einstellung*) the mental life of other persons, rests on the fact that the emotive and intellectual contents of consciousness which reproduce the mental life of other persons are copyings within ourselves, occasioned by the movements of other persons and the products of their mental life (1258-59), Erdmann was nevertheless able to distinguish not only these motor reactions as expressions of psychic life from the products of these movements, as historical sources of every kind, but also to distinguish psychological understanding strictly speaking from objective understanding.

At least in regard to *speech*, understanding it, in Erdmann's view, has a richer function than that of putting us into the inner mental life of other persons. It also serves—to some extent even exclusively, so that for us the experience of the com-

municator, strictly speaking, loses its significance—for the transmission of an intellectual content which is objective, scientific, artistic, or practical. Thus, for example,
history in the narrow sense, as economic, legal, and political history, history of the
sciences and even of religion and of philosophical ideas, is focused not so much on
creative individuals and the individual conditions of their development as on the
historically operative make-up of their works (1265). One can only regret that these
embryonic questions, which are very valuable for a deepening of the problem of
understanding, remained undeveloped in Erdmann, even in their empirically psychological form. But it should not be denied that, in formulating them, Erdmann stressed
yet again the necessity and timeliness for philosophy of undertaking a deeper analysis of all of these themes.

Finally, contemporary psychology also puts forward the problem of understanding in connection with the application of the experimental method to the study
of the so-called "higher" psychic processes in the area of thinking—primarily in the
Würzburg School of experimental psychology.[7] These investigations have a rather
special and *sui generis* place with regard to our question. As experimental investigations, they are by their nature extremely remote from the above-mentioned type
of work in descriptive psychology which aims at the depiction of psychic experiences in their fullness and concreteness. But at the same time they are freer from
preconceived hypotheses and theories than is explanatory psychology. In a certain
sense they also claim to be descriptive in character, descriptive at least of those experiences which accompany the grasping of a problem on the part of the person to
whom it is given, and that person's seeking of an answer. Consequently this is not,
as in descriptive psychology, a depiction of experience in its natural setting, but a
certain abstraction of the act being studied from the experience as a whole by means
of analysis and preliminary definitions. The very organization of the artificial conditions, in which the process that is proposed for study stands out in its purity, calls for
preliminary definitions.

The result was that in the [psychological] experiments which studied thinking,
judging, etc., the process of understanding either appeared as secondary and supple-
mentary to other acts of experiencing of this type, or else, even if it was the object of
special attention, it was submerged in the general investigation of thinking as set out
in the preliminary definitions, which limited the person being experimented on by
the use of so-called "instructions." The result is something similar to what we have
seen in Prantl: understanding is a function of reason or pure thinking and therefore
in the analysis of reason itself the specificity of understanding, in the strict sense,
becomes blurred. There remain only certain very general and pale outlines.

But there is a specific feature of these investigations which the psychologist
should regard as a shortcoming but which, in the hands of the philosopher, can turn
these investigations into material which will be useful for him. It is understandable
why psychologists greeted the works of the Würzburg School with suspicion and
even with a certain hostility: "pure" thinking, the *actus purus*, was not at all the kind
of empirical reality that they were used to dealing with. And the more the new inves-

tigators insisted on the solidity of their data, the more apparent it became that they were importing non-psychological categories into psychology. Psychologists were urged to approach psychic factors with a non-psychological interest. It would have been easier for empirical psychologists to reconcile themselves to the importing into psychology of even metaphysical motifs, but this *non-real* psychological factor was, and *should* have been, alien to them.

On the other hand, the philosophers could easily recognize something of *their own* in this "new" kind of psychology—something not real either empirically or metaphysically, but their own as being ideal. The innovators could be inspired by the hope that they were securing for psychology the carrying out of its ancient, even if illegitimate, claim to play the role of a basic science. The philosophers could not fail to harden themselves against these unjustified claims. But, by the nature of the case, the further and deeper the work of the new investigators proceeds, the clearer it will be to impartial observers, whether psychologists or philosophers, that this work is abandoning the terrain of psychology, that its experiments are being displaced by *analysis*, and the introspection which accompanies its experiments is being replaced by *reflection*. These experimental psychologists are borrowing more and more of the terminological apparatus of philosophy. We shall see that now, as a result, philosophy too has something to gain from this "psychology" in exchange for those services which it has had occasion to render to this new psychology.[8]

(b) Insofar as the psychological consideration of the problem of understanding goes beyond the framework of experimental-psychological investigation, insofar as motifs of fundamental and logical investigation operate within it, to that extent we are already proceeding to the second aspect in which hermeneutical problems appear to the contemporary philosophical consciousness. In the first instance, *linguistics*[9] has here rendered a great service to philosophy. As linguistic interest in questions of semasiology has developed and as the conviction has grown that linguistics could not cope with these questions using either its own psychological resources or those at its disposal, it had to turn, at least for the principles for solving them, to psychology, logic, and philosophy. At first, however, linguistics could not find anything in them except for general explanatory theories based on association and apperception. But linguistics itself inspired a more specialized consideration of its semasiological themes.

Martinak's book[10] was almost the first direct response to such interests from the side of psychology. Questions of sign and meaning had been put forward even earlier by Stöhr.[11] But the turning point with respect to philosophy was the publication of Husserl's *Logical Investigations*,[12] which linked the elaboration of semasiological questions to the objective logic of truth in the spirit of Bolzano, on the one hand, and with the fundamental theory of *meaning* as idea in Lotze's modified sense,[13] on the other. In the same year as Husserl's *Logical Investigations* there appeared a book by another prominent student of Brentano, namely Meinong,[14] in which philosophical importance is also assigned to the question of the role of sign, meaning, and understanding, although this question is examined with far less subtlety and skill than in

Husserl. But the highest point that has been reached in the fundamental elaboration of questions of semasiology is to be found in the books of Marty and Gomperz,[15] both of which were published in 1908. The first of these books strikes one with the elegance and subtlety of its analysis, and the second with its thorough historical documentation and its ability, one might say, to exhibit the entire history of philosophical searchings in the light of semasiology.

We will lean heavily on all of these works below when we have occasion to examine strictly logical and methodological questions in the course of our investigation of the fundamental question of understanding, questions which in my view will complete the fundamental investigation and become suitably clear and firm only when grounded in the latter [viz., understanding]. But for the immediate purposes of a fundamental analysis of understanding itself they can render only a partial and for the most part indirect service: more through the classification and filiation of problems which arise on the soil of understanding than through an exhibition of the essence of understanding itself.

In this connection one must point out not so much a defect as an inadequacy of the above-mentioned works, which, however—as we must note—does not spring exclusively from the predetermined character of the themes which were suggested by the logical and epistemological aspect of these investigations. And here we encounter the predetermined character of the themes of understanding through the more general themes of thought, knowledge, etc. The themes of understanding stand out when seen from this point of view, but they should be examined from all sides, and, moreover, they should themselves be made the center from which there will radiate various points of view upon various problems standing on the periphery of the problem of understanding.

There is in these investigations another gap—a small point generally speaking, but of the first importance for us. The analysis of semasiological problems in these investigations is not placed in a close and intimate union with the methodological problems of the human sciences and of *history*, which led to them. Although this is a specific lack, it also has certain general consequences. For we expect that, by illuminating the questions of historical methodology in the light of understanding, we will illuminate all other methodological questions as well. But just this freshness, the spirit of spirit itself, does not yet make itself felt in many of the philosophical conclusions of contemporary semasiology. This creates a peculiar situation. Dilthey and others who valued the vivifying role of understanding for history and the human sciences did not discover in the circle expressed in the formula "experience-expression-understanding" a key to the circle of philosophical thought as a whole. The authors of these fundamental semasiological investigations failed to see that the latter should be carried out through the life of spirit itself in order to be embodied in a philosophically vital and concrete way.

With this last rebuke, incidentally, we ourselves go beyond the limits of that aspect to which the logically methodological search should be limited, i.e., we proceed to a new aspect, which we called "fundamental" above and which has not yet been formulated as a task with sufficient definiteness. Nevertheless there remains the fact of the underestimation of the role which semasiology could have played here if its position in regard to the human sciences had been taken into account. Semasiology remains, but only in its abstract significance. It is not even clear just what place it should occupy among philosophical problems.

Thus in Husserl, for example, questions of semasiology tend to get lost among the other problems discussed in his *Logical Investigations*, and one senses that he feels freer when he proceeds from "expression" to an analysis of what is expressed, an analysis of the life of "pure" consciousness itself and the relations of "pure" ideas. On the contrary, in Gomperz, for example, we find what is evidently the most radical solution of the question of the place of semasiology: it is a basic part of his "noology," and this creates the impression of something artificial and strained. Such a "reform" in the organization of philosophical knowledge is felt as unnecessary, forced, and above all completely ungrounded. Such a grounding, which rationally defines the place of semasiology itself in the system of philosophical thought, can—I am convinced—be achieved only through an elucidation of its role in the organization of the human sciences.

(c) But we must repeat once more what has just been said: the elucidation of all these questions, as well as the demands which are made upon this elucidation, lead beyond the limits of the strictly methodological aspect of the hermeneutical problem and presuppose a deeper, a very deep analysis in principle of the act of understanding, which lies at the base of all these problems. One reason for this is the excessively static character of semasiology itself, which cannot find a place for itself within philosophical knowledge, and its excessive dryness, which fails to sense the significance of its very close contact and kinship with the vital spirit of the human sciences. And this is the reason for the absence of a comprehensive philosophical analysis of understanding in its vital efficacy, its dynamic character, its all-penetrating rational spirituality. The psychological analyses of understanding—however exhaustive they may seem—always carry the imprint of the empirical limitedness and relativity which is present in them from the very beginning. They themselves need a philosophical grounding in principle.

One must take as one's point of departure a fundamental analysis of understanding; only then can one hope for a rigorous and complete theoretical construction, and a methodology based on it—in the first instance for the historical sciences and then for the whole of semasiological logic as it will appear after the confirmation of its general propositions in the light of historical methodology. Such a historical logic, however, will be "historical" in the broad philosophical sense. As applied to the particular objects of the human sciences, it must be subjected to further specification. The circle is completed: through spirit we make our way to what is concretely universal, on the basis of which we solve the special problems of that same spirit. These particular tasks, which, by the way, psychology can also pose, as is obvious, are its own proper tasks. Psychology should concern itself with drawing what it needs from the general source that we see in a fundamental analysis of understanding.

Thus, in the first instance, we have the fundamental problem of understanding in all its breadth. Then comes logic in the light of a semasiology enlivened by the hermeneutical spirit. And finally there are the objective specifications of this logic. The problem of understanding in this form is nothing but the problem of spirit itself: spirit and understanding are mutually related, as an object is related to the act which is directed upon it. That content, of which spirit as an object is the bearer, is for understanding a rational content. Understanding can be directed only upon reason. *Spirit as the object of understanding is rational spirit.*

To the best of my knowledge, the problem in this form is posed here for the first time,[16] and I should like to make some further remarks, partly to explain, partly to justify, the inner sequence and consistency of my further exposition. I should like to call special attention to the following point: In both an analysis of principle and a logical analysis, given such a general formulation of the theme, one must not limit oneself only to the *primary* propositions in order then to leap directly to the details of particular historical objects. Here, as elsewhere, one should not neglect the *axiomata media*. But the essential thing, to which I attach the greatest significance, even the only significance, is not how I shall succeed in formulating these axioms but whether I shall succeed in showing their *transforming* philosophical role with the greatest possible clarity. Perhaps their content will be wholly rejected, but their organizational role must be allowed.

I consider the realization of ideal elements the most important thing in this transformation. Understanding is not just a grasping of ideas—this, I think, is firmly established—but the grasping of realized ideas. Only in this sense can one talk about reality itself as history, for history has to do only with what has been realized. The reason which understands is not an abstract reason but a reason which has been realized in this history. Furthermore, only in this sense can one speak of rational reality. And, what is most important, only in this sense can one speak of *absolute reality*. Only in relation to what has become, what is historical, what has been realized, can one employ this concept without fear of a *contradictio in adjecto*. The absolute reality of the transcendent is unconditional; the absolute reality of the ideal is a destruction of the ideal; the absolute reality of what becomes is an illusion; only the absolute reality of the historical is truth. We move from sensuous reality, as something enigmatic, to its ideal foundation in order to resolve this enigma by bestowing sense upon reality, by attending to the reason which is realized and embodied in reality itself.

If understanding is the way of grasping spirit, questions about the reality of the "external world," the reality of "other persons," and the reality "of my own self" come to stand on the same level for philosophy. In the final analysis—and, consequently, from the very beginning of the investigation—this is a single problem: the problem of a spiritual historical reality. Historical reality, as we have said, is something which has been realized but at the same time is also something which is being realized and is subject to [future] realization. In a word, this is a continuous process. However, this process or movement is not mechanical but theoretical: it is an actualization, embodiment, realization of the idea. I do not think that from our knowledge of how it has been realized, and our knowledge of its rationality, we can learn how history Is to be realized in the future. I think quite the reverse—that if we attempted to realize it on the basis of such knowledge, we would commit an evil deed: we would put an end to our free and unlimited creativity. We would simply eliminate the possibility of history as being further realized. We would put an end to it.

The only lesson we could learn from our study of past history would be that we should bestir ourselves and realize what has not yet been realized. But this is tantamount to deriving from our study of the past only the lesson that one cannot and should not derive any lesson from that study. Thus, at one blow, from beginning to end, everything in philosophy remains pure: intuition, thinking, and understanding. Our only concern, which is as much a human concern as a philosophical one, is to protect this purity. Dogma and opinion are inclined to turn it into an instrument, to give their own assertions a pragmatic application. But this is itself a matter of opinion. Philosophy, in contrast, should defend the freedom of opinion itself, for the pragmatic application of any one opinion hampers the freedom of all the rest, lays upon them pragmatic legal restrictions and then subjects them to moral condemnation as well.

Philosophy protects the freedom of every opinion, and therefore, whenever an opinion appears, it should proclaim "Opinion!" in order not to allow that opinion to put on the dress of knowledge, something which is alien to it and does not belong to it, and in order not to allow it to present itself as though it could lay claim to a recognition which excludes every other opinion. It is not opinions which are dangerous but opinions masquerading as knowledge. Whoever truly cherishes knowledge will not call it opinion. All this is particularly applicable to assertions of every kind about reality. Philosophy itself does not err at this point in distinguishing between opinion and knowledge; neither does a philosopher as such err, but a human being can err. Simple philosophical honesty therefore demands that we, at least, warn others: perhaps I myself err and take my own opinion for knowledge;—watch out and do not take my opinion for knowledge . . . But, also, do not take knowledge for my opinion! . . .

July 6, 1918

Notes

1. The analysis of all of these theories is the subject of the second volume of my *Investigations* (*Issledovanii*).

Ed. Note: Shpet here refers to a text, small portions of which were incorporated into what was conceived as the second part (published in Russia only in 2002) of his *History as a Problem of Logic*.

2. Hermann Swoboda, "Verstehen und Begreifen. Eine psychologische Untersuchung," *Vierteljahrsschrift für wissenschaftliche Philosophie und Soziologie*, Vol. 27, New Series II (1903), No. 2 and 3, 131: "'Verstehen' und 'Begreifen' sind keine wissenschaftlichen Termini."

3. Guthmunder Finnbogason, *Den sympatiske Forstaaelse* (Copenhagen, 1911).

Gustav Shpet

4. Theodor Elsenhans, *Die Aufgabe einer Psychologie der Deutung als Vorarbeit für die Geisteswissenschaften* (Giessen, 1904). As the author himself notes in another place, in this lecture he comes close, on certain points, to Dilthey (cf. *Fries und Kant*, Pt. 2 [Giessen, 1906]: 83n.).

5. Cf. also Theodor Elsenhans, *Lehrbuch der Psychologie* (Tübingen, 1912): 342-44.

6. Benno Erdmann, "Erkennen und Verstehen." Proceedings of the Royal Prussian Academy of Sciences. (Berlin, 1912): 1240-71.

7. The most important works of this school, of immediate interest for us, are: Karl Marbe, *Experimentell-psychologische Untersuchungen über das Urteil* (Leipzig, 1901); Clifton O. Taylor, "Über das Verstehen von Worten und Sätzen,"*Zeitschrift für Psychologie und Physiologie der Sinnesorgane*, Vol. 40 (1906), No. 4; August Wilhelm Messer, "Experimentell-psychologische Untersuchungen über das Denken," *Archiv für die gesamte Psychologie*, Vol. 8 (1906), Nos. 1 and 2; by the same author, *Empfindung und Denken* (Leipzig, 1908); Karl Bühler, "Tatsachen und Probleme zu einer Psychologie der Denkvorgänge. I. Über Gedanken," *Archiv für die gesamte Psychologie*, Vol. 9 (1907), No. 4; Kurt Koffka, *Zur Analyse der Vorstellungen und ihrer Gesetze* (Leipzig, 1912); Otto Selz, *Über die Gesetze des geordneten Denkverlaufs* (Stuttgart, 1913).

8. Therefore Husserl was wrong when he reproached experimental psychology for its tendency to take on the role of a fundamental philosophical science. If experimental psychology displayed such tendencies, that was precisely because it had ceased to be psychology. However, Messer was even more wrong (cf. his "Husserls Phänomenologie in ihrem Verhältnis zur Psychologie," *Archiv für die gesamte Psychologie*, Vol. 13 (1911), Nos. 2 and 3; see also his *Empfindung und Denken*, 11; compare also 33, 56, 147, 158, 164ff, 171, where he took it into his head to prove that a "pure" psychology which does not take a natural-scientific approach to its subject matter is philosophy. This is the "logicism" in psychology which was so violently opposed by Wundt. In general, Wundt and the psychologists (see Konstantin N. Kornilov, "Konflikt dvukh eksperimental'no-psikhologicheskikh shkol" in the Chelpanov Festschrift, *G. I. Chelpanovu: Stat'i po filosofii i psikhologii*, Moscow, 1916) challenge the very *methodology* of the new experimental psychology and here they are neither strong nor persuasive, but their criticism is evidently motivated by a correct sense of the loss of psychology itself and its *methodology*. Introspection and experiment are essentially—and not just with respect to a given situation—something fundamentally different from reflection and analysis.

9. For bibliography see Hermann Paul, *Prinzipien der Sprachgeschichte* [1880], 4th ed. (Halle, 1909): 74-75n.

10. Eduard Martinak, *Psychologische Untersuchungen zur Bedeutungslehre* (Leipzig, 1901). Frege's article "Über Sinn und Bedeutung" pursues different aims and stands quite apart in this entire literature (Gottlob Frege, "Über Sinn und Bedeutung," *Zeitschrift für Philosophie und philosophische Kritik* [New Series] 100.1 [1892]). In general, it is chiefly the merit of the *Austrian* psychologists and philosophers to have brought questions of semasiology into the orbit of philosophy and to have elaborated them from the point of view of psychology, logic and philosophy. I explain this primarily in terms of the strong influence on Austrian psychology and logic of English logic (especially Mill's logic), a logic which did not break the connection between logic and the theory of terms and propositions or the connection between the psychological theory of thought and the theory of language—in contrast to Kantian and post-Kantian formalism in logic. The influence of the rediscovered Bolzano was secondary and fell on hospitable soil that had already been prepared.

11. Adolf Stöhr, *Umriss einer Theorie der Namen* (Leipzig and Vienna, 1889). See also his more recent book *Lehrbuch der Logik* (Leipzig and Vienna, 1910).

12. Edmund Husserl, *Logische Untersuchungen,* Vol II (Halle, 1901; 2nd ed. 1913); see esp. the First Investigation: "Ausdruck und Bedeutung."

13. Cf. R. H. Lotze, *Logik* (2nd ed. [Leipzig], 1880): 507, 521.

14. Alexius von Meinong, *Über Annahmen* (1901, 2nd ed. [Leipzig], 1910).

15. Anton Marty, *Untersuchungen zur Grundlegung der allgemeinen Grammatik und Sprachphilosophie,* Vol. I (Halle, 1908); Heinrich Gomperz, *Weltanschauungslehre,* Vol. II: *Noologie,* 1st Half (*Semasiologie*) (Jena, 1908).

16. I made several veiled allusions to this in my book *Iavlenie i smysl* (Moscow, 1914). I have expressed certain of these ideas more openly in my essay "Mudrost' ili razum?" ["Wisdom or Reason?"], *Mysl' i slovo,* Vol. I (1917): 1-69.

Ed. Note: *Iavlenie i smysl* has been trans. as *Appearance and Sense* by Thomas Nemeth (Dordrecht, 1991).

Introduction to Shpet's "O granitsakh nauchnogo literaturovedeniia" ("On the Limits of Scientific Literary Scholarship")

Dušan Radunović and Galin Tihanov

Gustav Shpet delivered this paper on 24 November and 1 December 1924 in Moscow, at the joint session of the Literary Section and the Department of Philosophy of the State Academy of Artistic Sciences (GAKhN). Here we publish a translation of the synopsis prepared by Shpet (Shpet 441-42). Readers should be aware of the covert addressee of Shpet's paper, the primary intention of which was to contest the arguments that had been advanced a month earlier by another researcher in the Department of Philosophy, the renowned classical scholar Boris Isaakovich Iarkho (1889-1942). Iarkho's paper, presented in two parts—on 24 and 31 October 1924 (cf. Akimova and Shapir xi-xii)—was originally entitled "On the Limits of Scientific Literary Scholarship," and Shpet's decision to maintain Iarkho's title in his critical response only testifies to the strong polemical charge of his arguments.

Iarkho, in his first address of 24 October, had made a radical plea (not necessarily typical for GAKhN's academic environment, which was not intolerant toward the sociological current in the study of literature represented by Kogan, Friche, and GAKhN's very active philosopher Liubov' Akselrod) for a scientific approach to literature, combining arguments drawn from a Herbartian proto-formalist aesthetics (that the work of art comprises various elements aesthetically relevant to the viewer's perception) and from positivism (that the ideal of exactness is to be found in the natural sciences, e. g., biology). As Shpet's hand-written marginalia on his copy of Iarkho's theses suggest, it was Iarkho's simplified positivism that triggered Shpet's response. Hence Shpet's first thesis directly challenges Iarkho's argument that "the litarary work of art is perceived and understood in the same way as any other phenomenon of the outer world" (Iarkho 684), and that it is therefore best approached with the analytic apparatus of the exact sciences. The literary work of art, Shpet replies, belongs to a semiotic ("significative," in his own parlance) field and thus cannot be studied in the same way in which the objective, materially given phenomena are. Given that the literary discourse is tropological rather than termino-logical (Shpet's statement was contributing here to the ongoing Russian debate on the distinctive features of the "poetic language" and the "literariness" of literature), the methodological tools for its appropriation should be found in "criticism and interpretation," rather than in the procedures of quantitative analysis. However, it is essential to note that Shpet does not oppose the need for a scientific approach to literature. On the contrary, he ardently supports the idea of a science of literature allied with linguistics (cf. theses 4 and 9), and by so doing comes close to the platform of the Russian Formalists, although, it has to be stressed, Shpet, unlike the Formalists, believes that the science of literature should also study the specific social functions of literature in the evolution of national cultures, especially its role as collective consciousness of the nation and a guardian of its traditions (theses 6 and 7). Thus his critique of Iarkho needs to be understood as a plea for an approach that would theoretically account not just for the material (immanent-formal) aspects of literature, but for the full complexity of its ontological status within culture.

Works Cited

Akimova, M.V., and M.I. Shapir. "Boris Isaakovich Iarkho i strategiia 'tochnogo literaturovedeniia.'" *Metodologiia tochnogo literaturovedeniia. Izbrannye trudy po teorii literatury.* By Boris Iarkho. Ed. Maksim Shapir. Moscow: Iazyki slavianskikh kul'tur, 2006. vii-xxxii.

Iarkho, Boris. "O granitsakh nauchnogo literaturovedeniia. Doklad A: Granitsy nauchnosti. Doklad B: Granitsy literaturovedeniia." *Iskusstvo kak vid znaniia. Izbrannye trudy po filosofii kul'tury.* By Gustav Shpet. Ed. T.G. Shchedrina. Moscow: ROSSPEN, 2007. 684-85.

Shpet, Gustav. "O granitsakh nauchnogo literaturovedeniia." *Slovar' khudozhestvennykh terminov. GAKhN. 1923-1929 gg.* Ed. I.M. Chubarov. Moscow: Logos-Al'tera and Ecce Homo, 2005. 441-42.

O granitsakh nauchnogo literaturovedeniia
(On the Limits of Scientific Literary Scholarship)

Gustav Shpet

*Translated from the Russian by Dušan Radunović and
Galin Tihanov*

1. The object of literary scholarship does not belong among the objects of the natural sciences; in defining the tasks of literary scholarship, analogies from the natural sciences are methodologically illicit [*nezakonomerny*].

2. The givenness of the object of literary scholarship is significative [*signifikativna-ia*], and not perceptive.

3. Literary scholarship is part of the encyclopaedia of philology and employs the heuristic methods of criticism and interpretation.

4. Detaching itself within philology from material history, and more generally from the so-called realia, literary scholarship, as a science of the "word," aligns itself with linguistics, which is what defines the problematic of literary scholarship.

5. The word, as an object of literary scholarship, is carved out from the linguistic word by way of delimitation: it is a word turned trope (as opposed to the word made term), an artistic word (as opposed to the pragmatic word), and a written one (as opposed to the spoken word).

6. The immanent necessity of the literary word is revealed in the analysis of the object of literature itself, the latter being a collective consciousness *sui generis*. Literary consciousness is the cultural self-consciousness of a nation; it surmounts the ethnic diversity of the dialects by creating a common literary language.

7. In respect of content, literature serves the purpose of preserving the cultural past of a nation; in respect of form, it serves the purpose of protecting the artistic form of the word from its degeneration in folklore [*v ustnoi slovesnosti*].

8. In its content, literature provides material for the social sciences in general; in order to make this material its object, literary scholarship requires a specific principle of selection.

9. The criteria of form define the problematic of literary scholarship; these criteria should be derived from an analysis of the structure of the word in its linguistic functions.

10. This problematic is distributed as follows: A) external forms: (i) indicative-significative forms (predominantly compositional and dispositional) are the subject of technical poetics (which comprises technical rhetoric); (ii) external expressive forms are the concern of stylistics (which is based on syntax as the doctrine of intonation-related coordinating [*intonatsionno-uporiadochivaiushchikh*] forms of the word); B) the entire content of these forms (Gehalt): (i) plot [*siuzhet*], as the ultimate matter, is the problem of comparative study ("historical poetics"); (ii) plot in its inner and dialectical forms of literary processing [*obrabotki*] is the problem of the interpretive history of literature and the theory of literature corresponding to it (literary scholarship proper or theoretical poetics, rhetoric) as a system of terms, nomenclature, and categories.

11. Literary scholarship naturally exceeds its own boundaries; on the one hand, in the direction of its empirical foundations, from where the farthest transition is towards general philosophical principles; and on the other hand, in the direction of the explanatory hypotheses of material history, from where the transition is towards metaphysical anticipations and world-view constructions.

12. The problem of the primary foundations and the methodology of literary scholarship is a particular problem of the philosophy and methodology of scientific knowledge.

Part Six

Bibliographies

Bibliography of Gustav Shpet's Published Works
(1901-2009)

Galin Tihanov

The bibliography encompasses Shpet's published works from 1901 (when his first scholarly translation appeared) to 2009. It is organized in the following sections: scholarly publications (subdivided into publications in Shpet's lifetime and posthumous publications); correspondence; personal documents; works in which Shpet figures as translator or editor; and finally, translations of Shpet's writings. Within each of these sections, the entries are organized in chronological order, according to the year of publication (and to the first letter of the title where several titles were published in the same year). To make the material more easily manageable, further chronological groupings are introduced in the largest section (Shpet's scholarly publications). To make the bibliography accessible to a wider scholarly constituency, in the section listing Shpet's publications as editor or translator the auxiliary bibliographical information is given in English translation, while the titles of the translations or editions are kept in Russian (in those infrequent instances where the Russian conveys or disambiguates auxiliary information that would have otherwise been lost, the original is kept and is reproduced in italics in square brackets). Republications or reprints are indicated but do not form separate entries, unless they contain a substantial proportion of previously unpublished material. Modern Russian spelling is used throughout (original prefixation forms are preserved, e.g. "izsledovanie"). The reader needs to keep in mind that until 1914 Shpet spelled his surname with a double *t*: *Shpett*; with the appearance of *Iavlenie i smysl*, he adopted the spelling *Shpet* (except in texts in German and English, where the *t* was still doubled).

For earlier bibliographies of Shpet's published works, see A.A. Mitiushin. "Bibliografiia pechatnykh trudov G. G. Shpeta." *Nachala* 1 (1992): 89-92, containing a total of 69 entries from 1901 to 1990, and L.V. Fedorova, "Pervye izdaniia rabot G. G. Shpeta." *Istoriia kak problema logiki. Kriticheskie i metodologicheskie issledovaniia. Materialy. V dvukh chastiakh.* Ed. V.S. Miasnikov. Moscow: Pamiatniki istoricheskoi mysli, 2002, 1166-67, which contains a total of 47 entries from 1903 to 2000. None of these two bibliographies include translations of Shpet's works. The present bibliography supplements Mitiushin's and Fedorova's bibliographies, both in the section listing Shpet's works published in his lifetime and in that listing the posthumous publications of his writings; it also corrects the inevitable inaccuracies and errors found in the two previous bibliographies. (Despite my best effort, I was unable to see and verify a small number of the entries included here.) It is a pleasant duty to acknowledge my significant debt to the work of my predecessors, particularly to the bibliography researched and compiled by Mitiushin. It is hoped that the present bibliography is exhaustive with regard to those of Shpet's publications that appeared in his lifetime.

G. T.

The following abbreviations are used throughout (and also in the list of literature on Gustav Shpet published in the present volume):

Arkhiv Epokhi: Tat'iana Shchedrina. *Arkhiv epokhi: tematicheskoe edinstvo russkoi filosofii*. Moscow: ROSSPEN, 2008.

Chpet 2008: *Gustave Chpet et son héritage aux sources russes du structuralisme et de la sémiotique*. Ed. Maryse Dennes. Special Issue of *Slavica Occitania* 26 (2008).

Filosofskie: G.G. Shpet. *Filosofskie etiudy*. Moscow: Progress, 1994.

FP: G.G. Shpet. *Filosofsko-psikhologicheskie trudy*. Ed. T.I. Artem'eva et al. Moscow: Nauka, 2005.

Iskusstvo: *Gustav Shpet. Iskusstvo kak vid znaniia. Izbrannye trudy po filosofii kul'tury*. Ed. T.G. Shchedrina. Moscow: ROSSPEN, 2007.

Istoriia: Gustav Shpet. *Istoriia kak problema logiki. Kriticheskie i metodologicheskie issledovaniia. Materialy. V dvukh chastiakh*. Ed. V.S. Miasnikov. Moscow: Pamiatniki istoricheskoi mysli, 2002.

KO: *Kriticheskoe obozrenie*.

MS: *Mysl' i slovo. Filosofskii ezhegodnik*. Ed. G. Shpet. I (*MS* I): Moscow: G.A. Leman and S.I. Sakharov, 1917; II.1 (*MS* II): Moscow: S.I. Sakharov, 1918-1921. [In fact, *MS* II was published in 1919; cf. M. K. Polivanov, "Ocherk biografii G.G. Shpeta", *Litsa. Biograficheskii al'manakh* 1 (1992): 7-43, here 25.]

Mysl': Gustav Shpet. *Mysl' i slovo. Izbrannye trudy*. Ed. T.G. Shchedrina. Moscow: ROSSPEN, 2005.

Natalis: Gustav Shpet. *Philosophia Natalis. Izbrannye psikhologo-pedagogicheskie trudy*. Ed. T.G. Shchedrina. Moscow: ROSSPEN, 2006.

Ocherk: Gustav Shpet. *Ocherk razvitiia russkoi filosofii. T. 2. Materialy*. Ed. T.G. Shchedrina. Moscow: ROSSPEN, 2009.

Psikhologiia: Gustav Shpet. *Psikhologiia sotsial'nogo bytiia. Izbrannye psikhologicheskie trudy.* Ed. T.D. Martsinkovskaia. Moscow and Voronezh: Institut prakticheskoi psikhologii and MODEK, 1996.

PT: Published partial translations.

R: Republications/reprints.

Shpet 1991: Shpetovskie *chteniia v Tomske, 1991. Tvorcheskoe nasledie G.G. Shpeta i sovremennye gumanitarnye issledovaniia.* Ed. O.G. Mazaeva. Tomsk: Izdatel'stvo Tomskogo universiteta, 1991.

Shpet 1992: *Nachala. Religiozno-filosofskii zhurnal* 1 (1992): 4-95. [A special issue on Gustav Shpet.]

Shpet 1995: *Shpet v Sibiri: ssylka i gibel'.* Ed. N.V. Serebrennikov et al. Tomsk: Vodolei, 1995.

Shpet 1997: *G.G. Shpet/Comprehensio. Vtorye Shpetovskie chteniia. Tvorcheskoe nasledie G.G. Shpeta i sovremennye filosofskie problemy.* Ed. O.G. Mazaeva. Tomsk: Vodolei, 1997.

Shpet 1999: *G.G. Shpet/Comprehensio. Tret'i Shpetovskie chteniia. Tvorcheskoe nasledie G.G. Shpeta i filosofiia XX veka.* Ed. O.G. Mazaeva, Tomsk: Vodolei, 1999.

Shpet 2000: *Gustav Gustavovich Shpet. Arkhivnye materialy. Vospominaniia. Stat'i.* Ed. T.D. Martsinkovskaia. Moscow: Smysl, 2000.

Shpet 2003: *Tvorcheskoe nasledie Gustava Gustavovicha Shpeta v kontekste filosofskikh problem formirovaniia istoriko-kul'turnogo soznaniia (mezhdistsiplinarnyi aspekt). G.G. Shpet/Comprehensio. Chetvertye Shpetovskie chteniia.* Ed. O.G. Mazaeva. Tomsk: Izdatel'stvo Tomskogo universiteta, 2003.

Shpet 2006: *Gustav Shpet i sovremennaia filosofiia gumanitarnogo znaniia.* Ed. T.G. Shchedrina et al. Moscow: Iazyki slavianskikh kul'tur, 2006.

Shpet 2007: G.G. Shpet. *Filosofiia i psikhologiia kul'tury: izbrannoe.* Ed. T.I. Artem'eva et al. Moscow: Nauka, 2007.

Shpet 2008: Gustav Shpet. *Ocherk razvitiia russkoi filosofii. I.* Ed. T.G. Shchedrina. Moscow: ROSSPEN, 2008.

Shpet 2009: *Gustav Shpet's Contribution to Philosophy and Cultural Theory.* Ed. Galin Tihanov. West Lafayette: Purdue UP, 2009.

Slovar': *Slovar' khudozhestvennykh terminov. GAKhN. 1923-1929 gg.* Ed. I.M. Chubarov. Moscow: Logos-Al'tera and Ecce Homo, 2005.

Sochineniia: G.G. Shpet. *Sochineniia.* Moscow: Pravda, 1989.

T: Published translations.

VFP: *Voprosy filosofii i psikhologii.*

A. In Russian

a) Scholarly Publications

In Shpet's Lifetime

1903-1904

1. [Review of] "Lipps, G.F. [Hans Lipps]. *Osnovy psikhofiziki*. Trans. G. Kotliar (St. Petersburg, 1903)." *VFP* 69 (1903): 732-33.

2. [Review of] "Rodzhers, A. [Arthur Rogers] *Kratkoe vvedenie v istoriiu novoi filosofii*. Trans. S.S. Zelinskii. Ed. Iu. I. Aikhenval'd (Moscow, 1903)." *VFP* 69 (1903): 728-32.

3. [Review of] "Chelpanov, G. *Mozg i dusha*. 2nd ed. (St. Petersburg, 1903)." *VFP* 70 (1903): 877-82.

4. [Review of] "Ium, D. [David Hume] *Izsledovanie chelovecheskogo razumeniia*. Trans. S.I. Tsereteli (St. Petersburg: Pirozhkov, 1902)." *Mir Bozhii* 11 (1903): 88-91.

5. [Review of] "*Zu Kants Gedächtnis: Zwölf Festgaben zu seinem 100-jährigen Todestage* (Berlin, 1904)." *VFP* 73 (1904): 406-18.

6. [Review of] "Kant, I. *Grezy dukhovidtsa, poiasnennye grezami metafizika*. Trans. B. Burdes. Ed. A.L. Volynskii (St. Petersburg, 1904)." *VFP* 74 (1904): 564-66.

7. [Review of] "Kant, I. *Kritika chistogo razuma*. Trans. N.M. Sokolov. 2nd ed. (St. Petersburg, 1902)." *VFP* 74 (1904): 550-64.

1905-1907

8. "Pamiat' v eksperimental'noi psikhologii." *Pedagogicheskaia mysl'*. Ed. I.A. Sikorskii and I.I. Glivenko. Kiev: Izd. kollegii Pavla Galagana, 1905. 2: 107-215.

9. "Problema prichinnosti u Iuma i Kanta." *Trudy Psikhologicheskoi seminarii pri universitete Sv. Vladimira. Filosofskie issledovaniia* 1.3 (1905): 1-16; 1.4 (1907): 1-208.

10. *Problema prichinnosti u Kanta i Iuma*. Kiev: Tipografiia Imperatorskogo universiteta, 1906. [Also published in *Universitetskiia izvestiia* [Kiev] 5 (1906): 1-16; 6 (1906): 17-49; 7 (1906): 51-82; 12 (1906): 83-164; 5 (1907): 165-203; cf. No. 9 above.]

11. [Review of] "Kant, I. *Kritika chistogo razuma*. Trans. N. Losskii (St. Petersburg, 1907)." *KO* 2 (1907): 39-40.

12. [Review of] "Polan, Fr. [Frédéric Paulhan] *Volia*. Trans. M.I. Vasil'eva (St. Petersburg, 1907)." *KO* 3 (1907): 23-25.

13. [Review of] "Forel', Avg. [August Forel] *Mozg i dusha*. Trans. B.I. Feinberg (St. Petersburg, 1908)." *KO* 4 (1907): 20-22.

1908-1911

14. [Review of] "Veimer [Hermann Weimer] *Istoriia pedagogiki*. Trans. K. Tiuleliev (St. Petersburg, 1908)." *KO* 5 (1908): 31-32.

15. [Review of] "Zigvart, Kh. [Christoph Sigwart] *Logika. T. 1*. Trans. I.A. Davydov (St. Petersburg, 1908)." *Russkaia mysl'* 9 (1908): 191-93.

16. [Review of] "Prodan, I.S. *Prakticheskoe rukovodstvo po psikhologii dlia VII klassov muzhskikh gimnazii i dlia samoobrazovaniia* (Khar'kov, 1908)." *KO* 4 (1909): 30-34.

17. "Predislovie." *Filosofiia kak osnova pedagogiki*. By P[aul] Natorp. Moscow: N.N. Klochkov, 1910. 3-8. [**R**: Paul' Natorp. *Izbrannye raboty*. Moscow: Territoriia budushchego, 2006. 297-301.]

18. "Skeptitsizm i dogmatizm Iuma." *VFP* 106 (1911): 1-18. [**R**: *Shpet 2000*: 95-111.]

1912

19. "Odin put' psikhologii i kuda on vedet." *Filosofskii sbornik. L'vu Mikhailovichu Lopatinu k tridtsatiletiiu nauchno-pedagogicheskoi deiatel'nosti ot Moskovskogo Psikhologicheskogo Obshchestva. 1881-1911*. Moscow: n.p., 1912. 245-64. [**R**: *Psikhologiia* 28-48; *Natalis* 247-63.]

20. *Logika. Lektsii, chitannye v 1911-1912 g. na Vysshikh zhensikh kursakh. Po zapiskam slushatel'nits. Chast' 1-2*. Moscow: Tipo-litografiia I. Kh. Kavykina, 1912. [litograph.]

1914-1915

21. *Iavlenie i smysl. Fenomenologiia kak osnovnaia nauka i eia problemy*. Moscow: Germes, 1914. [**R**: Tomsk: Vodolei, 1996; *FP* 308-414. A version based on Shpet's personal copy of the first edition, containing a small number of handwritten additions by Shpet, was published by T.G. Shchedrina in *Mysl* 34-188. **T**: English, 1991; Bulgarian, 2003. **PT**: Hungarian, 1997; German, 2003.]

22. "Filosofskoe nasledstvo P.D. Iurkevicha (K sorokaletiiu so dnia smerti)." *VFP* 125 (1914): 653-727. [**R**: As a separate brochure (Moscow: I. N. Kushnerev, 1915); P.D. Iurkevich. *Filosofskie proizvedeniia*. Ed. A.I. Abramov and I.V. Borisova. Moscow: Pravda, 1990. 578-638; *Ocherk* 306-61.]

23. "K istorii ratsionalizma XVIII veka (otryvok)." *VFP* 126 (1915): 1-61.

24. "Kriticheskie zametki k probleme psikhicheskoi prichinnosti (Po povodu knigi V. V. Zen'kovskogo "Problema psikhicheskoi prichinnosti," Kiev, 1914)." *VFP* 127 (1915): 283-313.

25. "Pervyi opyt logiki istoricheskikh nauk (K istorii ratsionalizma XVIII veka)." *VFP* 128 (1915): 378-438.

1916

26. *Istoriia kak problema logiki. Kriticheskiia i metodologicheskiia izsledovaniia. Chast' I. Materialy.* Moscow: T-vo tipografii A. I. Mamontova, 1916. [**R:** *Istoriia* 35-512.]

27. "Istoriia kak problema logiki. Kriticheskiia i metodologicheskiia izsledovaniia. Chast' I. Materialy. M., 1916. (Avtoreferat)." *Istoricheskie izvestiia* 1 (1916): 69-75. [**R:** *MS* I: 416-21.]

28. "Filosofiia i istoriia: Rech'." *VFP* 134 (1916): 427-39. [**R:** *Vestnik Moskovskogo universiteta. Seriia 7. Filosofiia* 3 (1994): 7-13; *Mysl* 191-200. **T:** English, 1998.]

29. "Kommentarii k odnoi kantovskoi fraze." [Published as an extended note to N.A. Umov's article "Evoliutsiia fizicheskikh nauk i ee ideinoe znachenie" in] N.A. Umov. *Sobranie sochinenii.* Ed. A.I. Bachinskii. Moscow: I.N. Kushnerev, 1916. 3: 647-50.

30. "Soznanie i ego sobstvennik (Zametki)." *Georgiiu Ivanovichu Chelpanovu ot uchastnikov ego seminariev v Kieve i Moskve. 1891-1916. Stat'i po filosofii i psikhologii.* Moscow: T-vo tipografii A.I. Mamontova, 1916. 156-210. [**R:** As a separate brochure (Moscow: n.p., 1916); *Filosofskie* 20-116; *Natalis* 264-310.]

1917

31. [with A.I. Bachinskii] "Fideizm prof. Khvol'sona" *MS* I: 379-88. [A review essay on O.D. Khvol'son. *Znanie i vera v fizike.* Petrograd, 1916.]

32. "Filosofiia Dzhoberti [Gioberti]" *MS* I: 297-367. [A review essay on V.F. Ern. *Filosofiia Dzhoberti.* Moscow, 1916.]

33. "Mudrost' ili razum?" *MS* I: 1-69. [**R:** *Filosofskie* 222-336; *Natalis* 311-65.]

34. "Nekotorye cherty iz predstavleniia N. O. Losskogo o prirode" *MS* I: 368-78. [A review essay on N.O. Losskii. *Materiia v sisteme organicheskogo mirovozzreniia.* Moscow, 1916.]

35. [Review of] "Ium [David Hume], *Izsledovanie o chelovecheskom ume* [Trans. S.I. Tsereteli. 2nd ed. Petersburg, 1916]." *MS* I: 394.

36. [Review of] "Giliarov [A.N.], *Rukovodstvo k izucheniiu filosofii* [Vol. 1: Kiev, 1916]." *MS* I: 394-400.

1918-1921

37. "Predmet i zadachi etnicheskoi psikhologii." *Psikhologicheskoe obozrenie* 1.1 (1917): 27-59; 1.2 (1917): 233-63; 1.3-4 (1918): 405-20.

38. "Skeptik i ego dusha (Etiud po filosofskoi interpretatsii)." *MS* II.1: 108-68. [Offprints dated Moscow, 1919; **R:** *Filosofskie nauki* 9 (1991): 85-136; *Filosofskie* 117-221; *Natalis* 366-416.]

39. "Filosofiia Lavrova." *"Forward!" Vpered! Sbornik statei, posviashchennykh pamiati Petra Lavrovicha Lavrova. 1900 g. 7-ogo Fevralia. 1920.* Ed. P. Vitiazev. Petrograd and Moscow: Kolos, 1920. 24-28. [**R**: *Ocherk* 428-33.]

40. "P.L. Lavrov i A.I. Gertsen." *"Forward!" Vpered! Sbornik statei, posviashchennykh pamiati Petra Lavrovicha Lavrova. 1900 g. 7-ogo Fevralia. 1920.* Ed. P. Vitiazev. Petrograd and Moscow: Kolos, 1920. 35-39. [**R**: *Ocherk* 434-38.]

41. "Differentsiatsiia postanovki teatral'nogo predstavleniia." *Kul'tura teatra* 7-8 (1921): 31-33. [**R**: *Sovremennaia dramaturgiia* 5 (1991): 202-04 and *Iskusstvo* 15-18; for an almost identical version based on a draft from Shpet's estate in the Russian State Library, see *Shpet 2000*: 43-46 and *Shpet 2007*: 425-27.]

42. *Filosofskoe mirovozzrenie Gertsena.* Petrograd: Kolos, 1921. [**R**: *Ocherk* 206-98.]

1922-1923

43. "Antropologizm Lavrova v svete istorii filosofii" [1919]. *P.L. Lavrov: stat'i, vospominaniia, materialy.* Petrograd: Kolos, 1922. 73-138. [**R**: *Ocherk* 439-508.]

44. "Istoriia, kak predmet logiki." *Nauchnye izvestiia Narkomprosa* 2 (1922): 1-35. [**R**: *Istoriko-filosofskii ezhegodnik 1988.* Moscow: Nauka, 1988. 290-320; *Mysl'* 212-47.]

45. *Ocherk razvitiia russkoi filosofii. Ch. 1.* Petrograd: Kolos, 1922. [**R**: *Sochineniia* 9-342; A.I. Vvedenskii et al. *Ocherki istorii russkoi filosofii.* Ed. B.V. Emel'ianov and K.N. Liubutin. Sverdlovsk: Izdatel'stvo Ural'skogo universiteta, 1991. 217-570; *FP* 72-307; *Shpet 2008*: 35-350. Partial reprint: Viktor Kravets. *Razgovor o Skovorode. S prilozheniem khrestomatii po skovorodovedeniiu.* Kiev: Proza, 2000. 210-24.]

46. *Esteticheskie fragmenty I.* Petrograd: Kolos, 1922; *II, III.* Petrograd: Kolos, 1923. [**R**: *Sochineniia* 343-472; *Shpet 2007*: 274-365; *Iskusstvo* 175-287. **T**: Italian, 1992/93; Japanese, 2004.]

47. "Teatr kak iskusstvo." *Masterstvo teatra. Vremennik Kamernogo teatra* 1-2 (1922-23): 31-55. [**R**: *Voprosy filosofii* 11 (1988): 77-91; *Iz istorii sovetskoi nauki o teatre: 20-e gody.* Ed. S.V. Stakhorskii. Moscow: GITIS, 1988. 32-52; *Psikhologiia* 413-37; *Shpet 2000*: 111-34; *Shpet 2007*: 394-410; *Iskusstvo* 19-39. **T**: English, 1989/90; German, 1996.]

48. "Problemy sovremennoi estetiki." *Iskusstvo* 1 (1923): 43-78. [**R**: *Psikhologiia* 373-412; *Shpet 2007*: 366-93; *Iskusstvo* 288-322. **T**: Italian, 1993.]

1926-1927

49. "K voprosu o postanovke nauchnoi raboty v oblasti iskusstvovedeniia." *Biulleteni GAKhN* 4-5 (1926): 3-30. [**R**: As a separate brochure (Moscow: GAKhN, 1927); *Shpet 2000*: 135-52; *Shpet 2007*: 411-22; *Iskusstvo* 149-63.]

50. "Literatura." *Giperborei*: 41-55. [A typewritten almanach published and disseminated in Moscow in 1926; two copies survive in RGALI. For a slightly differ-

ent version of this article (1929), published in 1982, see below under "Posthumous publications."]

51. *Vvedenie v etnicheskuiu psikhologiiu. Vyp. 1.* Moscow: Gosudarstvennaia akademiia khudozhestvennykh nauk, 1927. [In fact, published in 1926; cf. Petritskii in *Shpet 1991:* 25 (entry listed below in the bibliography of works on Shpet). **R**: *Sochineniia* 473-574; *Psikhologiia* 261-372; St. Petersburg: Aleteiia, 1996; *FP* 3-71; *Natalis* 417-500. **T**: Bulgarian, 2003.]

52. *Vnutrenniaia forma slova (etiudy i variatsii na temy Gumbol'ta* [sic]*).* Moscow: Gosudarstvennaia akademiia khudozhestvennykh nauk, 1927 (Istoriia i teoriia iskusstv. Vypusk vos'moi). [**R**: *Psikhologiia* 49-260; Ivanovo: Ivanovskii gosudarstvennyi universitet, 1999; Moscow: URSS, 2003; Moscow: KomKniga, 2006; *Shpet 2007:* 3-144; *Iskusstvo* 325-501; Moscow: Librokom, 2009. **T**: French, 2007; **PT**: Hungarian, 1978.]

1932

53. [Signed "G.G-n"]. *Granat: entsiklopedicheskii slovar'.* 7th ed. Moscow and Leningrad: Granat, 1932. 50: 378-80. [An entry on Shpet's philosophy written by Shpet.]

Posthumous publications

1959-1992

54. "Ot perevodchika" [1937]. *Fenomenologiia dukha.* By G.W.F. Gegel' [Hegel]. Trans. G. Shpet. (G.W.F. Gegel' [Hegel]. *Sochineniia. T. 4*). Moscow: Akademiia Nauk SSSR, Institut Filosofii, 1959. xlvi-xlviii [unsigned].

55. "Literatura" [1929]. Ed. A.A. Mitiushin. *Uchennye zapiski tartuskogo gosudarstvennogo universiteta* 576 (1982): 150-58 (*Trudy po znakovym sistemam* 15). [**R**: *Iskusstvo* 164-72; *Shpet 2007*: 443-50. A slightly different version (edited by N.S. Antonova) was published under the same title as an appendix to *Istoriia* 1133-36 and republished in *Slovar'* 253-59.]

56. "Germenevtika i ee problemy" [Completed in July 1918]. Ed. A.A. Mitiushin and E.V. Pasternak. *Kontekst 1989.* Moscow: Nauka, 1989. 231-67; *Kontekst 1990.* Moscow: Nauka, 1990. 219-59; *Kontekst 1991.* Moscow: Nauka, 1991. 215-55; *Kontekst 1992.* Moscow: Nauka, 1993. 251-84. [**R**: *Shpet 2007:* 145-273. A textologically improved version, restoring minor omissions, was edited and published by Tat'iana Shchedrina in *Mysl'* 248-418. Several translations are available, some of them made either before or largely simultaneously with the preparation of the first publication in Russian. **T**: German, 1993; Croatian, 2006; **PT**: Hungarian, 1983; English, 1999 and 2009 (the latter in the present volume); Slovene, 2000.]

57. [With V. Porzhezinskii and G. Chelpanov] "Dokladnaia zapiska ob uchrezhdenii kabineta etnicheskoi i sotsial'noi psikhologii" [1 February 1920]. *Voprosy psikhologii* 4 (1990): 159-60.

58. "K voprosu o gegel'ianstve Belinskogo" [1923]. Ed. L.V. Fedorova. *Voprosy filosofii* 7 (1991): 115-76. [**R**: *Ocherk* 100-84.]

59. "Rabota po filosofii" [Most likely 1914-1916; title given at the time of publication]. Ed. I.M. Chubarov. *Logos* 2 (1991): 215-33. [**R**: *Shpet 1992*: 31-49. Ed. M. Venditti and L. Fedorova; *Vestnik Moskovskogo universiteta. Seriia 7. Filosofiia* 2 (1995): 22-36. **T**: English, 1998.]

60. "Shpet (Stat'ia dlia entsiklopedicheskogo slovaria "Granat")" [June 1929]. *Shpet 1992*: 50-52. [Shpet's manuscript version of the article he published in 1932; see entry No. 53 above.]

2000

61. "Doklad v Komissii po organizatsii Akademii fizicheskoi kul'tury" [1921]. *Shpet 2000*: 63-67.

62. "Iskusstvo kak vid znaniia." Ed. T.D. Martsinkovskaia. *Dekorativnoe iskusstvo* 2-4 (1996): 26-27. [Synopsis of a paper presented by Shpet at GAKhN in April 1926. **R**: *Shpet 2000*: 47-52, under the title "Iskusstvo kak vid znaniia (tezisy doklada)"; *Shpet 2007*: 427-31; different from No. 89 below.]

63. "Konspekt besedy o nakazanii" [Undated]. *Shpet 2000*: 68-69.

64. "Material po organizatsii kabineta etnicheskoi psikhologii pri Etnolingvisticheskom otdele fakul'teta obshchestvennykh nauk Moskovskogo universiteta. Zaiavlenie Shpeta" [Most likely 1919-20]. *Shpet 2000*: 70-71. [**R**: *FP* 439-40.]

65. Materialy k lektsionnomu kursu "Vvedenie v izuchenie etnicheskoi psikhologii" [1921]. *Shpet 2000*: 71-82.

66. "Plan 'Biograficheskoi biblioteki filosofov'" [1920]. *Shpet 2000*: 86-90. [**R**: *FP* 436-39.]

67. "Plan issledovatel'skoi raboty v Institute iskusstvovedeniia" [1926]. *Shpet 2000*: 61-63. [**R**: *Shpet 2007*: 433-34.]

68. "Plan serii knig pod obschim zaglaviem 'Moralisty'" [1920]. *Shpet 2000*: 90-92.

69. "Podgotovitel'nye materialy k khrestomatii po istorii psikhologii" [1917]. *Shpet 2000*: 82-85. [**R**: *FP* 433-36.]

70. "Poznanie i iskusstvo (konspekt doklada)" [1926]. *Shpet 2000*: 52-54. [**R**: *Shpet 2007*: 431-33; *Iskusstvo* 101-02, under the title "Poznanie i iskusstvo (tezisy doklada)."]

71. "Poznanie i iskusstvo (tezisy doklada)" [1926]. *Shpet 2000*: 54-61. [**R**: A textologically improved version was published by T.G. Shchedrina, under the title "Poznanie i iskusstvo (konspekt doklada)": *Iskusstvo* 95-100.]

2002

72. "Istochniki disertatsii [sic] Chernyshevskogo" [1929]. Ed. L.V. Fedorova. *Novoe literaturnoe obozrenie* 53 (2002): 6-45. [46-48 commentary and notes by Fedorova; **R**: *Ocherk* 362-416.]

73. *Istoriia kak problema logiki. Kriticheskie i metodologicheskie issledovaniia. Materialy. V dvukh chastiakh.* Ed. V.S. Miasnikov. Moscow: Pamiatniki istoricheskoi mysli, 2002. [Contains a reprint (35-512) of Shpet's *Istoriia kak problema logiki. Kriticheskiia i metodologicheskiia izsledovaniia. Chast' I. Materialy.* Moscow: Tovarishchestvo tipografii A.I. Mamontova, 1916 and the first full publication (prepared by L.V. Fedorova and I.M. Chubarov) of the second part of this work (547-1131), which had remained unpublished at the time; ch. 7 ("Vil'gel'm Dil'tei") of the second part (836-916) was first published (edited by M. Litvinovich and I. Chubarov) in *2 teksta o Vil'gel'me Dil'tee. I. G. Shpet. Istoriia kak problema logiki. II. Vil'gel'm Dil'tei. II. M. Khaidegger. Issledovatel'skaia rabota Vil'gel'ma Dil'teia i bor'ba za istoricheskoe mirovozzrenie v nashi dni. Desiat' dokaldov, prochitannykh v Kassele (1925 g.).* Moscow: Gnozis, 1995. 7-136.]

2004

74. "Istoriia kak problema logiki: razvernutyi plan III toma i nabroski IV toma" [Most likely 1917-18 or shortly afterwards]. Ed. T.G. Shchedrina. *"Ia pishu kak ekho drugogo . . ." Ocherki intellektual'noi biografii Gustava Shpeta.* By Tat'iana G. Shchedrina. Moscow: Progress-Traditsiia, 2004. 341-53. [**R**: *Mysl'* 201-11.]

75. "Konspekt kursa lektsii po istorii nauk" [1917-18]. Ed. S.V. Chernen'ko and T.G. Shchedrina. *Epistemologiia i filosofiia nauki* 2 (2004): 217-33. [**R** (with expanded commentaries by Tat'iana Shchedrina): *Arkhiv epokhi* 262-83.]

76. "Opyt populiarizatsii filosofii Gegelia" [1918]. Ed. T.G. Shchedrina. *"Ia pishu kak ekho drugogo . . ." Ocherki intellektual'noi biografii Gustava Shpeta.* By Tat'iana G. Shchedrina. Moscow: Progress-Traditsiia, 2004. 281-322. [Shpet's unfinished review of I.A. Il'in's two-volume monograph *Filosofiia Gegelia.*]

77. "Rabochie zametki k stat'iam L.I. Shestova: "Memnto mori (po povodu teorii poznaniia Edmunda Gusserlia)" i "Samoochevidnye istiny" [1917 or shortly afterwards]. Ed. T.G. Shchedrina. *"Ia pishu kak ekho drugogo . . ." Ocherki intellektual'noi biografii Gustava Shpeta.* By Tat'iana G. Shchedrina. Moscow: Progress-Traditsiia, 2004. 323-40.

2005

78. "Geneticheskii metod" [Second half of the 1920s]. Ed. I.M. Chubarov. *Slovar'* 108-11.

79. "Iazyk i smysl" [Most likely 1921-25]. Ed. T.G. Shechdrina [Notes by T.G. Shchedrina, T.A. Dmitriev and I.M. Chubarov]. *Mysl'* 470-668. [A portion of Part I

appeared under the title "Znak-znachenie kak otnoshenie *sui generis* i ego sistema" in *Voprosy filosofii* 12 (2002): 79-92 and in T.G. Shchedrina. *"Ia pishu kak ekho drugogo . . ." Ocherki intellektual'noi biografii Gustava Shpeta*. Moscow: Progress-Traditsiia, 2004. 354-78; Part II was first published in *Logos* 7 (1996): 81-122; 1 (1998): 9-52. **PT** (preceding the publication in Russian): Italian, 1994.]

80. "O granitsakh nauchnogo literaturovedeniia." *Slovar'* 441-42. [Synopsis of a paper delivered by Shpet at GAKhN in 1924; **R**: *Iskusstvo* 682-83. The text was first published in M.I. Kagan. *O khode istorii*. Ed. V.L. Makhlin. Moscow: Iazyki slavianskoi kul'tury, 2004. 569-70, where it was wrongly attributed to Matvei Kagan. **T**: English, 2009 (in the present volume).]

81. "Rabochii variant glavy o V.G. Belinskom" [May 1923; title given by the editors of the volume]. *FP* 417-33 (notes 450-51).

2006

82. "Gerbert Spenser [Herbert Spencer] i ego pedagogicheskie idei" [1913-14]. Ed. T.G. Shchedrina. *Natalis* 28-138.

83. "K voprosu o prepodavanii filosofii v srednei shkole" [1904]. Ed. T.G. Shchedrina. *Natalis* 23-24.

84. "K voprosu o prepodavanii filosofskoi propedevtiki v srednei shkole" [1906; signed with Shpet's pseudonym "Lord Genry"]. Ed. T.G. Shchedrina. *Natalis* 25-27.

85. "Psikhicheskaia antropologiia" [Most likely 1916-17. Extensive notes towards a larger work]. Ed. T.G. Shchedrina. *Natalis* 583-89.

86. "Rabota po psikhologii" [1907]. Ed. T.G. Shchedrina. *Natalis* 141-246.

87. "Sotsializm ili gumanizm" [late 1910s]. Ed. T.G. Shchedrina. *Kosmopolis* 1 (2006): 77-90. [**R** (with expanded commentaries by Tat'iana Shchedrina): *Arkhiv epokhi* 236-54.]

2007

88. "Chto takoe metodologiia nauk?" [Synopsis of a paper, most likely around 1917]. *Shpet 2007*: 451-53.

89. "Iskusstvo kak vid znaniia (etiud)" [1927]. Ed. T.G. Shchedrina. *Iskusstvo* 112-48. [Different from No. 62 above; for an abridged publication, see *Kul'turno-istoricheskaia psikhologiia* 4 (2006): 25-34.]

90. "Konspekt doklada o p'ese U. Shekspira [William Shakespeare] *Iulii Tsezar* [*Julius Caesar*]," sdelannogo dlia Malogo Teatra" [1920]. *Shpet 2007*: 434-43.

91. "Krizis filosofii" [1920]. Ed. T.G. Shchedrina. *Issledovaniia po istorii russkoi mysli: ezhegodnik* 7 (2007): 92-102. [**R**: "Konspekt doklada G. G. Shpeta 'Krizis filosofii.'" *Arkhiv epokhi* 228-35; *Ocherk* 532-36.]

92. "O granitsakh nauchnogo literaturovedeniia (konspekt doklada)" [1924]. Ed. T.G. Shchedrina. *Iskusstvo* 40-48.

93. "O razdelenii iskusstv (rabochie zametki i vypiski)." Ed. T.G. Shchedrina. *Iskusstvo* 103-11.

94. "Zametki k stat'e 'Roman'" [1924]. Ed. T.G. Shchedrina. *Iskusstvo* 49-89. [An abridged version published in *Voprosy filosofii* 7 (2007): 86-101.]

95. "Zametki o muzyke" [Not earlier than 1925]. Ed. T.G. Shchedrina. *Iskusstvo* 90-94.

2008

96. "Chernovik plana kursa lektsii G.G. Shpeta 'Istoriia nauchnoi mysli'" [1921]. Ed. T.G. Shchedrina. *Arkhiv epokhi* 255-61.

97. "Dokladnaia zapiska G.G. Shpeta po sotsial'noi pedagogike" [1921]. Ed. T.G. Shchedrina. *Arkhiv epokhi* 284-89.

98. "[Unpublished review of] S. Frank, *Dusha cheloveka. Opyt vvedeniia v filosof-skuiu psikhologiiu* [1917]". Ed. T.G. Shchedrina. *Arkhiv epokhi* 127-28.

2009

99. "Glava 'Bez lineek': plan i zametki." Ed. T.G. Shchedrina. *Ocherk* 57-74.

100. "Glava 'Pereval': plan i zametki." Ed. T.G. Shchedrina. *Ocherk* 75-99.

101. "Konspekt knigi A.N. Pypina 'Kharakteristika literaturnykh mnenii ot dvadt-satykh do piatidesiatykh godov' (SPb., 1890)." Ed. T.G. Shchedrina. *Ocherk* 590-92.

102. "Konspekt knigi F.M. Dostoevskogo 'Besy.'" Ed. T.G. Shchedrina. *Ocherk* 548-89.

103. "Konspekt 'Ocherka' s deleniem na glavy." Ed. T.G. Shchedrina. *Ocherk* 24-56.

104. "Konspekt serii statei A.A. Skabichevskogo 'Ocherki umstvennogo razvitiia nashego obshchestva. 1825-1860.'" Ed. T.G. Shchedrina. *Ocherk* 593-617.

105. "Konspekt sochinenii P.A. Viazemskogo." Ed. T.G. Shchedrina. *Ocherk* 539-47.

106. "'Ocherk razvitiia russkoi filosofii': plan." Ed. T.G. Shchedrina. *Ocherk* 21-23. [First published by Shchedrina in her book *"Ia pishu kak ekho drugogo . . ." Ocherki intellektual'noi biografii Gustava Shpeta*. Moscow: Progress-Traditsiia, 2004. 37-40.]

107. "Otdel'nye zametki." Ed. T.G. Shchedrina. *Ocherk* 509-31.

108. "Zametki k paragrafam o Belinskom." Ed. T.G. Shchedrina. *Ocherk* 185-205.

109. "Zametki k paragrafam o Chernyshevskom." Ed. T.G. Shchedrina. *Ocherk* 417-27.

110. "Zametki k paragrafu 'Filosofsko-istoricheskoe reshenie problemy narodnosti u slavianofilov i u Gertsena.'" Ed. T.G. Shchedrina. *Ocherk* 299-305.

b) Shpet's correspondence

111. "Pis'ma k G.G. Shpetu." Ed. Marina Shtorkh. *Shpet 1992*: 63-69. [Three letters and a postcard to Shpet from Boris Bugaev (Andrei Belyi); and letters to Shpet by N. Luzin (1), D. Zaslavskii (1), F. Berezhkov (2), and L. Grossman (2).]

112. "Shpet v Gettingene." Ed. I.M. Chubarov. *Logos* 3 (1992): 243-63. [Contains letters to Shpet by Georgii Chelpanov (3), Lev Shestov (1), Boris Iakovenko (4), Sofiia L'vovna Shatenshtein-Veitsman (1), and Roman Jakobson (2). The selection of Shestov's and Jakobson's letters is superceded by the fuller versions in the 2005 volume of Shpet's correspondence (see entry further below).]

113. "Pis'mo A.F. Loseva k G.G. Shpetu." Ed. Marina Shtorkh. *Nachala* 3 (1993): 50-51. [A letter to Shpet by Aleksei Losev.]

114. *Edmund Husserl Briefwechsel. Vol. 3: Die Göttinger Schule*. Ed. Karl Schuhmann and Elisabeth Schuhmann. Dordrecht: Kluwer, 1994. 527-44; 598-600 (notes). [Contains Shpet's letters to Husserl (23 November 1913–10 June 1918) and Husserl's letters to Shpet, as well as a letter from Husserl's wife Malvine to Shpet. **T**: Russian (*Logos* 3 (1992): 233-42— Husserl's letters translated from the originals *before* the 1994 publication in German; 7 (1996): 123-33— Shpet's letters translated from the 1994 German publication).]

115. *Shpet v Sibiri: ssylka i gibel'*. Ed. N.V. Serebrennikov et al. Tomsk: Vodolei, 1995. [The fullest available selection of Shpet's letters from Siberia (beginning with two letters from the journey to Eniseisk—1 and 3 July 1935—and ending with a letter from Tomsk dated 25 October 1937). Contains letters by Shpet to his wife Nataliia; his children Margarita, Lenora, Marina, and Sergei; and a letter to Liubov' Gurevich; supercedes the publication of two letters by Shpet to his children Marina and Sergei in *Shpet 1992*: 55-61.]

116. "Perepiska G.G. Shpeta." *Shpet 2000*: 23-28. [Contains letters to Shpet by P.P. Blonskii (3) and M.M. Rubinshtein (1), as well as summaries of letters by T.I. Rainov and G.I. Chelpanov, along with letters by Shpet to his mother (two of 1910 and one of 1913); the publication of Shpet's 1910 letters to his mother is superceded by the fuller versions in the 2005 volume of Shpet's correspondence (see entry further below).]

117. "Iz perepiski s G.G. Shpetom." *Pokhod vremeni*. Vol. 2. *Stat'i i esse*. By Boris Gornung. Moscow: RGGU, 2001. 392-97. [Two letters by Boris Gornung to Gustav Shpet, dated 23 August 1925 (392-95) and 3 February 1926 (396-97).]

118. Shpet, Gustav. "Pis'mo Stalinu" [November 1935]. Ed. E.V. Pasternak. *Shpet 2003*: 586-92. [A letter to Stalin that Shpet probably did not send; a shorter draft appeared in *Shpet 1995*: 72-74.]

119. *Gustav Shpet: zhizn' v pis'makh. Epistoliarnoe nasledie*. Ed. T.G. Shchedrina. Moscow: ROSSPEN, 2005. [The largest available selection of Gustav Shpet's letters; includes letters by Shpet to his mother; to Nataliia Guchkova (later Nataliia Shpet);

to his children Lenora, Marina, and Sergei; to E.M. Metner; Iu. K. Baltrushaitis; N.I. Ignatova; E.N. Konshina; M.O. Gershenzon; D.M. Petrushevskii; F.I. Vitiazev-Sedenko. As far as the period before Shpet's exile in 1935 is concerned, this publication supercedes the partial (at times also abridged) publication of his letters to his mother (of 1910); to Nataliia Guchkova; N.I. Ignatova; Iu. K. Baltrushaitis; and D. Petrushevskii, in: *Istoriko-filosofskii ezhegodnik 1988*. Moscow: Nauka, 1988. 120-25; *Nachala* 3 (1993): 37-49; *Shpet 1997*: 243-45; *Russkaia mysl'* 4269 (13-19 May 1999): 19; *Shpet 2000*: 28; *Novyi mir* 1 (2004): 143-57; *Pushkinskii sbornik*. Ed. I. Loshchilov and I. Surat. Moscow: Tri kvadrata, 2005. 356-60. The volume also contains letters to Shpet by his mother; L.I. Shestov; N.I. Ignatova; E.N. Konshina; N.O. Losskii; I.I. Lapshin; D.M. Petrushevskii; F.I. Vitiazev-Sedenko; and Roman Jakobson. The publication of Jakobson's six letters supercedes the publication of two of his letters in *Logos* 3 (1992): 257, while the full publication of Shestov's letters supercedes the selections that appeared in *Logos* 3 (1992): 249; *Shpet 1997*: 245-49; and *Shpet 1999*: 212-30.]

120. Shor, E.D. "Pis'ma G.G. Shpetu i neizvestnomu parizhskomu korrespondentu." Ed. V. Iantsen. *Shpet 2006*: 403-12. [403-05 a letter to Shpet by E.D. Shor of 1 December 1923.]

121. Bulgakov, Sergei. [A letter to Gustav Shpet of 1906, published by T.G. Shchedrina in] *Russkoe bogoslovie v evropeiskom kontekste: S. N. Bulgakov i zapadnaia religiozno-filosofskaia mysl'*. Ed. V.N. Porus. Moscow: Bibleisko-Bogoslovskii Institut sv. Apostola Andreia, 2006. 199. [**R**: *Arkhiv epokhi 56-57*.]

122. Trubetskoi, Evgenii. [A letter to Gustav Shpet of 1907, published by T.G. Shchedrina in] *Vorporsy filosofii* 11 (2007): 72. [**R**: *Arkhiv epokhi 105-06*.]

123. Krivtsova, A., and Evgenii Lann. [Extracts from a letter to Shpet dated 5 June 1931, published by T.G. Shchedrina in] *Arkhiv epokhi* 333 n. 20.

124. Gurevich, Liubov'. [Extracts from a letter to Shpet dated 5 February 1932, published by T.G. Shchedrina in] *Arkhiv epokhi* 327 n. 5.

125. Smirnov, Aleksandr. [Extracts from a letter to Shpet dated 27 June 1933, published by T.G. Shchedrina in] *Arkhiv epokhi* 336 n. 26.

126. "Pis'mo G.G. Shpeta k L. B. Kamenevu" (12 January 1934). *Arkhiv epokhi* 338-44.

127. Shpet, Gustav, Krivtsova, A., and Evgenii Lann. [Extracts from a letter to Lev Kamenev dated 4 April 1934, published by T.G. Shchedrina in] *Arkhiv epokhi* 328 n. 6.

128. "Pis'mo G.G. Shpeta k L.B. Kamenevu" (19 April 1934). *Arkhiv epokhi* 344-45.

129. Smirnov, Aleksandr. [A letter to Gustav Shpet dated 2 November 1934, published by T.G. Shchedrina in] *Arkhiv epokhi* 346 n. 58.

130. "T.I. Rainov i G.G. Shpet: perepiska o 'vnutrennei forme slova.'" Ed. N.K. Gavriushin. *Issledovaniia po istorii russkoi mysli: ezhegodnik* 8 (2009): 127-39. [In-

cludes a letter by Timofei Rainov to Shpet dated 13 November 1927 (134-37) and Shpet's response of 20 November 1927 (137-39); both letters discuss Shpet's book *The Inner Form of the Word*; Gavriushin first published these two letters in 1987 as part of a larger selection of Rainov's correspondence.]

c) Personal documents and poems authored and/or signed by Shpet

131. "Zaiavlenie" [4 June 1937. A statement by Shpet submitted to the public prosecutor's office, published in] M.K. Polivanov. "Ocherk biografii G.G. Shpeta." *Litsa. Biograficheskii al'manakh* 1 (1992): 39-41. [**R**: *Shpet 1995*: 189-90.]

132. "Anketa arestovannogo" [27 October 1937. A questionnaire filled by Shpet after his re-arrest]. *Shpet 1995*: 268-70.

133. "Protokol doprosa" [1 November 1937. A record of Shpet's (first) interrogation on that day]. *Shpet 1995*: 270-71.

134. "Protokol doprosa" [1 November 1937. A record of Shpet's (second) interrogation on that day]. *Shpet 1995*: 272-75.

135. "Avtobiografiia" [1922. A *curriculum vitae* by Shpet]. *Shpet 2000*: 18. [**R**: *Shpet 2007*: 460.]

136. "Anketa" [23 April 1925. A questionnaire filled by Shpet]. *Shpet 2000*: 19. [**R**: *Shpet 2007*: 461.]

137. "Nochnoi koshsmar" ["Nightmare," a poem written by Shpet on 3 September 1921]. Ed. T.G. Shchedrina. *Iskusstvo* 602-03.

138. "Otvety na voprosy ankety A. Borovogo, 1908 g." [Answers to a questionnaire, 1908]. *Voprosy psikhologii* 3 (2009): 121-22.

d) Translations and editorships

139. L. Vol'tman [Ludwig Woltmann]. *Sistema moral'nogo soznaniia v sviazi s otnosheniem kriticheskoi filosofii k darvinizmu i sotsializmu*. Trans. from the German V. Mikhailov and G. Shpett. Ed. M.M. Filippov. St. Petersburg: Ziabitskii and Piatin, 1901.

140. G.I. Chelpanov. *O sovremennykh filosofskikh napravleniiakh: publichnyia lektsii, chitannyia v osennem polugodii 1902 goda*. Ed. [*Izdal*] Gustav Shpett. Kiev: Tipografiia Petra Barskago, 1902.

141. R. Eisler [Rudolf Eisler]. *Osnovnye polozheniia teorii poznaniia*. Trans. from the German G. Shpett. Kiev: V.A. Prosianichenko, 1902.

142. G. Rikkert [Heinrich Rickert]. *Vvedenie v transtsendental'nuiu filosofiiu. Predmet poznaniia*. Trans. from the 2nd ed. G. Shpett. Kiev: V.A. Prosianichenko, 1904.

143. I. Ditsgen [Joseph Dietzgen]. *Teoriia poznaniia v svete marksizma.* Trans. from the German V. Budzilevich. Ed. G. Shpett. Kiev: Pravda, 1907. [Shpet also supplied brief notes.]

144. A. Bine [Alfred Binet]. *Sovremennye idei o detiakh.* Trans. from the French. Ed. G.G. Shpett. Moscow: Kosmos, 1910.

145. V. Dzhems [William James]. *Vselennaia s pliuralisticheskoi tochki zreniia.* Trans. from the English B. Osipov and O. Rumer. Ed. G.G. Shpett. Moscow: Kosmos, 1911.

146. F. Enrikves [Federigo Enriques]. *Problema nauki. Chast'. I.* Trans. from the Italian. Ed. A.I. Bachinskii and G.G. Shpett. Moscow: Kosmos, 1911.

147. B. Bozanket [Bernard Bosanquet]. *Osnovaniia logiki: Populiarnye lektsii.* Trans. from the French. Ed. G. Shpet. Moscow: Germes, 1914.

148. Dzh. F. Staut [George Frederic Stout]. *Analiticheskaia psikhologiia. T. 1.* [*Analytic Psychology*] 2nd ed. Trans. from the English A.K. Rachinskii. Ed. G.G. Shpet. Moscow and Petrograd: Gosudarstvennoe izdatel'stvo, 1923.

149. Alkei [Alcaeus]. "Kogda Latona svetlogo otroka . . ." [A fragment from Alcaeus in Shpet's translation] *Germes* [A typescript journal published in Moscow in 1922-24] 3 (September 1923): 90. [**R**: L.V. Gornung. "Moi vospominaniia o professore Gustave Gustavoviche Shpete." *Shestye Tynianovskie chteniia. Tezisy dokladov i materialy dlia obsuzhdeniia.* Riga-Moscow: n.p., 1992. 178-79.]

150. Platon [Plato]. "V zvezdy gliadish', moia Zvezdochka . . ." [A distich by Plato in Gustav Shpet's translation] *Germes* [A typescript journal published in Moscow in 1922-24] 3 (September 1923): 89. [**R**: *Mnemozina: Al'manakh poezii i kritiki.* Moscow, 1924. 6 (a typescript almanac, a single issue of which appeared in 1924); L. V. Gornung. "Moi vospominaniia o professore Gustave Gustavoviche Shpete." *Shestye Tynianovskie chteniia. Tezisy dokladov i materialy dlia obsuzhdeniia.* Riga-Moscow: n.p., 1992. 178.]

151. V. Dil'tei [Wilhelm Dilthey]. *Opisatel'naia psikhologiia.* Trans. from the German E.D. Zaitseva. Ed. G.G. Shpet. Moscow: Russkii knizhnik, 1924.

152. Ch. Dikkens [Charles Dickens]. *Posmertnye zapiski Pikvikskogo kluba. Roman. Sokrashchennyi perevod s angliiskogo* [*The Pickwick Papers* (abridged translation from the English)]. Ed. A.G. [Gornfel'd] and G. Sh.[Shpet]. Moscow-Leningrad: Molodaia gvardiia, 1932.

153. Dzh. G. Bairon [George Gordon Byron]. *Misterii.* Translated by G. Shpet in keeping with the meters of the orginal [*razmerami podlinnika*]. Introduction and commentary by P.S. Kogan. Moscow and Leningrad: Academia, 1933. [Shpet's translation of Byron's "Manfred," "Cain," and "Heaven and Earth"; includes also notes by Shpet.]

154. Ch. Dikkens [Charles Dickens]. *Tiazhelye vremena* [*Hard Times*]. Trans. G. Shpet. Moscow: OGIZ, 1933. [**R**: Moscow, 1935 (without mention of Shpet's name).]

155. Ch. Dikkens [Charles Dickens]. *Holodnyi dom (Dlia detei starshego vozrosta i podrostkov)* [*Bleak House* (For older children and adolescents)]. Abridged translation by G. Shpet. Moscow: Molodaia gvardiia, 1933.

156. Leo Tolstoy. *Anna Karenina.* 2 vols. Trans. Constance Garnett. Ed. Bernard Guilbert Guerney and Gustavus Spett, with an introduction by Anatole Lunacharsky, and with wood engravings by Nikolas Piskariov. Moscow: Published for the Members of the Limited Editions Club of New York by the State Publishing House for Fiction and Poetry, 1933. [**R**: Cambridge, England: The UP, 1951.]

157. U.M. Tekkerei [W.M. Thackeray]. *Sobranie sochinenii* [Collected Writings]. 2 vols. Ed. G. Shpet. Moscow and Leningrad: Academia, 1933-34. [Shpet also wrote the notes to *Vanity Fair.*]

158. Ch. Dikkens [Charles Dickens]. *Posmertnye zapiski Pikvikskogo kluba* [*The Pickwick Papers*]. 3 vols. Trans. from the English A.V. Krivtsova and E.L. Lann. With the participation of and commentaries by G.G. Shpet. Moscow and Leningrad: Academia, 1933-34. [Shpet's commentary occupies the third volume (1934). **R**: Small portions of the commentary are available in *Psikhologiia* 438-84; for a full reprint, see Gustav Shpet. "Kommentarii k romanu Charl'za Dikkensa 'Posmertnye zapiski Pikvikskogo kluba.'" *Posmertnye zapiski Pikvikskogo kluba. Roman.* By Charlz Dikkens (Charles Dickens). Moscow: Nezavisimaia gazeta, 2000. 573-812.]

159. *Bol'shoi nemetsko-russkii slovar'. T. 1, A-K.* Pod redaktsiei E.A. Meier [Elisabeth Meyer], pri uchastii v redaktsionnoi rabote A.G. Gabrichevskogo, L. Iu. Gorodetskoi, A.G. Levental', N.N. Liamina, N.E. Mamuna, M.A. Petrovskogo, D.S. Usova, A.G. Chelpanova, G.G. Shpeta, B.I. Iarkho. Moscow: OGIZ RSFSR, 1934.

160. Dzh. G. Bairon [George Gordon Byron]. *Lirika i satira.* Ed. M.N. Rozanov. Moscow: Goslitizdat, 1935. [Contains on 241-62 "Bronzovyi vek," Shpet's translation of Byron's "Age of Bronze".]

161. Dzh. Berkli [George Berkeley]. *Tri razgovora mezhdu Gilasom i Filonusom* [*Three Dialogues between Hylas and Philonous*]. Moscow: Sotsekgiz, 1937. [Since Shpet translated this text while in exile, his name is not mentioned in the book.]

162. G.W.F. Gegel' [Hegel]. *Fenomenologiia dukha* [*Phänomenologie des Geistes*] (G.W.F. Gegel' [Hegel]. *Sochineniia T. 4*). Trans. G. Shpet. Moscow: Akademiia Nauk SSSR, Institut Filosofii, 1959. [**R**: Moscow: Nauka and RAN, 2000; St. Petersburg: Nauka, 1992 and 2002.]

163. A. Tennison [Alfred Tennyson]. "Enokh Arden" ["Enoch Arden"]. *Shpet 1995*: 17-38. [Translated by Shpet in Eniseisk in September-October 1935 but only published sixty years later by his daughter Marina Shtorkh.]

B. In Translation

a) In English

1. "Theatre as Art" [Trans. Michel Vale]. *Soviet Studies in Philosophy* 28.3 (Winter 1989-90): 61-88. [Translation of "Teatr kak iskusstvo".]

2. *Appearance and Sense: Phenomenology as the Fundamental Science and Its Problems.* Trans. Thomas Nemeth. Dordrecht: Kluwer, 1991. [Translation of *Iavlenie i smysl. Fenomenologiia kak osnovnaia nauka i eia problemy.* Moscow: Germes, 1914.]

3. "A Work on Philosophy" [Trans. Michel Vale]. *Russian Studies in Philosophy* 35.4 (1997): 43-59. [Translation of "Rabota po filosofii".]

4. "On Various Meanings of the Term "Form"" [Trans. John E. Bowlt]. *Experiment. A Journal of Russian Culture* 3 (1997): 194-99. [Translation of the synopsis and the discussion of Shpet's paper "O razlichnykh znacheniiakh termina 'formy,'" which he gave at GAKhN in July 1923. *So far the only publication of this text in any language.*]

5. "The Purge of Gustav Shpet." *Experiment. A Journal of Russian Culture* 3 (1997): 299-305. [Contains extracts, including a longer statement by Shpet (300-02), from the minutes of a session (4 June 1930) of the Commission conducting the purges at GAKhN, along with the text of the Resolution issued on 16 July 1930. *So far Shpet's statement has not been published in any other language.*]

6. "Philosophy and History." Trans. Isobel Martin. *Philosophical Writings* [Durham, England] 9 (1998): 40-48. [Translation of "Filosofiia i istoriia: Rech'."]

7. "On Wilhelm Dilthey's Concept of the Human Sciences." Trans. Erika Freiberger and George L. Kline. *Russian Studies in Philosophy* 37.4 (1999): 53-61. [Translation of excerpts from "Germenevtika i ee problemy" ("Hermeneutics and Its Problems").]

8. "Augustin"; "Simmel"; "The Contemporary Situation."; "Swoboda." Trans. Erika Freiberger. Ed. George L. Kline. *Gustav Shpet's Contribution to Philosophy and Cultural Theory.* Ed. Galin Tihanov. West Lafayette: Purdue UP, 2009. 223-45. [Translation of excerpts from "Germenevtika i ee problemy" ("Hermeneutics and Its Problems") in the present volume.]

9. "On the Limits of Scientific Literary Scholarship." Trans. Dušan Radunović and Galin Tihanov. *Gustav Shpet's Contribution to Philosophy and Cultural Theory.* Ed. Galin Tihanov. West Lafayette: Purdue UP, 2009. 248-49. [Translation in the present volume of the synopsis of "O granitsakh nauchnogo literaturovedeniia," a paper delivered by Shpet in 1924 at GAKhN.]

b) In German

10. *Die Hermeneutik und ihre Probleme (Moskau 1918)*. Trans. Erika Freiberger and Alexander Haardt. Ed. Alexander Haardt and Roland Daube-Schackat. Freiburg and Munich: Alber, 1993. [Translation of "Germenevtika i ee problemy."]

11. "Theater als Kunst." Trans. Walter Koschmal and Herta Schmid. *Balagan* 2.1 (1996): 62-87. [Translation of "Teatr kak iskusstvo."]

12. "Die Idee einer Grundlagenwissenschaft." Trans. Ulrich Schmid. *Russische Religionsphilosphen des 20. Jahrhunderts*. Ed. Ulrich Schmid. Freiburg: Herder, 2003. 270-75. [Translation of "Ideia osnovnoi nauki," a speech delivered by Shpet in January 1914 and included by him as a foreword to *Iavlenie i smysl.*]

c) In Italian

13. "Frammenti di estetica." Trans. Erica Klein and Anna Romei Longhena. *Kamen'. Rivista semestrale di poesia e filosofia* 2.2 (October 1992): 7-46; 3.3 (May 1993): 7-61; 3.4 (December 1993): 7-48. [Translation of *Esteticheskie fragmenty* (a new translation, by Margherita De Michiel and Stefania Sini, is forthcoming).]

14. "I problemi dell'estetica contemporanea." Trans. Maria Ghidini. *Poetiche ed estetiche del primo Novecento in Russia*. Ed. A. Dioletta Siclari. Parma: Edizioni Zara, 1993. 183-217. [Translation of "Problemy sovremennoi estetiki."]

15. "Linguaggio e senso. 1924-25." Trans. Michela Venditti. *Slavia* 3.4 (1994): 28-36. [Translation of an extract from "Iazyk i smysl."]

d) In Hungarian

16. "A belső költőőforma." Trans. István Orosz. *Helikon* 24.1-2 (1978): 65-83. [Translation of the chapter "Vnutrenniaia poeticheskaia forma" from *Vnutrenniaia forma slova.*]

17. "A hermeneutika és problémái (Részletek). Trans. István Orosz. *Helikon* 29.2 (1983): 218-42. [Translation of extracts from "Germenevtika i ee problemy."]

18. "Értelem és megértés." Trans. Gábor Sisák. *Helikon* 43.3 (1997): 273-91. [Translation of ch. 7 ("Smysl i urazumenie") from *Iavlenie i smysl.*]

e) In French

19. *La Forme Interne du Mot. Études et variations sur des thèmes de Humboldt*. Trans. Nicolas Zavialoff. Paris: Kimé, 2007. [French translation of *Vnutrenniaia forma slova*. Three more of Shpet's works are forthcoming in French translation, the result of concerted effort led by Porf. Maryse Dennes at the University of Bordeaux: "Le Sceptique et son âme." Trans. Françoise Teppe (French translation of "Skeptik

i ego dusha"); *Le Phénomène et le sens*. Trans. Maryse Dennes et Françoise Teppe (French translation of *Iavlenie i smysl*); "La Conscience et son propriétaire." Trans. Françoise Teppe (French translation of "Soznanie i ego sobstvennik").]

f) In Other Languages

20. "Hermenevtika in njeni problemi." Trans. Alfred Leskovec. *Phainomena* 9.33-34 (2000): 95-107. [Slovene translation of extracts from "Germenevtika i ee problemy."]

21. *Fenomenologiia. Etnicheska psikhologiia*. Trans. Aneta Ivanova. Sofia: Kritika i khumanizum, 2003. [Bulgarian translation of *Iavlenie i smysl* and *Vvedenie v etnicheskuiu psikhologiiu*.]

22. *Bigaku dansho*. Trans. Bin Kato. Tokyo: Suisei-sha, 2004. [Japanese translation of *Esteticheskie fragmenty*.]

23. *Hermeneutika i njezini problemi*. Trans. Josip Užarević. Zagreb: Breza, 2006. [Croatian translation of "Germenevtika i ee problemy."]

Literature on Gustav Shpet (1915-2009)

Galin Tihanov

The bibliography consists of titles in Russian and in other languages. The titles in Russian are organized in the following sections: monographs; dissertations; edited volumes; special issues; articles and reviews. Within each section, the entries are listed in chronological order, according to the date of publication; entries with the same date of publication are organized alphabetically, by the author's surname and by title (if more than one entry is available by the same author). This is also the principle followed when listing titles in other languages. To make the material more easily manageable, further chronological groupings are created in the large section containing articles and reviews in Russian. For earlier bibliographies of literature on Shpet, see I.L. Belen'kii, "Iz literatury o G.G. Shpete" *Nachala* 1 (1992): 92-93, comprising a total of 24 entries from 1922 to 1991 (it lists only two works on Shpet published in his lifetime); M. Venditti, "Zapadnoevropeiskaia nauchnaia literatura o Shpete i ego tvorchestve." *Nachala* 1 (1992): 94, with 10 entries spanning the period 1983-88; and Maryse Dennes's "Principales Publications sur Gustave Chpet en Russe," in *Slavica Occitania* 26 (2008): 515-27 (the earliest publication listed by Dennes appeared in 1970; Vashestov's article listed there as published in 1964 was actually published in 1984), as well as her bibliography of works on Shpet in languages other than Russian (529-33), comprising 50 entries spanning the period 1971-2008. It is a pleasant duty to acknowledge my significant debt to the work of my predecessors. Although I have endeavored to expand significantly the included material, this bibliography is not exhaustive. (The reader will notice the telling gap in the list of works on Shpet in the Soviet Union from 1929 (when Shpet became the target of a purging campaign at GAKhN) through to 1970—and the growing attention he has been enjoying since the mid-1980s.) Clarificfations about the content of a particular entry are given in square brackets, and only in those rare instances where the title does not refer directly to Shpet. For a list of the abbreviations used here, see "Bibliography of Gustav Shpet's Published Works (1901-2009)."

G.T.

A. In Russian

a) Monographs

1. Zinchenko, Vladimir. *Mysl' i slovo Gustava Shpeta: vozvrashchenie iz izgnaniia.* Moscow: Izdatel'stvo URAO, 2000 [**PT**: English, 2000].

2. Patrakhina, Tat'iana. *Gustav Shpet: ot fenomenologii k geremenevtike.* Ekaterinburg: Izdatel'stvo Ural'skogo universiteta, 2004.

3. Schastlivtseva, E.A. *Logika Zigvarta v ponimanii Shpeta.* Moscow: Kompaniia Sputnik +, 2004.

4. Shchedrina, Tat'iana G. *"Ia pishu kak ekho drugogo. . ." Ocherki intellektual'noi biografii Gustava Shpeta.* Moscow: Progress-Traditsiia, 2004.

5. Emel'ianov, Boris. *N.A. Berdiaev, P.A. Florenskii, G.G. Shpet.* Ekaterinburg: Diskurs-Pi, 2005.

6. Schastlivtseva, E.A. *Ocherki fenomenologii Gustava Shpeta.* St. Petersburg: Infoda, 2005.

7. Loshchevskii, K.V., and O.A. Koval'. *Gustav Shpet: mezhdu fenomenologiei i germenevtikoi.* St. Petersburg: Izdatel'stvo Sankt-Peterburgskogo gosudarstvennogo universiteta, 2006.

8. Schastlivtseva, E.A. *Edmund Gusserl': intellektual'nye batalii s Gustavom Shpetom.* St. Petersburg: Info-da, 2006.

9. Schastlivtseva, E.A. *Fenomenologicheskaia kontseptsiia Gustava Shpeta.* St. Petersburg: Info-da, 2006.

10. Schastlivtseva, E.A. *Vvedenie v "Istoriiu kak problemu logiki" Gustava Shpeta: posobie dlia studentov.* Kirov: n.p., 2006.

11. Shchedrina, T.G. *Arkhiv epokhi: tematicheskoe edinstvo russkoi filosofii.* Moscow: ROSSSPEN, 2008.

b) Dissertations

12. Iushmanova, T.N. *Nekotorye problemy kritiki germenevtiki kak metoda filosofsko-esteticheskikh interpretatsii kul'tury (Kriticheskii analiz idealisticheskikh germenevticheskikh kontseptsii Gustava Shpeta i Polia Rikera* [Paul Ricoeur]*).* Moscow: MGU, 1984.

13. Fedorova. L.V. *G.G. Shpet kak istorik russkoi filosofii.* Moscow: Akademiia obshchestvennykh nauk, 1991.

14. Valeitenok, V.V. *Problema iazyka v filosofii Gustava Shpeta.* Minsk: Belorusskii gosudarstvennyi universitet, 1992.

15. Krasil'nikov, S.E. *Istoriia kak problema logiki v filosofii istorii G. Shpeta*. Penza: Penzenskii gosudarstvennyi universitet, 1993.

16. Chernen'kaia, S.V. *Filosofskaia germenevtika G.G. Shpeta*. Moscow: MGU, 1999.

17. Mazur, S. Iu. *Obosnovanie gumanitarnogo znaniia v filosofii G.G. Shpeta: Logicheskii i metodologicheskii aspekty*. Moscow: RGGU, 2000.

18. Sal'nikov, E.V. *Germenevticheskaia kontseptsiia v filosofii G.G. Shpeta*. Moscow: Moskovskii pedagogicheskii gosudarstvennyi universitet, 2000.

19. Schastlivtseva, E.A. *Ideinye istoki i osnovaniia fenomenologii Shpeta*. Moscow: Moskovskii pedagogicheskii gosudarstvennyi universitet, 2003.

20. Shchedrina, T.G. *Filosofsko-metodologicheskii proekt Gustava Shpeta*. Moscow: Moskovskii pedagogicheskii gosudarstvennyi universitet, 2003.

21. Voronkov, V. V. *Problema soznaniia v filosofii V. S. Solov'eva, S. L. Franka i G.G. Shpeta: Sravnitel'nyi istoriko-filosofskii analiz*. Moscow: MGU, 2003.

22. Patrakhina, T.N. *Germenevticheskaia filosofiia G.G. Shpeta*. Ekaterinburg: Institut filosofii i prava Ural'skogo otdeleniia RAN, 2005.

c) Edited Volumes

23. *Shpetovskie chteniia v Tomske, 1991. Tvorcheskoe nasledie G.G. Shpeta i sovremennye gumanitarnye issledovaniia*. Ed. O.G. Mazaeva. Tomsk: Izdatel'stvo Tomskogo universiteta, 1991.

24. *Shpet v Sibiri: ssylka i gibel'*. Ed. N.V. Serebrennikov et al. Tomsk: Vodolei, 1995.

25. *G.G. Shpet/Comprehensio. Vtorye Shpetovskie chteniia. Tvorcheskoe nasledie G.G. Shpeta i sovremennye filosofskie problemy*. Ed. O.G. Mazaeva. Tomsk: Vodolei, 1997.

26. *G.G. Shpet/Comprehensio. Tret'i Shpetovskie chteniia. Tvorcheskoe nasledie G.G. Shpeta i filosofiia XX veka*. Ed. O.G. Mazaeva. Tomsk: Vodolei, 1999.

27. *Gustav Gustavovich Shpet. Arkhivnye materialy. Vospominaniia. Stat'i*. Ed. T.D. Martsinkovskaia. Moscow: Smysl, 2000.

28. *Tvorcheskoe nasledie Gustava Gustavovicha Shpeta v kontekste filosofskikh problem formirovaniia istoriko-kul'turnogo soznaniia (mezhdistsiplinarnyi aspekt). G.G. Shpet/Comprehensio. Chetvertye Shpetovskie chteniia*. Ed. O.G. Mazaeva. Tomsk: Izdatel'stvo Tomskogo universiteta, 2003.

29. *Gustav Shpet i sovremennaia filosofiia gumanitarnogo znaniia*. Ed. T.G. Shchedrina et al. Moscow: Iazyki slavianskikh kul'tur, 2006.

30. *Tvorcheskoe nasledie G.G. Shpeta v kontekste sovremennogo gumanitarnogo znaniia. Comprehensio: Piatye Shpetovskie chteniia.* Ed. O.G. Mazaeva. Tomsk: Izdatel'stvo Tomskogo universiteta, 2009.

d) Special Issues

31. *Nachala. Religiozno-filosofskii zhurnal* 1 (1992): 4-95.

32. *Voprosy psikhologii* 3 (2009): 65-122.

e) Articles and Reviews

In Shpet's Lifetime

1915-1922

33. Blonskii, P.P. "G. Shpet, 'Iavlenie i smysl.'" *Golos Moskvy* 65 (19 March 1915): 6. [A review of Shpet's book *Iavlenie i smysl* (*Appearance and Sense*).]

34. Kuznetsov, K.A. "Po povodu knigi G. Shpeta 'Iavlenie i smysl.'" *Izvestiia Odesskogo bibliograficheskogo obshchestva pri Novorosiiskom universitete* 4.1 (1915): 2-4. [A review of Shpet's book *Iavlenie i smysl* (*Appearance and Sense*).]

35. P.K. "Shpet, G. *Filosofskoe nasledstvo P.D. Iurkevicha. K sorokaletiiu ego smer-ti.* M., 1915." *Khristianskaia mysl'* 6 (1916): 141-42. [A review of Shpet's study of Iurkevich.]

36. Chelpanov, G. "Obzor knigi G. Shpeta 'Istoriia kak problema logiki. Ch. I. Mate-rialy.'" *Voprosy filosofii i psikhologii* 134 (1916): 316-24. [A review essay on Shpet's *Istoriia kak problema logiki* (*History as a Problem of Logic*).]

37. Ern, V. "Problema istorii (Po povodu dissertatsii G.G. Shpeta "Istoriia kak pro-blema logiki")." *Zhurnal Ministerstva Narodnogo Prosveshcheniia. Novaia Seriia* 6 (1917): 314-30. [A review essay on Shpet's *Istoriia kak problema logiki* (*History as a Problem of Logic*).]

38. Rainov, T. "Shpet, G.G. *Istoriia kak problema logiki. Kriticheskie i metodolog-icheskie issledovaniia. Chast' 1. Materialy,* M., 1916." *Vestnik Evropy* 1 (1917): 418-21. [A review essay on Shpet's *Istoriia kak problema logiki* (*History as a Problem of Logic*).]

39. Florovskii, G.V. "Gustav Shpet. Filosofskoe mirovozzrenie Gertsena. Knigoizdatel'stvo 'Kolos.' Petrograd, 1921." *Russkaia mysl'* [Prague and Berlin] 8-12 (1922): 228-31. [A review of Shpet's book *Filosofskoe mirovozzrenie Gertsena* (*Herzen's Philosophical Outlook*).]

40. Ivanovskii, V.N. "Logika istorii kak ontologiia edinichnogo." *Trudy Belarussko-go universiteta* 1 (1922): 14-25; 2-3 (1922): 35-49. [A review essay on Shpet's *Is-toriia kak problema logiki* (*History as a Problem of Logic*).]

1923

41. Belenson, Aleksandr. "Fragmenty." *Zhizn' iskusstva* 13 (888) (2 April 1923): 3-4. [A review of Shpet's *Esteticheskie fragmenty (Aesthetic Fragments)*. **R**: *Russkii ekspresionizm. Teoriia. Praktika. Kritika*. Ed. V.N. Terekhina. Moscow: IMLI RAN, 2005. 459-61.]

42. Florovskii, G.V. "G. Shpet, Ocherk razvitiia russkoi filosofii. Pervaia chast'. Petrograd, 1922." *Russkaia mysl'* [Prague and Berlin] 6-8 (1923): 424-31. [A review of Shpet's *Ocherk razvitiia russkoi filosofii. Ch. 1* (Outline of the Development of Russian Philosophy, Part I) within Florovskii's larger review article (419-31), which also deals with Ershov's *Puti razvitiia filosofii v Rossii* and Iakovenko's *Ocherki russkoi filosofii*.]

43. Gizetti, A. "Erudit i diletant (Po povodu dvukh filosofskikh knig)." *Zapsiki Peredvizhnogo Teatra P.P. Gaideburova i N.F. Skarskoi* 63 (22 October 1923): 8. [A review of Shpet's *Ocherk razvitiia russkoi filosofii. Ch. 1* (Outline of the Development of Russian Philosophy, Part I) and Kukliarskii's *Kritika tvorcheskogo soznaniia*.]

44. Nechkina, M.V. "G. Shpet, Ocherk razvitiia russkoi filosofii. Pervaia chast'. Petrograd, 1922." *Kazanskii bibliofil* 4 (1923): 105-08. [A review of Shpet's *Ocherk razvitiia russkoi filosofii. Ch. 1* (Outline of the Development of Russian Philosophy, Part I).]

45. Preobrazhenskii, P. "Gustav Shpet, Ocherk razvitiia russkoi filosofii. Pervaia chast'. Petrograd, 1922." *Pechat' i revoliutsiia* 3 (1923): 209-12. [A review of Shpet's *Ocherk razvitiia russkoi filosofii. Ch. 1* (Outline of the Development of Russian Philosophy, Part I).]

46. Prokof'ev, P.[D. Tschiževskij]. "G. Shpet, Ocherk razvitiia russkoi filosofii. Pervaia chast'. Petrograd, 1922." *Sovremenniia zapiski* [Paris] 18 (1923): 454-57. [A review of Shpet's *Ocherk razvitiia russkoi filosofii. Ch. 1* (Outline of the Development of Russian Philosophy, Part I). **R**: *Shpet 2006*: 385-89.]

1924-1928

47. Veidle, Vladimir [Signed V.V.]. "G. Shpet, Esteticheskie fragmenty." *Russkii sovremennik* 2 (1924): 302. [A review of Shpet's *Esteticheskie fragmenty (Aesthetic Fragments)*.]

48. Vinokur, G.O. "Shpet, G. Esteticheskie fragmenty, 1922-1923. I-III." *Chet i nechet: Al'manakh poezii i kritiki*. Moscow: Avtorskoe izd-e, 1925. 44-46. [A review of Shpet's *Esteticheskie fragmenty (Aesthetic Fragments)*; **R**: G.O. Vinokur. *Filologicheskie issledovaniia: Lingvistika i poetika*. Ed. M.I. Shapir and T.G. Vinokur. Moscow: Nauka, 1990. 87-88.]

49. Asmus, Valentin. "Filosofiia iazyka Vil'gel'ma Gumbol'dta v interpretatsii prof. G.G. Shpeta." *Vestnik Kommunisticheskoi akademii* 23 (1927): 250-65. [A review essay on Shpet's *Vnutrenniaia forma slova (The Inner Form of the Word)*.]

50. Lutokhin, D. "G. Shpet. Vvedenie v etnicheskuiu psikhologiiu." *Volia Rossii* [Prague] 8-9 (1927): 212-13. [A review of Shpet's *Vvedenie v etnicheskuiu psikhologiiu, Vyp. 1* (Introduction to Ethnic Psychology, Part I).]

51. Grigor'ev, M.S. "Vnutrenniaia forma slova." *Literatura i marksizm* 1.6 (1928): 3-42. [A review essay on Shpet's *Vnutrenniaia forma slova* (*The Inner Form of the Word*).]

After Shpet's Death

1950-1984

52. Zen'kovskii, V.V. *Istoriia russkoi filosofii*. Paris: YMCA Press, 1950. 2: 369-72. [A brief and as a whole unsympathetic account.]

53. Asmus, Valentin "Shpet, Gustav Gustavovich." *Filosofskaia entsiklopediia*. Moscow: Sovetskaia entsiklopediia, 1970. 5: 519-20.

54. Ivanov, V.V. "Shpet, G.G." *Kratkaia literaturnaia entsiklopediia*. Moscow: Sovetskaia entsiklopediia, 1975. 8: 782-83.

55. Ivanov, V.V. *Ocherki po istorii semiotiki v SSSR*. Moscow: Nauka, 1976. [On Shpet 267-70; 273.]

56. "Arkhiv Gustava Gustavovicha Shpeta (1879-1940)." *Zapiski otdela rukopisei GB SSSR im. V. I. Lenina* 39 (1978): 145-46. [A brief description of Shpet's papers preserved in the Russian State Library, f. 718 (written before the precise year of Shpet's death was known).]

57. Mitiushin, A.A. "Shpet, Gustav Gustavovich." *Bol'shaia Sovetskaia Entsiklopediia*. 3rd ed. Moscow: Sovetskaia entsiklopediia, 1978. 29: 469.

58. Iushmanova, T.N. "Semioticheskaia model' kul'tury v filosofksо-esteticheskoi kontseptsii Gustava Shpeta." *Nekotorye voprosy istorii i teorii estetiki: Filosofsko-esteticheskii sbornik*. Moscow. 4 (1981): 16-27.

59. Mitiushin, A.A. "O stat'e G. Shpeta 'Literatura.'" *Trudy po znakovym sistemam* 15 (1982): 149-50.

60. Guseva, A.V. "Kontseptsiia istoricheskogo soznaniia G.G. Shpeta." *IV Vsesoiuznye filosofskie chteniia molodykh uchennykh: Tezisy dokladov. Vol. 10: K. Marks* [Marx] *i sovremennost': filosofiia, sotsiologiia, ideologiia*. Ed. V.A. Malinin et al. Moscow: n.p., 1984. 48-50.

61. Vashestov, A.G. "Kontseptsiia 'novoi' kul'tury G.G. Shpeta: kriticheskii analiz." *IV Vsesoiuznye filosofskie chteniia molodykh uchennykh: Tezisy dokladov. Vol. 3: Filosofiia, politika, kul'tura*. Moscow: n.p., 1984. 87-90.

62. Vashestov, A.G. "Kritika fenomenologicheskogo metoda G.G. Shpeta." *Nekotorye voprosy istoriko-filosofskoi nauki (Po materialam konferentsii)*. Ed. Anatolii Kosichev et al. Moscow: Izdatel'stvo MGU, 1984. 51-59.

1988

63. Iakovlev, A.A. "K publikatsii stat'i G.G. Shpeta 'Istoriia kak predmet logiki.'" *Istoriko-filosofskii ezhegodnik 1988*. Moscow: Nauka, 1988. 288-89.

64. Mitiushin, A.A. "G. Shpet i ego mesto v istorii otechestvennoi psikhologii." *Vestnik MGU. Seriia 14. Psikhologiia* 2 (1988): 33-42.

65. Mitiushin, A.A. "Iz arkhiva Gustava Shpeta: voprosy istoricheskogo poznaniia i polemika s Badenskoi shkoloi." *Voprosy istorii estestvoznaniia i tekhniki* 3 (1988): 114-28. [Contains a letter (1928) by Shpet to D.M. Petrushevskii (120-25).]

66. Mitiushin, A.A. "Kommentarii" *Voprosy filosofii* 11 (1988): 91-92. [Commentary on Shpet's article "Teatr kak iskusstvo."]

67. Mitiushin, A.A. "Tvorchestvo G. Shpeta i problema istolkovaniia deistvitel'nosti." *Voprosy filosofii* 11 (1988): 93-104.

68. Pasternak, E.V. "Pamiati Gustava Gustavovicha Shpeta." *Voprosy filosofii* 11 (1988): 72-76.

69. Stakhorskii, S.V. "Kommentarii" *Iz istorii sovetskoi nauki o teatre: 20-e gody*. Ed. S.V. Stakhorskii. Moscow: GITIS, 1988. 216-24. [Commentary on Shpet's article "Teatr kak iskusstvo."]

1989

70. Mitiushin, A.A. "Ob issleodovanii G.G. Shpeta 'Germenevtika i ee problemy.'" *Kontekst 1989*. Moscow: Nauka, 1989. 229-30.

71. Mitiushin, A.A. "Printsipy etnicheskoi piskhologii v traktovke G. G. Shpeta." *Sovetskaia etnografiia* 6 (1989): 67-75.

72. Pasternak, E.V. "G.G. Shpet." *Sochineniia*. By G.G. Shpet. Moscow: Pravda, 1989. 3-8.

73. Serebrennikov, N.V. "Novye dannye o gibeli G.G. Shpeta." *Russkaia mysl'* [Paris] 3778 (2 June 1989): 13.

1990

74. Fedorova, L.F. "Neizvestnaia rabota o P.L. Lavrove." *Otechestvennaia filosofiia* 5 (1990): 153-55.

75. Losev, A.F. *Strast' k dialektike. Literaturnye razmishleniia filosofa*. Moscow: Sovetskii pisatel', 1990. [44-45 a brief, unsympathetic memoir of Shpet.]

76. Poizner, B.N. "Na otkrytie memorial'noi doski Gustavu Shpetu." *Press-biulleten' Sibirskogo Informatsionnogo Agentstva* 3 (1990): 8-9.

77. Polivanov, M.K. "O sud'be G.G. Shpeta." *Voprosy filosofii* 6 (1990): 160-64. [**R**: M.K. Polivanov. *Tainaia svoboda*. Ed. A.A. Baranovich-Polovanova. Moscow: Matematicheskii institut im. V.A. Steklova RAN, 2006. 87-97.]

78. Svas'ian, Karen. "Gustav Gustavovich Shpet." *Literaturnaia gazeta* 7 (14 February 1990): 5. [**R**: K.A. Svas'ian. *Rastozhdestvleniia*. Moscow: Evidentis, 2006. 252-67 (contains several footnotes added in 2006).]

1991

79. Bilyk, A.M., and Ia. M. Bylik. "K voprosu o razvitii filosofii na Ukraine v XVI-XVIII stoletiiakh." *Shpet 1991*: 42-44. [Shpet on the history of philosophy in Ukraine.]

80. Burova, I.N. "O postanovke nekotorykh filosofskikh problem v rabotakh G.G. Shpeta." *Shpet 1991*: 45-49.

81. Emel'ianov, B.V., and V.L. Livshits. "Neizdannaia rukopis' G.G. Shpeta 'Istochniki dissertatsii Chernyshevskogo.'" *Shpet 1991*: 40-42.

82. Evdokimov, P.G. "Gustav Shpet i problemy natsional'nogo soznaniia." *Shpet 1991*: 26-30.

83. Fedorova, L.V. "G. Shpet kak istroik russkoi filosofii." *Shpet 1991*: 32-36.

84. Freiberger, Erika. "Gustav Shpet: semiotika i germenevtika." *Shpet 1991*: 135-45. [Russian translation of Erika Freiberger's article in *Semiotica Ausrtiaca* (1987).]

85. Freiberger, Erika. "Filosofskaia lingvistika: V. Gumbol'dt i G.G. Shpet (semioticheskaia teoriia o vnutrennei forme)." *Shpet 1991*: 115-26.

86. Freiberger, Erika. "Vklad Shpeta v razvitie semioticheskoi estetiki." *Shpet 1991*: 160-71. [Russian translation of Erika Freiberger's paper at the 1986 International Shpet Symposium in Bad Homburg (Germany); this seems to be the only publication of the paper in any language.]

87. Freiberger-Sheikholeslami, Erika. "Gustav G. Shpet: fenomenologicheskaia semiotika i germenevtika." *Shpet 1991*: 145-60. [Russian translation of Erika Freiberger-Sheiholeslami's article in *Semiotic Theory and Practice: Proceedings of the Third International Congress of the IASS, Palermo, 1984* (1988).]

88. Freiberger-Sheikholeslami, Erika. "Gustav Shpet: teoriia interpretatsii kak teoriia ponimaniia." *Shpet 1991*: 127-34. [Russian translation of Erika Freiberger-Sheiholeslami's article in *American Contributions to the Tenth International Congress of Slavists. Sofia, September 1988* (1988).]

89. Freiberger-Sheikholeslami, Erika. "Vil'gel'm Gumbol'dt i Gustav Shpet: vnutrenniaia forma slova." *Shpet 1991*: 109-14.

90. Griaznov, A.F. "Sinteticheskaia filosfiia iazyka Gustava Shpeta." *Shpet 1991*: 65-67.

91. Iashchuk, A.N. "Problema istorii v filosofskom tvorchestve G.G. Shpeta." *Shpet 1991*: 83-85.

92. Kholstinin, R.N. "Filosofiia kak znanie-interpretatsiia G. Shpeta." *Shpet 1991*: 54-57.

93. Khvoshnianskaia, S.M., and V.M. Isakov. "Filosfiia iskusstva." *Shpet 1991*: 77-80. [On Shpet's philosophy of art.]

94. Kupreeva, I.V. "Tema 'Istoriia kak problema logiki' v filosofii Shpeta." *Shpet 1991*: 80-83.

95. Kuznetsov, V.G. "Germenevticheskaia fenomenologiia v kontekste filosofskikh vozzrenii Gustava Gustavovicha Shpeta." *Logos* 2 (1991): 199-214.

96. Mazaeva, O.G. "G.G. Shpet i A. Belyi: fenomenologicheskaia traditsiia v russkoi kul'ture." *Shpet 1991*: 50-53.

97. Meshcheriakova, E.I. "G. Shpet—sovremennoi teorii i praktike psikhologii." *Shpet 1991*: 30-31.

98. Novikova, T.M. "G.G. Shpet i fenomenologiia." *Shpet 1991*: 57-59.

99. Petritskii, V.A. "K tvorcheskoi biografii G.G. Shpeta (po materialam ekzempliara "Vvedeniia v etnicheskuiu psikhologiiu" s inskriptom filosofa)." *Shpet 1991*: 21-26.

100. Poizner, B.N. "Skeptik v otsenke Shpeta i vnutrenniaia forma tvorchestva." *Shpet 1991*: 88-95.

101. Povtoreva, S.M., and I.V. Shalyshkina. "Mnogoobrazie istolkovanii poniatiia "dukh" v proizvedeniiakh G.G. Shpeta." *Shpet 1991*: 15-18.

102. Serebrennikov, N.V. "Printsipy organizatsii teksta v 'Ocherke razvitiia russkoi filosofii' Shpeta." *Shpet 1991*: 44-45.

103. Shcheglov, V.V. "Ontologicheskaia interpretatsiia fenomenov kul'tury v filosofii G. G. Shpeta." *Vestnik Moskovskogo universiteta. Seriia 7. Filosofiia* 6 (1991): 40-44.

104. Shteiner, Petr [Peter Steiner]. "Gustav Shpet i Prazhskaia shkola: kontseptual'nye ramki dlia iazykovogo issledovaniia." *Shpet 1991*: 96-109 [Russian translation of Peter Steiner's 1990 article "Gustav Špet and the Prague School: Conceptual Frames for the Study of Language."]

105. Stakhorskii, Sergei. "Gustav Shpet." *Sovremennaia dramaturgiia* 5 (1991): 197-202.

106. Suleimanova, L.A. "K voprosu o printsipakh etnicheskoi psikhologii." *Shpet 1991*: 18-21.

107. Tomilov, V.G. "Gustav Shpet i stalinskii mif o russkoi filosofii." *Shpet 1991*: 36-40.

108. Turkulets, A.V. "Istoriko-logicheskie idei G.G. Shpeta." *Shpet 1991*: 86-88.

109. Venditti, M. [Michela Venditti]. "Rol' iazyka i ego otnoshenie k germenevtike v issledovaniiakh G.G. Shpeta." *Shpet 1991*: 68-72.

110. Volkov, A.G. "G. Shpet i B. Asaf'ev: slovo i intonatsiia." *Shpet 1991*: 75-77.

1992

111. [Author unknown]. "Ob 'Esteticheskikh fragmentakh' G.G. Shpeta" [1926]. Ed. M.K. Polivanov. *Shpet 1992*: 70-88.

112. Belen'kii, I.L. "Iz literatury o G.G. Shpete." *Shpet 1992*: 92-93.

113. Chubarov, I.M. "Shpet v Gettingene. Predislovie k publikatsii pisem G.I. Chelpanova, L.I. Shestova, B.V. Iakovenko, R.O. Iakobsona i dr." *Logos* 3 (1992): 243-46.

114. Gidini, Kandida [Maria Candida Ghidini]. "Osobennosti germenevtiki G.G. Shpeta." *Nachala* 2 (1992): 13-18.

115. Gornung, L.V. "Moi vospominaniia o professore Gustave Gustavoviche Shpete." [With notes by K.M. Polivanov]. *Shestye Tynianovskie chteniia. Tezisy dokladov i materialy dlia obsuzhdeniia*. Riga and Moscow: n.p., 1992. 172-85.

116. Kalinichenko. V.V. "Gustav Shpet: ot fenomenologii k germenevtike." *Logos* 3 (1992): 37-61.

117. Mazaeva, O.G., and B.N. Poizner. "Pervye Shpetovskie chteniia." *Shpet 1992*: 94-95.

118. Mitiushin, A.A. "Bibliografiia pechatnykh trudov G.G. Shpeta." *Shpet 1992*: 89-92.

119. Mitiushin, A.A. "O tom, kak "delaetsia" istoriia russkoi filosofii (Kommentarii k stat'e "Shpet")." *Shpet 1992*: 52-54.

120. Polivanov, M.K. "Ocherk biografii G.G. Shpeta." *Litsa. Biograficheskii al'manakh* 1 (1992): 7-43. [**R**: M.K. Polivanov. *Tainaia svoboda*. Ed. A.A. Baranovich-Polovanova. Moscow: Matematicheskii institut im. V.A. Steklova RAN, 2006. 97-141.]

121. Polivanov, M.K. "Ocherk biografii G. G. Shpeta." *Shpet 1992*: 4-25. [Abridged version of the article under the same title published in *Litsa* 1 (1992).]

122. Shtorkh, M.G. "Nemnogo proshlogo." *Shpet 1992*: 62-63. [On Shpet's contacts with Andrei Belyi, Nikolai Luzin, D. Zaslavskii, Fedor Berezhkov, and Leonid Grossman.]

123. Venditti, M. [Michela Venditti]. "Ob izuchenii tvorchestva G.G. Shpeta v stranakh Zapadnoi Evropy i Ameriki." *Shpet 1992*: 93-94. [Includes a bibliography of articles on Shpet in English, German, and French (10 entries in total, covering the period 1983-1988).]

124. Venditti, M. [Michela Venditti], and L.V. Fedorova. "V poiskakh tochnogo smysla (Predislovie k publikatsii)." *Shpet 1992*: 26-30. [Foreword to the posthumous publication of Shpet's "Rabota po filosofii."]

1993

125. Gur'ianova, M.A. "Vnutrenniaia forma slova v kontseptsii G.G. Shpeta." *Iz istorii nauki o iazyke. Mezhvuzovskii sbornik. Pamiati Iu. S. Maslova.* Ed. L.V. Sakharnyi. St Petersburg: Izdatel'stvo Sankt-Peterburgskogo universiteta, 1993. 54-69.

126. Serebrennikov, N.V. "O printsipakh organizatsii materiala v 'Ocherke razvitiia russkoi filosofii' Shpeta." *Traditsii v kontekste russkoi kul'tury: Sbornik statei i materialov.* Ed. V.A. Koshelev and A.V. Chernov. Cherepovets: Izd-vo ChGPI im. A.V. Lunacharskogo, 1993. 1: 16-19.

1994

127. Kuznetsov, V.G. and A.A. Mitiushin. "Primechaniia." *Filosofskie etiudy.* By G.G. Shpet. Moscow: Progress, 1994. 337-71. [Notes by Kuznetsov (337-49 on Shpet's essays "Soznanie i ego sobstvennik" and "Skeptik i ego dusha," and by Mitiushin (349-71) on Shpet's essay "Mudrost' ili razum?"]

128. Polivanov, M.K. "Gustav Shpet." *Filosofskie etiudy.* By G.G. Shpet. Moscow: Progress, 1994. 3-19.

129. Portnov, A.N. "G.G. Shpet: ot vnutrennei formy k smyslu." *Iazyk i soznanie: osnovnye paradigmy issledovaniia problemy v filosofii XIX-XX vv.* By A.N. Portnov. Ivanovo: Ivanovskii gosudarstvennyi universitet, 1994. 299-321.

130. Shcheglov, V.V. "Filosofiia smysla Gustava Shpeta." *Vestnik Moskovskogo universiteta. Seriia 7. Filosofiia* 3 (1994): 3-6.

1995

131. Chubarov, I.M. "Shpet." *Russkaia filosofiia. Slovar'.* Ed. M.A. Maslin. Moscow: Respublika, 1995. 623-24.

132. "Dokumenty." *Shpet 1995*: 256-304. [A selection of documents pertaining to Shpet's arrest, trial, exile, retrial, death, and rehabilitation.]

133. "Khronologiia zhizni G.G. Shpeta perioda arestov i ssylki 1935-1937 gg." *Shpet 1995*: 321-27.

134. Kogan, L.A. "Neprochitannaia stranitsa (G.G. Shpet—direktor Instituta nauchnoi filosofii: 1921-1923)." *Voprosy filosofii* 10 (1995): 95-105. [**T**: English, 1999.]

135. Martsinkovskaia, T.D. "Gustav Shpet." *50 vydaiushchikhsia psikhologov mira.* Ed. T.D. Martsinkovskaia and M.G. Iaroshevskii. Moscow: Mezhdunarodnaia pedagogicheskaia akademiia, 1995. 60-65. [**R**: *100 vydaiushchikhsia psikhologov mira* (Moscow, 1997) 122-28.]

136. Moiseev, V.I. "Shpet, Gustav Gustavovich." *Russkaia filosofiia. Malyi entsiklopedicheskii slovar'.* Moscow: Nauka, 1995. 603-08.

137. "On byl slishkom trezvym analitikom . . ." *Shpet 1995*: 305-15. [A record of the discussion at the evening in memory of Shpet, Tomsk, 17 November 1989.]

138. Pasternak, E.V. "Shpet, Gustav." *Sto russkikh filosofov: biograficheskii slovar'.* Ed. A.D. Sukhov. Moscow: Mirta, 1995. 303-06.

139. Poizner, B.N. "K godovshchine ubiistva Gustava Shpeta." *Shpet 1995*: 317-18.

140. Polivanov, M.K. "Zhizn' i trudy G. G. Shpeta." *Shpet 1995*: 5-15.

141. Rodi, F. [Frithjof Rodi]. "Germenevticheskaia logika v fenomenologicheskoi perspektive: Georg Mish [Misch], Hans Lipps i Gustav Shpet." *Nachala* 7 (1995): 41-46.

142. Shtorkh, M.G. "V Sibir' i iz Sibiri." *Shpet 1995*: 212-52.

143. Vilenchik, S.V. "Vospominaniia o G.G. Shpete." *Shpet 1995*: 253-55.

1996

144. Borisov, E.V. ""Iavlenie i smysl" G. Shpeta v kontekste razvitiia fenomenologii E. Gusserlia." *Iavlenie i smysl*. By Gustav Shpet. Tomsk: Vodolei, 1996. 183-91.

145. Emel'ianov, Boris V. "Gustav Gustavovich Shpet." *Ocherki russkoi filosofii: uchebnoe posobie*. By B.V. Emel'ianov. Ekaterinburg: Ural'skii gosudarstvennyi universitet. 1996. 51-59.

146. Martsinkovskaia, T.D. "Gustav Gustavovich Shpet—zhizn' kak problema tvorchestva." *Psikhologiia* 5-27.

147. Martsinkovskaia, T.D. ["Kommentarii"] *Dekorativnoe iskusstvo* 2-4 (1996): 28-29. [Commentary on the synopsis of Shpet's paper "Iskusstvo kak vid znaniia" (1926).]

148. Shtorkh, Marina. "Otkrytoe pis'mo v redaktsiiu zhurnala 'Logos.'" *Logos* 7 (1996): 212-15. [Contains interesting details of Shpet's biography.]

1997

149. Boiko, V.A. "Kontseptual'no-stilisticheskoe edinstvo 'Ocherka razvitiia russkoi filosofii' G.G. Shpeta." *Shpet 1997*: 195-98.

150. Chubarov, I.M. "Modifikatsiia fenomenologicheskoi paradigmy ponimaniia soznaniia v proekte germenevticheskoi dialektiki Gustava Gustavovicha Shpeta." *Shpet 1997*: 27-33.

151. Doroshenko, N.M. "G.G. Shpet o zadachakh logiki i metodologii istorii." *Shpet 1997*: 173-74.

152. Fedorova, L.V. "G. Shpet i A. Gertsen: ob istokakh istorizma i relaizma." *Shpet 1997*: 198-200.

153. Freiberger, Erika. "Gustav Shpet." *Shpet 1997*: 13-21. [Russian translation of Erika Freiberger's article in *Semiotics 1983* (1987).]

154. Freiberger, Erika. "Lingvisticheskie izyskaniia Rossiiskoi Akademii khudoz-hestvennykh nauk." *Shpet 1997*: 250-55. [Russian translation of Erika Freiberger's article in *Penn Review of Linguistics* 5 (1981).]

155. Fritiof, Rodi. [Frithjof Rodi]. "Programma 'germenevticheskoi logiki.' Sravnitel'nyi analiz podkhodov Gustava Shpeta i Georga Misha [Misch]." *Shpet 1997*: 36-50.

156. Gidini, Maria. [Maria Candida Ghidini]. "Slovo i real'nost'. K voprosu o rekon-struktsii filosofiia iazyka Gustava Shpeta." *Shpet 1997*: 51-98.

157. Gorbyleva, Zh. V. "Struktura i rechevaia kontaminatsiia: vnutrennee i vnesh-nee." *Shpet 1997*: 138-45. [On Shpet's concept of inner form.]

158. Inishev, I.N. "Mesto G.G. Shpeta v fenomenologicheskom dvizhenii." *Shpet 1997*: 21-24.

159. Iushmanova, T.N. "Germenevtika: iskusstvo perezhivaniia kul'tury." *Shpet 1997*: 98-102.

160. Khan, Anna [Anna Han]. "Poetika i filosofiia: Boris Pasternak i Gustav Shpet (Vvedenie k teme)." *Studia Slavica Academiae Scientiarum Hungaricae* 42 (1997): 301-16.

161. Kniazev, M.O. "O Gustave Shpete, filosofe, ne uplyvshem na 'filosofskom parokhode.'" *Russkaia mysl'* [Paris] 4195 (1997): 8.

162. Martsinkovskaia, T.D. "G.G. Shpet." *Vydaiushchiesia psikhologi Moskvy*. Ed. V.V. Rubtsov and M.G. Iaroshevskii. Moscow: n.p., 1997. 89-108. [**R**: 2007, same pagination.]

163. Martsinkovskaia, T.D. "Pamiati G.G. Shpeta." *Voprosy psikhologii* 5 (1997): 89-91.

164. Martsinkovskaia, T.D. "Problema psikhologii sotsial'nogo bytiia v tvorchestve G.G. Shpeta." *Voprosy iskusstvoznaniia* 2 (1997): 50-60.

165. Mazaeva, O.G. "Izuchenie tvorcheskogo naslediia G.G. Shpeta: itogi i perspe-ktivy." *Shpet 1997*: 3-10.

166. Persianov, Georgii [Protoierei]. "Gustav Shpet: Fenomenologiia Dukha i khris-tianskaia kul'tura." *Shpet 1997*: 201-12.

167. Poizner, B.N. "'Podrazhanie po vospominaniiu' i ustoichivost' kul'tury." *Shpet 1997*: 220-29. [Discussion of some aspects of Shpet's *Aesthetic Fragments* in their relevance for cultural theory.]

168. Polishchuk, A.V. "Predstavleniia o kul'ture v 'Ocherke razvitiia russkoi filoso-fii.'" *Shpet 1997*: 212-14.

169. Savin, A.E. "Interpretatsiia i kritika G.G. Shpetom filosofii Ed. Gusserlia." *Shpet 1997*: 24-27.

170. Serebrennikov, N.V. "Vzgliad na 'Esteticheskie fragmenty' Shpeta i nechto o L've Shestove." *Shpet 1997*: 191-92.

171. Stepanenko, S.B. "Gustav Shpet: fenomenologiia i semiotika." *Shpet 1997*: 130-36.

172. Sukhushin, D.V. "G.G. Shpet—L. V. Shestov o prirode i zadachakh filosofii." *Shpet 1997*: 186-90.

173. Surovtsev, V.A. "K voprosu o lektsiiakh po logike G.G. Shpeta 1911-1912 gg." *Shpet 1997*: 233-35.

174. Sycheva, S.G. "G.G. Shpet: Dukh i iazyk, forma i smysl." *Shpet 1997*: 136-38.

175. Syrov, V.N. "G.G. Shpet i problemy istoricheskogo poznaniia." *Shpet 1997*: 175-86.

176. Tartynov, M.G. "Germenevticheskii razum v kontseptsii ponimaniia G. Shpeta." *Shpet 1997*: 50-51.

177. Venditti, Mikela [Michela Venditti]. "Teatr kak korreliat poezii." *Shpet 1997*: 217-19. [On Shpet's theory of theatre.]

178. Zaikova, Ia. V. "Filosofiia iazyka G. Shpeta i filosofskii iazyk L. Shestova." *Shpet 1997*: 192-95.

179. Zhitkov, G.N. "Nekotorye aspekty fenomenologii G.G. Shpeta." *Shpet 1997*: 34-36.

1998

180. Babich, V.V. "Dialog poetik: Andrei Belyi, G.G. Shpet i M.M. Bakhtin." *Dialog. Karnaval. Khronotop* 1 (1998): 5-54.

181. Chubarov, I.M. "Gustav Gustavovich Shpet." *Antologiia fenomenologicheskoi filosofii v Rossii*. Ed. I.M. Chubarov. Moscow: Logos "Gnozis" RFO, 1998. 1: 315-20.

182. Pocheptsov, Georgii. *Istoriia russkoi semiotiki*. Moscow: Labirint, 1998. [179-93 on Shpet's hermeneutics and semiotics.]

183. Poleva, N.S. "Problema vnutrennei formy v trudakh uchenykh GAKhN." *Voprosy iskusstvoznaniia* 1 (1998): 280-95. [On Shpet's impact amongst the art historians associated with GAKhN.]

1999

184. Barbashina, E., and V. Boiko. "O poniatii predmetnosti u Gustava Shpeta i ob odnom pragmaticheskom moduse fenomenologicheskikh issledovanii smysla." *Shpet 1999*: 48-53.

185. Bazhanov, V., and N. Baranets. "Obraz filosofii v XX veke: G.G. Shpet o ponimanii i prirode filosofii." *Shpet 1999*: 115-16.

186. Chernen'kaia, S. "Poniatie vnutrennei formy V. Gumbol'dta i interpretatsiia G. Shpeta." *Shpet 1999*. 75-78.

187. Chubarov, I. "K voprosu ob otnoshenii germenevticheskoi dialektiki G.G. Shpeta k klassicheskoi germenevtike i problematike intersub ektivnosti u Ed. Gusserlia." *Shpet 1999*: 12-20.

188. Denn, Mariz [Maryse Dennes]. "Mesto 'tela' i kritika klassicheskoi psikhologii v proizvedenii Gustava Shpeta 'Vvedenie v etnicheskuiu piskhologiiu.'" *Logos* 2 (1999): 122-29.

189. Epina, L. "G.G. Shpet i problema ponimaniia russkoi filosofii XIX v." *Shpet 1999*: 180-87.

190. Garaeva, G. "Tendentsii russkoi filosofii: sovremennoe sostoianie i istoriko-filosofskii vzgliad G.G. Shpeta." *Shpet 1999*: 187-89.

191. Gidini, M.K. [Maria Candida Ghidini]. "Problema lichnosti mezhdu fenomenologiei i istoriei: vliianie Gustava Shpeta na raboty Grigoriia Vinokura dvadtsatykh godov." *Shpet 1999*: 163-73.

192. Gurko, E. "Fenomenologicheskaia reduktsiia v interpretatsii G.G. Shpeta i Ia. Patochki." *Shpet 1999*: 8-12.

193. Iashchuk, A. "Istorichnost' i 'osnovnaia nauka': V. Dil'tei i G.G. Shpet." *Shpet 1999*: 20-26.

194. Inishev, I. "Proekt germenevticheskoi fenomenologii v rabote G.G. Shpeta 'Iavlenie i smysl.'" *Shpet 1999*: 72-74.

195. Iurkshtovich, E. "Osobennosti esteticheskikh vozzrenii G. Shpeta." *Shpet 1999*: 107-12.

196. Khan, Anna [Anna Han]. "Boris Pasternak i Gustav Shpet. Opyt sopostavitel'noi kharakteristiki." *Wiener Slawistischer Almanach* 43 (1999): 27-67.

197. Krasil'nikov, M. "Shpet o Radishcheve." *Shpet 1999*: 189-93.

198. Lukina, N. "Filosofskoe nasledie G. Shpeta i stanovlenie sotsiokul'turnoi strategii poznaniia." *Shpet 1999*: 118-22.

199. Martsinkovskaia, T.D. "Problema esteticheskikh perezhivanii v kontseptsii G. Shpeta." *Voprosy psikhologii* 6 (1999): 31-38.

200. Mazaeva, O. "Issledovanie tvorchestva G.G. Shpeta (po materialam Shpetfonda v g. Tomske)." *Shpet 1999*: 3-8.

201. Niakash, T. [Tünde Nykas]. "Esteticheskie vozzreniia Gustava Shpeta i nekotorye osobennosti poetiki postsimvolizma." *Shpet 1999*: 136-45.

202. Noskov, A. "G.G. Shpet o russkoi filosofii." *Shpet 1999*: 174-80.

203. Poizner, B. "Istoriia kak predmet sinteziruiushchikh nauk." *Shpet 1999*: 123-33. [On Shpet's importance for a philosophy of the historical sciences.]

204. Portnov, A.N. "Filosofiia iazyka G.G. Shpeta." *Vnutreniaia forma slova*. By Gustav Shpet. Ivanovo: Ivanovskii gosudarstvennyi universitet, 1999. 287-304.

205. Sal'nikov, E. "Razrabotka germenevticheskikh kategorii v russkoi filosofii nachala XX veka (G.G. Shpet i A.F. Losev)." *Shpet 1999*: 197-202.

206. Savin, A. "Postanovka problemy iazyka v fenomenologicheskoi filosofii Gustava Gustavovicha Shpeta." *Shpet 1999*: 27-31.

207. Schmid, G. [Herta Schmid]. "Iz stat'i: 'Gustav Shpet: proekt germenevticheskogo napisaniia istorii literatury.'" *Shpet 1999*: 146-57. [Abridged Russian translation of Herta Schmid's article published in *Wiener Slawistischer Almanach* 32 (1993).]

208. Shchedrina, T. "Dialogichnost' obshchestvennogo soznaniia. Aspekty metodologii gumanitarnogo issledovaniia v rabote G. Shpeta 'Soznanie i ego sobstvennik.'" *Shpet 1999*: 116-18.

209. Shcheglov, V. "Filosofsko-metodologicheskie osobennosti ponimaniia G.G. Shpetom 'polozhitel'noi nauki.'" *Shpet 1999*: 112-14.

210. Shcheglova, L. "G.G. Shpet o tvorcheskoi aristokratii v Rossii nachala XIX veka." *Shpet 1999*: 193-96.

211. Sheirman, E. "Otnoshenie dialekticheskikh novatsii G.G. Shpcta i A.F. Loseva k fenomenologicheskomu proektu." *Shpet 1999*: 202-04.

212. Shtorkh, Marina, and Anna Margolis. "Neizvestnyi Shpet." *Russkaia mysl'* [Paris] 4269 (13-19 May 1999): 19.

213. Soldatova, D. "Problema 'Ia' v triadichnom kontrsootnoshenii." *Shpet 1999*: 46-48. [On Shpet's philosophy of the subject.]

214. Stepanenko, S. "G. Shpet: fenomenologiia i poniatie filosofii." *Shpet 1999*: 44-46.

215. Sukhushin, D. "Traditsiia—novatsiia. G. Shpet—L. Shestov." *Shpet 1999*: 210-12.

216. Sycheva, S. "Poniatie vnutrennei formy u G. Shpeta." *Shpet 1999*: 78-82.

217. Venditti, M [Michela Venditti]. "Ponimanie Shpetom literatury i nekotorye zamechaniia k ego Kommentariiam k 'Posmertnym zapiskam Pikvikskogo kluba Ch. Dikkensa.'" *Shpet 1999*: 157-63.

218. Volkov, A. "Slovo i sotsial'naia real'nost' v fenomenologii G. Shpeta." *Shpet 1999*: 60-66.

219. Zinchenko, E. "Shpet protiv ego-logii Gusserlia." *Shpet 1999*: 35-38.

220. Zinchenko, V. "G.G. Shpet i M.M. Bakhtin." *Voprosy psikhologii* 6 (1999): 110-18.

2000

221. "Arkhivnye materialy." *Shpet 2000*: 15-30. [Various documents related to Shpet's life.]

222. Chubarov, I.M. "K voprosu ob otnoshenii germenevticheskoi dialektiki Gustava Gustavovicha Shpeta k klasicheskoi germenevtike i problematike pozdnego Gusserlia [Husserl]." *Antologiia fenomenologicheskoi filosofii v Rossii*. Ed. I.M. Chubarov. Vol. 2. Moscow: Logos and "Progress-Traditsiia," 2000. 37-47.

223. Iaroshevskii, M.G. "Versiia G.G. Shpeta o russkoi 'oppozitsionnoi intelligentsii.'" *Shpet 2000*: 329-34.

224. Maksimova, T.G. "Iz vospominanii" [Recorded by T. Bogdanova]. *Shpet 2000*: 155-69. [Memoirs by one of Shpet's daughters.]

225. Martsinkovskaia, T.D. "G.G. Shpet: vzgliad iz budushchego." *Shpet 2000*: 270-83.

226. Martsinkovskaia, T.D. "Gustav Shpet kak istorik psikhologii." *Shpet 2000*: 250-69.

227. Martsinkovskaia, T.D. "Problema esteticheskikh perezhivanii v kontseptsii G.G. Shpeta." *Shpet 2000*: 236-49.

228. Mikhailov, A.V. "Sovremennaia istoricheskaia poetika i nauchno-filosofskoe nasledie Gustava Gustavovicha Shpeta (1879-1940)." *Obratnyi perevod*. By A.V. Mikhailov. Ed. D.R. Petrov and S. Iu. Khurumov. Moscow: Iazyki russkoi kul'tury, 2000. 526-34. [Posthumous publication of a text written by Mikhailov before the precise year of Shpet's death (1937) became known; **R**: Aleksandr Mikhailov. *Izbrannoe: Istoricheskaia poetika i geremenevtika*. St. Petersburg: Izd-vo S.-Peterburgskogo universiteta, 2006.]

229. Mil'don, V.I. "Avtobiograficheskoe v tvorchestve G.G. Shpeta (nabroski k psikhologicheskomu portretu)." *Shpet 2000*: 295-303.

230. Mil'don, V.I. "Simpaticheskoe ponimanie: teoriia poeticheskoi rechi v ponimanii G.G. Shpeta." *Shpet 2000*: 284-94.

231. Poleva, N.S. "Osnovnye daty biografii G.G. Shpeta." *Shpet 2000*: 5-14.

232. Poleva, N.S. "Vnutrenniaia forma khudozhestvennogo proizvedeniia kak predmet nauchnogo issledovaniia." *Shpet 2000*: 304-19. [On Shpet's concept of inner form in the context of GAKhN's theoretical pursuits.]

233. Severtseva, O.S. "G.G. Shpet: fragmenty biografii." *Shpet 2000*: 170-82.

234. Severtseva, O.S. "Kommentarii k materialam sledstvennykh del sotrudnikov GAKhN." *Shpet 2000*: 31-40. [On Shpet's purge, arrest, trial, and exile in the wider context of GAKhN's persecution and closure.]

235. Shchedrina, T.G. "Razvitie idei istorii v filosofii Gustava Shpeta." *Filosofskie issledovaniia* 4 (2000): 175-86.

236. Stefanenko, T.G. "G.G. Shpet i etnopsikhologiia kontsa XX veka." *Shpet 2000*: 320-29.

237. Stepun, Fedor. *Byvshee i nesbyvsheesia.* 2nd ed. St. Petersburg: Aleteiia, 2000. [On Shpet 148-49; originally published in German.]

238. Zhdan, A.N. "Fenomen Shpeta: o roli metodologii v nauchnom issledovanii." *Shpet 2000*: 195-202.

239. Zhdan, A.N. "G.G. Shpet i sovremennaia psikhologiia." *Shpet 2000*: 185-95.

240. Zinchenko, V.P. "Gustav Gustavovich Shpet: vozvrashchenie iz izgnaniia." *Shpet 2000*: 203-35.

2001

241. Denn, Mariz [Maryse Dennes]. "Nasledie Vl. Solov'eva i russkoi religioznoi mysli v rabotakh G. Shpeta." *Solov'evskii sbornik.* Ed. I. Borisova and A. Kozyrev. Moscow: Fenomenologiia-Germenevtika, 2001. 135-44.

242. Lektorskii, V.A. "Nemetskaia filosofiia i rossiiskaia gumanitarnaia mysl': S.L. Rubinshtein i G.G. Shpet." *Voprosy filosofii* 10 (2001): 129-39. [R: *Shpet 2006*: 62-81.]

243. Marchenko, O.V. "Shpet, Gustav." *Novaia filosofskaia entsiklopediia v chetyrekh tomakh.* Ed. V.S. Stepin et al. Moscow: Mysl', 2001. 4: 394-95.

244. Osuka, F., and T. Kiube, "Transformatsiia kontseptsii 'simvola' i 'lingvisticheskii povorot' v filosofii iazyka (teoriia iazyka G.G. Shpeta i A.F. Loseva)." *Russkaia kul'tura na poroge novogo veka.* Ed. Tetsuo Mochizuki et al. Saporo: Slavic Research Centre, 2001. 211-32.

245. Shchedrina, T.G. "Ideiia 'sobornosti' v interpretatsii G.G. Shpeta." *Russkaia filosofiia: mnogoobrazie v edinstve. Materialy VII Rosiiskogo simpoziuma istorikov russkoi filosofii.* Ed. P.V. Kalitin et al. Moscow: EkoPress-2000, 2001. 243-48.

2002

246. Alekseev, A.P., and V.G. Kuznetsov. "Shpet, Gustav Gustavovich." *Filosofy Rossii XIX-XX stoletii. Biografii. Idei. Trudy.* Ed. P.V. Alekseev. Moscow: Akademicheskii proekt, 2002. 1101-03.

247. Chubarov, I. "Dil'tei [Dilthey] i Shpet. Granitsy germenevtiki." *Germenevtika, psikhologiia, istoriia.* Ed. Nikolai Plotnikov. Moscow: Tri kvadrata, 2002. 160-76.248. Denn, Mariz [Maryse Dennes]. "Imiaslavie i ego filosofskie proroki: ot substituta glossolalii k obosnovaniiu vremennosti." *Voprosy filosofii* 12 (2002): 93-104. [A discussion of Losev's and Shpet's views on language and temporality.]

249. Fedorova, L.V. "Gustav Shpet o russkoi kul'ture: evropeiskoe bytie ili vostochnyi anabioz?" *Vostok-Zapad. Istoriko-literaturnyi al'manakh: 2002.* Ed. V.S. Miasnikov. Moscow: Izdatel'skaia firma "Vostochnaia literatura" RAN, 2002. 163-83.

250. [Fedorova, L.V.] "Pervye izdaniia rabot G.G. Shpeta." *Istoriia* 1166-67.

251. Miasnikov, V.S. "Gustav Shpet: trudy i gody." *Istoriia* 5-32.

252. Samoikina, A.A. "Problema sub 'ekta i sub' ektivnosti v fenomenologii Shpeta." *Sbornik tezisov Tret'ego Vserosiiskogo filosofskogo kongressa.* Ed. G.V. Drach et al. Rostov: Izdatel'stvo Severo-Kavkazskogo nauchnogo tsentra vysshei shkoly, 2002. 361-62.

253. Shchedrina, T.G. "Sobornaia 'sfera razgovora' russkikh filosofov (Vladimir Solov'ev i Gustav Shpet)." *Solov'evskie issledovaniia* 4 (2002): 19-38.

254. Shchedrina, T.G. "U istokov russkoi semiotiki i strukturalizma (issledovanie semeinogo arkhiva Gustava Shpeta)." *Voprosy filosofii* 12 (2002): 75-78.

255. Shchedrina, T.G. "Vybor Gustava Shpeta: 'Ostat'sia, chtoby deistvovat' . . .' (po materialam pisem i dnevnikov)." *Russkaia filosofiia i vlast' (k 80-letiiu "filosofskogo parokhoda")*: *Materialy VI Vserossiiskoi nauchnoi zaochnoi konferentsii.* Ed. B.V. Emel'ianov and O.B. Ionaitis. Ekaterinburg: Ural'skii gosudarstvennyi universitet, 2002: 59-63.

256. Shtorkh, M.G. "V Rossii dobrogo cheloveka staviat vyshe obrazovannogo" *Izvestiia. Prilozhenie "Nauka."* 22 February 2002. [An interview with Shpet's daughter, Marina Shtorkh, conducted by Natal'ia Ivanova-Gladil'shchikova.]

2003

257. Antipov, G.A. "Aktual'nost' Gustava Shpeta." *Shpet 2003*: 172-79.

258. Bukovskaia, N.V. "Gustav Shpet: demarkatsiia mudrosti i razuma." *Shpet 2003*: 38-44.

259. Denn, Mariz [Maryse Dennes]. "Izuchenie tvorchestva G.G. Shpeta vo Frantsii." *Shpet 2003*: 501-05.

260. Denn, Mariz [Maryse Dennes]. "Rol' i znachenie ssylki na nominalizm v tekste G. Shpeta 'Iavlenie i smysl.'" *Shpet 2003*: 24-37.

261. Egorov, B.F. "G.G. Shpet o russkoi kul'ture XIX veka." *Shpet 2003*: 319-26.

262. Epina, L.V. "Tvorchestvo G.G. Shpeta i problemy metodologii istoriko-filosofskikh issledovanii." *Shpet 2003*: 486-90.

263. Ermakov, V.S. "Shpet." *Spravochnik po istorii filosofii: khornologicheskii, personifitsiorvannyi.* By V.S. Ermakov. St. Petersburg: Soiuz, 2003. 262-63.

264. Gidini, Maria Kandida [Maria Candida Ghidini]. "Spetsifika esteticheskogo predmeta: otreshennoe bytie u Shpeta i u Bakhtina." *Shpet 2003*: 370-78.

265. Gornova, G.V. "'Ia-tsentr' zhiznennogo mira." *Shpet 2003*: 168-71. [On Shpet's philosophy of the subject.]

266. Iakovenko, B.V. *Istoriia russkoi filosofii.* Trans. M.F. Solodukhina. Moscow:

Respublika, 2003. [On Shpet 381-82; 430-31; originally published in Czech in 1938.]

267. Iurkshtkovich, E.A. "Vozmozhnosti germenevtiki kak metoda ratsional'nogo myshleniia v filosofii G. Shpeta." *Shpet 2003*: 124-32.

268. Karpitskii, N.N. "Fenomenologiia istoricheskogo stanovleniia." *Shpet 2003*: 455-65. [On the implications of Shpet's concept of inner form for a phenomenological philosophy of history.]

269. Kelle, V. Zh. "Istoriografiia i istochnikovedenie. Istoriia kak nauka v traktovke G.G. Shpeta." *Novaia i noveishaia istoriia* 2 (2003): 148-64.

270. Khan [Han], Anna. "Boris Pasternak i Gustav Shpet: lingvofilosofskii aspekt sopostavleniia." *Shpet 2003*: 340-69.

271. Khlebnikov, M.V. "K voprosu o russkom konservatizme (opyt fenomenologii v ponimanii otechestvennogo filosofstvovaniia)." *Shpet 2003*: 481-85. [On Shpet's usefulness for understanding Russian conservatism.]

272. Kirilenko, E.I. "Printsipy vnutrennei formy i problema telesnosti." *Shpet 2003*: 210-16. [On the implications of Shpet's concept of inner form for a philosophy of the body.]

273. Kuz'min, A.A. "Fenomenologiia lichnosti v filosofii E. Gusserlia i G.G. Shpeta." *Shpet 2003*: 88-93.

274. Maksimenko, L.A. "Problema pervichnogo znaniia v filosofii G.G. Shpeta." *Shpet 2003*: 49-51.

275. Margolis, E.L. "Homo semanticus. Aktualizatsiia lingvisticheskikh idei G.G. Shpeta v rabotakh Anny Vezhbitskoi [Wierzbicka]." *Shpet 2003*: 254-67.

276. Meshcheriakova, T.V. "K voprosu ob opredelenii poniatiia 'istoricheskaia individual'nost'.'" *Shpet 2003*: 466-69. [On Shpet's philosophy of history and individuality.]

277. Mikhailov, I.A. "Germenevticheskaia logika G. Shpeta i G. Lippsa." *Shpet 2003*: 114-23.

278. Misik, M.A. "Poetika istorii: predely istoricheskoi reprezentatsii." *Shpet 2003*: 444-54. [Explores possible parallels between Shpet and Hayden White on the philosophy and logic of historiography.]

279. Naiman, E.A. "'Sovremennye povtoreniia' Gustava Shpeta." *Shpet 2003*: 387-93.

280. Orekhov, S.I. "Filosofiia i filosofstvovanie po G.G. Shpetu." *Shpet 2003*: 45-48.

281. Patrakhina, T.N. "O vliianii G. G. Shpeta na formirovanie strukturnoi lingvistiki v Rossii." *Shpet 2003*: 249-53.

282. Podshibiakina, L.V. "Fenomenologicheskoe prisustvie smysla." *Shpet 2003*: 244-48. [On Shpet's phenomenology of sense.]

283. Poizner, B.N. "Dukh naroda: Shpet o Pushkine." *Shpet 2003*: 331-39.

284. Sal'nikov, E.V. "Osnovnye polozheniia germenevticheskoi logiki G.G. Shpeta." *Shpet 2003*: 133-38.

285. Samoikina, A.A. "Razvitie gusserlevskogo poniatiia smysla v filosofii G. Shpeta." *Shpet 2003*: 240-43.

286. Savin, A.E. "Poniatie reduktsii v 'Ideiakh I' E. Gusserlia i 'Iavlenii i smysle' G.G. Shpeta." *Shpet 2003*: 15-23.

287. Schastlivtseva, E. "Gustav Shpet: ekzistentsial'no-ontologicheskie motivy tvorchestva Gertsena." *Chelovek i Vselennaia* 6 (2003): 184-88.

288. Serebrennikov, N.V. "Shpet kak literaturnyi kritik." *Shpet 2003*: 327-30.

289. Shchedrina, T.G. "Arkhiv kak kommunikativnyi kontekst v istoriko-filosofskoi rekonstruktsii: Issledovanie rukopisnykh materialov Gustava Shpeta." *Filosofskii vek. Al'manakh* 24 (2003): 256-63.

290. Shchedrina, T.G. "Filosofiia Platona v interpretatsii Vladimira Solov'eva i Gustava Shpeta." *Solov'evskie issledovaniia* 7 (2003): 50-60.

291. Shchedrina, T.G. "Idei Gustava Shpeta v problemnom pole sovremennykh filosofskikh diskussii." *Shpet 2003*: 491-500.

292. Shchedrina, T.G. "Kommunikativnoe prostranstvo russkogo filosofskogo soobshchestva (opyt rekonstruktsii filosofskogo arkhiva Gustava Shpeta)." *Voprosy filosofii* 8 (2003): 106-18.

293. Shchedrina, T.G. "'Razgovor' s filosofom (po materialam semeinogo arkhiva Gustava Shpeta)." *Kul'turologiia. Daidzhest* (RAN INION) 1 (2003): 193-213.

294. Shtorkh, M.G. "Gustav Shpet i Iurgis Baltrushaitis (po materialam semeinogo arkhiva G. Shpeta)." *Shpet 2003*: 580-85.

295. Soldatova, D.V. "Deistvitel'nost' v trudakh Shpeta: ot fenomenologicheskogo k germenevticheskomu rassmotreniiu." *Shpet 2003*: 221-26.

296. Stepanov, E.A. "Predposylki dialogichnogo ponimaniia slova u Gustava Shpeta." *Shpet 2003*: 139-44.

297. Sukhanov, V.A. "Problema esteticheskoi real'nosti v rabotakh G.G. Shpeta i M.M. Bakhtina." *Shpet 2003*: 379-86.

298. Sukhushin, DV. "Problema interpretatsii spetsifiki filosofii v tvorchestve G. Shpeta i L. Shestova." *Shpet 2003*: 514-22.

299. Tarnapol'skaia, G.M. "Problema smysloporozhdeniia v filosofii iazyka G. Shpeta." *Shpet 2003*: 268-72.

300. Venditti, Mikela [Michela]. "Filosofiia P.D. Iurkevicha v istolkovanii V.S. Solov'eva i G.G. Shpeta." *Shpet 2003*: 506-13.

301. Viakhireva, S.R. "Simmetrichnyi dialog shpetovskogo slova i asimmetrichnyi dialog arabskogo slova." *Shpet 2003*: 273-81.

302. Volkov, A.G. "G. Shpet—Zh. [Jacques] Derrida: ot ocharovaniia slovom k razocharovaniiu v pis'me." *Shpet 2003*: 394-402.

303. Vozilov, V.V. "G.G. Shpet i evoliutsiia predstavlenii o russkom nigilizme." *Shpet 2003*: 470-80.

2004

304. Chubarov, I.M. "Simvol, affekt i mazokhizm. Obrazy revoliutsii u A. Belogo i A. Bloka." *Novoe literaturnoe obozrenie* 65 (2004): 131-47. [133-36 on Shpet's negative assessment of Blok and praise for Belyi.]

305. Nikolaev, N.I. "Bakhtin, Nevel'skaia shkola filosofii i kul'turnaia istoriia 1920-kh godov." *Bakhtinskii sbornik* 5 (2004): 210-80. [On Shpet 228-29; 266-67 and Section 3: "Filosofskaia germenevtika: G.G. Shpet i M.M. Bakhtin" (268-72).]

306. Samoikina, A.A. "Kantovskie motivy v tvorchestve G.G. Shpeta." *Filosofiia Kanta i sovremennost'*. Ed. A.I. Aleshin. Moscow: Izdatel'stvo RGGU, 2004. 128-33.

307. Serebrennikov, N.V. "Shpet, Gustav Gustavovich." *Tomsk ot A do Ia. Kratkaia entsiklopediia goroda*. Ed. N.M. Dmitrienko. Tomsk: Izdatel'stvo nauchno-tekhnicheskoi literatury, 2004. 422–23.

308. Shchedrina, T.G. "Gustav Shpet kak filosof nauki." *Epistemologiia i filosofiia nauki* 2 (2004): 212-16.

309. Shtainer, P. [Peter Steiner]. "*Tropos logikos*: filosofiia istorii Gustava Shpeta." *Voprosy filosofii* 4 (2004): 154-63. [Russian translation of Steiner's 2003 article "*Tropos Logikos*: Gustav Shpet's Philosophy of History."]

310. Zenkin, Sergei. "Forma vnutrenniaia i vneshniaia (Sud'ba odnoi kategorii v russkoi teorii XX v.)." *Russkaia teoriia 1920-1930-e gody*. Ed. S. Zenkin. Moscow: RGGU, 2004. 147-67. [156-58 on Shpet's concept of inner form.]

2005

311. Chernysheva, A.V. "Problema istolkovaniia deistvitel'nosti v filosofii iazyka G.G. Shpeta." *Filosofiia i budushchee tsivilizatsii: Tezisy dokladov i vystuplenii IV Rossiiskogo filosofkogo kongressa*. Ed. V.A. Sadovnichii et al. Vol. 2. Moscow: Sovremennye tetradi, 2005. 345-46.

312. Fedorova, L.V., and T.G. Shchedrina. "[Review of] *Tvorcheskoe nasledie Gustava Gustavovicha Shpeta v kontekste filosofskikh problem formirovaniia istoriko-kul'turnogo soznaniia (mezhdistsiplinarnyi aspekt). G.G. Shpet/Comprehensio.*

Chetvertye Shpetovskie chteniia. Ed. O.G. Mazaeva. Tomsk: Izdatel'stvo Tomskogo universiteta, 2003." *Voprosy filosofii* 1 (2005): 176-78.

313. Kantor, V. "Gustav Shpet: russkaia filosofiia kak pokazatel' evropeizatsii Rossii." *Vestnik Evropy* 13-14 (2004-05): 191-206.

314. Kantor, V. "Gustav Shpet: russkaia filosofiia v kontekste kul'tury." *Voprosy literatury* 3 (2005): 263-92.

315. Martsinkovskaia, T.D. "G.G. Shpet: parafraz na sovremennuiu temu." *FP* 454-68. [T: French, 2008.]

316. Shchedrina, T.G. "A.S. Pushkin v filosofskom nasledii Gustava Shpeta." *Pushkinskii sbornik.* Ed. I. Loshchilov and I. Surat. Moscow: Tri kvadrata, 2005. 350-55.

317. Shchedrina, T.G. "Gustav Shpet i sovremennaia filosofiia gumanitarnogo znaniia." *Voprosy filosofii* 3 (2005): 167-74. [Conference report on the 2004 Moscow Shpet conference, the proceedings of which were published in 2006 as *Gustav Shpet i sovremennaia filosofiia gumanitarnogo znaniia.*]

318. Shchedrina, Tat'iana. "Gustav Shpet: put' filosofa." *Mysl* 5-32.

319. Shchedrina, Tat'iana. "Gustav Shpet: zhizn' v pis'makh." *Gustav Shpet: zhizn' v pis'makh. Epistoliarnoe nasledie.* Ed. T.G. Shchedrina. Moscow: ROSSPEN, 2005. 5-14.

320. Shchedrina, Tat'iana. "Kommentarii." *Gustav Shpet: zhizn' v pis'makh. Epistoliarnoe nasledie.* Ed. T.G. Shchedrina. Moscow: ROSSPEN, 2005. 509-697.

321. Shchedrina, T.G. "Zhiznennyi mir Gustava Shpeta (Razgovor v pis'makh)." *Vestnik Evropy* 13-14 (2004-05): 207-18.

322. Shiian, A.A. "Shpet kak platonik." *Δόξα /Doksa. Zbirnik naukovikh prats' z filosofii ta filologii.* Ed. N.A. Ivanova-Georgievska and V.L. Levchenko. Vol. 8. Odessa: ONU im. I.I. Mechnikova, 2005. 123-29.

323. Venditti, Mikela [Michela Venditti]. "Obrazy 'Afin i Ierusalima' u G. Shpeta, L. Shestova i S. Averintseva." *Biulleten' Biblioteki istorii russkoi filosofii i kul'tury "Dom A. F. Loseva."* 2 (2005): 68-71.

324. Zhivov, V. "Apologiia Gertsena v fenomenologicheskom ispolnenii ("Filosofskoe mirovozzrenie Gertsena" G.G. Shpeta)." *Novoe literaturnoe obozrenie* 71 (2005): 166-74. [T: English, 2005.]

2006

325. Binevskii, A.A. "Ratsionalizm filosofii Gustava Shpeta: mezhdu evropeiskoi i vostochnoi traditsiiami." *Shpet 2006*: 330-39.

326. Chernysheva, A.V. "Filosofiia iazyka G.G. Shpeta kak osnova nauki o iazyke." *Obshchestvo—Iazyk—Kul'tura: aktual'nye problemy vzaimodeistviia v XXI veke.* Ed. A. Ia. Bagrova et al. Moscow: Moskovskii institut lingvistiki, 2006. 54-55.

327. Chubarov, I.M. "'Serdechnye' iskazheniia v prostranstve estetiki: Gustav Shpet i Lev Vygotskii." *Shpet 2006*: 221-35.

328. Denn, M. [Maryse Dennes]. "Logika tvorcheskogo akta v filosofii Gustava Shpeta." *Shpet 2006*: 236-50.

329. Fedorova, L.V. "Tema filosofii i zhizni v tvorchestve G. Shpeta (istoriko-filos-ofskii aspect)." *Shpet 2006*: 340-50.

330. Iantsen, V. "D.I. Chizhevskii, E.D. Shor i G.G. Shpet." *Shpet 2006*: 357-82.

331. Kantor, V.K. "Gustav Shpet kak istorik russkoi filosofii." *Shpet 2006*: 269-301. [**R**: *Shpet 2008*: 5-34.]

332. Makhlin, V.L. "Taina filologov." *Shpet 2006*: 187-220. [Mostly on Shpet and the Bakhtin Circle.]

333. Martsinkovskaia, T.D. "Problemy istorii psikhologii v trudakh G.G. Shpeta." *Metodologiia i istoriia psikhologii* 2 (2006): 37-43.

334. Mikeshina, L.A. "Gustav Shpet i sovremennaia filosofiia nauki." *Shpet 2006*: 21-61.

335. Mikeshina, L.A. "Gustav Shpet i sovremennaia metodologiia sotsial'no-guman-itarnykh nauk." *Epistemologiia i filosofiia nauki* 1 (2006): 16-37.

336. Mukhamadiev, R. Sh. "Gustav Shpet: problemy germenevticheskoi logiki." *Vestnik Moskovskogo universiteta. Seriia. 7. Filosofiia* 5 (2006): 33-43.

337. Plotnikov, N.S. "Antropologiia ili istoriia. Polemika G.G. Shpeta s V. Dil'teem [Dilthey] po povodu osnovanii gumanitarnykh nauk." *Shpet 2006*: 171-86.

338. Porus, V.N. "Spor o ratsionalizme: filosofiia i kul'tura (E. Gusserl' [Husserl], L. Shestov i G. Shpet)." *Shpet 2006*: 146-67.

339. Pruzhinin, B.I. "Mezhdu kontekstom otkrytiia i kontekstom obosnovaniia: me-todologiia nauki Gustava Shpeta." *Shpet 2006*: 135-45.

340. Reznichenko, A.I. "Gustav Shpet, Pavel Florenskii i "pole filosofii"." *Shpet 2006*: 351-57.

341. Schastlivtsev, R.A. "Vnutrenniaia forma slova kak gumanitarnyi universum (tekstologicheskii analiz)." *Shpet 2006*: 251-60. [On Shpet's *Vnutrenniaia forma slova.*]

342. Shchderina, T.G. "Arkhiv Gustava Shpeta kak fenomen kul'turno-istoricheskoi psikhologii. Predislovie k publikatsii stat'i G.G. Shpeta "Iskusstvo kak vid znaniia." *Kul'turno-istoricheskaia psikhologiia* 4 (2006): 22-24.

343. Shchedrina, T.G. "Kommentarii." *Natalis* 501-606.

344. Shchedrina, T.G. "Kommuniaktivnoe prostranstvo russkogo filosofskogo soo-bshchestva (opyt arkhivnoi rekonstruktsii filosofskogo arkhiva Gustava Shpeta)." *Shpet 2006*: 302-23.

345. Shchedrina, T.G. "Sergei Bulgakov i Gustav Shpet: razgovor o sobornosti." *Russkoe bogoslovie v evropeiskom kontekste: S. N. Bulgakov i zapadnaia religiozno-filosofskaia mysl'*. Ed. V.N. Porus. Moscow: Bibleisko-Bogoslovskii Institut sv. Apostola Andreia, 2006. 198-204.

346. Shchedrina, T.G. "Tematicheskie linii russkoi filosofii: Pavel Florenskii i Gustav Shpet." *Na puti k sinteticheskomu edinstvu evropeiskoi kul'tury: filosofsko-bogoslovskoe nasledie P.A. Florenskogo i sovremennost'*. Ed. V.N. Porus. Moscow: Bibleisko-Bogoslovskii Institut sv. Apostola Andreia, 2006. 156-63.

347. Shchedrina, T.G. "Vybor filosofa: pochemu Gustav Shpet ostalsia v Rossii?" *Kosmopolis* 1 (2006): 72-77. [Introduction to the publication of Shpet's paper "Sotsializm ili gumanizm."]

348. Shtorkh, M.G. (née Shpet). "Gustav Shpet v vospominaniiakh sovremennikov i uchenikov." *Shpet 2006*: 324-29.

349. Soldatova, D.V. "Propedevticheskoe znachenie fenomenologii dlia gumanitarnogo poznaniia." *Shpet 2006*: 261-66.

350. Zinchenko, V.P. "Geterogenez mysli: podkhody L.S. Vygotskogo i G.G. Shpeta." *Shpet 2006*: 82-134.

351. Zinchenko, V. P. "Zhizn' v mysle i slove." *Natalis* 5-20.

2007

352. Chubarov, I.M. "V poiskakh "drugogo" istorizma: Nitsshe [Nietzsche] i Shpet." *Logos* 63 (2007): 4-16.

353. Iusim, Ev. V. "[Note on Shpet's article] "Differentsiatsiia postanovki teatral'nogo predstavleniia"." *Shpet 2007*: 463-64.

354. Martsinkovskaia, T.D. "Problema vnutrennei formy khudozhestvennogo proizvedeniia v rabotakh G.G. Shpeta." *Metodologiia i istoriia psikhologii* 2 (2007): 21-28.

355. Martsinkovskaia, T.D. "Psikhologiia i filosofiia iskusstva G.G. Shpeta." *Shpet 2007*: 465-74.

356. Pruzhinin, B., and T.G. Shchedrina. "V poiskakh epistemologii obshcheniia: Nikolai Berdiaev—Gustav Shpet—Lev Shestov." *N. A. Berdiaev i edinstvo evropeiskogo dukha*. Ed. V.N. Porus. Moscow: Bibleisko-Bogoslovskii Institut sv. Apostola Andreia, 2007. 69-79.

357. Shchedrina, T.G. "'Chto nasha zhizn'—Roman!" *Voprosy filosofii* 7 (2007): 82-86. [A brief study of Shpet's notes on the novel.]

358. Shchedrina, T.G. "Ekzistentsial'nye motivy istoricheskoi pamiati: Evgenii Trubetskoi i Gustav Shpet." *Voprosy filosofii* 11 (2007): 66-72.

359. Shchedrina, T.G. "Filosofskii arkhiv Gustava Shpeta: opyt istoriko-filsofskoi rekontsruktsii." *Issledovaniia po istorii russkoi mysli: ezhegodnik* 7 (2007): 81-92.

360. Shchedrina, T.G. "Idei Gustava Shpeta v kontekste fenomenologicheskoi estetiki." *Iskusstvo* 7-12.

361. Shchedrina, T.G. "Kommentarii." *Iskusstvo* 502-681.

362. Shchedrina, T.G. "Shpet, Gustav Gustavovich." *Kul'turologiia. Entsiklopediia v dvukh tomakh.* Vol. 2. Moscow: ROSSPEN, 2007. 998-1000.

2008

363. Chubarov, I. "Gustav Shpet i Vladimir Solov'ev: kriticheskoe nasledovanie." *Novoe litraturnoe obozrenie* 91 (2008): 9-22.

364. Gidini, M. [Maria Candida Ghidini] "Tekushchie zadachi i vechnye problemy: Gustav Shpet i ego shkola v Gosudarstvennoi akademii khudozhestvennykh nauk." *Novoe litraturnoe obozrenie* 91 (2008): 23-34.

365. Ioffe, D. "Passivnoe protivostoianie diamatu na puti k ontologii i fenomenologii: Imiaslavie i kriticheskoe neogumbol'dtianstvo (russkie religioznye filosofy i Gustav Shpet)." *Russian Literature* 63 (2008): 63.2/3/4: 293-366.

366. Medvedev, N. "G.G. Shpet (1879-1937)". *Otzvuk myslei blagorodnykh.* Ed. A.I. Iudin and N.M. Averin. Tambov: Izdatel'skii dom TGU im. G.R. Derzhavina, 2008. 215-27.

367. Shchedrina, T.G. "Chetyre pis'ma L.B. Kamenevu, ili rol' Gustava Shpeta v perevodakh Shekspira." *Novoe literaturnoe obozrenie* 92 (2008): 81-103. [**R:** *Arkhiv epokhi.*]

368. Shchedrina, T.G. "Kommentarii." *Shpet 2008*: 351-566.

369. Tihanov, Galin. "Mnogoobrazie po nevole, ili neskhozhie zhizni Gustava Shpeta." *Novoe litraturnoe obozrenie* 91 (2008): 35-63. [Russian translation of Tihanov's 2008 article "Multifariousness under Duress: Gustav Shpet's Scattered Lives."]

370. Tul'chinskii, G.L. "G.G. Shpet: perspektiva logiki soderzhaniia (smysla)." *Sovremennaia logika: problemy teorii, istorii i primeneniia v nauke* 8 (2008): 398-401.

2009

371. Aristov V.V. "G.G. Shpet i proekt sozdaniia im Akademii Moskovskogo khudozestvennogo teatra." *Voprosy psikhologii* 3 (2009): 108-15.

372. Chubarov, I.M. "Mezhdu bessmyslitsei i absurdom: status futurizma i bespredmetnogo iskusstva v esteticheskikh teoriiakh 20-kh gg. (V. Shklovskii, L. Vygotskii, V. Kandinskii, G. Shpet i GAKhN)." *Voprosy filosofii* 4 (2009): 114-25.

373. Chubarov, I.M. "Problema sub ektivnosti v germenevticheskoi filosofii G.G. Shpeta." *Issledovaniia po istorii russkoi mysli: ezhegodnik* 8 (2009): 41-69.

374. Denn, M. [Maryse Dennes]. "Estetika Gustava Shpeta i ego kritika russkogo futurizma." *Voprosy psikhologii* 3 (2009): 82-87.

375. Dmitriev, Aleksandr. "Kak sdelana 'formal'no-filosofskaia shkola' (ili pochemu ne sostoialsia moskovskii formalizm?)." *Issledovaniia po istorii russkoi mysli: ezhegodnik* 8 (2009): 70-95. [85-94 on Shpet.]

376. Gavriushin, N.K. "Poniatie 'perezhivaniia' v trudakh G.G. Shpeta (predvaritel'nye zametki)." *Issledovaniia po istorii russkoi mysli: ezhegodnik* 8 (2009): 96-105.

377. Martsinkovskaia, T.D. "Gustav Shpet—syn svoego vremeni i nash sovremennik." *Voprosy psikhologii* 3 (2009): 65-71.

378. Molchanov, Viktor. "Ot chistogo soznaniia k sotsial'noi veshchi. Semanticheskii i kontseptual'nyi aspekty problemy Ia u Gustava Shpeta." *Issledovaniia po istorii russkoi mysli: ezhegodnik* 8 (2009): 11-40.

379. Plotnikov, Nikolai. "Kritika rossiiskogo razuma. Zametki po povodu novogo izdaniia 'Ocherka russkoi filosofii' G.G. Shpeta." *Issledovaniia po istorii russkoi mysli: ezhegodnik* 8 (2009): 173-86.

380. Plotnikov, Nikolai. "Ot romanticheskoi germenevtiki k fenomenologii iazyka: Fridrikh Shleiermakher [Friedrich Schleiermacher]—Pavel Florenskii—Gustav Shpet." *Voprosy filosofii* 4 (2009): 107-13.

381. Shchedrina, T.G. "Kommentarii." *Ocherk* 618-827.

382. Shchedrina, T.G. "Predislovie." *Ocherk* 5-18.

383. Stefanenko T.G. "Etnopsikhologiia G.G. Shpeta v XXI v." *Voprosy psikhologii* 3 (2009): 103-07.

384. Steiner, P. "Uz ne parodiia li on?" *Voprosy psikhologii* 3 (2009): 88-96. [Russian translation of Steiner's 2009 article "'But Isn't He a Parody?' Gustav Shpet's *Aesthetic Fragments*, III."]

385. Tihanov, G. "Gustav Shpet v zerkale Georgiia Florovskogo (1922-1959)." *Issledovaniia po istorii russkoi mysli: ezhegodnik* 8 (2009): 140-49.

386. Vel'mezova, Ekaterina, and Tat'iana Shchedrina. "Sharl' Balli i Gustav Shpet v russko-evropeiskom nauchnom razgovore (opyt rekonstruktsii "arkhiva epokhi")." *Issledovaniia po istorii russkoi mysli: ezhegodnik* 8 (2009): 106-26. [Russian translation of the two authors' 2008 article "Charles Bally et Gustav Shpet en dialogue: en reconstruisant les archives de l'époque."]

387. "Vospominaniia T.G. Maksimovoi-Shpet ob otse." *Voprosy psikhologii* 3 (2009): 116-21.

388. Zav'ialov, N. [Nicolas Zavialoff] "Razvitie poniatiia 'vnutrenniaia forma slova' G.G. Shpeta v kognitivnykh naukakh." *Voprosy psikhologii* 3 (2009): 97-103.

389. Zinchenko, V.P. "Otvet psikhologa fiziologam ("Rabota po psikhologii" G.G. Shpeta)." *Voprosy psikhologii* 3 (2009): 72-82.

B. Literature on Shpet in other Languages
a) In English

1. Lossky, N.O. *History of Russian Philosophy*. New York: International Universities Press, 1951. 324-25. [A brief and rather mixed evaluation of Shpet's philosophy.]

2. Zenkovsky, V.V. *A History of Russian Philosophy*. Trans. George L. Kline. New York: Columbia UP, 1953. 829-33. [A brief and on the whole unsympathetic account.]

3. Scanlan, James P. "Shpet, Gustav Gustavovich." *Encyclopaedia of Philosophy*. Ed. Paul Edwards. Vol. 7. New York: Macmillan, 1967. 433-34.

4. Prat, Naftali. "Orthodox Philosophy of Language in Russia." *Studies in Soviet Thought* 20 (1979): 1-21. [11-13 on Shpet's philosophy of language.]

5. Freiberger-Sheikholeslami, Erika. "Forgotten Pioneers of Soviet Semiotics." *Semiotics 1980*. Ed. Michael Herzfeld and Margot D. Lenhart. New York and London: Plenum, 1980. 156-63. [A discussion of Shpet's work in the context of GAKhN's research on language and form.]

6. Freiberger-Sheikholeslami, Erika. "Linguistic Contributions of the Russian Academy for Study of the Arts in the 1920s." *Penn Review of Linguistics* 5 (1981): 22-27. [A discussion of Shpet's work on the philosophy of language in the context of GA-KhN's theoretical concerns.]

7. Freiberger, Erika. "Philosophical Linguistics: W. v. Humboldt and G.G. Shpet (A semiotic theory of inner form)." *Penn Review of Linguistics* 7 (1983): 95-105.

8. Freiberger-Sheikholeslami, Erika. "Gustav G. Špet: Hermeneutical Logic and Philosophical Semiotics." *Semiotics 1984*. Ed. John Deely. Lanham, MD: UP of America, 1985. 381-91.

9. Freiberger-Sheikholeslami, Erika. "Gustav G. Špet." *Semiotics 1983*. Ed. Jonathan Evans and John Deely. Lanham, MD: UP of America, 1987. 145-54.

10. Freiberger-Sheikholeslami, Erika. "Gustav G. Špet: Phenomenological Semiotics and Hermeneutics." *Semiotic Theory and Practice: Proceedings of the Third International Congress of the IASS, Palermo, 1984*. Ed. Michael Herzfeld and Lucio Melazzo. Berlin and New York: Mouton de Gruyter, 1988. 279-92.

11. Freiberger-Sheikholeslami, Erika. "Gustav G. Špet's theory of interpretation as a theory of understanding." *American Contributions to the Tenth International Congress of Slavists. Sofia, September 1988. Literature*. Ed. Jane Gary Harris. Columbus: Slavica, 1988. 167-72.

12. Mitiushin, A.A. "Commentary" [On Shpet's article "Theatre as Art." Trans. Michel Vale] *Soviet Studies in Philosophy* 28.3 (Winter 1989-90): 89-91. [Translation of A. Mitiushin, "Kommentarii." *Voprosy filosofii* 11 (1988): 91-92.]

13. Pasternak, E.V. "In Memory of Gustav Gustavovich Shpet." [Trans. Michel Vale] *Soviet Studies in Philosophy* 28.3 (Winter 1989-90): 52-60. [Translation of E. Pasternak, "Pamiati Gustava Gustavovicha Shpeta." *Voprosy filosofii* 11 (1988): 72-76.]

14. Steiner, Peter. "Gustav Špet and the Prague School: Conceptual Frames for the Study of Language." *Semantic Analysis of Literary Texts. To Honour Jan van der Eng on the Occasion of His 65th Birthday.* Ed. Eric de Haard, Thomas Langerak and Willem G. Weststeijn. Amsterdam: Elsevier, 1990. 553-62. [T: Russian, 1991; Czech, 1993; prepublication translations into Japanese (1988) and French (1988).]

15. Haardt, Alexander. "Gustav Špet's *Appearance and Sense* and Phenomenology in Russia." *Appearance and Sense: Phenomenology as the Fundamental Science and Its Problems.* By Gustav Shpet. Trans. Thomas Nemeth. Dordrecht: Kluwer, 1991. xvii-xxxi.

16. Haardt, Alexander. "Gustav Špet's *Aesthetic Fragments* and Roman Ingarden's literary theory: two designs for a phenomenological aesthetics." *Wiener Slawistischer Almanach* 27 (1991): 17-31.

17. Nemeth, Thomas. "Translator's Introduction." *Appearance and Sense: Phenomenology as the Fundamental Science and Its Problems.* By Gustav Shpet. Trans. Thomas Nemeth. Dordrecht: Kluwer, 1991. ix-xv.

18. Scanlan, James P. "Phenomenology in Russia: The Contribution of Gustav Shpet." *Man and World* 26 (1993): 467-75. [Review essay on the English translation (1991) of Shpet's *Iavlenie i smysl.*]

19. Nemeth, Thomas. "Husserl, Shpet and Losev." *The Slavonic and East European Review* 73.1 (1995): 100-05. [Review article.]

20. Kline, George L. "Meditations of a Russian Neo-Husserlian: Gustav Shpet's "The Skeptic and His Soul." *Phenomenology and Skepticism: Essays in Honor of James M. Edie.* Ed. Brice R. Wachterhauser. Evanston: Northwestern UP, 1996. 144-63; 249-54 (notes).

21. Bowlt, John E. "RAKhN on Trial: The Purge of Gustav Shpet." *Experiment. A Journal of Russian Culture* 3 (1997): 295-98.

22. Cassedy, Steven. "Gustav Shpet and Phenomenology in an Orthodox Key." *Studies in East European Thought* 49 (1997): 81-108. [R: *Shpet 2009*: 94-110.]

23. Durst, Elizabeth. "Gustav Shpet." *Experiment. A Journal of Russian Culture* 3 (1997): 189-93.

24. Kuznetsov, V.G. "Introduction to the Publication of G.G. Shpet's 'A Work on Philosophy.'" [Trans. Michel Vale] *Russian Studies in Philosophy* 35.4 (1997): 39-42.

[Translation of V. Kuznetsov, "Predislovie k publikatsii 'Raboty po filosofii' G.G. Shpeta." *Vestnik Moskovskogo universiteta. Seriia 7. Filosofiia* 2 (1995): 19-22.]

25. Haardt, Alexander. "Shpet, Gustav Gustavovich." *Routledge Encyclopedia of Philosophy.* Ed. Edward Craig. Vol. 8. London and New York: Routledge, 1998. 754-58.

26. Smith, Michael G. *Language and Power in the Creation of the USSR, 1917-1953.* Berlin and New York: Mouton de Gruyter, 1998. [Ch. 3: "G.G. Shpet, Linguistic Structure, and the Eurasian Imperative in Soviet Language Reform."]

27. Kline, George L. "Gustav G. Shpet as Interpreter of Hegel." *Archiwum historii filozofii i myśli społecznej* 44 (1999): 181-90.

28. Kogan, L.A. "An Unread Page. G.G. Shpet as Director of the Institute of Scientific Philosophy, 1921-23." *Russian Studies in Philosophy* 37.4 (1999): 38-52. [Translation of L. Kogan, "Neprochitannaia stranitsa (G.G. Shpet—direktor Instituta nauchnoi filosofii: 1921-1923)." *Voprosy filosofii* 10 (1995): 95-105.]

29. Kuznetsov, V.G. "The Role of Hermeneutic Phenomenology in Grounding the Affirmative Philosophy of Gustav Gustavovich Shpet." Trans. Benjamin Hale. *Russian Studies in Philosophy* 37.4 (1999): 62-90.

30. Polivanov, M.K. "An Outline of G.G. Shpet's Biography." *Russian Studies in Philosophy* 37.4 (1999): 6-37. [Translation of Polivanov's "Ocherk biografii G.G. Shpeta." *Litsa. Biograficheskii al'manakh* 1 (1992): 7-43.]

31. Wertsch, James V. "Editor's Introduction." *Journal of Russian and East European Psychology* 38.4 (2000): 3-7; 38.5 (2000): 3-5. [Introduction to the English translation of Chapters I-XV of Zinchenko's monograph (listed below); of particular interest to Shpet scholars is the part published in 38.4 (2000): 3-7.]

32. Zinchenko, V.P. "The Thought and Word of Gustav Shpet (Return from Exile)." Trans. Vladimir Talny. *Journal of Russian and East European Psychology* 38.4 (2000): 10-68; 38.5 (2000): 6-71. [Translation of Chapters I-XV of Zinchenko's 2000 monograph on Shpet (see full entry under literature on Shpet in Russian).]

33. Steiner, Peter. "*Tropos Logikos*: Gustav Shpet's Philosophy of History." *Slavic Review* 62.2 (2003): 343-58. [**R**: *Shpet 2003*: 558-79; *Shpet 2009*: 11-25; **T**: Russian, 2004; Czech, 2008.]

34. Ermishin, O.T. "On Two Conceptions of Russian Philosophy: V.V. Zenkovsky, B.V. Iakovenko, G.G. Shpet." *Russian Studies in Philosophy* 43.3 (2004): 81-89.

35. Seifrid, Thomas. *The Word Made Self. Russian Writings on Language, 1860-1930.* Ithaca and London: Cornell UP, 2005. [Extensive discussion of Shpet in ch. 4: "Through the Prism of Phenomenology."]

36. Shiyan, Anna. "Phenomenological Problems in Shpet's Creative Work." *Russia and Phenomenological Tradition. Proceedings of the International Conference.* Ed. A.A. Volokovykh. St. Petersburg: St. Petersburg School of Religion and Philosophy. 2005. 160-65.

37. Zhivov, V. "A Phenomenological Apologia for Herzen (Herzen's "Philosophical World Outlook" by G. Shpet)." Trans. Aram Yavrumyan. *Social Sciences* [Moscow] 36.4 (2005): 99-107. [English translation of Zhivov's 2005 article "Apologiia Gertsena v fenomenologicheskom ispolnenii ("Filosofskoe mirovozzrenie Gertsena" G.G. Shpeta)."]

38. Haardt, Alexander. "Shpet, Gustav Gustavovich (1879-1937)." *Encyclopedia of Philosophy*. Ed. Donald Borchert. 2nd ed. Vol. 9. Detroit: Macmillan Reference, 2006. 17-20. [Largely identical with Haardt's 1998 article in the *Routledge Encyclopedia of Philosophy* (see entry above).]

39. Tihanov, Galin. "Gustav Shpet: Literature and Aesthetics from the Silver Age to the 1930s." *Primerjalna književnost* [Ljubljana] 29.2 (2006): 1-19.

40. Zinchenko, Vladimir. "Thought and Word: the Approaches of L.S. Vygotsky and G.G. Shpet." *The Cambridge Companion to Vygotsky*. Ed. Harry Daniels, Michael Cole, James V. Wertsch. Cambridge: Cambridge UP, 2007. 212-45.

41. Tihanov, Galin. "Multifariousness under Duress: Gustav Shpet's Scattered Lives." *Russian Literature* 63 (2008): 63.2/3/4: 259-92. [T: Russian, 2008.]

42. Bird, Robert. "The Hermeneutic Triangle: Gustav Shpet's Aesthetics in Context." *Shpet 2009*: 28-44.

43. Brandist, Craig. "Problems of Sense, Significance and Validity in the Work of Shpet and the Bakhtin Circle." *Shpet 2009*: 192-206.

44. Dennes, Maryse. "Vladimir Solovev and the Legacy of Russian Religious Thought in the Works of Gustav Shpet." *Shpet 2009*: 115-22.

45. Grier, Philip. "Gustav Shpet and the Semiotics of 'Living Discourse.'" *International Journal for the Semiotics of Law* 22.1 (2009): 61-68.

46. Haardt, Alexander. "Shpet's *Aesthetic Fragments* and Sartre's Literary Theory— a 'Dialectical Interpretation.'" *Shpet 2009*: 169-78.

47. Kline, George L. "Introduction to Excerpts from Shpet's "Hermeneutics and Its Problems." *Shpet 2009*: 221-22.

48. Kline, George L. "Shpet as Translator of Hegel's *Phänomenologie des Geistes*." *Shpet 2009*: 140-56.

49. Nemeth, Thomas. "Shpet's Departure from Husserl." *Shpet 2009*: 125-39.

50. Radunović, Dušan. "Semiotics in Voloshinov and Shpet." *Shpet 2009*: 207-18.

51. Radunović, Dušan, and Galin Tihanov. "Introduction to Shpet's Paper 'On the Limits of Scientific Literary Scholarship.'" *Shpet 2009*: 246-47.

52. Scanlan, James P. "The Fate of Philosophy in Russia: Gustav Shpet's Studies in the History of Russian Thought." *Shpet 2009*: 83-97.

53. Schmid, Ulrich. "The Objective Sense of History: Shpet's Synthesis of Hegel, Cieszkowski, Herzen, and Husserl." *Shpet 2009*: 157-68.

54. Seifrid, Thomas. "Sign and/vs. Essence in Shpet." *Shpet 2009*: 181-91.

55. Steiner, Peter. "'But Isn't He a Parody?' Gustav Shpet's *Aesthetic Fragments*, III." *Slavonica* 15.1 (2009): 3-10. [**T**: Russian, 2009.]

56. Tihanov, Galin. "Bibliography of Gustav Shpet's Published Works (1901-2009)." *Shpet 2009*: 253-72.

57. Tihanov, Galin. "Gustav Shpet's Life and Works: Introduction to the Volume." *Shpet 2009*: 1-12.

58. Tihanov, Galin. "Gustav Shpet's Literary and Theatre Affiliations." *Shpet 2009*: 56-80.

59. Tihanov, Galin. "Literature on Gustav Shpet (1915-2009)." *Shpet 2009*: 273-312.

60. Zinchenko, Vladimir, and James V. Wertsch. "Gustav Shpet's Influence on Psychology." *Shpet 2009*: 45-55.

b) In German

61. Goerdt, Wilhelm. *Russische Philosophie: Zugänge und Durchblicke*. Freiburg: Alber, 1984. 594-96; 715-16. [A general outline of Shpet's philosophy and of his contribution as a historian of Russian thought.]

62. Eismann, Wolfgang. "Einleitung. Zur Geschichte des obraz-Begriffes in der russischen und sowjetischen Literaturwissenschaft." *Einführung in allgemeine Probleme der Semiotik*. By Vjacheslav Vsevolodovich Ivanov. Ed. Wolfgang Eismann. Trans. Brigitte Eidemüller and Wolfgang Eismann. Tübingen: Gunter Narr, 1985. 1-45. [On Shpet 20-26.]

63. Eismann, Wolfgang. *Von der Volkskunst zur proletarischen Kunst. Theorien zur Sprache der Literatur in Rußland und der Sowjetunion*. Munich: Otto Sagner, 1986. 217-34. [Ch. 4: "Das Primat der ästhetischen Einstellung. Der Teil als Repräsentant des Ganzen. Zur Aesthetik und Poetik G.G. Špets".]

64. Freiberger, Erika. "Gustav Špet: Semiotik und Hermeneutik" [1986]. *Semiotica Austriaca*. Ed. Jeff Bernard. Vienna: ÖGS, 1987. 111-18.

65. Haardt, Alexander. "Phänomenologie und strukturelle Sprachanalyse bei Gustav Špet. Zur russischen Husserl-Interpretation der zwanziger Jahre." *Phänomenologische Forschungen* 21 (1988): 167-98.

66. Rodi, Frithjof. "Hermeneutische Logik im Umfeld der Phänomenologie: Georg Misch, Hans Lipps, Gustav Špet." *Phänomenologie im Widerstreit. Zum 50. Todestag Edmund Husserls*. Ed. Christoph Jamme and Otto Pöggeler. Frankfurt am Main: Suhrkamp, 1989. 352-72. [**R**: F. Rodi. *Erkenntnis des Erkannten. Zur Hermeneutik des 19. und 20. Jahrhunderts*. Frankfurt am Main: Suhrkamp, 1990. 147-67; **T**: Italian, 1996.]

67. Daube-Schakat, Ronald, and Frithjof Rodi, "Nachwort." *Die Hermeneutik und ihre Probleme (Moskau 1918)*. By Gustav Shpet. Trans. Erika Freiberger and Alexander Haardt. Ed. Alexander Haardt and Roland Daube-Schackat. Freiburg and Munich: Alber, 1993. 285-94.

68. Haardt, Alexander. *Husserl in Rußland. Phänomenologie der Sprache und Kunst bei Gustav Špet und Aleksej Losev*, Munich: Wilhelm Fink, 1993.

69. Schmid, Herta. "Gustav Špets Entwurf einer hermeneutischen Literaturgeschichtsschreibung." *Wiener Slawistischer Almanach* 32 (1993): 33-68.

70. Plotnikov, Nikolaj. "Phänomenologische Erschließung der russischen Philosophie." *Philosophische Rundschau* 41.4 (1994): 328-37. [Review essay on recent publications in English and German by and on Gustav Shpet.]

71. Müller, H. "Kurzgefasste Worte von der Gedenksstunde des verstorbenen Philosophen Gustav Gustavowitsch Spet." [15 November 1989] *Shpet 1995*: 319-20.

72. Haardt, Alexander. "Gustav Špets *Ästhetische Fragmente* und Jean-Paul Sartres Essays *Was ist Literatur?*—Zum Beschreibungspluralismus in der Literaturphänomenologie." *Russische Philosophie im 20. Jahrhundert*. Ed. Klaus-Dieter Eichler and Ulrich Johannes Schneider. Leipzig: Leipziger Universitätsverlag, 1996. 109-21.

73. Möckel, Christian. "Das Problem des Verstehens von sprachlichen Ausdrücken: Zur Rezeption von Edmund Husserls 1. Logischen Untersuchungen durch Gustav Špet." *Recherches Husserliennes* 5 (1996): 53-81.

74. Möckel, Christian. "Zu Špets Husserl-Kritik in der Hermeneutik-Schrift. Das Problem des Verstehens von sprachlichen Ausdrücken." *Russische Philosophie im 20. Jahrhundert*. Ed. Klaus-Dieter Eichler and Ulrich Johannes Schneider. Leipzig: Leipziger Universitätsverlag, 1996. 96-105.

75. Schmid, Herta. "Gustav Špets Theatertheorie im Kontext der historischen Avantgarde der Künste." *Balagan* 2.1 (1996): 88-116.

76. Groys, Boris. "Špet und die Entsubjektivierung des Bewusstseins (Solov'ev, Askol'dov, Bachtin)." *Russisches Denken im europäischen Dialog*. Ed. Maria Deppermann. Innsbruck and Vienna: Studien-Verlag, 1998. 122-50.

77. Schmid, Ulrich. "Gustav Špet. Porträt." *Russische Religionsphilosphen des 20. Jahrhunderts*. Ed. Ulrich Schmid. Freiburg: Herder, 2003. 265-69.

78. Chubarov, Igor. "Die Oberfläche des literarischen Dings als Grenze zwischen Sinn und Nonsense (Andrej Belyj, V. Šklovskij, V. Kandinskij, L. Vygotskij, G. Špet und Futurismus). *Fraktur. Gestörte ästhetische Präsenz in Avantgarde und Spätavantgarde*. Ed. Anke Hennig, Brigitte Obermayr and Georg Witte. *Wiener Slawistischer Almanach* (Sonderband) 63 (2006): 127-41.

79. Eismann, Wolfgang. "Gustav Špets Kritik und semiotische Neubegründung der Völkerpsychologie." *Name und Person. Beiträge zur russischen Philosophie des Namens*. Ed. Holger Kuße. Munich: Otto Sagner, 2006. 39-58.

80. Plotnikov, Nikolaj. "Ein Kapitel aus der Geschichte des Strukturbegriffs. Gustav Špet als Vermittler zwischen Phänomenologie, Hermeneutik und Strukturalaismus." *Archiv für Begriffsgeschichte* 48 (2006): 191-201.

81. Plotnikov, Nikolaj. "Name—Sinn—Person. Zur hermeneutischen Dimension der Sprachphilosophie bei Pavel Florenskij und Gustav Špet." *Name und Person. Beiträge zur russischen Philosophie des Namens*. Ed. Holger Kuße. Munich: Otto Sagner, 2006. 111-23.

82. Plotnikov, Nikolaj. "Anthropologie versus Geschichte. Gustav Špets Konzeption einer hermeneutischen Wissenschaftstheorie im Kontext seiner Dilthey-Rezeption." *Dilthey und die hermeneutische Wende in der Philosophie. Wirkungsgeschichtliche Aspekte seines Werkes*. Ed. Gudrun Kühne-Bertram and Frithjof Rodi. Göttingen: Vandenhoeck & Ruprecht, 2008. 187-204.

c) In French

83. Zenkovsky, Basile. *Histoire de la philosophie russe*. Vol. 2. Paris: Gallimard, 1955. 391-93.

84. Steiner, Peter. "Gustav Shpet et l'Ecole de Prague: cadres conceptuels pour l'étude de la langue." *Centres et périphéries: Bruxelle–Prague et l'espace culturel européen*. Ed. Jan Rubeš. Brussels: Yellow Now and Liege: R. Vervinckt, 1988. 81-94. [French prepublication of Steiner's 1990 article "Gustav Špet and the Prague School: Conceptual Frames for the Study of Language."]

85. Kline, G.L. "La philosophie en Union soviétique autour de 1930." *Histoire de la literature russe*. Ed. E. Etkind et al. Vol. 3. *Gels et dégels*. Paris: Fayard, 1990. 259-63.

86. Dennes, Maryse. "L'influence de Husserl en Russie au début du XXème siècle et son impact sur les émigrés russes de Prague." *Jakobson entre l'Est et l'Ouest, 1915-1939. Un épisode de l'histoire de la culture européenne*. Ed. Françoise Gadet and Patrick Lausanne: Cahiers de l'ILSL, no. 9, 1997. 47-68. [See sections 3 ("R. Jakobson et l'héritage de G. Špet", 55-57) and 4 ("Autres Caractéristiques de l'œuvre de Špet", 58-62).]

87. Dennes, Maryse. *Husserl—Heidegger. Influence de leur œuvre en Russie*. Paris: L'Harmattan, 1998. [69-170 on Shpet.]

88. Pighetti, N. "Gustav Shpet. De la phénoménologie à une 'dialectique herméneutique.'" *Revue de Métaphysique et de Morale* 3 (1999): 333-50.

89. Dennes, Maryse. "Vitesse de la parole et deployment du discourse: de la *Glorification du Nom* à un fondement de temporalité." *Modernités russes* (Special issue "Vitesse et Modernité") 2 (2000): 223-42. [A discussion of Losev and Shpet on language.]

90. Dennes, Maryse. "L'école russe de phénoménologie et son influence sur le Cercle linguistique de Prague: Gustav Chpet et Roman Jakobson." *Prague entre l'Est et l'Ouest—l'émigration russe en Tchécoslovaquie, 1920-1938*. Ed. Milan Burda. Paris: L'Harmattan, 2001. 32-63.

91. Dennes, Maryse. "La place du corps et la critique de la psychologie classique dans *L'introduction à la psychologie ethnique* de Gustav Chpet." *Slavica Occitania* 18 (2004): 89-102.

92. Dennes, Maryse. "De la 'structure du mot' à la 'forme interne' chez Gustav Špet." *Revue Germanique internationale* 3 (2006): 77-92.

93. Dennes, Maryse. "La fin de la modernité et le retour au classicisme dans le *Fragments esthétiques* de Gustav Chpet." *Modernités russes* (Special issue "La Fin de la Modernité") 6 (2006): 53-66.

94. Dennes, Maryse. "Le Renouveau de l'hermeneutique à travers la reprise en compte de l'oeuvre de Gustav Chpet." *Chroniques slaves* 2 (2006): 173-83.

95. Zenkine, Serge. "Forme interne, forme externe. Les transformations d'une catégorie dans la théorie russe du XXe siècle." *Revue Germanique internationale* 3 (2006): 63-76. [70-72 on Shpet's concept of inner form; French version of Zenkin's 2004 article "Forma vnutrenniaia i vneshniaia (Sud'ba odnoi kategorii v russkoi teorii XX v.)".]

96. Dennes, Maryse. "Préface." *La Forme Interne du Mot. Études et variations sur des thèmes de Humboldt*. By Gustav Shpet. Trans. Nicolas Zavialoff. Paris: Kimé, 2007. 7-13.

97. Zavialoff, Nicolas. "L'actualité de la notion de forme interne chez Gustav Chpet." *La Forme Interne du Mot. Études et variations sur des thèmes de Humboldt*. By Gustav Shpet. Trans. Nicolas Zavialoff. Paris: Kimé, 2007. 15-51.

98. Zavialoff, Nicolas. "Corps socialisé et corps biologique." *La Forme Interne du Mot. Études et variations sur des thèmes de Humboldt*. By Gustav Shpet. Trans. Nicolas Zavialoff. Paris: Kimé, 2007. 279-300.

99. Ageeva, Inna. "V. Vološinov et G. Špet: deux points de vue sur la sémiotique." *Langage et pensée: Union Soviétique années 1920-1930*. Ed. P. Seriot and J. Friedrich. Lausanne: Université de Lausanne, 2008 (*Cahiers de l'ILSL*, no. 24). 101-12.

100. Anisimova-Frappé, Natalia. "Gustave Chpet et le problème de la forme interne du mot: ouverture à la linguistique." *Chpet 2008*: 89-95.

101. Aristov, Vladimir. "Gustave Chpet, la forme interne et sa signification pour la poétique et la poésie contemporaines." *Chpet 2008*: 405-18.

102. Avtonomova, Natalia. "Les principes épistémologiques de la critique de l'ethnodéterminisme." *Chpet 2008*: 373-85. [On Shpet's ethnic psychology.]

103. Azarova, Natalia. "Deux experiences de traduction philosophique: la *Phénoménologie de l'Esprit* de Hegel dans la traduction russe de G. Chpet et dans la traduction française de A. Kojève." *Chpet 2008*: 253-69.

104. Chtchetkina-Rocher, Nadejda. "Herméneutique de la temporalité et de la forme musicale chez Gustave Chpet." *Chpet 2008*: 281-98.

105. Chubarov, Igor. "Analyse comparé de la comprehension de la subjectivité chez G. Deleuze et chez G. Chpet." *Chpet 2008*: 333-43.

106. Dennes, Maryse. "Avant-Propos." *Chpet 2008*: 13-18.

107. Dennes, Maryse. "La structure du mot et de l'expression dans l'œuvre de Gustave Chpet, et sa signification pour l'histoire du structuralisme." *Chpet 2008*: 19-30.

108. Dennes, Maryse. "Špet et Potebnja." *Autour du skaz. Nicolas Leskov et ses héritiers*. Ed. Catherine Géry. Paris: Institut d'études slaves, 2008. 211-29.

109. Feshchenko, Vladimir. "G. Chpet et la tradition cachée de la sémiotique profonde en Russie." *Chpet 2008*: 127-38.

110. Flack, Patrick. "Dans l'ombre du structuralisme (Chklovski, Merleau-Ponty . . . et Chpet?)" *Chpet 2008*: 393-403.

111. Ghidini, Maria Candida. "Trois publications du Département de Philosophie du GAKhN: Variations sur le thème de la forme interne." *Chpet 2008*: 109-25.

112. Gogotishvili, Lioudmila. "G. Chpet et M. Bakhtine: Divergences attendues et rapprochements inattendus." *Chpet 2008*: 49-62.

113. Gruebel, Rainer. "Esthétique de la poésie et esthétique de la prose. Gustave Chpet et Mikhail Bakhtine." *Chpet 2008*: 63-73.

114. Guseltseva, Marina. "La signification de la réflexion méthodologique de G. Chpet pour la psychologie contemporaine." *Chpet 2008*: 427-36.

115. Ioffe, Denis. "Gustave Chpet, la religion et le problème du signe (Glorificatiion du nom *vs* phénoménologie et sémiologie)." *Chpet 2008*: 149-59.

116. Khorouji, Sergueï. "Aux limites de la phénoménologie: Chpet, Husserl et l'intentionalité dans le monde de la pratique spirituelle." *Chpet 2008*: 359-71.

117. Kochan, Ewa. "Gustave Chpet: la philosophie de l'homme et de la culture." *Chpet 2008*: 271-79.

118. Komorowska, Ewa. "L'actualité des conceptions scientifiques de Gustave Chpet dans le contexte de la linguistique contemporaine." *Chpet 2008*: 387-92.

119. Lyusyy, Aleksandr. "De la logique de l'histoire aux genres de l'histoire." *Chpet 2008*: 419-25. [On the implications of Shpet' work for historiography and philosophy of history.]

120. Martsinkovskaïa, Tatiana. "Gustave Chpet: paraphrase d'un thème contemporain." *Chpet 2008*: 437-47.

121. Mazaeva, Olga. "G. Chpet et A. Biély dans l'horizon phénoménologique de l'Âge d'argent." *Chpet 2008*: 161-72.

122. Molchanov, Victor. "Le problème du "Moi" chez G. Chpet: l'expérience et l'interprétation." *Chpet 2008*: 213-24.

123. Novikov, Vladimir. "'Il vaut mieux Chpet que jamais.' Chpet et Tynianov." *Chpet 2008*: 173-79.

124. Novikova, Olga. "Chpet écrivain: l'interaction du moi et de la pensée dans ses travaux." *Chpet 2008*: 225-32.

125. Poleva, Natalia. "L'influence des travaux de G. Chpet sur l'étude des problèmes de la forme artistique, dans la cadre de l'Académie d'État de Sciences Artistiques (GAKhN). *Chpet 2008*: 97-107.

126. Pruzhinin, Boris. "Perspective sémiotique de la méthodologie des sciences humaines chez Gustave Chpet." *Chpet 2008*: 201-11.

127. Shchedrina, Tatiana. "Gustave Chpet et les problèmes actuels de la philosophie des sciences humaines." *Chpet 2008*: 301-12.

128. Shchedrina, Tatiana, and Ekaterina Velmezova. "Charles Bally et Gustav Shpet en dialogue: en reconstruisant les archives de l'époque." *Langage et pensée: Union Soviétique années 1920-1930*. Ed. P. Seriot and J. Friedrich. Lausanne: Université de Lausanne, 2008 (*Cahiers de l'ILSL*, no. 24). 237-51. [**T**: Russian, 2009.]

129. Shiyan, Anna. "Les fondements ontologiques de la philosophie du langage du 'dernier' Chpet." *Chpet 2008*: 243-52.

130. Steiner, Peter. "La formule mathématique de la beauté dans les *Fragments esthétiques* de Gustave Chpet: un simple jeu ou une affaire sérieuse?" *Chpet 2008*: 233-41.

131. Tihanov, Galin. "Gustave Chpet: Problèmes théoriques de literature et de theatre dans les années 1920 (le CLM et le GAKhN)." *Chpet 2008*: 33-48.

132. Trybowska, Marta. "La pensée de Gustave Chpet et l'anthropologie polonaise: Chpet et Ingarden." *Chpet 2008*: 191-98.

133. Tulchinsky, Grigory. "Gustave Chpet et les nouvelles perspectives du paradigme des sciences humaines: le texte en tant qu'intonation de l'être ou l'autre rationalité de la sémiotiques." 345-58.

134. Vasiliev, Nikolaï. "G. Chpet et M. Bakhtine: aux sources de la métalangue du 'cercle de Bakhtine.'" *Chpet 2008*: 75-87.

135. Velmezova, Ékatérina. "Sémantique et sémiotique chez Gustave Chpet et Nikolaï Marr." *Chpet 2008*: 139-48.

136. Venditti, Michela. "La forme interne du mot chez G. Chpet et A. Marty." *Chpet 2008*: 181-90.

137. Zavialoff, Nicolas. "Actualité et perspectives de la notion de forme interne chez G. Chpet (en psychologie et sciences cognitives)." *Chpet 2008*: 449-93.

138. Zinchenko, Vladimir. "Le creuset de Wilhelm von Humboldt et la forme interne de Gustave Chpet dans le contexte du problème de la creation." *Chpet 2008*: 313-32.

d) In Italian

139. Ghidini, Maria Candida. "La parola e la realità: Per una ricostruzione della filosofia del linguaggio di Gustav Špet." *Rivista di filosofia neoscolastica* 83.1-2 (1991): 142-88.

140. Ghidini, Maria Candida. "Il pensiero linguistico di Gustav Špet." *L'analisi linguistica e letteraria* 1 (1993): 245-63.

141. Ghidini, Maria Candida. "La forza reale del possibile. Il pensiero estetico di Gustav Špet." *Poetiche ed estetiche del primo Novecento in Russia.* Ed. A. Dioletta Siclari. Parma: Edizioni Zara, 1993. 151-81.

142. Vladimirskaja, Olga. "Postfazione." *Kamen'. Rivista semestrale di poesia e filosofia* 3.4 (December 1993): 49-54. [Afterword to the Italian translation of Shpet's *Esteticheskie fragmenty.*]

143. Mitiushin, A.A. "La sfera del linguaggio nella concezione logica di Špet." Trans. Michela Venditti. *Slavia* 3.4 (1994): 20-27.

144. Siciliani de Cumis, Nicola. "Per Gustav' Špet." *Slavia* 3.4 (1994): 14-16.

145. Venditti, Michela. "Il primo convegno sovietico su Špet." *Slavia* 3.4 (1994): 37-43.

146. Venditti, Michela. "La teoria del linguaggio di G.G.Špet." *Slavia* 3.4 (1994): 17-19.

147. Rodi, Frithjof, "Logica ermeneutica nei dintorni della fenomenologia: Georg Misch, Hans Lipps, Gustav Shpet." *"Conoscenza del conosciuto." Sull'ermeneutica del XIX e XX secolo.* By Frithjof Rodi. Milan: Franco Angeli, 1996. 135-53. [Italian translation of Rodi's 1989 article "Hermeneutische Logik im Umfeld der Phänomenologie: Georg Misch, Hans Lipps, Gustav Špet."]

148. De Michiel, Margherita. *"G.G. Shpet: la storia come oggetto della semiotica." Janus. Quaderni del Circolo Glossematico* 5 (2005): 147-60.

149. Ghidini, Maria Candida, "G. Shpet." *Dizionario Bompiani degli autori.* Milano: Bompiani, 2006. 4226-27.

e) In Hungarian

150. Nyírő, Lajos. "Kutatási irányok az 1920-as évek szovjet irodalomtudományában" ["Main directions in the Soviet literary research of the 1920s"]. *Helikon* [Special issue edited by Lajos Nyírő and Anna Han] 24.1-2 (1978): 4-21. [On Shpet and GA-KhN 4-8; 13; 20.]

151. Mityusin, A.A. "Gusztav Spet filozófiai hermeneutikájának alaptételei" ["The Foundations of Shpet's Philosophical Hermeneutics"]. *Helikon* 29.2 (1983): 204-17.

152. Gránicz, István. "Hermeneutika az orosz századelőn, utána és ma" ["Hermeneutics in Russia at the Beginning of the 20th Century, Afterwards, and Today"]. *Helikon* [Special issue edited by István Gránicz and Anna Han] 43.3 (1997): 163-77. [On Shpet 170-72; **R**: Gránicz, István. *A nyelvészeti poétika útjai és lehetőségei* (*The Roads and Prospects of Linguistic Poetics*). Budapest: Balassi Kiadó, 2002. 25-49 (on Shpet 39-40).]

153. Han, Anna. "Útban a fenomenológiától a hermeneutikáig: Gusztav Spet esztétikai rendszere" ["On the Way from Phenomenology to Hermeneutics: The System of Gustav Shpet's Aesthetic Views"]. *Helikon* [Special issue edited by István Gránicz and Anna Han] 43.3 (1997): 195-236.

154. Kovács, Árpád. "A szó diszkurzív poétikája" ["A Discursive Poetics of the Word"]. *Helikon* 45.1-2 (1999): 5-35. [On Shpet 18-25.]

155. Kovács, Árpád. "A filológiai aktus" ["A Filological Act"]. *Literatura* 4 (2002): 395-426. [On Shpet 397-401.]

156. Kovács, Árpád. "A szó filológiai és poétikai megközelítésben" ["The Word in the Light of Philology and Theoretical Poetics"]. *Poétika és nyelvelmélet. Válogatás Aleksszandr Potebnya, Aleksszandr Veszelovszkij, Olga Frejdenberg elméleti műveiből. Szerkesztette és a kísérő tanulmányt írta Kovács Árpád* [*Poetics and Theory of Language. A Selection of Texts by A. Potebnia, A. Veselovsky, and O. Freidenberg*]. Ed. A. Kovács. Budapest: Argumentum, 2002. 335-400. [On Shpet 339-45; 380-87.]

f) In Croatian

157. Schmid, Herta. "G. Špet/ruska avangarde" ["G. Shpet/The Russian Avant-Garde"]. *Pojmovnik ruske avangarde. Peti svezak*. Ed. Aleksandar Flaker and Dubravka Ugrešić. Zagreb: Zavod za znanost o književnosti Filosofkog fakulteta u Zagrebu, 1987. 85-109.

158. Han, Anna. "Boris Pasternak i Gustav Špet: Pokušaj usporedne karakterizacije" ["Boris Pasternak and Gustav Shpet: An Attempt at a Parallel Characterization"]. Trans. Josip Užarević. *Filozofska Istraživanja* 69.18/2 (1998): 311-39.

159. Pavić, Željko. "'Hermeneutička logika' i teorija razumijevanja kod Gustava Gustavoviča Špeta" ["The 'Hermeneutic Logic' and the Theory of Comprehension in Gustav Gustavovich Shpet"]. *Filozofska Istraživanja* 93.2 (1998): 481-504.

160. Užarević, Josip. "Hermenutički obrat Gustava Špeta" ["Gustav Shpet's Hermeneutic Turn"]. *Hermeneutika i njezini problemi*. By Gustav Shpet. Trans. Josip
Užarević. Zagreb: Breza, 2006. 204-20.

g) In Other Languages

161. Steiner, Peter. "Gustav Špet a Pražská škola: Pojmové základy zkoumání řeči."
Filosofický časopis 41.4 (1993): 595-606. [Czech translation of Steiner's 1990
article "Gustav Špet and the Prague School: Conceptual Frames for the Study of
Language."]

162. Oesch, Erna. "Gustav Shpet ja venäläinen fenomenologia" ["Gustav Shpet and
Russian Phenomenology"]. *Niin & Näin* 1 (1995): 12-13. [In Finnish.]

163. Kebuladze, V.I. "Fenomenologichne poniatia intelektual'noi intuitsii ta iogo ob-
gruntuvannia u filosofii Gustava Shpeta" ["The Phenomenological Concept of Intellectual Intuition and its Grounding in Gustav Shpet's Philosophy"]. *Naukovi zapiski*
20 (2002): 86-90. [In Ukrainian.]

164. Teokharov, Vladimir. "Gustav Shpet. Ideiiata za osnovnata filosofksa
nauka" ["Gustav Shpet: The Idea of the Fundamental Philosophical Science"].
Fenomenologiia. Etnicheska psikhologiia. By Gustav Shpet. Trans. Aneta Ivanova.
Sofia: Kritika i khumanizum, 2003. 7-20. [In Bulgarian.]

165. Steiner, Peter. "Tropos logikos. Filozofie historiografie   Gustava Špeta."
Dějiny—teorie—kritika 2 (2008): 237-54. [Czech translation of Steiner's 2003 article "*Tropos Logikos*: Gustav Shpet's Philosophy of History."]

Contributors

Robert Bird teaches in the Department of Slavic Languages and Literatures at the University of Chicago. His major interests include the literature and thought of Russian modernism, the cinema of Andrei Tarkovsky, and philosophical and theological aesthetics. Among his publications are two books, *The Russian Prospero: The Creative Universe of Viacheslav Ivanov* (University of Wisconsin Press) and *Andrei Rublev* (BFI Classics), and several major translations, including *On Spiritual Unity: A Slavophile Anthology* (with Boris Jakim) and Viacheslav Ivanov's *Selected Essays* (in collaboration with Michael Wachtel).

Craig Brandist teaches in the Department of Russian and Slavonic Studies at the University of Sheffield. Among his publications are the monographs *Carnival Culture and the Soviet Modernist Novel* (1996), *The Bakhtin Circle: Philosophy, Culture and Politics* (2002) and the co-edited volumes *Materializing Bakhtin* (2000, with Galin Tihanov) and *The Bakhtin Circle: In the Master's Absence* (2004, with David Shepherd and Galin Tihanov). He has been director of the major research project *The Rise of Sociological Linguistics in the Soviet Union, 1917–1938: Institutions, Ideas and Agendas*, funded by the Arts and Humanities Research Council (UK).

Steven Cassedy teaches Slavic and Comparative Literature at the University of California, San Diego. He has written about modern literary criticism, American Jewish culture, aesthetics, Christian theology, music, philosophy, and Russian literature. His most recent book is *Dostoevsky's Religion*. He is currently working on a comprehensive history of the turn of the twentieth century in the West.

Maryse Dennes teaches Russian literature, culture, and intellectual history at the University Michel de Montaigne Bordeaux 3. Her main field of expertise is Russian philosophy and intellectual history in its interaction with German phenomenology. She is the author of 85 scholarly publications, among which is a book on Husserl's and Heidegger's impact on Russian philosophy, as well as numerous studies of Shpet, Solov'ev, Losev, Florensky, and Sergei Bulgakov. She is the co-author of the French translation of Shpet's *Iavlenie i smysl* (forthcoming) and has also translated the poetry of Mayakovsky and Tsvetaeva, modern Slovak poetry and Russian scholarly prose. In 2007 she organized an International Conference on Gustav Shpet in Bordeaux and published the proceedings the following year in French (*Slavica Occitania*, 26). She is an honorary member of the Zenkovsky Society of Historians of Russian Philosophy in Moscow and Chevalier de l'Ordre des Palmes académiques.

Alexander Haardt teaches Post-Mediaeval Philosophy at the University of Bochum, Germany. Born in Vienna, he studied philosophy, Slavic Studies, and Indology at Vienna and Frankfurt. His doctoral thesis was on Kant, while his habilitation resulted in a book on Husserl's reception in Russia, with particular focus on Shpet and Losev (1993). In 1998-2000 he was President of the German Society for Phenomenological Research. Haardt is the author of numerous publications on the history of phenomenology of language and art in Germany, France, and Russia; he is also co-editor of the German translation of Shpet's "Germenevtika i ee problemy" (1993).

George L. Kline has taught philosophy at Bryn Mawr College (Pennsylvania), and teaches history at Clemson University (South Carolina). He is the author of *Spinoza in Soviet Philosophy* (1952, rpt. 1981) and *Religious and Anti-Religious Thought in Russia* (1968); editor of *Soviet Education* (1957) and *European Philosophy Today* (1965); co-editor of *Russian Philosophy*, 3 vols. (1965, rpt. 1976, 1984), *Iosif Brodskii: Ostanovka v pustyne* [*Joseph Brodsky: A Halt in the Wilderness*] (1970, rpt. 1988, 2000) and *Philosophical Sovietology: The Pursuit of a Science* (1988); translator of V. V. Zenkovsky, *A History of Russian Philosophy*, 2 vols. (1953, rpt. 2003), *Boris Pasternak: Seven Poems* (1969, 1972), and *Joseph Brodsky: Selected Poems* (1973, 1974). Kline has also written on Spinoza, Vico, Hegel, Marx, Nietzsche, Whitehead, Lukács, Kolakowski, Losev, and Shpet. He is an honorary member of the Zenkovsky Society of Historians of Russian Philosophy in Moscow.

Thomas Nemeth holds a doctorate in philosophy from the University of Louvain, Belgium. His postdoctoral studies took him to Australia (University of Melbourne) and to Germany where he was Research Fellow of the Alexander von Humboldt Foundation. He has published *Gramsci's Philosophy: a Critical Study* (1980) and several articles on Kant and Husserl in Russia. He is the translator of Gustav Shpet's *Appearance and Sense* (1991) and serves presently as subject editor for Russian philosophy at the Internet Encyclopaedia of Philosophy, to which he has also contributed a number of entries.

Dušan Radunović teaches European literature and intellectual history at the University of Essex. He holds BA and MA degrees in Comparative Literature and Literary Theory from the University of Belgrade and has earned a PhD (University of Sheffield, 2008) on the intersection of social and cognitive trends in the Russian humanities of the 1910s and 1920s. His research interests include twentieth-century Russian and European intellectual history, and literature and film theory; he has written and presented widely on these subjects. He has previously taught at the Universities of Sheffield and Bristol.

James P. Scanlan has taught philosophy at Ohio State University, Columbus. He received his B.A. (1948), M.A. (1950) and Ph.D. (1956) degrees from the University of Chicago. A specialist in the history of Russian thought, he is the author of many articles on individual Russian thinkers of the nineteenth and twentieth centuries and the author, translator, editor, or co-editor of many volumes in the field, including *Russian Philosophy* (3 vols., 1967), *Marxism in the USSR: A Critical Survey of Current Soviet Thought* (1985), and *Russian Thought after Communism: The Recovery of a Philosophical Heritage* (1994). His most recent book is *Dostoevsky the Thinker* (2002).

Ulrich Schmid teaches Russian literature, culture, and intellectual history at St Gallen University, Switzerland, having previously held a Chair in Russian at the University of Bochum and appointments at the Universities of Basel and Berne. He studied at the Universities of Zurich, Heidelberg, and Leningrad. In 1995 he was a Visiting Fellow at Harvard University. Since 1993 he contributes regularly to the feuilleton of *Neue Zürcher Zeitung*. His research interests include Russian intellectual history, nationalism in interwar Eastern Europe, and media theory. In 2003 he published a collection of Russian philosophical texts in German translation, ranging from Losskii, Frank, Bulgakov, Ern and Trubetskoi to Losev and Shpet. He is the author of books on Sologub and on the history of autobiographical discourse in Russia.

Thomas Seifrid teaches Slavic Languages and Literatures at the University of Southern California. He was born in Aurora, Illinois; on receiving a B.S. in Wildlife Biology with a Major in Russian in 1978 from the University of Montana, he completed his graduate study in the field of Russian literature at Cornell University, receiving his Ph.D. there in 1984. His *The Word Made Self*, a study of Russian philosophy of language in the early twentieth century, is published by Cornell UP (2005). He is also the author of *Andrei Platonov. Uncertainties of Spirit* (1992) and of many articles on Russian literature and culture, and has a secondary (but avid) interest in Polish language and culture. He lives in Los Angeles with his wife and son.

Peter Steiner teaches Slavic Languages and Literatures at the University of Pennsylvania. He is the author of *Russian Formalism: A Metapoetics* (1984), translated into Italian, Spanish, Japanese, and Bulgarian, and *The Deserts of Bohemia: Czech*

Fiction and Its Social Context (2000). His most recent publications include an extended Introduction to Vaclav Havel's *The Beggar's Opera* (2001; Japanese version 2002).

Galin Tihanov teaches Comparative Literature and Intellectual History and is Co-Director of the Research Institute for Cosmopolitan Cultures at The University of Manchester. He holds doctorates in Bulgarian literature (Sofia, 1996) and in Comparative Literature (Oxford, 1998). His publications include *The Master and the Slave: Lukács, Bakhtin, and the Ideas of Their Time* (2000), two books on Bulgarian literature (1994 and 1998), co-edited volumes on Bakhtin and the Bakhtin Circle (2000 and 2004) and on Robert Musil (2007), a guest-edited issue on Russian avant-garde photography and visual culture (*History of Photography*, 2000), as well as numerous articles on German, Russian, and East-European intellectual and cultural history, and on various issues in comparative literature. He has been Research Fellow of the Alexander von Humboldt Foundation and of the George Soros Foundation, Visiting Professor of Comparative Literature at Yale University and Fellow at Collegium Budapest and the Wissenschaftskolleg zu Berlin. He is Honorary Chair of the Committee on Literary Theory of the International Comparative Literature Association.

James V. Wertsch teaches at Washington University in St. Louis. After obtaining his Ph.D. from the University of Chicago in 1975, he spent the following year as a postdoctoral fellow in Moscow. He has held faculty positions at Northwestern University, the University of California, San Diego, Clark University, and Washington University, as well as visiting positions at the University of Utrecht, Moscow State University, the University of Seville, and the Scandinavian Collegium for Advanced Study in Social Sciences. Wertsch's publications include *Vygotsky and the Social Formation of Mind* (1985); *Voices of the Mind: A Sociocultural Approach to Mediated Action* (1991); *Mind as Action* (1998), and *Voices of Collective Remembering* (2002). His research is concerned with language, thought, and culture, with a special focus on text, collective memory, and identity. Wertsch holds honorary degrees from Linköping University and Oslo University and is an honorary member of the Russian Academy of Education.

Vladimir Zinchenko teaches at the State University–Higher School of Economics (Gosudarstvennyi universitet–Vysshaia shkola ekonomiki) in Moscow. On defending his Ph.D. on perception and action at Leningrad University, he became Head of the Department of Ergonomics at the Institute of Technical Aesthetics in Moscow and later organized and chaired the Department of Labor and Engineering Psychology at Moscow State University, as well as the Department of Ergonomics at the Moscow Institute of Radio-Engineering, Electronics and Automation. He is full member of the Russian Academy of Education and the author of about 400 scholarly publications. His main research interests are developmental psychology and the microstructure of human motor performance. He is also editor-in-chief of the Russian journal of cultural-historical psychology.

Index

318